The Origins of English Revenge Tragedy

Edinburgh Critical Studies in Renaissance Culture

Series Editor: Lorna Hutson

Titles available in the series

Open Subjects: English Renaissance Republicans, Modern Selfhoods and the Virtue of Vulnerability
James Kuzner

The Phantom of Chance: From Fortune to Randomness in Seventeenth-Century French Literature
John D. Lyons

Don Quixote in the Archives: Madness and Literature in Early Modern Spain
Dale Shuger

Untutored Lines: The Making of the English Epyllion
William P. Weaver

The Girlhood of Shakespeare's Sisters: Gender, Transgression, Adolescence
Jennifer Higginbotham

Friendship's Shadows: Women's Friendship and the Politics of Betrayal in England, 1640–1705
Penelope Anderson

Inventions of the Skin: The Painted Body in Early English Drama, 1400–1642
Andrea Ria Stevens

Performing Economic Thought: English Drama and Mercantile Writing, 1600–1642
Bradley D. Ryner

Forgetting Differences: Tragedy, Historiography and the French Wars of Religion
Andrea Frisch

Listening for Theatrical Form in Early Modern England
Allison Deutermann

Theatrical Milton: Politics and Poetics of the Staged Body
Brendan Prawdzik

Legal Reform in English Renaissance Literature
Virginia Lee Strain

The Origins of English Revenge Tragedy
George Oppitz-Trotman

Visit the Edinburgh Critical Studies in Renaissance Culture website at www.edinburghuniversitypress.com/series/ECSRC

The Origins of English Revenge Tragedy

George Oppitz-Trotman

University Press

Edinburgh University Press is one of the leading university presses in the UK. We publish academic books and journals in our selected subject areas across the humanities and social sciences, combining cutting-edge scholarship with high editorial and production values to produce academic works of lasting importance. For more information visit our website: edinburghuniversitypress.com

© George Oppitz-Trotman, 2019, 2021

First published in hardback by Edinburgh University Press 2019

Edinburgh University Press Ltd
The Tun – Holyrood Road
12(2f) Jackson's Entry
Edinburgh EH8 8PJ

Typeset in 10.5/13 Adobe Sabon by
Servis Filmsetting Ltd, Stockport, Cheshire

A CIP record for this book is available from the British Library

ISBN 978 1 4744 4171 1 (hardback)
ISBN 978 1 4744 4172 8 (paperback)
ISBN 978 1 4744 4173 5 (webready PDF)
ISBN 978 1 4744 4174 2 (epub)

The right of George Oppitz-Trotman to be identified as the author of this work has been asserted in accordance with the Copyright, Designs and Patents Act 1988, and the Copyright and Related Rights Regulations 2003 (SI No. 2498).

Contents

Illustrations	vii
Acknowledgements	viii
Series Editor's Preface	x
Abbreviations	xiii
Introduction	1
1. Verge	27
2. Points	64
3. A Brief Interlude of Vice	101
4. Servants	126
5. Figures	164
6. Bare Facts, Endless Tragedies	204
Bibliography	221
Index	249

I am, with you.

Illustrations

Figure 2.1 'A *prinse faut faire contreprinse, comme est icy monstré par ce Lieutenant au Prevost.*' Henry de Sainct Didier, *Traicté contenant les secrets du premier livre sur l'espée seule* (Paris, 1573), fol.64^v. © The British Library Board: General Reference Collection 63.a.18.   78

Figure 2.2 '*Es kompt aber manchmal, das ihr zwene zusammen kommen, die da geschwinde im Rappier sind.*' Michael Hundt, *Ein new künstliches Fechtbuch im Rappier* (Leipzig, 1611), Sig. R3. © Herzog August Bibliothek Wolfenbüttel: A: 31 Bell. (2).   84

Figure 4.1 Frontispiece, '*A Horrible Creuel and Bloudy Murther*, committed at Putney in Surrey on the 21 of Aprill last, 1614, being Thursday, upon the body of Edward Hall *a Miller of the same parish*, Done by the hands of *John Selling, Peeter Pet* and *Edward Streater*, his servants' (London, 1614). © Bodleian Library: 4° G 29(5) Art.   144

Figure 5.1 Georges de la Tour, *L'Apparition de l'Ange à Saint Joseph* (c.1643). © Nantes-Métropole, Musée d'Arts. Photography: C. Clos. Inventory Nr 642.   179

Acknowledgements

Research for this book was made possible by grants from the AHRC, Corpus Christi College and the University of Cambridge, the British Academy and the Alexander von Humboldt Foundation. The research leading to these results has also received funding from the European Research Council under the European Union's Seventh Framework Programme (FP7/2007-2013)/ERC grant agreement no. 617849.

Various excerpts from this work were read to audiences in Cambridge and Norwich, and earlier drafts to symposia in Exeter, Oxford, Rotterdam, St Andrews, Stratford-upon-Avon and York. Chapter 3 is based on research that was published in an early, compressed form as 'Staging Vice and Acting Evil: Theatre and Antitheatre in Sixteenth-Century England', in Peter Clarke and Charlotte Methuen (eds), *The Church and Literature*, Studies in Church History 48 (Woodbridge, 2012), 156–69.

I owe thanks to friends, colleagues and teachers of all kinds. I should especially like to thank Gavin Alexander, Tom Day, Katherine Dow, Kathy Eden, Ben Etherington, Tony Gash, Priyamvada Gopal, Joel Halcomb, Rachel Heard, David Hillman, Rachel Holmes, Joe Jarrett, Mary Laven, Raphael Lyne, Tim Marshall, Drew Milne, Subha Mukherji, Josh Robinson, Toby Sleigh-Johnson, Simon Sandall, Jason Scott-Warren, Elizabeth Swann, Hillary Taylor, Eva Urban, Daniel Wakelin, Peter Womack, Andy Wood, Andrew Zurcher and my brother, Fred. I also thank Hillary Taylor and Keith Wrightson for allowing me to read and cite unpublished papers. James Dale, Ersev Ersoy, Michelle Houston, Rebecca Mackenzie and Adela Rauchova at Edinburgh University Press have been very accommodating and efficient. Two anonymous readers for the Press gave me perspective on this work at an important stage, and the vigilant copy-editing of Nicola Wood spared me countless mortifications. Lorna Hutson has been an inspiring editor and touchstone. John Kerrigan was there at the inception of this book a decade ago. His unstinting moral support and intellectual generosity have seen it through almost every incarnation.

Much of the basic argumentation was worked out during long, contented nights in the second home I was given by Erika and Reinhold Oppitz. I will always remember what they did for me. It is only with appalling slowness that I have come to appreciate some of the sacrifices made for me by my parents, Alex Schofield and John Trotman, and I know there will be many of which I still know nothing. Were it not for Gesine this work would never have been started, nor would it be what it is. But for Milly it would likely have languished in the shade; she fetched me into the light. Maud, Ned: this is what George was doing in the shed that summer.

I cannot give adequate thanks for the numberless acts of love, lessons both moral and intellectual, favours intended and haphazard, concessions and gifts momentous and tiny, encouragements, rebukes and examples that have shaped this work. It is common to note that such debts cannot be added up, let alone expressed and repaid. Perhaps it is secretly possessive to address them as if they were obligational. Perhaps I cannot thank you for this book because it is not completely mine, but ours.

Series Editor's Preface

Edinburgh Critical Studies in Renaissance Culture may, as a series title, provoke some surprise. On the one hand, the choice of the word 'culture' (rather than, say, 'literature') suggests that writers in this series subscribe to the now widespread assumption that the 'literary' is not isolable, as a mode of signifying, from other signifying practices that make up what we call 'culture'. On the other hand, most of the critical work in English literary studies of the period 1500–1700 which endorses this idea has rejected the older identification of the period as 'the Renaissance', with its implicit homage to the myth of essential and universal Man coming to stand (in all his sovereign individuality) at the centre of a new world picture. In other words, the term 'culture' in the place of 'literature' leads us to expect the words 'early modern' in the place of 'Renaissance'. Why, then, 'Edinburgh Critical Studies in *Renaissance Culture*'?

The answer to that question lies at the heart of what distinguishes this critical series and defines its parameters. As Terence Cave has argued, the term 'early modern', though admirably egalitarian in conception, has had the unfortunate effect of essentialising the modern, that is, of positing 'the advent of a once-and-for-all modernity' which is the deictic 'here and now' from which we look back.[1] The phrase 'early modern', that is to say, forecloses the possibility of other modernities, other futures that might have arisen, narrowing the scope of what we may learn from the past by construing it as a narrative leading inevitably to Western modernity, to 'us'. *Edinburgh Critical Studies in Renaissance Culture* aims rather to shift the emphasis from a story of progress – early modern to modern – to series of critical encounters and conversations with the past, which may reveal to us some surprising alternatives buried within texts familiarly construed as episodes on the way to certain identifying features of our endlessly fascinating modernity. In keeping with

---

[1] Terence Cave, 'Locating the Early Modern', *Paragraph* 29:1 (2006), 12–26, 14.

one aspect of the etymology of 'Renaissance' or 'Rinascimento' as 'rebirth', moreover, this series features books that explore and interpret anew elements of the critical encounter between writers of the period 1500–1700 and texts of Greco-Roman literature, rhetoric, politics, law, oeconomics, *eros* and friendship.

The term 'culture', then, indicates a license to study and scrutinise objects other than literary ones, and to be more inclusive about both the forms and the material and political stakes of making meaning both in the past and in the present. 'Culture' permits a realisation of the benefits to be reaped after two decades of interdisciplinary enrichment in the arts. No longer are historians naïve about textual criticism, about rhetoric, literary theory or about readerships; likewise, literary critics trained in close reading now also turn easily to court archives, to legal texts, and to the historians' debates about the languages of political and religious thought. Social historians look at printed pamphlets with an eye for narrative structure; literary critics look at court records with awareness of the problems of authority, mediation and institutional procedure. Within these developments, modes of research that became unfashionable and discredited in the 1980s – for example, studies in classical or vernacular 'source texts', or studies of literary 'influence' across linguistic, confessional and geographical boundaries – have acquired a new critical edge and relevance as the convergence of the disciplines enables the unfolding of new cultural histories (that is to say, what was once studied merely as 'literary influence' may now be studied as a fraught cultural encounter). The term 'Renaissance' thus retains the relevance of the idea of consciousness and critique within these textual engagements of past and present, and, while it foregrounds the Western European experience, is intended to provoke comparativist study of wider global perspectives rather than to promote the 'universality' of a local, if far-reaching, historical phenomenon. Finally, as traditional pedagogic boundaries between 'Medieval' and 'Renaissance' are being called into question by cross disciplinary work emphasising the 'reformation' of social and cultural forms, so this series, while foregrounding the encounter with the classical past, is self-conscious about the ways in which that past is assimilated to the projects of Reformation and Counter-Reformation, spiritual, political and domestic, that finally transformed Christendom into Europe.

Individual books in this series vary in methodology and approach, sometimes blending the sensitivity of close literary analysis with incisive, informed and urgent theoretical argument, at other times offering critiques of grand narratives of the period by their work in manuscript transmission, or in the archives of legal, social and architectural history, or by social histories of gender and childhood. What all these books have in common, however, is the capacity to offer compelling, well-documented and lucidly written critical accounts of how writers and thinkers in the period 1500–1700 reshaped, transformed and critiqued the texts and practices of their world, prompting new perspectives on what we think we have learned from them.

Lorna Hutson

Abbreviations

Aristotle, *Works* Jonathan Barnes (ed.), *The Complete Works of Aristotle*, 2 vols (Oxford, 1984). Bekker numbering is indicated by section marks [§]: Immanuel Bekker (ed.), *Aristotelis Opera*, 5 vols (Berlin, 1831).

Benjamin, *GS* Rolf Tiedemann and Hermann Schweppenhäuser (eds), *Gesammelte Schriften*, 7 vols (Frankfurt a. M., 1972-89).

Chambers, *ES* E. K. Chambers, *The Elizabethan Stage*, 4 vols (Oxford, 1923).

Hamlet William Shakespeare, *The Tragical History of Hamlet, Prince of Denmark*, ed. Ann Thompson and Neil Taylor (London, 2006). Citations of the first quarto [Q1] and the first folio [F] refer to Ann Thompson and Neil Taylor (eds), *Hamlet: The Texts of 1603 and 1623* (London, 2006).

Middleton, *Works* Gary Taylor and John Lavagnino et al. (eds), *Thomas Middleton. The Collected Works* (Oxford, 2007). *RT* refers to *The Revenger's Tragedy*, ed. MacDonald P. Jackson, in this edition.

MSC *Malone Society: Collections*, 17 vols (Oxford, 1907–).

ST Thomas Kyd, *The Spanish Tragedy*, ed. Clara Calvo and Jesús Tronch (London, 2013).

Webster, *Works* David Gunby, David Carnegie, Antony Hammond and MacDonald P. Jackson (eds), *The Works of John Webster. An Old-Spelling Critical Edition*, 3 vols (Cambridge, 2004). *Duchess* and *WD* refer to *The Duchess of Malfi* and *The White Devil* in this edition, I.

Let us continue to chase spirits back into their bodies.

Gillian Rose

Introduction

> If finished works only become what they are because their being is a process of becoming, they are in turn dependent on forms in which that process crystallises: interpretation, commentary, critique. These are not merely brought to bear on works by those who concern themselves with them, but are the scene [*Schauplatz*] of the historical agitation of artworks in themselves, and thus forms in their own right.[1]
>
> Theodor W. Adorno, *Ästhetische Theorie*

Moments before his death, Hamlet looks into our future: 'O God, Horatio, what a wounded name, / Things standing thus unknown, shall I leave behind me!' (*Hamlet* V.ii.328–9). Hamlet's 'name' seems to mean reputation, honour, fame – what Cassio in *Othello* calls 'the immortal part of myself'.[2] Honour in early modern England was sometimes imagined to be woundable, like a second body. A neo-Platonic distinction between Hamlet's self and his fame cannot be upheld, however, because Hamlet *is* the legacy he is concerned to protect. Hamlet anticipates that unless Horatio gives a proper report of events – unless his friend makes them known to 'th' yet unknowing world' (363) – he will be misremembered, malformed, disfigured. The play ends with Horatio on the cusp of fulfilling this dying wish, 'from his mouth whose voice will draw no more' (376). The yet unknowing world of the Danish court, reconstituted under Fortinbras, will go out and become an 'audience' (371) to a tale 'of carnal, bloody and unnatural acts, / Of accidental judgments, casual slaughters', and, one assumes, the rest (365–6). But what sort of story would that be, which makes things sufficiently known that Hamlet can be whole? Readers and audiences have been invited to speculate upon a narrative compassing all the uncertainties and diversions of the play they are still struggling to process, a play so unruly, discursive and quibbling that its conversion back into a monological history must surely seem improbable. *Hamlet* has projected the question of its hero's identity forward into its manifold future retellings, rereadings, restagings.

Although there is certainly some sort of conspicuous brilliance at work here, the issue of whether William Shakespeare had quite this effect in mind is nugatory. The simultaneous projection and experience of legacy is indelibly proper to an encounter with the play. Somehow *Hamlet* speculates upon, or folds into itself, the very confusion I feel reading those lines. The play has also pre-empted my attempt to understand and judge the terms on which Hamlet was able to attain his vengeance: 'O God, Horatio, what a wounded name / Things standing thus unknown [. . .]' The implied contrast – 'things known' and 'things unknown' – fails. Even after close inspection of the play's catastrophe, the condition of the name of 'Hamlet' remains fundamentally uncertain, the marks of his intention hieroglyphic.

Sudden interventions like this against the reader's presumption of their disinvolvement in the afterlife or survival of the work – that which Walter Benjamin referred to variously as its *Nachleben* ('afterlife'), *Überleben* ('survival') and especially *Fortleben* ('continuing life') with its connotations of presence and futurity – have always exercised a special fascination. *Antony and Cleopatra* (1607; 1623) supplies a comparable moment of historical vertigo. 'The quick comedians / Extemporally will stage us and present / Our Alexandrian revels'. Again, the fictional psychosocial concern is with honour: the heroes have anticipated their removal to Rome and the humiliation which awaits them there. Again, it is impossible to sustain that meaning without a collapse of temporal distance. The collapse is double. On the one hand, the 'historical' Cleopatra is worrying about the player standing upon the stage of the Globe or Blackfriars in around 1607, speaking those lines as Cleopatra. This would have had the oblique political advantage of representing London as a new Rome, at the expense of the players. On the other, that performance is arrayed next to our own encounters with these characters in a single continuous afterlife: our readings and watchings of various Cleopatras all number among the acts of remembrance she is shown to fear. 'How many times shall Caesar bleed in sport?', wonders Brutus in *Julius Caesar*. Cleopatra is concerned with which Cleopatra you are thinking of. Even more perplexingly, Cleopatra is worried that Cleopatra might be improvised into something else, 'extemporally' staged.[3]

In common academic parlance, such ingenuities are termed examples of 'metatheatre' or 'metadrama'. I will show how that greatly impoverishes them. It is clear enough that Cleopatra's lines, like those in *Hamlet*, are doing something more mysterious and potentially consequential than signalling a wry consciousness of self-artifice. These figures are speculating upon all their future figurations; the play, upon an afterlife in which my writing these sentences, and your reading of them – now –

will participate. The usual word for these acts of confused remembrance is culture. What we do not possess is a word for who or what Hamlet *is* when he worries how he will be remembered. After all, having observed the tautology, one is left to wonder who is capable of having uttered it. Because Hamlet is mythic – a real person who never existed, as Friedrich Gundolf had it – he seems familiar enough for this to seem a strange way of putting it.[4] I must nevertheless credit a stubborn bemusement whenever I find myself, students, or colleagues speaking about early modern characters as if they were real people. Although it is now uncommon for such pronouncements to have anything of naivety about them, I think it highly doubtful that the processes and contingencies involved in even the most ironic resuscitations really are as deeply understood as they might be.

This book might be said to outline a poetics of figuration. I hope that by the end it will be clearer what the term 'figuration' might involve, but 'poetics', precisely because it trips off the tongue with such suspicious ease, requires some qualification. Poetics has among other things been described as poetry's concepts and theories of itself, an account which, as Josh Robinson has recently suggested, 'contains the beginnings' of a link to 'subjective experience, reflection on and formulation of these concepts'. 'The experience of poetry,' continues Robinson, 'frequently contains within itself something that seems to go beyond the bounds of what we think of as experience', spurring or beginning reflection on the implications of that experience.[5] 'Poetics' refers less to a theoretical corpus ancillary to, or attendant upon, poetry, than to the potential of poetry to expand and rupture the conceptual frameworks in which it is apprehended or presented. If the experience of poetry discovers within itself the constraining limits of that experience via an encounter with the 'objectivity' of a poetic object, at the same time it must be an iron rule that there could be no poetics without experience. Poetics dissolves a strict antinomy of literary objectivity and critical subjectivity. If that is the chief reason why the retention of the term 'poetics' is desirable, its object ('poetry') enters into a tension with the object of this book ('drama') precisely because of the way it muffles this potential. Except in the limited, pejorative sense, there is no such thing as 'theatrics'. When it encounters the fraught relation between theatre and dramatic poetry 'poetics' tends necessarily to instate and instantiate an Aristotelian notion of that relation. But to brick up early modern plays either in a dichotomy of poetry and performance, or within the politics of cultural supersession (the written over the oral; the elite over the popular), is potentially to effect more severe injuries to the attempt to understand the experience of making and encountering dramatic figures. For it is the contention here that the work we do in animating dramatic figures in our minds is a thinking back into the terms on which they were, or could be, originally figured. Figuration is involved in the historical imagination even where it seems most difficult. In fact, it is at exactly those moments in the experience of reading early modern drama (even 'dramatic poetry') when its figures seem strangest, the encounter with them most alienating, and our conceptual apparatus most inadequate, that we face the burden of the past most nearly head-on.

Disfigurements

What cultures do with texts is part of textuality. The apparent ease and frequency with which dramatic characters are figured in those societies where historical printed drama in English is read and discussed gives the lie to the dogma that they are probably sufficient as bare textual formations. 'Characters,' writes Stephen Orgel, digesting one side of a familiar debate, 'are not people, they are elements of a linguistic structure, lines in a drama, and more basically, words on a page.'[6] This view has been opposed chiefly in terms of 'authority'.[7] In one of the most influential formulations, this is expressed as the contest of 'author's pen' and 'actor's voice', Shakespearean terms lending Robert Weimann the title of his book.[8] It is instructive to observe how some of the chief participants in the contest of 'literary' Shakespeare and 'theatrical' Shakespeare agreed on the place where they should fight, because it helps explain why problems of figuration, such as those adduced above, receive so little attention.

Weimann developed a bifocal view of drama as immersed in a struggle between authors and performers to reserve to themselves a position as original forces of dramatic production. In expounding this fertile argument, his work gravitated to those moments where the exchange of authority seemed most conspicuous, in prologues and epilogues;[9] towards what he termed 'the threshold experience', with direct reference to the anthropologist Victor Turner's concept of liminality.[10] This destination – 'liminality' (and the more glamorous 'indeterminacy') – seems to lack any power of description that does not land back at that destination. To describe a phenomenon as 'liminal' is usually to claim or defend the validity of a concept of liminality, rather than to cast light on the specific ambiguities of the moment in question. Part of the dysfunction of 'liminality' can be seen in what Turner's concept does to theatre history. Professional theatre distinguishes itself from all other sorts of social drama, but through 'liminality' it is paraded as just one more example of ritual.¹¹ Discussing this same problem from the perspective of anthropology, Catherine Bell observes that 'an initial focus on the performative aspects of ritual easily leads to the difficulty of being unable to distinguish how ritual is not the same as dramatic theater'.¹² Weimann's account of dramatic authority, while often very nuanced locally, is prone to welcome this ultimate effacement of difference because of its debts not only to Turner but to particular elements in early twentieth-century German philology. These debts are touched on in a later chapter.

In his equally influential volume *Shakespeare as Literary Dramatist* (2003), Lukas Erne was able to accommodate Weimann's account by interpreting it as a response to 'plays' rival modes of existence' or what Leah Marcus termed 'competing forms of communication'.¹³ Although faintly tendentious, this was not a misrepresentation of Weimann's argument. An antinomy of orality and literacy has long shaped the argument about what drama is, and had been restated as Weimann's (Shakespeare's) 'author's pen' and 'actor's voice'.¹⁴ Character was either written by a playwright or spoken by an actor; in most cases, the argument then proceeds, it is the record of their contest and collaboration. Construing dramatic figures in terms of this polarity leaves dramatic *person* rather orphaned, or at least rather naked, somewhere in what Weimann calls 'the inexhaustible terrain of *and* between present players' bodies and absent, verbally certified representations'.¹⁵ As William Worthen suspects, even those critics most attentive to textual fragmentation of Hamlet's name probably remain in the 'orbit' of character criticism.¹⁶ Above all, there is here the presumption that the identity of dramatic person is secured by those parts of the creative process in which critics, readers and audiences are largely uninvolved. But the verbally certified representations of Hamlet and Cleopatra, as we can see, evince a worry about how they will be remembered, that is, mentally bodied. If the problems of embodiment are deemed proper only to one side of things, to the zone of orality and performance, how do we speak of the way in which Hamlet's or Cleopatra's fears about being represented onstage require us to body them forth as persons in texts?

Rhetoricians called it *prosopopoeia*, a word which means 'the making of a face', but may perhaps with more justice be described as the effect of 'a mask put on something that may not even have a face'.¹⁷ Gavin Alexander introduces it as 'the speaking figure', thereby penning it somewhat unwillingly back into the terrain of orality-literacy.¹⁸ In 1589 George Puttenham glossed prosopopoeia without any reference to *voice* at all, as the figuration of person (albeit by a notional orator). It was 'the Counterfeit in personation', either the feigning of a person or the attribution of a human quality to 'insensible things'.[19] There is a lot to the slip from the one to the other. This too is glimpsed in the problem of Hamlet's 'wounded name', which inflicts a deanimation of its speaker, the transformation of him into an insensible thing, a mere title; and into inorganic stuff, his honour (an artificial 'body'). Naturally this contributes to the illusion that he is real, but not without engendering a crisis of prosopopoeic function. Aside from the personification or voicing of inanimate and inhuman things, classic accounts of prosopopoeia following Quintilian tend to emphasise a contraction of space: the making present of someone from somewhere else. But in the earliest extant descriptions, prosopopoeia referred just as readily to a historical relation, a 'figural mechanism'.[20] Demetrius of Phalerum gave the example of Plato speaking to children 'in the name of their ancestors' in his *Menexenus*.[21] Puttenham thought the best historical examples were prosopopoeial, 'the lively image of our deare forefathers'.[22] It is not far from there to the tomb of Agamemnon; and not far from there either to Tantalus, Pelops, Clotho. Revenge tends always toward prosopopoeial complication. In revenge narratives prosopopoeia ('face-making') shades frequently into eidolopoeia ('icon-making'), 'which maketh a persone knowne though dedde, and not able to speake'. This is what Horatio seems to promise when he promises 'to speak / from his mouth whose voice will draw no more' (V.ii.375–6).[23] Some contemporaries sensibly assumed that the public theatre was the most powerful eidolopoetic instrument of all. 'How would it have joyed brave *Talbot*,' wondered Thomas Nashe in *Pierce Penniless* (1592), 'to thinke that after he had lyne two hundred yeares in his Tombe, hee should triumph againe on the Stage, and have his bones newe embalmed with the teares of ten thousand spectators.'[24] The basic figure of eidolopoeia, Richard Rainolde thought, had been 'set forthe of Euripides, upon the persone of Polidorus dedde, whose spirite entereth at the Prologue of the tragedie'.[25]

English revenge tragedy is prone to enmesh figures with history, figuration with difficulties of right remembrance, restitution, reconstitution, fulfilment. Of all early modern drama, it most entangles theatre in dead matter – and its dead figures in a problem of theatre appearance. Meanwhile, in the presence of the revenger, the figural work of reading becomes both more salient and more problematic; the jargon of liminality and textuality, hollow. Orgel observes that it is 'very difficult to think of character' as linguistic constructs 'when those words on a page are being embodied in actors on a stage'.[26] That might be an understatement. To behold a silenced Lavinia in *Titus Andronicus* and think only 'that's a linguistic construct' is not only difficult but idiotic. Is it only in a theatre that this unthinking is difficult? If that were true, it would seemingly be impossible to feel pity (or even the possibility of feeling pity) reading drama at home. In his *Rhetoric*, Aristotle suggested that we can pity only those we recognise as sufficiently like us for their suffering to be prospectively ours; but that if they are too close to us then it is not pity we feel, but our own pain.[27] As Gabriel Zoran notes, this account holds that the theatre makes the 'reality of the characters' sufficiently *strong* 'because it is physically represented', but that their inhabitation of 'a mimetic world' keeps those figures sufficiently *distant* for us to feel pity without actual pain or fear.[28]

To feel pity reading by a desk light is then to hold more arduously in mind this other world, but it is also to encounter tragic persons in configurations Aristotle could not anticipate but Shakespeare and his colleagues possibly could. Bodies and materials of a variable and uncertain kind must speculatively supplement 'the words on a page' if any meaningful recognition, however temporary, is to occur at a scene of reading. Accounts of textual sufficiency like Orgel's ignore the mimetic impulse of drama. If a polyglottal alien found a copy of the second quarto of *Hamlet* floating in the void, and did to it something we might recognise as reading, perhaps character would indeed safely remain 'elements of a linguistic structure, lines in a drama [. . .] words on a page'. In practice, part of knowing how to recognise Hamlet is knowing that his world is a mimesis of a part of ours, in a different time, and that perhaps he moved through it a little like us. A separate part of dramatic recognition is the feeling that he is something else entirely. Again, *Hamlet* is shooting off ahead of us, asking us to differentiate Hamlet from Old Hamlet, the human figure from the figure of something else, albeit their names often appear in the same way 'on the page'.

As Randall McLeod's avatar reminds us, speech tags are not in fact to be trusted at all: their consistency was an eighteenth-century editorial invention. Is Claudius 'Claudius', as he is in his first speech tag in Q2 – or 'King'? And if 'King' (which Hamlet disputes), then how might he be distinguished from the Player King ('King' in Q2), who allegorises not 'Claudius' but Old Hamlet (the king)?[29] A description of the fragmentation and editorial reconstruction of dramatic name usually precedes or anticipates an assault on the ramparts of 'character', as it does in some of McLeod's essays. But if the discernment of dramatic person is a struggle, that struggle is not solely produced by inconsistencies or fallacies of textual denotation. Strip away the strange convention of dramatis-personae lists, and the burdensomeness of identifying dramatic person is not vanquished along with 'character'.[30] On the contrary, it calls more plainly for investigation – not least because we will still attempt that identification, and it seems in part to motivate or potentiate our continued engagement with this corpus. There will never be an account of textual history so complete as to dissuade us from trying to relate to most dramatic figures as something other than reality effects. As Michael Bristol claims, 'interpretative practices of this kind seem obvious and sensitive ways to respond to [Shakespeare's] plays'. 'It is reasonable to think about literary characters the way we think about real people,' he goes on, 'because that is how we actually make sense of stories.'[31] That is not what is argued here. I am instead interested in why early modern plays so often expose the premises and limits of that comparison. The clearly separate question of what the 'Ghost' is bleeds into the issue of who or what 'Hamlet' or any other dramatic figure can be said to be. Recognition of dramatic person contains a secret effort of the historical imagination. For us to work hard to obtain the possibility of entertaining pity is to calculate the resemblance characters bear to us. To peer even for a second at the terms of that supposition – the quality and plausibility of resemblance – is to encounter a problem of historical distance. In this way figuration always involves a question of origin.

The position to be attained temporarily here does not concern pity itself, then, but the recognition of another which may be a necessary premise (rather than corollary) of its effect. For us to respond to these mimetic worlds, their figures must be provisionally recognised. To ignore the problem of recognition involves restricting that encounter, by an inhuman effort, to a purely semantic realm, successfully imagining, or desiring to imagine, a Hamlet without any human dimensions at all, his person nothing more than a rhetorical effect with no necessary relation to speaking and talking humans we have known and may wish to know. It is very questionable whether such a reduction is either practical or desirable. By bracketing off the experience of figuring plays, it may be impossible to say why they are still read, as I have already implied. However, that is not the central concern of this book. A more provocative thesis is instead advanced, namely that parenthesisation of the figurations involved in reading makes it significantly more difficult not only to entertain revengers in their own world but also to understand how they were originally made out of ours.

This argument is detained and prejudicated by the simplest account of misrecognition, in which linguistic constructs or theatrical fictions are misrecognised as persons from ignorance or for delight, or in co-mixture thereof. Even Bertolt Brecht admitted that theatre could not do without enjoyment: it requires 'no other passport but fun, but this it must have'.[32] He also assumed, rightly, that the (mis)recognition of dramatic bodies was a problem and an opportunity not wholly absorbed by pleasure, even as it concerned at its core the status of the work of the professional entertainer. That assumption implicates theatrical disguise in problems of political recognition and economic personhood, and it is therefore anything but straightforward. Anti-theatre following Plato in the *Republic* had assumed that acting ('imitation') was not a trade and therefore not an identity. The imitator could not imitate many things as well as he could imitate one (namely an occupation; trade; social function), and was therefore not to be welcomed into Kallipolis: 'no one in our city is two or more people simultaneously, since each does only one job'.[33] The question of the recognition of the imitator therefore has a long history, and must be somewhat distinguished from the issue of the pleasures produced by fiction. Plato also introduced the problem of imitation as the self-concealment of the poet, informing a later set of assumptions about what recognition of a figure like Hamlet really involves. Elizabeth Montagu, writing in the eighteenth century, was certainly not alone in supposing that Shakespeare possessed 'the art of the Dervise, in the Arabian tales, who could throw his soul into the body of another man'.[34] To pursue recognition on such terms is of course to retreat ultimately to the realm of voice and the 'bifold authority' irresolution. The task, then, is to avoid getting misrecognition all wrong from the start. Reading *Hamlet* as a play is to encounter its invitation to recognise figures within a space different from ours. To be recognised, figures must – of course – be figured, and figured not with entire freedom but in some sort of nervous, distendable affinity with the figurations attempted or ruined by the play.

The question here is not of belief or disbelief (its 'suspension'), but whether the eidetic necessarily supplements the semantic in drama; how particular plays manage and challenge this supplementation; and how this relates to their temporality and our ability to respond to them as artefacts of the past. As Maurice Merleau-Ponty observed, it is impossible 'to conceive a perceptible place in which I am not myself present'.[35] Brenda Machosky elaborates: 'The imaginative space of literature [. . .] must *appear*, and that appearance, is, by definition, phenomenological' – but 'the phenomenology of literary or artistic space is *a peculiar kind of appearance*'.[36] To attribute to Hamlet or any other dramatic character even a quantum of life in grammar and syntax is to imagine, however fleetingly and changeably, and always in cognisance of textual materiality, a special sort of scene in which they do and say things before us, even if, as Merleau-Ponty goes on, they 'recede beyond their immediately given aspects'.[37] It is to presume that they have (and therefore to *lend* them) some sort of pneumatic body. It is – after all – to imagine that they possess voice, albeit without the distinction of an actual voice. Even if the cognitive necessity of this might be arguable, it is certain that people do something like it all the time and that much critical literature presumes work of this sort even where it is not explicitly at issue.

Perhaps, like Horatio, we pronounce Hamlet's words 'from his mouth' (V.ii.378). There have been times I have found myself almost involuntarily mouthing them. Again, the affective relation potentiated here is augured by Hamlet himself: 'Absent thee from felicity awhile,' he tells Horatio, 'And in this harsh world draw thy breath in pain / To tell my story' (331–3). Hamlet's speech may be native to the play, spoken in the air of a 'harsh world', but it is routinely, and apparently easily, removed from it. 'I heard thee speak me a speech once – but it was never acted, or, if it was, not above once' (II.ii.372–3). This movability of voice (the speakability of a speech) is again anticipated as the play draws close to its end, in the somewhat ironical light of a politic convenience or convention. Fortinbras metaphorically acquires Hamlet's tongue, sound, mouth: 'He has my dying voice' (340). The metaphorical sense – the actual donation of Hamlet's royal voice – is strengthened by his suppressed acknowledgement that his nomination of Fortinbras is likely superfluous: 'I do prophesy th'election lights / On Fortinbras' (339–40). Hamlet is opposing this symbolism or metaphor of voice to his own actual speech, emanating from a physical body, or rather, from all the bodies that Hamlet has ever had and ever will have.

Although Stephen Greenblatt memorably inaugurated the New Historicism with 'the desire to speak with the dead', the more basic critical effort seems to involve giving the dead a voice.[38] 'We should never talk about the thing,' suggests Michel Serres in a larger provocation, 'but make it, let it speak.'[39] Compared to voice in lyric poetry, dramatic voice cascades less willingly into pure, non-human sound, or into a problem thereof. If language seems sometimes to require 'both voice, *and* the devocalisation of voice', dramatic language tends to call more strenuously for a *revocalisation*:[40] work to return sounded language to a human origin. Revenge tragedy implicates this work in narrative, grief, memory and a pantheon of troublesome bodies. 'He shrieks,' states a distracted Hieronimo, remembering his son in Thomas Kyd's *The Spanish Tragedy* (c.1587): 'I heard, and yet methinks I hear, / His dismal outcry echo in the air' (*ST* 107–8). Echoes and revoicings of that sort sound in cultural afterlives. 'I thinke your voice would serve for Hieronimo,' an apprentice is told by 'Richard Burbage' in *The Return from Parnassus* (1606): 'observe me how I act it and then imitate mee'.[41] English tragedies are often plagued by crises of audibility, their scenes resounding with voices of uncertain provenance. Hearing an echo in a ruin, Antonio of John Webster's *The Duchess of Malfi* (c.1612) gives a start: ''Tis very like my wives voice'. 'Ay, wifes-voyce,' comes the response (*Duchess*,

V.iii.26). Reading dramatic speech not only involves the prospective reconciliation of poetry's sound to poetry's sense, but the desire to attribute voice to human figures who not only speak but stride, leap, dance, kiss, fight, fall – as they could and did in the past. Webster urges us to entertain two thoughts at once: that dramatic speech echoes as we speak into it, and that dramatic speech is the artificial residue of sounds voiced by other humans in an ever stranger past.

To read drama carefully is then to meet its invitations to create, and then think in, of and through figures. Early modern English plays often seem determined to make that even more laborious than it already is. Hosting their fictions involves a sense of dragging around lumps of dead matter in the mental background, the bad conscience of 'character': 'What have you done, my lord, with the dead body?' (*Hamlet*, IV.ii.4). The figures made by reading drama appear and disappear, but those of revenge tragedy are usually as confusingly fleshy as they are confusingly spectral. Reading revenge tragedies – violent plays of blood and burial – means supplying words with bodies, bodies which do things and to which things are done. The possibly ethical dimensions of this work indict the presumption that it can be achieved with a facile wink. It takes real effort 'fancifully' to imagine the Duchess of Malfi being strangled. To explore how those bodies are made imaginable is to begin a basically historical enquiry into the relation of those texts to dead human beings; into *our* relation to those dead human beings as it is mediated by those texts.

Revenge tragedy is preoccupied with the physical, intellectual, rhetorical labour involved in remembering bodies. It tends to interfere with routine procedures of comprehension by enmeshing figuration – the recognition or misrecognition of figures who move and speak – in specific ethical and political circumstances. 'Remembering,' as William Ian Miller and many of these plays remind us, 'is a richly obligational notion.'[42] By variously distending, collapsing and confusing the interval between the first scene of violence and its recreation by the avenger, revenge tragedy implicitly calls into question the fixed distance critics like to impose between themselves and the literary historical events they would examine, because in it the distinction between interpretation and remembering is purposefully confused. The prosopopeia involved in contemporary reception of early modern plays, even at its most delinquent, suggests and prompts enquiry into the terms on which it is possible and desirable. In making figuration an issue of memory and resurrection, revenge tragedy has gained, in the course of its afterlives, the potential to prosecute the innocence with which its figures appear in literary histories.

To ask who Hamlet is when he voices his proleptic concern that we will misrecognise him is to ask about all the figures he has ever been, their relation to us, and the dimensions in which 'Hamlet' could originally have existed. This book will show that to ask the last question is to ask about Hamlet's original actor, Burbage and 'Burbage', sometimes his actual physical dimensions, his dexterity and speed, the values attributed to his presumed skill within early modern society, and so forth; and that it is practically impossible to exclude that question from the interrogation of Hamlet's 'name'. The most important evidence is supplied by Hamlet: the account he gives of himself; its paradoxes, deficiencies and tautologies. Under pressure, his testimony shifts the blame from moral being to theatre circumstance. That deviation is an early modern tragic speciality. Bosola is asked how he came to stab Antonio in *The Duchess of Malfi*: he describes it as 'Such a mistake as I have often seene / In a play' (*Duchess*, V.v.93–4). Such mistakes are semi-literal in that they allude both to the artificiality of repeatable narrative and to the way theatrical performance involves real accident. Why should the action of revenge tragedy so often merge with its theatrical grounds, and its characters with their actors – and as conspicuously as it does? Why should their *anagnorises* so often coincide with the perception of theatrical artifice? One part of the explanation may be basic: 'There is a sense,' writes John Kerrigan in *Revenge Tragedy*, 'in which theatrical "doing" gravitates, quite naturally, towards revenge.'[43] Revenge makes a scene, but it also starts a plot. Perhaps to understand the scene and the plot means just that. Perhaps Bosola's self-reflection cannot be other than a consideration of theatrical accident because the contingencies of revenge naturally resemble those of the theatre it originated. As Kerrigan continues, revengers seem distinct from most tragic protagonists because the revenger's 'predicament is imposed on him, and to know this is part of his plight [. . .] he is forced to adopt a role'.[44]

Actors, scenes, plots and roles do not mean the same thing through history. To be in London in 1614 or Athens in 458 BC is to have a different understanding of accidents and mistakes, theatrical or otherwise. European theatre changed irrevocably during the sixteenth century. In England the changes were not very much more sudden than elsewhere, but they were unique in their consequences for dramatic art. Amateur performances were suppressed; licences mandated; public theatres opened; theatre commercialised. The relatively few remaining actors were prized for skill, were even 'professional' (although that is mostly a later concept). The 'common' in 'common player' – an epithet shared with prostitutes, innkeepers, attorneys, wage labourers and others – originally meant 'available to or for the public'; 'generally available'.[45] This was contradictory, because it can be argued that the common player was created before there was a market of theatre-goers, and that he himself had to work both to produce and retain his public. What it meant was that to be an actor was to pursue a trade, and that there was no necessary connection between who the player was, what he was asked to play, and whom he played for. The relation of fiction to society, of theatrical figures to those who paid to encounter them, had been disturbed forever, a cataclysm which spurred, shaped and sometimes confounded dramatic art. 'The rise of English drama in the Tudor period and its Elizabethan triumph,' claimed George Steiner in *The Death of Tragedy*, 'restored to the notion of tragedy the implications of actual dramatic performance.' How did this give rise to an alternative to tragedy – what Steiner calls a 'rival form', the history of which is still 'obscure'?[46]

As Steiner's allusion to 'actual dramatic performance' attests, the obvious place to seek this momentous change is in the new ways tragedy was encountered, the premises and grounds of its transmission. But might the continuing formal obscurity of the history of early modern tragedy not originate in these, the terms of the same alteration? This is where a simple notion of historical objectivity – in this instance, the notion of an objective cultural discontinuity – comes unstuck. Assuming it has indeed become impossible to recognise tragic figures properly, the task is then to describe how early *modern* tragedy is digested by those living a 'modernity' that first *appears* in *early* modern tragedy. Put like that, it is easy to see why some versions of the response could tend toward solipsism or (perhaps even worse) heritage. To really investigate the circumstances of our own encounter with historic tragic drama is to inaugurate a wholly different sort of enquiry, into the reasons why early modern tragedy became so invested in exploring dialectics of misrecognition, its interest in its own phenomena. For convenience, this contradiction might be said simply to reveal a contest and co-action of figuration and historical origin.

Just as the persecution of theatre in the sixteenth century supplied the social conditions in which complex and powerful theatre could thrive, so the alleged baseness and negligibility of the common player resourced richly individuated characters. This durable relationship propelled dilemmas of figuration into dramatic art and its futures. Thinking not only of performance prospects but of literary afterlives, some English playwrights no doubt anticipated a few of the conundrums that would arise in literary drama from such a dialectic and took great advantage of them. Revenge tragedy proved an especially adequate medium – full of apparitions, corpses, simulacra, monuments, flesh, combining difficulties of interior figuration with ethics, atavism and memory in such a way as to interfere directly in literary afterlives. *The Origins of English Revenge Tragedy* assumes, then, that Hamlet's prediction was both knowing and correct. His name is 'wounded'. The play is always inflicting and avenging that injury. I conjecture that *recognition* of tragic character, tragic scene and tragic props is *misrecognition*; and that in revenge tragedy the potential identity of tragic recognition and theatrical misrecognition – a radically new premise – is a paramount concern.[47]

Origins

Although this book calls on a plethora of historical materials to show how revenge plays were shaped by social, economic and religious upheaval, it departs from the historicist tradition to which – readers may at this point be startled to learn – it often contributes. It is concerned not only with the moral, political and historical content of English revenge plays but with some of the serious epistemological obstacles standing in the way of its explanatory retrieval and digestion. This book is therefore both phenomenological record, in that it explores the scope of misrecognition in reading revenge plays; and historical encounter, because it shows how such difficulties were created within the fabric of tragic theatre by contradiction and asynchronicity in early modern English society and culture. Origins always refer to an effort of historical thinking – but are encountered as constellations.

The Origins of English Revenge Tragedy does not directly concern poetic originality; it poses a separate set of questions.[48] Neither does it treat origins simply in terms of precedent or influence. The meaning of the titular 'origin(s)' draws on a distinction made by Walter Benjamin in his 1928 book *Ursprung des deutschen Trauerspiels* (*Origin of the German Mourning Play*):

> Origin [*Ursprung*], although a thoroughly historical category, nevertheless has nothing in common with genesis [*Entstehung*]. Origin does not mean the process by which the existent [*Entsprungenen*] came to be, but rather the becoming and fading away of the emergent [*Entspringendes*].[49]

Benjamin's idea of 'origin(s)' has the effect of transforming literary history into a dialectic of appearance that is also historical. A form's origin is that which combines both 'becoming' and 'disappearance', involving both its 'pre- and post-history'. Both of these are present together in, or constitute, the 'work'.[50] The term *Ursprung* includes both the circumstances of the work's production and the phenomenological experience of encountering and interpreting it. Benjamin thought that it was in this combination that baroque drama acquired its artistic 'semblance'. This book is impelled via Benjamin towards a hidden vantage point from which the tradition of English revenge tragedy can be seen to complicate figuration in such a way that at its most artfully inorganic it becomes 'expressionless' (*Ausdruckslos*), mask-like, capable of turning a basic enquiry into literary historical origins into anxious physiognomy. In this way I uphold, in most instances, a connection between the unity of early modern dramatic art and its theatricality. One aim of this book is to contradict the assumption that theatrical performance and literary unity are mutually exclusive.

The Origins of English Revenge Tragedy is related to *Ursprung des deutschen Trauerspiels* in the same way a cousin twice removed is related to the distant family member he has asked to loan him money. Possibly the reader would be right to look at any family resemblance with hesitation, even with a nagging suspicion that someone was being exploited. It is nonetheless difficult to overstate quite how often this book responds to elements of Benjamin's thought. Explicit dialogue is rare, but that silence has proven the only adequate response to an influence so enveloping that it might otherwise have interfered with the separate tasks I pursue. To begin an anatomy of the debt would include observing that the first chapter indirectly develops Benjamin's preoccupation with the contradictory court as the basic tragic space; the second, his observation that the end of *Hamlet* is involved in a problem of fateful props; the third, his interest in the 'comic person'; the fourth, his concentration on the intriguer; the fifth, his investigation of corpses and ghosts. In each of these cases, their origins in specific critiques of Benjamin's book are no longer specifiable and may now be merely of occult interest. Each chapter was shaped by the challenges posed by early modern English materials rather than by any attempt to respond persuasively to specific difficulties in making sense of Benjamin's account of baroque allegory.

Benjamin's *Ursprung* has inspired the general argument of this book, which is that the literary and social geneses of English revenge tragedy, its cultural and material grounds, cannot be untangled from the way they appear and are made to appear in plays. Of only distant secondary interest is the response, contained in Benjamin's discussion of *Ursprung*, to neo-Kantian attempts – including those of Hermann Cohen, Franz Rosenzweig, William Windelband and Heinrich Rickert – to ground both philosophy and historiography in a logic of the origin.[51] That body of work created an antinomy of the singular (viz. causation) and the repetitious (viz. universal laws). Benjamin sought to think both at once. This aspect is relevant only insofar as it has obliquely motivated a determination to think together both the singularity of the dramatic artwork and its repetitious dramatisations. The account of origin in Benjamin's introduction includes a strongly eschatological element, including the notion that the artwork has received the imprint of a divine origin, appearing as the seal of its authenticity. I am more interested in the unlived afterlife of the term *Ursprung*. Benjamin's elaboration of a concept of origin directly preceded his encounter with historical materialism. The work on *Trauerspiel* was finished in the same year he read György Lukács's *History and Class Consciousness*. More importantly, his friendship with Brecht began only months later.[52] One motive of the present book was the thought that the actor was a missing category in Benjamin's account of baroque drama. Had he been pressed on it a few years later, I suggest he might have conceded that *schuldbeladenen Physis* ('guilt-laden nature'), the original sin of the bare human, and even the immanence of the world represented by the drama at question, its apparent non-access to a world beyond itself, aligned with distrust of material theatre circumstances and the sinful bodies of its players. Perhaps, with Brecht, he might have thought all this a theatre problem. 'In violent actions,' he had suggested in *Ursprung des deutschen Trauerspiels*, 'the *theatrical* speaks with especial force.'[53]

Although informed by wide reading in philosophical aesthetics and critical theory, this is not a book which parades its influences as a set of propositions or concepts, edible or inedible slices of marching theoretical pie. Instead its formulation of tasks, and its attitude towards solving them, has been shaped by reflections upon a sprawling and somewhat Frankensteinian theoretical corpus. It belongs in the most general sense to a tradition of dialectical thought, especially (but not exclusively) in German. Instead of setting the materials of this book out at a distance from me and then executing *a priori* 'scientific' concepts upon them, or arraigning them under a heading or under the rubric of a specific academic debate, the aim is to show how at their best the plays considered here occlude historical distance and call into question the very terms on which we might form concepts to explain them. I have sought to find a mode of criticism appropriate to each task, as it has presented itself. Accordingly, relevant scholarly literatures are deployed topically, as and when they bear on separately derived questions.

A Dark Lantern

Despite its complicated investigatory premises, the chapters of this book respond to Socratic questions. What is a 'Knight Marshal'? Where does Hieronimo's revenge happen? How does Hamlet effect revenge? What is

Claudius stabbed with? Who is Revenge? What is a 'servant'? Is Bosola good? Do ghosts have bodies? What is a tragic corpse? In trying to answer those and other ordinary queries, the structure of *The Origins of English Revenge Tragedy* has become sprawling and rather baroque itself. The crookedness of some of its paths – and not merely convention – obliges me to help the reader with navigation.

In its first two chapters, this book explores dialectics of action in *The Spanish Tragedy* and *Hamlet*. Hingeing on a shorter chapter centred on the figure of the 'Vice', the later chapters shift from a dialectics of action to a dialectics of figuration. That structure is not rigid. The chapters of this book can be read independently, even if they mutually support and develop one another. They sometimes approach the same phenomenon, whether play, scene, word or figure, from different angles or at new ranges, with the intention of creating enlightening parallax and telescoping effects. 'Verge' centres on Thomas Kyd's *The Spanish Tragedy*; 'Points', on *Hamlet*; 'A Brief Interlude of Vice' ranges across numerous sixteenth-century plays, tracing a path through *Horestes* to Kyd and Shakespeare. 'Servants' takes its scenes of service largely from revenge plays after *Hamlet*, especially *Hoffmann, The Revenger's Tragedy, 'Tis Pity She's a Whore, The Duchess of Malfi* and *The Changeling*. 'Figures', which of all the chapters is perhaps most dependent on those around it, concentrates largely on *The Duchess*, but like so much of my thought here is also drawn backwards by, or bends sometimes almost unwillingly towards, *Hamlet*.[54] Theodor W. Adorno thought rightly that the great artwork was both a thing of terror and the promise of happiness. *Hamlet* exerts, even at more extreme distances, a special gravity which bears one back, again and again, to its alien and shifting surfaces. I have tried my best not to write yet another book about *Hamlet*, but it is left to the reader to decide how successfully.

Origins is preoccupied with nonsynchronism, anachronism and archaism, in several related senses. The first sense is likely most familiar. Dramatic texts record historical contradictions obtaining during the period of their composition and original performances. Each chapter broaches an important and central problem of discontinuity in early modern English social, economic, religious or cultural history. The first, second, and fourth chapters all engage their material in the context of major debates within the historiography of sixteenth-century society. 'Verge' shows how *The Spanish Tragedy* clears a space for a new sort of tragic drama not by making a *tabula rasa* but by situating its action within an ancient and possibly dysfunctional jurisdiction. Kyd's play implicated revenge tragedy in the increasingly fraught contest between the common law and royal prerogative, as well as in dilemmas of office-holding and 'crises of jurisdiction'.⁵⁵ 'Points' explores the anachronistic introduction of the rapier into ancient tragic materials. It traces a conflict between feudal honour and middling sort civility, and the development of yet inchoate legal categories of manslaughter and chance.⁵⁶ 'A Brief Interlude' finds that the paradoxes of the sixteenth-century 'Vice' arose partly from the transformation of religious allegory into typological social criticism; partly from confessional dispute about images.⁵⁷ 'Servants' shows how the attempt to comprehend the waged servant through the paternalistic image of the loyal retainer gave rise to a violent scepticism about identity, and a concern to find ways of reliably judging appearance.⁵⁸ 'Figures' tackles perhaps the most salient 'anachronism' of all: Renaissance. It illustrates how the recovery of classical epistemologies of figure and image compromised distinctions between the dead, the living and the ghostly on the early modern tragic scene.

The second sense of non-synchronism or anachronism, inseparable from the first in my account, concerns the figure of the actor or 'player'. I argue that the common player appeared in fictional worlds, and was introduced to them by playwrights, as a force of ambiguous contemporisation; but that, conversely, the modern reader encounters the player, at the scene of literary character's failure or insufficiency, as a figure from another time who must appear ever more ancient. Chief amongst the recurrent themes here is the connection between the social identity of the common player in early modern England and the epistemological difficulty of the reader's encounter with shapes, bodies and figures in printed tragedies. The figure of the player is present throughout – here emerging onto the scene and there receding into its shadows. He is many things in this book, including: a real person and persons who lived in the past; a new occupation; a shapeless abstraction; the material side of character; the agent of revenge past and future. In 'Verge', Hieronimo slowly acquires the aspect of an actor playing a royal officer. In 'Points', the player appears during the presentation of physical skill in the climactic sword fight, so that the question of whether Hamlet, the character, really intends and attains a revenge is deferred. 'A Brief Interlude' traces the sixteenth-century connections between the Vice and the common player, showing how in later revenge plays the uncertain origins of revenge morality have been translated into a crisis of theatrical materiality. 'Servants' explores how the common player, himself a servant, appears in servant intriguers prominent in later revenge plays, creating a problem of misrecognition that can be shown to have both social historical origins and theoretical repercussions. Finally, in 'Figures' it is argued that the uncertain residues and materials of ghosts and corpses in revenge tragedy translate the problem of the player's body – its presence and absence – semi-literally into the matter of tradition.

Because I am concerned with the player as he is assigned value in early modern printed sources and as he appears and disappears in play-texts, he possesses only a partial reality in this book. Actors were real people and their history is important, but I am interested in clearing a space for understanding how that history shapes figures in play-texts rather than in writing that history again. This is a book about the partiality of the player's presence in dramatic literature and the epistemological consequences. Although at least some of those consequences are here understood with close reference to the social history of the common player and the history of the early modern English theatres, this is not a work of theatre history or social history. Nonetheless, often where it is most intensely concerned with especially literary questions, *Origins* approaches theatre history. In 'Verge', the fraught symbiosis of theatre space with political and legal bounds is ultimately linked to the theatre-historical context of the early 1590s, with reference also to the theatre itinerancy I have written about elsewhere.[59] In 'Points', I enquire into the materiality of props. 'Vice' essentially concerns the commercialisation of theatre in the 1570s and 1580s. 'Servants' attends to the curious position of the common player at the bounds of the household, with reference to his legal implication in discourses of service. 'Figures' suggests, among other things, that conditions of stage lighting in the past continue to constrain and animate the reader's ability to envisage tragic persons. Such matters notwithstanding, this is not a book closely concerned with the history of the professional companies and its important intricacies of repertory, rivalry, patronage, or financial reciprocity.[60] It proposes that difficulties of literary epistemology are often difficulties of early modern history in disguise, mediated by the prospective presence of the Elizabethan and Jacobean actor. It involves procedures of thought that arise from and remain essentially concerned with the properties of literary encounter, and cannot easily be assimilated into so-called performance studies. *The Origins of English Revenge Tragedy* explores some of the implications of treating early modern drama not as the reflection or container of early modern history, but its manifestation.

Revenge Tragedy

Revenge tragedy can be taken as an object of enquiry, but it cannot be construed as a discrete field or set of texts. This seeming contradiction helps explain why the term revenge tragedy has been retained at all.

The improbability of anybody taking 'revenge tragedy' entirely literally is a positive advantage. 'Ideas relate to things like constellations to stars,' wrote Benjamin.[61] Revenge tragedy here is an idea of that sort, its phenomena straining the eyes as the constellation is sought. Eye-strain, as a later chapter will suggest, can be positively virtuous. In its time, *phenomena* referred only to celestial apparition.[62] Even the most didactic star charts, whether consulted by sunshine or candlelight, originate in, and maintain a friendship with, the amazed, enquiring gaze into the night sky, 'this wonderful & incomprehensible huge frame of God's work proponed to our senses'.[63] Benjamin's image could hardly be more proper to the baroque. Back then, stargazing was not yet known as the first contemplation of history.[64]

Revenge tragedy is implicated not only in indefinite literary and dramaturgical traditions, but in ongoing traditions of reading and interpreting that *The Origins of English Revenge Tragedy* speaks back (and forward) into, the sediment accrued and still accruing, the afterlives of plays. A concept of 'revenge tragedy' is maintained and disseminated in seminar rooms, lecture halls and academic texts. Some terms seem to survive any amount of qualification, which is perplexing to the sociologist but less so to the historian. Despite efforts, like those of John Kerrigan and Linda Woodbridge, to compass the vast literature of revenge thinking in which revenge tragedy takes its place, the constellation 'revenge tragedy', viewed from within early modern studies, remains more or less congruent with Thorndike's 1902 classification of 'a distinct species of the tragedy of blood'.[65] That classification was not entirely artificial. An idea about a distinctive tragic matter involving revenge was conspicuously present to English playwrights in the 1590s and beyond, without its being adequately defined.

Even if there were a specific material to which one could refer later plays of revenge, the terms on which revenge tragedy was present can never be fully determined by the literary historian. An early version of *Hamlet*, whether written by Thomas Kyd, William Shakespeare, someone else, or in collaboration, is lost. That loss makes the intertextual or genealogical relationship between *The Spanish Tragedy* and the extant Hamlet plays insoluble – a grimace without a cat. The mysterious status of the lost play is the source of endless scholarly disagreements. That the lost play or plays possess the quality of myth is contained in the name for it: the *ur*-Hamlet. The Germanic prefix refers to the primitive and originary; Woodbridge refers to 'the primordial slime from which Shakespearean tragedy emerged'.[66] The relationship of *The Spanish Tragedy* to *Hamlet* is only complicated by the 1602 Additions to *The Spanish Tragedy* that it seems possible Shakespeare authored or co-authored, even if treated as what Woodbridge characterises as an exquisite evolution out of 'sensationalist forbears'.⁶⁷ The origins of English revenge tragedy, considered as literary historical beginnings, are therefore benighted. They are uncertainly implicated, nonetheless, in the extraordinary emergence in England of dramatic art and expert theatre in the 1590s. This is just one of the ways in which origins suffer a transposition, giving way to a swarm of other questions which reshape them.

If the extant Shakespearean *Hamlets* can be thought of as somehow antithetical to an original revenge play through which a convention was inaugurated, then that convention must have expired in infancy. Most of the plays assigned to the corpus by academic convention were produced in the two decades after *Hamlet*, so that revenge tragedy must somehow include 'anti-revenge tragedy'. Given that genre is so closely married to issues of convention and the maintenance of convention, that may seem an alarming proposition. Reference to a convention of English 'revenge tragedy' refers above all to Thomas Kyd's *The Spanish Tragedy*. Kyd's play was pivotal because its success and novelty established a space. This was a prospectively literal space: the space of the public playhouse, implicated in legal, economic and political spaces; grounds and territory where classical origins might be managed. It was a space that could be extended and worked upon by other playwrights writing within an emergent tradition of secular English tragedy. Once one looks at that space more closely, as I do in the first chapter, convention stops being the right word altogether. It is not, therefore, contradictory to set out 'revenge tragedy' as a speculative category and to allow for the possibility that the ethics of reciprocal violence are treated with similar complexity in plays that could not easily be called revenge plays. *Pari passu*, it may be impossible to say anything interesting about revenge tragedy and not at the same time say something potentially interesting about early modern tragedy – which is exactly what Lily Campbell suggested in the 1930s.⁶⁸ Still, it would be unwise to construe revenge tragedy as a *species* of tragedy. Benjamin held that any reference to baroque 'tragedy' involved a category mistake: the wrong-headed application of neo-Aristotelian rules to an inappropriate object. Others argue that at some point in early modernity, tragedy became literally impossible.⁶⁹ Here, again, we face questions of origin that mesh historical causation and literary appearance. These questions are best confronted within the derelict arena of revenge tragedy – upon its blood-stained grounds.

Notes

1. Theodor W. Adorno, *Ästhetische Theorie*, in Rolf Tiedemann et al. (eds), *Gesammelte Schriften*, 20 vols (Frankfurt, 1986), 7: 289.
2. William Shakespeare, *Othello*, ed. E. A. J. Honigmann (London, 2006), II.iii.259.
3. William Shakespeare, *Antony and Cleopatra*, ed. John Wilders, Arden 3rd ser. (London, 1995), V.ii.215–17; William Shakespeare, *Julius Caesar*, ed. David Daniell, Arden 3rd ser. (London, 2011), III.i.114.
4. Friedrich Gundolf, *Shakespeare und der deutsche Geist* (Berlin, 1920), 319.
5. Gerald L. Bruns, *The Material of Poetry. Sketches for a Philosophical Poetics* (Athens, 2005), 4; Josh Robinson, *Adorno's Poetics of Form* (New York, 2018), 17.
6. Stephen Orgel, 'What is a Character?', *Text* 8 (1995), 101–8, at 102.
7. See W. B. Worthen, 'Drama, Performativity, and Performance', *PMLA* 113:5 (Oct., 1998), 1093–107.
8. Robert Weimann, *Author's Pen and Actor's Voice. Playing and Writing in Shakespeare's Theatre* (Cambridge, 2000).
9. Cf. Robert Weimann and Douglas Bruster, *Shakespeare and the Power of Performance: Stage and Page in the Elizabethan Theatre* (Cambridge, 2008).
10. Weimann, *Author's Pen and Actor's Voice*, 244.
11. *Contra* Victor Turner, *From Ritual to Theatre. The Human Seriousness of Play* (New York, 1982). In the conclusion to his influential book, Turner refers to 'the loops of the horizontal figure eight [. . .] the relationships of opposition and synthesis between social drama and aesthetic drama' (121), as if this were a purely theoretical relationship of ambiguity without any historical variance. He also restates his theory that staged drama is 'liminoid' – 'suffused with freedom' – in being entertainment (120). 'When we act on the stage, whatever our stage may be' (122) is the point from which his theoretical assimilation of commercial theatre as a 'subjunctive world' must begin. Theatre historians are rightly interested in what the stage is, where it is, who is on it, how it is made, and when it was used: these constitute proper foundations not only for a history of theatre, but for a theory of it.
12. Catherine Bell, *Ritual Theory, Ritual Practice* (Oxford, 1992), 42–3.
13. Lukas Erne, *Shakespeare as Literary Dramatist* (Cambridge, 2003), 221; Leah S. Marcus, *Unediting the Renaissance. Shakespeare, Marlowe, Milton* (London, 1996), 137.
14. See Walter J. Ong, *Orality and Literacy: The Technologizing of the Word* (New York, 1982).
15. Weimann, *Author's Pen, Actor's Voice*, 250.
16. William Worthen, *Print and the Poetics of Modern Drama* (Cambridge, 2005), 32.
17. Michael Riffaterre, 'Prosopopeia', *Yale French Studies* 69 (1985), 107–23, at 108.

18. Gavin Alexander, 'Prosopopoeia: The Speaking Figure', in Sylvia Adamson, Gavin Alexander and Katrin Ettenhube (eds), *Renaissance Figures of Speech* (Cambridge, 2007), 97–112; esp. 107: '*Prosopopoeia* allows its users to adopt the voices of others.'
19. George Puttenham, *The Arte of English Poesie* (London, 1589), 200.
20. See James J. Paxson, *The Poetics of Personification* (Cambridge, 1994), 14.
21. R. Rhys Roberts (ed.), *Demetrius on Style. The Greek Text of Demetrius De Elocutione Edited after the Paris Manuscript* (Cambridge, 1902), §265–6.
22. Puttenham, *Arte*, 245.
23. Richard Rainolde, *The Foundacion of Rhetoric* (London, 1563), fol. xlix^v. F gives the oft-preferred 'whose voice will draw on more' (F: V.ii.347).
24. Thomas Nashe, *Pierce Penilesse his Supplication to the Divell* (London, 1592), Sig. F3.
25. Rainolde, *Foundacion of Rhetoric*, fol. xlix^v.
26. Orgel, 'What is a Character?', 102.
27. Aristotle, *Rhetoric*, trans. W. Rhys Roberts, in Aristotle, *Works* 2: 2008 [§1386*17–25].
28. Gabriel Zoran, *Bodies of Speech. Text and Textuality in Aristotle* (Cambridge, 2014), 72.
29. Random Cloud, 'What's the Bastard's Name?', in George Walton Williams (ed.), *Shakespeare's Speech-Headings* (Newark, 1997), 133–209, at 162. Also see Peter Stallybrass, 'Naming, Renaming and Unnaming in the Shakespearean Quartos and Folio', in Andrew Murphy (ed.), *The Renaissance Text. Theory, Editing, Textuality* (Manchester, 2000), 108–34, at 118–19; Lukas Erne, *Shakespeare's Modern Collaborators* (London, 2008), 40.
30. Random Cloud, '"The very names of the Persons": Editing and the Invention of Dramatick Character', in David Scott Kastan and Peter Stallybrass (eds), *Staging the Renaissance. Reinterpretations of Elizabethan and Jacobean Drama* (New York, 1991), 88–96, at 95.
31. Michael Bristol, 'How Many Children Did She Have?', in John J. Joughlin (ed.), *Philosophical Shakespeares* (London, 2005), 19–34, at 20.
32. Bertolt Brecht, *Kleines Organon für das Theater*, in *Gesammelte Werke*, 20 vols (Frankfurt a.M., 1967), 16: 663.
33. Plato, *Republic*, trans. G. M. A. Grube, rev. C. D. C. Reeve, in John M. Cooper (ed.), *Plato. Complete Works* (Indianapolis, 1997), 1033 [III.394–6].
34. Elizabeth Montagu, *An Essay on the Writings and Genius of Shakespeare* (London, 1810), 15.
35. Maurice Merleau-Ponty, 'The Primacy of Perception and its Philosophical Consequences', trans. James M. Edie, in James M. Edie (ed.), *The Primacy of Perception and Other Essays on Phenomenological Psychology, The Philosophy of Art, History and Politics* (Evanston, 1964), 12–42, at 16.
36. Brenda Machosky, *Structures of Appearing. Allegory & the Work of Literature* (New York, 2013), 2. The second emphasis is mine.
37. Merleau-Ponty, 'Primacy', 16.
38. Stephen Greenblatt, *Shakespearean Negotiations. The Circulation of Social Energy in Renaissance England* (Berkeley, 1988), 1.

39. Michel Serres, *Statues. The Second Book of Foundations*, trans. Randolph Burks (London, 2015), 90.
40. David Nowell Smith, *On Voice in Poetry. The Work of Animation* (Houndmills, 2015), 17.
41. Anon., *The Returne from Parnassus* (London, 1606), Sig. G3.
42. William Ian Miller, *Eye for an Eye* (Cambridge, 2006), 97.
43. John Kerrigan, *Revenge Tragedy. From Aeschylus to Armageddon* (Oxford, 1996), 4.
44. Kerrigan, *Revenge Tragedy*, 12.
45. A. W. B. Simpson, *A History of the Common Law of Contract. The Rise of the Action of Assumpsit* (Oxford, 1975), 230.
46. George Steiner, *The Death of Tragedy* (New Haven, 1996), 13; 21.
47. In this I break with notions of objectivity as they obtain in some traditions of materialism. See Gillian Rose, *Hegel contra Sociology* (London, 2009), 44: 'In Hegel's thought "spirit" means the structure of recognition or misrecognition in a society'; 79: 'In a society based on private property relations, art, too, becomes a form of misrecognition. For if intuition predominates over the concept, art can only re-present a real social relation not a real unity'; 81: 'Art is the re-presentation of the kind of recognition or misrecognition prevalent in a society, of its spirit, in the "medium of intuition".'
48. For a response to the other question, see John Kerrigan, *Shakespeare's Originality* (Oxford, 2018).
49. Walter Benjamin, *Ursprung des deutschen Trauerspiels*, in Benjamin, GS I/i: 226.
50. Benjamin, *Ursprung*, GS 1/i: 226.
51. Beatrice Hanssen, 'Philosophy at its Origin: Walter Benjamin's Prologue to the *Ursprung des deutschen Trauerspiels*', MLN 110:4 (Sept. 1995), 808–29, esp. 821–6.
52. Erdmut Wizisla, *Benjamin und Brecht. Die Geschichte einer Freundschaft* (Frankfurt a.M., 2004), 55–63.
53. Benjamin, *Ursprung*, GS 1/i: 231.
54. The bounds of revenge tragedy are blurry enough that a book trying to construe and compass the 'entire' field would lose focus. Certain dramas are excluded for convenience because the complications they introduce would have taken the book away from its main business. Like George Chapman's *The Revenge of Bussy D'Ambois*, John Marston's *Antonio's Revenge* is left out because of its strong association with the children's companies. Although *Titus Andronicus* is sometimes represented as Shakespeare's earliest extant attempt to broach the ground opened up by Kyd, it seems to me to pursue an experimental agenda so distinctive as to have demanded an entirely separate chapter on affect. Cyril Tourneur's *The Atheist's Tragedy* may never have been performed, and, again, its explicitly antithetical concerns are special enough to have taken serious discussion beyond the scope of the task and into separate qualification. There are other examples. I am content to have restricted my argument largely to what is usually imagined the 'spine' of early modern revenge tragedy – Kyd, Shakespeare, Middleton, Webster – not least because I consider much of what I have to say about the core of this tragic canon almost entirely new.

55. Bradin Cormack, *A Power to Do Justice. Jurisdiction, English Literature, and the Rise of Common Law, 1509–1625* (Chicago, 2007), 1. On the common law and royal prerogative, see John Baker, *The Reinvention of Magna Carta 1216–1616* (Cambridge, 2017), Chap. 5. For some main themes in the historiography pertaining to Tudor office-holding, see Anthony J. Fletcher, 'Honour, Reputation and Local Officeholding in Elizabethan and Stuart England', in Anthony J. Fletcher and John Stevenson (eds), *Order and Disorder in Early Modern England* (Cambridge, 1985), 92–115; Patrick Collinson, 'The Monarchical Republic of Queen Elizabeth I', *Bulletin of the John Rylands University Library of Manchester* 69:2 (1987), 394–424; Mark Goldie, 'The Unacknowledged Republic: Officeholding in Early Modern England', in Tim Harris (ed.), *The Politics of the Excluded, c.1500–1850* (New York, 2001), 153–94.
56. On the rise of civility, see (for example) Norbert Elias, *The Civilizing Process*, trans. Edmund Jephcott (Oxford, 1994); Anna Bryson, *From Courtesy to Civility: Changing Codes of Conduct in Early Modern England* (Oxford, 1998).
57. On the sinfulness of images, see Patrick Collinson, *From Iconoclasm to Iconophobia: The Cultural Impact of the Second English Reformation* (Reading, 1986); Margaret Aston, 'Iconoclasm in England: Official and Clandestine', in Clifford Davidson and Ann Eljenholm Nichols (eds), *Iconoclasm vs. Art and Drama* (Kalamazoo, 1989), 47–91; Michael O'Connell, *The Idolatrous Eye. Iconoclasm and Theater in Early Modern England* (Oxford, 2000).
58. The debates in English social history arising from Marx's concepts of original [*ursprüngliche*] accumulation and the wage economy are probably sufficiently familiar to need no introduction. An important early stimulus to my thinking about the dialectic of service and vagrancy in early modern England was Patricia Fumerton's *Unsettled. The Culture of Mobility and the Working Poor in Early Modern England* (Chicago, 2006).
59. See George Oppitz-Trotman, *Stages of Loss. The English Comedians and their Reception* (forthcoming).
60. This is not proper to my task here. Elsewhere (*supra*) I explore misrecognition of theatre in a different sense and directly engage such questions from within a theatre-historical tradition.
61. Benjamin, *Ursprung*, 218.
62. See Francis Bacon, *Novum Organum*, in Graham Rees and Maria Wakely (eds), *The Oxford Francis Bacon, Vol. 11: The Instauratio Magna Part II: Novum Organum and Associated Texts* (Oxford, 2004), 98.
63. Thomas Digges, *A Perfit Description of the Cælestiall Orbes*, in Leonard Digges, *A Prognostication Everlasting* (London, 1576), Sig. N3^v.
64. On the variously decorative, rigorous and specialised star-maps of the sixteenth and seventeenth centuries, mimeses of an inchoate science, see Anna Friedman Herlihy, 'Renaissance Star Charts', in David Woodward (ed.), *The History of Cartography, Volume Three, Part 1: Cartography in the European Renaissance* (Chicago, 2007), 99–122, at 99.
65. John Kerrigan, *Revenge Tragedy*; Linda Woodbridge, *English Revenge Drama: Money, Resistance, Equality* (Cambridge, 2010); A. H. Thorndike, 'The Relations of *Hamlet* to Contemporary Revenge Plays', *PMLA* 17:2

(1902), 125–220, at 125. Cf. Emma Smith (ed.), *Five Revenge Tragedies. Kyd, Shakespeare, Marston, Chettle, Middleton* (London, 2012).
66. Woodbridge, *English Revenge Drama*, 3.
67. Woodbridge, *Revenge Drama*, 3. On Shakespeare's hand in the Additions, see Hugh Craig, *Shakespeare, Computers, and the Mystery of Authorship* (Cambridge, 2009), Chap. 8; Douglas Bruster, 'Shakespearean Spellings and Handwriting in the Additional Passages Printed in the 1602 *Spanish Tragedy*', *Notes & Queries* 60:3 (2013), 420–4; Gary Taylor, 'Did Shakespeare Write *The Spanish Tragedy* Additions?', in Gary Taylor and Gabriel Egan (eds), *The New Oxford Shakespeare: Authorship Companion* (Oxford, 2017), Chap. 15.
68. Lily B. Campbell, 'Theories of Revenge in Renaissance England', *Modern Philology* 28:3 (Feb., 1931), 281–96.
69. Steiner, *The Death of Tragedy*; Lionel Abel, *Metatheatre. A New View of Dramatic Form* (New York, 1963).

Chapter 1

Verge

> For as for the first wrong, it doth but offend the law;
> but the revenge of that wrong putteth the law out of office.
> Francis Bacon, 'Of Revenge'

In the wake of the fiasco of the 1589 counter-armada led by Francis Drake and John Norris, the Tudor government gave consideration to the return of diseased sailors:

> Forasmuch as it is found by good proofe, that many persons which have served of late on the Seas, in the journey towardes Spayne and Portingall, in coming from Plimmouth, and other Portes of the Realme, have fallen sicke by the way, and divers died as infected with the plague: And that it is likely that many will have purpose to come from the said Navie, to the Citie of London, and so consequently to the Court, whereby danger of infection may come to her Majesties housholde, and so approche to her sacred person. Therefore it is commaunded [. . .] if any such person shall contrary to this commandement, from this day being the xxii. of this moneth of July, attempt to come either to the Court, or within the Verge, and shall not immediately upon knowledge hereof depart with convenient speede, the same shall be apprehended by the Knight Marshall and his Deputies, or by any Justice or Constable dwelling within the Verge, and shall bee committed to the Marshalsea [. . .][1]

It is likely that the authors of this directive feared that the sailors would bring suits or protests to court: many of those who had fought the Armada and had then been kept in service for the subsequent expedition were never paid, and there were almost riotous displays in London when they returned.[2] So the Privy Council instructed the knight marshal to make sure none of those contagious and possibly disruptive men came within the Verge, and to imprison or expel them if they did.

Hieronimo, the chief protagonist of *The Spanish Tragedy* (c.1589), has a very specific office: Knight Marshal of Spain. There was no such office in the Spanish court. In England, however, the knight marshal was an ancient ennoblement.[3] Not only was the knight marshal responsible for the administration and security of the royal household, he was also associated with an unusual court known as the Court of the Marshalsea or the Court of the Verge, with jurisdiction over crimes occurring within and around the royal residence. The potential significance of Hieronimo's exact function within the political court he eventually destroys, and to a lesser degree the involvement of the play in the history of Tudor office-holding, has received remarkably little notice, let alone sustained attention. Lukas Erne observes merely that 'Hieronimo [...] holds the office of Knight Marshal of Spain and is supreme judge of the country in which he tries in vain to obtain justice.'[4] To Frank Whigham he is a 'worthy state officer'; to Andrew Gurr, 'Spain's chief justicer'.[5] Derek Dunne has recently explored, in more detail, the paradox of the exclusion of Hieronimo from the mechanisms of justice in which, as an officer of state, he is involved. Dunne thereby expounds the traditional premise that the play shows the larger historical conflict of a middling sort with a prospectively defunct aristocracy.[6] As Dunne states, the character's role 'as Knight Marshal doubtless heightens the irony in his pursuit of bloody vengeance'. His role 'is compromised' even as it is a job 'that all agree he is well suited to'.[7] But what did the office of knight marshal really involve? Exactly what sort of legal function was at stake, and within whose jurisdiction does Hieronimo's revenge actually happen?

These questions have never been properly asked, let alone answered. Early in the afterlife of the play, 'knight marshal' was taken for a generic title, whence the ballad published in 1620: 'I Marshall was in prime of yeares, / And wonne great honour in the fielde'.[8] The wrong assumption that Hieronimo's marshaldom referred to historic *martial* accomplishment is therefore very old, even though it is not availed by the text. It was adopted uncritically by later critics, and has obstructed scholarly enquiry into Hieronimo's legal position, to which it is only relevant insofar as *martial law* is concerned.[9] The ancient role of the knight marshal in enforcing ordinances within medieval English armies gave rise to multiple analogous positions, for example in camp: this can be seen in late sixteenth-century notices about the punishment of offenders therein.[10] The old role of the knight marshal as the executive force in the Verge may also explain why the position of marshal became a feature of common law court structure. Familiarity with those more generic offices has understandably led to looser descriptions of Hieronimo's role than his specific title encourages. Lorna Hutson describes Hieronimo's 'public-spirited care', his 'conscientiousness as public servant', his 'judicial efforts' and power as 'judge and plaintiff', but the avenger's role as knight marshal makes him more (or less) than a sergeant-at-law, and more (or less) than the Pauline 'minister of God' with which John Kerrigan associates him.[11] James Shapiro refers only in passing to Hieronimo being called upon to fulfil a double function: 'both to "punish such as do transgress" [...] within the verge of the court, and to provide royal entertainment', observing correctly that this is the governing logic of the play's climactic scene.[12] Kerrigan somewhat mischievously suggests that 'Hieronimo's playlet makes a deposition'.[13] Some of these are good approximations, but none of them quite gets to the nub. Hieronimo is, as Katherine Eisaman Maus glosses from the *OED*, 'an officer of the royal household with judicial authority over the palace and its environs'.[14] This seems to be as detailed a description as has ever been furnished of the actual position of one of the most famous and formative characters in English drama. The spatial logic of what is often reckoned 'the most influential play of the early modern English theater', and with it the legal and social dimensions of its hero's revenge, have remained fundamentally opaque.[15]

This chapter defines Hieronimo's office and explores its many confusing implications. As specific as that office is, understanding it leads one not into a secure arena of legal rationality or allegorical satire, but down a rabbit-hole where myriad aspects of social space, historical and theoretical or conjectural, crowd in upon interpretation of the play. In co-ordinating these various spaces, I seek to set out the grounds of the tragic mode inaugurated by *The Spanish Tragedy* by working that administrative and rather bureaucratic gesture of critical clearance or boundary-setting into an exploration of origins, grounds and jurisdictions social, poetic and theatrical. I argue that *The Spanish Tragedy* implicates the tradition of revenge tragedy in a basic problem of space and place; and that registering the crisis of space that emerges at the fictional level of the play means registering how the play itself works upon, and lays claim to, its own grounds. Attending to the absent circumstance of the Verge in *The Spanish Tragedy* means figuring the spaces past and future, historical and speculative, in which the drama did happen and could happen.

Placita Aule Regis

The jurisdiction of the marshal and steward over crimes committed within the *verge* or *marshalcy* were set down in the *Articuli super Cartas* of 1301, under the pretence of confirming an ancient right but in the context of an attempt to limit abuses of royal prerogative and bolster the liberties of *Magna Carta*.[16] The 'verge' or 'marshalsea' was an area comprising the twelve miles (*duodecim leucarum*) around the monarch. It is from this approximate zone that Shakespeare's Henry V banishes Falstaff at the end of *2 Henry IV*, a detail that in its specific inaccuracy (ten miles rather than twelve) may indicate both the durability of the idea and its disrepair as the sixteenth century ended.[17] The Court of the Marshalsea, or 'pleas of the royal palace and residence of the lord king, [heard] before the steward and the marshal' (*placita coronae aulae hospitii domini regis coram seneschallo et marischallo*), originally possessed a general jurisdiction governed only by the spatial degree of the Verge, covering thereby all felonies and trespasses that had been committed within that space – provided that the case could be concluded before the departure of the sovereign, which removed the Verge and so removed the crime from its ambit.

In Edward Coke's translation of the *Articuli*, such cases should be pleaded 'speedily from day to day, so that they may be pleaded and determined before that the king depart out of the limits of the same verge where the trespass was done'.[18] 'And if it so be that they cannot be determined within the limits of the same verge, then shall the same pleas cease before the steward, and the plaintiffs shall have recourse to the common law,' the articles continued. This made the Verge not only a spatial but a temporal limit. Beyond its alleged venerability, the court was intended to answer the problem that common law coroners had no right to investigate violent crimes within the Verge, as endangering the king's rights. This provision was reflected in sixteenth-century practice too: 'In case of mans death within the vierge it shalbe commaunded to the Coroner of [that] countrey that hee together with the Coroner of the kinges house, do make the inquiry and inroll it.'[19] In other words, the jurisdiction of the court combined a care for sovereign rights with a concern for access to justice.[20] Contestations of that jurisdiction were necessarily involved in a negotiation with the terms of royal sovereignty and its interaction with common law wisdom.

Such was the Marshalsea's importance and prominence as the sixteenth century began, that it is the first of the ancient courts named in Fitzherbert's *Diversite de courtz*.[21] Some took it to be the oldest court in the kingdom. Over the course of its history, it had become 'a court of regular resort for small suits in the metropolis' when the monarch was there, and a great expedient to plaintiffs in the provinces, who could take advantage of the sovereign's proximity to pursue their claims with greater alacrity. Cases may usually have been handled in just a few days. By the 1590s, the Court of the Verge was embroiled in controversies surrounding the possibility of pursuing the same matter in multiple courts, and may well have acquired a stronger association with London.

At the start of the seventeenth century it was a heavily constrained and probably rather disenchanted place. At the height of the popularity of *The Spanish Tragedy*, the effort to define the Court of the Verge as an inferior court, and the effort to circumscribe its authority with reference to the more usual common law courts, was in full swing.[22] In particular its authority over 'trespasses within the Verge', for which Edward had given the court an ambiguous remit, would face increasing challenge from the King's Bench, before which significant appeals from judgements made in the Marshalsea Court were heard.[23] The twelfth-century separation of the King's Bench from the *curia regis* may well have brought into being the legal power of the steward and marshal to effect justice in and around the royal household; this break was probably caused by the itinerancy of the Anglo-Norman kings.[24] In the Court of the Verge, the sovereign could continue to eclipse local jurisdictions, as seemed both practical and proper, despite the King's Bench sitting elsewhere. By the mid-1590s at the latest, the King's Bench was seeking to constrain the powers of what must have seemed to those at the bleeding edge of common law to have become an archaic institution, and to bring its judgements under the purview of a superior court. 'The difference between them,' declared George Croke in one of the sharpest arguments for its inferiority, is that 'one of them [...] *sequitur personam Regis* [follows the person of the king]: but otherwise it is [...] the King Bench which acts *in persona regis* [in the person of the king]'.[25]

In 1497 Henry VII had directed the Court of the Verge to focus on conspiracies to assassinate the king or his ministers and to administer punishment to the agents of such treachery.[26] Furthermore, 33 Hen. VIII. c.12, 'An Act for Murder and Malicious Bloodshed, within the Court', brought all treasons, murders, manslaughters and 'malicious strikings' occurring 'within the Limits of the King's Palace or House, or other House or Houses, where and when his Majesty is there demurrant and abiding' fully under the control of the Court of Marshalsea. It upheld the 'Liberty and Jurisdiction of the *Marshalsey* Court and Circuit of the Verge' to prosecute and judge any felonies and trespasses whatsoever.[27] The Act also specified the removal of the right hand of any who had shed blood within the Verge. In a notorious case, recorded by John Stow, Sir Edmond Knevet received this very sentence – but was pardoned.[28] Dozens of prisoners had been condemned to die by the knight marshal in 1536, without trial.[29] During the paranoid summer of 1549, the knight marshal rode through London 'with the trumpett and the common cryer afore' him, making a proclamation that 'rebels and upsterrers' be apprehended 'without any enditement or arraignment'.[30] A decade later, records show the knight marshal being called on to assist in the interrogation and torture of two men suspected of robbing a widow in London; possibly the first notice of the Elizabethan Privy Council sanctioning the rack. In 1581, 'two other priests' imprisoned with Edmund Campion, possibly Ralph Sherwin and Alexander Briant, were put under the charge of the knight marshal, by warrant, following torture or the threat of torture.[31] The knight marshal was apparently active in such matters in the late Tudor period too. John Ardern complained to Robert Cecil in 1596 that the knight marshal, suspecting him of treason, had without warrant searched his house and imprisoned him in the Marshalsea.[32]

As it was once so memorably put, 'treason is a crime which has a vague circumference, and more than one centre'.[33] The obscurity of that law under the Tudors forbids too strong an insistence on the role of the knight marshal in discovering and punishing treason.[34] What is certain is that he and his men were responsible for maintaining order, security and peace around the monarch, and that this responsibility naturally extended to the prosecution of treasonous conspiracy in a general and often arbitrary way.[35] As in the past, the Verge 'served as a focal point for the enforcement of public order in the area around the king'.[36] Several of the aforementioned cases hint that the Court of the Verge was used in the sixteenth century as a convenient instrument of proper legal detention or inquisition when the case against prisoners was slight. Indeed, there is evidence that the jurisdiction and prison of that court were employed in such a way by the King's Bench at other times.[37] Under Elizabeth I, the knight marshal continued to act as he had in the Middle Ages, as 'the chief disciplinarian of the court'.[38] Perhaps even more pertinent than any of the occasions already adduced was the case of Thomas Appletree, who in July 1579 was sentenced to be executed for accidentally discharging an arquebus upon the queen from the boat he and his friends were rowing along the Thames. He earned a royal pardon with a speech given, like Pedringano, with a halter around his neck; in it, he apologised to his master Henry Carey, who had been appointed knight marshal just for that day so that he could discharge the punishment – implicitly so as to mitigate 'slander[s] of the cause' that 'some evil disposed persons' had circulated against him.[39]

In 1598 the Privy Council suggested to the earl marshal, Robert Devereux, Earl of Essex, that an office of provost marshal be created to deal with 'certain rogues, vagabonds and other dissolute persons' alleged to have 'committed such violences [. . .] as the ordinary course of justice sufficeth not to suppress them'. Essex drafted a reply that was concerned to protect (and possibly extend) the 'ancient office' of earl marshal that he held, observing that 'the Knight Marshal, who is indeed but the K. Provost Marshal and is called in France *Grand Provost de l'Hostel*, hath been used in those kind of services'.[40] Essex was upholding an old concession of martial law, by which a knight or soldier could be appointed to act in the earl marshal's stead: this seems to have been a separate derivation of the same household office. The confusing origins of the office of earl marshal (its scope, and the etymology of the word 'marshal') formed the subject of a session of the Society of Antiquaries in the early seventeenth century; Robert Cotton thought knights marshal were *praepositi marescallorum* ('surrogates of the marshals').[41]

Although its officers may technically have been but delegates for two of the great officers of state (the earl marshal and the lord high steward), the Marshalsea Court acquired its jurisdiction and authority from the presence of the sovereign, preserving the ancient concept of the monarch as *fons justitiae*:[42] 'Justice, O justice: justice gentle King' (*ST* III.xii.62). When the monarch would 'rest, tarry, abide, or make his repose' somewhere, the Verge was created.[43] It was 'a bounded Court'.[44] It related to the limits of court or household, and alleged the primacy of the royal court and the royal household. The chief constraint that lawyers sought to impose on the court in the latter half of the sixteenth century was that the steward and marshal possess jurisdiction only over those trespasses and felonies involving 'certain particular persons', namely members of the royal household or officers of the royal court; and not the 'general authority' they had enjoyed 'in ancient time'.[45] This revision would eventually prevail, albeit the reference to 'ancient time' was probably spurious, the generality of the privilege being (as Coke et al. almost certainly knew) disused rather than simply obsolete.

Such changes eroded the close connection preserved by the Court of the Verge between the royal court and a space of absolute royal justice, a *court*. '*Curia* could mean a place, a body of men, an institution, or a jurisdiction,' writes John Baker: 'and perhaps all four at once.'[46] The sixteenth-century Court of the Verge was the very outline of that paradox. 'The Court was not so much a place or even an idea as a process of negotiation,' adds Robert Zaller. 'At its most precise it was a jurisdictional liberty bounded by a verge [. . .] but precision, legal or otherwise, meant little in an experimental monarchy that was constantly on the move,' he goes on: 'It might be said that modern bureaucracy sprang up in the abandoned tenements of royalty.'[47] As Baker notes, the word 'court' derived not from *curia* but from *cohors*, meaning 'enclosed yard', via the French *cour* – albeit that distinction was quickly lost.[48] But the Marshalsea Court did indeed acquire ever more definite physical parameters. Its perimeter gradually became a fixture of London cultural and legal topography rather than a dynamic and moving space. In the

1580s and 1590s this later identity was still a way off, but attempts to constrain the jurisdiction already presaged this future.

Against the grain of this managed decline, the Marshalsea Court was revived as the Court of the Verge of the King's Palace in mid-1611, after complaints were made to Parliament that its suppression had reduced the court fees previously enjoyed by certain members. Taking up a judgeship in this new tribunal, Francis Bacon gave an extraordinary address to its Grand Jury:

> *David* saith (who was a king) *The wicked man shall not abide in my house*; as taking knowledge that it was impossible for Kings to extend their care to banish wickedness over all their land or empire, but yet at least they ought to undertake to God for their house. We see further that the Law doth so esteem the dignity of the King's settled mansion-house, as it hath laid unto it a plot of twelve miles round (which we call the Verge) to a special and exempted jurisdiction depending upon his person and great officers. This is as a half-pace, or carpet, spread about the King's Chair of Estate, which therefore ought to be cleared and voided more than other places of the kingdom; for if offences shall be shrouded under the King's wings, what hope is there of discipline and good justice in more remote parts[?][49]

Perhaps Bacon's rhetoric was fired by the abuses to which the Marshalsea had recently been put: in 1610, the Howard family had attempted to remove their friend Edward Morgan from Newgate to the Verge, following his killing of John Egerton, hoping for a more favourable decision.[50] Bacon vanquished all quiddities touching the jurisdiction of this revived court by re-establishing it by royal prerogative, alluding to models of sacral kingship. This may explain the unusual extent and vehemence of the King's Bench judgement in *The Case of the Marshalsea*, concluded the following year. With renewed concern as to its scope, the institution was remade the 'Palace Court' in 1630. The Marshalsea prison would gain infamy in later years as a gaol for debtors, reflecting perhaps the frequency with which debt pleas were heard in the old court; while the so-called 'Verge of the Court' would operate (paradoxically) as a liberty and sanctuary for debtors.[51]

Throughout the period in question, then, from the 1580s through the 1600s, the office of knight marshal was linked by jurisdiction and long history to questions of sovereignty, household space and the physical extent of an entirely undisturbable royal peace.[52] It involved the investigation of treasonous intent, and violent enforcement of penalty. The Verge was a distinct and ancient space when *The Spanish Tragedy* was written and performed – both a ruin and one of the most prospectively 'perfect' places in England. Bacon assumed in 1611 that the steward and marshal's ancient power over any crime committed near the royal palace had never been superseded or cancelled, only disused.⁵³ In proceeding to map this uncertain jurisdiction onto *The Spanish Tragedy*, one does not call on a peripheral curiosity in the museum of legal history, but upon an ancient and potent zone in which action and redress could be understood with combined reference to mythologies of royal justice and procedures of common law; a place in which cries of anguish reverberated with an especial clarity. 'This plot of ground, which is the Kings Carpet,' affirmed Bacon, 'ought not to be stained with blood, crying in the Ears of God and the King.'⁵⁴

This Plot

If the blood of Hieronimo's murdered son Horatio cries out in *The Spanish Tragedy*, it echoes in a tragic verge – but is heard by neither God nor King. That contemporaries may have assumed that Hieronimo's office was deeply significant can perhaps be inferred from the dumb show opening the prequel to *The Spanish Tragedy* called *The Spanish Comedy, or The First Parte of Ieronimo* (1605), which Lukas Erne persuasively argues is an expansion of Kyd's lost *Don Horatio*, 'the first half of a continuous and interrelated diptych', into a play suitable for performance by the Children of the Chapel:⁵⁵

> *Sound a Signate and passe ouer the stage. Enter at one dore* The king of Spaine, Duke of Castile, Duke Medina, Lorenzo, *and* Rogero: *at another doore,* Andrea, Horatio, *and* Ieronimo, Ieronimo *kneeles downe, and the* King *creates him marshall of Spaine:* Lorenzo *putes on his spurres, and* Andrea *his sword, the* King *goes along with* Ieronimo *to his house. After a long signate is sounded, enter all the nobles, with couerd dishes, to the banquet. Exit Omnes. That done Enter all agen as before.*⁵⁶

'Frolick Ieronimo,' the King of Spain utters:⁵⁷ 'thou art now confirmd / Marshall of Spain, by all the dewe / And customary rights unto thy office' (*ST* I.i.1–3). Hieronimo calls on his son Horatio to genuflect with him before the sovereign from whom he has received 'this high staffe of office' (5–8). 'Staffe' is probably more specific than it seems: *verge* came from *virga*, meaning 'wand of office', 'yard' and 'rod', with necessary connection to *virgate* ('yardland') by way of the simultaneous use of the wand or rod as a symbol of authority and a means of measuring the physical extent of that authority. This ancient connection between the staff of authority and its ambit (*desous la vierge*) appears to have been standard in late sixteenth-century England: 'Verge hath also another signification, and is used for a sticke, or rodde, whereby one is admitted tenent, and holding it in his hand sweareth fealtie unto the Lord of a maner: who for that cause is called Tenent by the verge.'⁵⁸ In fact there is no distinction to be upheld between the two senses of *verge*: 'It is so called, because the marshal *portat virgam (quae signat pacem) coram Rege per spatium 12 leucarum*', or 'bears the rod (which designates peace) for a space of twelve miles before the king'.⁵⁹

The Spanish Tragedy involves the Spanish and Portuguese courts. It accesses anti-Catholic feeling which was at its height in the mid-/late-1580s, and English fear of the Iberian Union. The play seems to belong to a group of plays of the late 1580s and early 1590s treating of Spanish and Portuguese subjects, including the Stukeley plays. Hieronimo studied in Toledo. In the wake of his disastrous petitioning of the King directly, Hieronimo receives petitioners and makes specific reference to having pleaded 'in causes as corregidor' before his marshalship. The *corregidores* – meaning, literally, 'correctors' – were the chief representatives of the Castilian state in Spanish provinces; their office is described in Jerónimo Castillo de Bobadilla's *Política para corregidores y señores de vassallos* (1597), and was known to English writers: 'Those that the Romaines did call Censors or judges, we do call Corregidores or Correctors [. . .] He should be maried, holden for honest, meanely ritch, nor infamed with covetousness.'⁶⁰

It is therefore plain that the play relies on a complex mesh of national and mythical courts and regions. Were it not for some other specifically English legal instruments which are adduced by the play, it could seem possible that Kyd had loosely translated into 'knight marshal' some other position in Spanish administration of which he had read or heard. An equivalent instance could in that case be found in Thomas Stocker's *A Tragicall Historie of the troubles and civile warres of the lowe Countries* (1583), a translation from the French version, called *Histoire des troubles et guerres civiles des Pays-Bas* (1582), of Adam Henricpetri's *Niderlendischer Ersten Kriegen [. . .]* (Basel, 1575). At the scene of the Count of Egmont's execution in 1568, Henricpetri describes *der Profoß* below the scaffold, which was laid in black velvet; the French gives *le Provost*. This was the same foreign office cited as an analogue by Essex in 1598. Stocker writes: 'Below the Scaffolde was the knight Marshall carrying a red wande in his hande, and the Hangman upon the Scaffolde.'⁶¹ Presumably the detail of the red verge encouraged the precision of the translation. There would have been nothing at all unusual in employing foreign materials to treat an English subject. Kyd's drama *Cornelia* (1594), a translation from Garnier's *Cornélie* (1574), has been recognised for the way it uses a loss of Roman liberties to explore English absolutism; Eugene Hill has argued that *The Spanish Tragedy* likewise 'evokes, foregrounds, and enacts a *translatio studii*'.⁶² Reviewing the murder of Serberine and the punishment of his killer Pedringano in *The Spanish Tragedy* will confirm that the Marshalsea Court – and therefore the Verge – is present to the play, and that Hieronimo's title is neither unspecific, immaterial, nor foreign.

Pedringano is instructed to meet his victim in Saint Luigi's Park: ''Tis here hard behind the house' (*ST* III.ii.84). Lorenzo repeats that instruction to the servant he sends to Serberine: 'Bid him forthwith meet / The prince and me at Saint Luigi's Park, / Behind the house' (95–6). Then he reveals his plan, which he makes in anxiety as to Hieronimo's 'sly enquiry' after Bel-imperia, and his 'suspicion': 'I'll spread the watch, / Upon precise commandment from the king, / Strongly to guard the place' (101–3). The emphasis on place is continued into the scene of murder: 'This place is free from all suspect,' observes Pedringano (III. iii.15). Serberine agrees after a fashion: 'How fit a place – if one were so dispos'd – / Methinks this corner is to close with one' (26–7). The Watch wonder why they have been instructed to patrol this place, for they were 'never wont to watch and ward / So near the duke, his brother's, house before' (20–1). Both the murderer and his victim stress the circumstance of place. As Cicero had it in *De Inventione*, 'in considering the place where the act was performed, account is taken of the opportunity the place seems to have afforded'.⁶³ Earlier, the play links Pedringano to Hieronimo's attempt to confirm the intelligence he has received from Bel-imperia. 'I therefore will by circumstances try, / What I can gather to confirm this writ,' declares the knight marshal; Pedringano enters mere moments later (*ST* III.ii.48–53). The most persuasive explanation for the insistent emphasis on location in the scene of Serberine's death, re-enforced by the spreading of the Watch to surveil and regulate that location, is that his murder takes place within the Verge. It is this spatial limit which will bring the sub-plot to bear directly on Hieronimo's pursuit of justice, because it provides him with the occasion on which to learn more about the crime. The deed is done; the Watch move in.

2 Watch
  Come, to the Marshal's with the murderer.
1 Watch
  On to Hieronimo's. Help me here
  To bring the murdered body with us too.
Pedringano
  Hieronimo? – Carry me before whom you will:
  Whate'er he be, I'll answer him and you.
                  (III.iii.43–7)

Hieronimo has authority to investigate the crime because he is knight marshal, and for this specific reason. That is why the Watch deliver Pedringano to him: his 'office asks / A care to punish such as do transgress' (III.vi.11–12).

The *transgression*, because it involves the knight marshal, regains its literal meaning of 'going over' or 'going beyond' a limit. Balthasar assures Lorenzo that he will 'haste the marshal-sessions' to see Pedringano dead (*ST* III.iv.33). Pedringano writes to his master from gaol, so Lorenzo sends false hope: 'And, though the marshal sessions be today, / Bid him not doubt of his delivery' (61–2). The final word is a vicious pun, combining the general sense of redemption or liberation with a legal term, meaning 'bring to trial', which coerces the former sense to mean 'delivery from life'. The action has the Verge as a circumstance, even if it is never mentioned: the rapidity with which the whole case proceeds stems perhaps from the court's reputation for speed. It is by its circumstance that Hieronimo finally comes across proof, when the Hangman brings him one of Pedringano's letters (III.vii.25). In this way, revenge – that 'putteth law out of office'[64] – invades and infects the office of knight marshal. An ancient English legal space is conjoined and implicitly arrayed together with the panoply of classical, mythical and hellish authorities with which Hieronimo frames his appeal to a justice outside society. Hieronimo remains officer of the court, but also plaintiff: 'I will go plain me to my lord the king, / And cry aloud for justice through the court' (69–70). In the word 'court' the ambiguity is sustained and compacted, to make a new space co-eval with the space of theatrical performance.

The first act of the play bounds the court and the space of action. The battle that directly precedes the action is said to have taken place 'where Spain and Portingale do jointly knit / Their frontiers, leaning on each other's bound' (*ST* I.ii.22–3).[65] Horatio, Lorenzo, their prisoner Balthazar, and the rest are described as 'marching on towards [the] royal seat' of Spain (104): their entrance but a few lines later recreates the stage as this seat or palace, which is then described in the round by the Spanish king's instruction to have the returnees 'march once more about these walls' (121), calling for a bit of stage action literally to encircle the space of royal conference. Much of the action of the early scenes involves Hieronimo silently attending the central spectacle of kingship. In that first construction of the court, Hieronimo's roles as father, subject and royal sergeant are unified. His reaction to discovering the murdered Horatio hints at the confusion introduced into this nexus of official, familial, even religious responsibilities by the act of violence: 'in my bower to lay the guilt on me' (II.v.11). Following the scene in which

Hieronimo breaks down before the assembled court, and 'surrender[s] up' his marshalship to 'marshal up the fiends of hell / To be avenged' (III.xii.75–6), Lorenzo speaks to the King: ''Tis requisite his office be resigned, / And given to one of more discretion' (95–6).

The sovereign demurs: 'We shall encrease his melanchollie so. / 'Tis best that we see further in it first: / Till when, our selfe will exempt the place.'[66] This is a crucial moment, because it is only by means of the royal prevarication that Hieronimo is later in a position to effect his revenge, and here something decisive has occurred with respect to his office. The final clause is difficult to gloss, chiefly because of the intransigent *exempt*; but there is a hidden trickiness in *Till*, which may mean 'while we wait for the outcome of our inquiry into Hieronomo's competence' or 'while we look into what has caused this outburst' , or even 'at which point'. *Exempt* (Latin: *eximo, eximere*: remove; take out; banish; dispose of; free or release) at first sight seems synonymous with 'hold vacant', and since the nineteenth century has sometimes been glossed or emended accordingly, but it is not.[67] Lorenzo has asked the King, not to fill the knight-marshalship, but to remove Hieronimo from it. It therefore makes little sense for him to receive a reply that can be paraphrased, 'No, we will not make Hieronimo resign, but we shall hold the office vacant.' More careful editors have sometimes supposed that a printer's error resulted in the loss of a 'not', making the line hypometrical. It is then to be corrected thus: 'Till when, our selfe will [not] exempt the place'.[68] There are many reasons to recommend that correction, but given that the line remained unaltered in successive editions, we are enjoined to consider the readings created by the difference because the line was only available in its original state to its early readers. It is also moderately likely that the error crept into later performances, if error it be.[69]

If one accepts the line as it is and does not interpolate a negative, there are two adequate readings: that the King will not remove Hieronimo from his office, but will remove (*exempt*) the power of that office – which is the same as the sovereign impossibly exempting himself from the Verge his presence creates and sustains; or that the King intends in his own person to uphold the dignity of the Verge (its *exemption*), without replacing its chief officer, who is himself exiled (*exempted*), as a consequence, from the very space on which his duty to the court is contingent.[70] Either gloss seems consistent with what happens. Hieronimo, despite having ineffectually surrendered or offered up the marshalship, and despite the sovereign having suspended its power, continues to act ambiguously as knight marshal, thereby contesting the Verge as a site of perfect reparation. Or, the Verge becomes a space from which Hieronimo himself is *exempted*: if the King alone maintains it, then a failure to access the King becomes alienation from the space of absolute justice said to surround him, and Lorenzo's power to intercept Hieronimo's suits becomes the definition of arbitrary and unchecked intervention in justice, rather than the general moral trespass for which it is otherwise taken. The effect is similar. Hieronimo's revenge is not separated from his office and its jurisdiction, but must appear both as destruction and reconstruction of the sacred, ancient space of royal justice; and with it, a reconfiguration of the purpose and identity of its marshal.

When one inserts the apparently missing 'not' – 'our selfe will [not] exempt the place' – a surprisingly similar range of possibilities is activated, because the flexibility of the intransitive *exempt* continues to work in unexpected ways whether it is in the negative or not. The King can then mean, 'We will not vacate or reserve this position, or use it for some other cause.' Possibly Lorenzo has hinted he should be the next knight marshal. But given the unique properties of the Verge, this is the same as to say, 'We will not leave this place,' which *exempt* also allows. This sense of *exempt* might indeed be encouraged insofar as it sounds like it could take *our selfe* as its object, since *exempt* was often used reflexively (as it still is). The departure of the sovereign would remove Hieronimo's authority were Hieronimo to remain. Hieronimo – like the audience – would have departed the Verge by standing still.

Inside, Outside

This pivotal and aporetic line bisects the action to follow. To bring into effect his revenge, to inhabit a place 'Till to revenge [he] know when, where, and how' (*ST* III.xiii.44), Hieronimo must learn to hold office in a different way. That it is narratively plausible that the murder will be revealed follows from providential expectation. In the 1592 pamphlet *The Murder of John Bowen*, with which Kyd used to be spuriously associated, the conspirators are overheard arguing about the crime years later and so brought to account: 'at length the Lorde will bring it out, for bloud is an unceassant crier in the eares of the Lord and he will not leave so vilde a thing unpunished'.[71] This providential logic of story naturally threatens to make the agency of the avenger into the mere appearance of agency. But Hieronimo acquires an especially memorable force as a new sort of protagonist because he expresses his agency as the choice to learn effective role-play. He turns his dutiful marshalship into mere disguise ('dissembling'), realising the promise of earlier, that the court could be exempted without him being removed from it.

The making of the knight marshal into a *persona* actualises Hieronimo's threat to the state, even as it shows as contiguous with the polysemous *exempt* in the mid-way scene. In Shirley's Websterian tragedy *The Cardinal* (1641), the audience is warned that 'There's treason in some hearts, whose faces are / Smooth to the state.'[72] Vindice in Middleton's *The Revenger's Tragedy* hopes to make his face into 'dauntless marble'.[73] Kyd's play had popularised this concern in the drama of the avenger's alienation from the court and his education in expedient pretence: 'Thus therefore will I rest me in unrest / Dissembling quiet in unquietness, / Not seeming that I know their villainies' (III.xiii.29–31). Not only does commitment to the dynamics of hiding and showing ('so long concealed / [. . .] venged or revealed', *ST* III.vii.47–8) lend Hieronimo motive force – but this commitment is provoked by an encounter with personated likeness. Hieronimo comes face to face with another grieving father, Don Bazulto: 'Thou art the lively image of my griefe: / Within thy face my sorrowes I may see' (161–2). For a moment Bazulto is proposed as an actor remembering Hieronimo: 'The lively portrait of my dying self' (85).

The cases heard before the knight marshal in *The Spanish Tragedy* are distinctively English: an action of debt; an action on the case; an action in trespass of ejectment ('*ejectione firmae* by a lease'). Bazulto is the fourth plaintiff. Prior to meeting that opposite father, Hieronimo's function in respect of those pleas, even before he tears up the writs and abandons the 'poor petitioners' who brought them, is deeply ambiguous (*ST* III.xiii.45–172). Hieronimo implies strongly that he is not to judge or direct those suits as an officer of that court, but argue them before the King as advocate: 'Now must I bear a face of gravity; / For thus I us'd, before my marshalship, / To plead in causes as corregidor' (56–8). In this way his regression from the office of knight marshal is shown initially as the return to a prior legal position (the *corregidor*), a trick which helps to image Hieronimo as advocate, judge and plaintiff in one. The petitioners also expect representation: 'There is not any advocate in Spain / That can prevail, or will take half the pain / That he will, in pursuit of equity' (52–4). That final word, as Mark Fortier shows, was at the heart of a long (and vain) struggle in the sixteenth century to reconcile law to justice.[74] In contradistinction to the other plaintiffs, whose suits concern property, and possibly even legal artifices of violent breach (*vi et armis* and *contra pacem*), Bazulto's supplication concerns an actual spilling of 'blood'. This connects his plea directly to the maintenance of the King's peace and its beginnings in the sanctity of the Verge.

In Bazulto, Hieronimo recognises himself; recognises himself, that is, as a plaintiff external to the court wherein justice may be got. In turn this provokes him to exit his *place* by twice running off-stage, and then reoccupying it in a different mode by returning (*ST* III.xiii.123–30). The 'face of gravity' with which Hieronimo equated official duty seems but glib next to the physiognomy of the father's Stoicism. The proper comportment and bearing of the royal office-holder becomes spurious and unbearable ('Though on this earth justice will not be found, / I'll down to hell [...]', 107–8). Hieronimo's place cannot be understood using the rubric of liminality or carnival, beneath which such close and even rather technical contradictions would vanish.[75] Hieronimo's situation recalls, from the *Mirror for Magistrates*, 'The Fall of Robert Tresilian' and the confusion awaiting those who 'wretchedly did wrest the sense of law':

> A chaunge more new or straunge, when was there ever séene,
> Then Judges from the Bench to come downe to the Barre,
> And counsaylours that were, most nigh to King and Quéene
> Exiled their countrey, from Court and counsayle farre.[76]

Hieronimo appears incorrupt; a confusion of 'place' and 'law' has been inflicted upon him. He has perceived that 'justice is exiled from the earth' (III.xiii.139) and that he is exiled from the secular court by injustice. To pursue revenge, Hieronimo must impersonate the person he no longer feels himself to be: knight marshal of Spain. Consequently, the Verge is sustained but transformed into a field of theatrical accomplishment where revenge is doubly 'plotted' (maliciously charted); and where the appearance of persons within the Verge can only be comprehended as theatrical semblance. The political and legal unit collapses into the theatrical scene.

That Hieronimo should appear as both judge and plaintiff throughout the second half of the play is one way in which the distinction between a boundary and the space it contains – 'within the Verge' and 'on the verge' – is shown to be illogical. The Verge is both boundary and interior space at the same time. *The Spanish Tragedy* explores it as a *quality* or even a *substance*.[77] By the end of the play, Hieronimo is both within the Verge and beyond its limit: the protagonist becomes extravagant indoors, an exile who cannot leave.[78] He appears physically outside the law: 'Where shall I run to breathe abroad my woes?' (III.vii.1). His 'ceaseless plaintes' and 'broken sighs', 'solliciting for justice and revenge', find 'the place impregnable'. Walls or enemies 'resist [his] woes', 'give [his] words no way' (4–18). The attempt to have his 'suit' heard by the King is physically intercepted by Lorenzo (III.xii.28). The stage business involved here is later reported to have reflected the continual interdiction of Hieronimo's *placita aule* ('pleas of the hall/palace'):

> It is suspected, and reported too,
> That thou, Lorenzo, wrongest Hieronimo,
> And in his suits towards his majesty
> Still keep'st him back, and seek'st to cross his suit.
>
> (III.xiv.53–6)

The ideal *locus* of absolute justice is undone by the villain's effective control over the circulation of people and information within it. The Verge is turned into a setting for the execution and enforcement of practical political reason after Machiavelli, but also remains a motive circumstance for the extrajudicial prosecution of injustice.

By referring to the Verge as a circumstance of the play, I tentatively invoke Lorna Hutson's description of the rhetorical strategies employed by sixteenth-century playwrights to enjoin spectators and readers to imagine spaces and times in which the actions that are shown can be interpreted in terms of intention, motivation and purpose – partly by way of explaining why it is irrelevant that the Verge is not explicitly mentioned in *The Spanish Tragedy*. In the chapter of Abraham Fraunce's *Lawyer's Logic* (1588) entitled 'Of the subject', passages from Plowden's *Commentaries* (1571) are used to explain the concept of the 'subject'. 'The subject is that whereunto some thing is adjoined,' writes Fraunce: 'The subject receiveth the adjunct, eyther in it, as the minde learning, the place the thing placed: or to it.' 'This is either affected by the thing adjoyned, as the body receiveth garments to it, and is of them affected,' he explains, 'or els it doth affect the thing adjoyned, as a sicke man receyveth unto him the physitian.'[79] Among the passages from Plowden used by Fraunce to expound these logical relations, the Verge appears as the very paradigm of a 'subject':

> In this realm there are diverse authorities, and none may exceed its limits and bounds. And therefore if the Marshal holds plea of a thing done out of the Verge [. . .] it shall be void, for [his] authority extends to a certain place, and within a certain precinct, and not elsewhere [. . .][80]

To describe the Verge as the 'subject' of *The Spanish Tragedy* is therefore to make a technical claim that educated men of the 1580s would have understood; Kyd himself may have been a legal scrivener like his father.[81] The detention of the Verge from the rather separate poetic project Kyd pursues in the language of the play only effects a light – albeit, as the play's literary-critical history shows, entirely adequate – concealment of the way explorations of grief, mythology and revenge work upon that jurisdiction as the *subject* of the play, bear upon it as the ground of its argument and its action.

It does not follow from this, and I do not wish to argue, that the hidden circumstance of the Verge shows that Kyd was specifically interested in making a satirical intervention in English political mythology, nor that he intended an allegory which identification of the presence of the Verge can finally unlock. Rather, I claim that in *The Spanish Tragedy* Kyd used the circumstance of the Verge to effect highly original changes to the way the relationship between legal, political and theatrical spaces of action could be imagined and actualised in drama and dramatic writing. The play creates a 'jurisdictional field' which informs the autonomy of the dramatic work, but which in its disrepair and obscurity conceals the political logic of its action even as other aspects of that logic become translucent when the Verge is recognised as its circumstance.[82] If the scene is capable of showing only part of the Verge, then the extra-mimetic world of *The Spanish Tragedy* must be contingent upon the hazy borders of the Verge that extend out beyond and around the scene, a *circumstance* (Latin: *circumstare*: to stand or gather around).[83] In framing or recognising the boundedness of the drama and its tragic matter, one is called on to imagine theatrical borders, just as the Verge remained a legal abstraction only up until the knight marshal made his appearance and enforced its presence in an actual space, and against or for actual persons.

The space engendered outside or beyond the limit of the Verge comes to seem identical with the space beyond the *fictional* scope of the drama, and therefore to acquire an affinity with the space of performance in which players appear as themselves. Hieronimo's recommitment to the Verge (or court), by which his revenge (in this case a pleading for the dead) is made possible, is the same as a recommitment to the world of fiction and role-inhabitation. The Verge unifies the dramatic work: in this sense, to postulate the Verge as the 'subject' of the play is to give a good answer to old questions about the tragic unity of *The Spanish Tragedy* and its relation to Tudor absolutism. But the fracturing and profanation of the Verge's spatial and temporal identity, which is exactly what the revenge plot effects, threatens the sovereignty which might otherwise attend that unity, invoking the provisional and prospectively defunct zone of its theatrical realisation.

The analogy of the Crown to the Verge, and of the Verge to its logical extension as a kingdom, was powerful and generative. In Shakespeare's *Richard II* (c.1595), Gaunt exploits the word to collapse royal exception into the pedantic register of land law, enforcing the comparison by making the Crown into a verge of meagre scope:

> A thousand flatterers sit within thy crown,
> Whose compass is no bigger than thy head;

And yet, incaged in so small a verge,
The waste is no whit lesser than thy land.[84]

If Thomas Kyd's concern with the Verge is more structural, William Shakespeare proves almost impossibly sensitive to the poetic and tonal opportunities actuated by the adoption of this old word into emerging registers. 'Verge' had by then become idiomatic as a way of describing circular bounds and interiors: in the verge escapements or crown-wheels of the mechanical clocks prevalent before Huygens;[85] the navigational cross-staff;[86] and applied geometry in general.[87] To describe Hieronimo as being 'on the verge of madness' participates in a discourse precipitated by the disappearance of the Verge, a disappearance registered by the term's absence in the play it locates.[88] The psychological crisis shown by *The Spanish Tragedy* emerged in the ruins of an ancient space of royal fiat and its progressive alienation, allegorisation and secularisation into 'the verge of reason', 'the verge of poetry', 'the verge of duty', 'the verge of eyelids', 'the verge of nature', or 'the Verge of Vice'. All such phrases appear first to have become idiomatic towards the end of the sixteenth century.[89]

The Orderly Household

The claim that *The Spanish Tragedy* reduces the sovereign Verge to theatrical *setting* comports with Walter Benjamin's account of the court in the baroque *Trauerspiel*.[90] What Bacon would maintain as the unblemished and pure 'half-pace' or 'carpet' of justice in and around the royal palace becomes the incidental show-place for intrigue. But that reduction is complicated by the way houses and households were invested with value in England, and by the deeply ambiguous position of the common player in respect of those houses and households.

The tragedy involves the resemblance of the stage to interiors and exteriors of houses. Hieronimo exits his house to discover his murdered son in II.v., a scene depicted in the frontispiece of the play adorning its title page after the seventh edition (1615), which may have been produced in direct reference to the 1602 Additions.[91] It places the tragedy ambiguously proximal to the house. The household predominates in *The Spanish Tragedy*, but is encountered largely from without. Belimperia – a parallel, encased avenger – drops a letter to Hieronimo from her exile there, above the stage; and Hieronimo, suspicions aroused, decides on the course of 'harkening near the Duke of Castile's house / [. . .] / To listen more' (III.ii.23–4; 50–2). The house becomes a strange and inaccessible zone once Hieronimo leaves its interior to find his dead son. Whispers, noises and mysterious letters emanate from within. Hieronimo's reaction is to allegorise the *domus*, palace, place, verge – with the effect that the revenge plot terrorises the microcosm–macrocosm relationship, obtaining in mainstream early modern political thought, between household and state.

Economics is the attempt to separate a branch of science from its origins in the law (νόμος) of the house (οἶκος): *oikonomía*. In Roman rhetoric the same word refers, as Kathy Eden notes, to *dispositio*: the arrangement of materials 'to accommodate the circumstances of the case'.[92] This carries us circuitously back to Fraunce's 'subject'. Within Christian Patristics, *oikonomía* refers (unstraightforwardly) to divine ordering of the human world; the unfolding reality of the Church.[93] It had been associated with episcopal discretion for centuries. This was how it came to describe ecclesiastical jurisdiction. Thus the canon lawyer Richard Cosin (who as the bishop of Worcester's chancellor certified Shakespeare's marriage to Anne Hathaway in 1582) could later call on St Peter's '*speciall oeconomie*', by which 'he was *publikely* to proceede to [the] *examination* and *condemnation* unto death' of Ananias and Sapphira for lying to the Holy Spirit (Acts 5). Why, Cosin asks, in line with centuries of Christian exegesis, should there be anything impious or arbitrary about Peter's enquiry, which caused the spontaneous deaths of the liars? 'For God doth as it were make Enquirie upon a crie of sinne coming into his eares.' Cosin therefore maintains the ancient connection between apostolic succession and the right to judge a truth revealed to the bishop by divine intercession or revelatory ordering (*oikonomía*).[94] When Hieronimo, in his capacity as knight marshal, comes by Pedringano's incriminating letter to Lorenzo, the disclosure prompts him to swear by 'sacred heavens', wondering that 'by this' a crime 'so closely smothered and so long concealed' would thus 'be venged or revealed' (*ST* III.vii.45–8). The final suggestive equivocation (revenged or revealed) implies exactly this potential identity of the discovery of truth and the right to punish. But if there is an exogenous ordering of the action, it is not divine but the indirect influence of Revenge, who has promised that 'the end is crown of every work well done' (II.vi.8). In this way the ordering of the action and authority within the scene seems to originate and remain within a secular political circle. A later chapter will explore in more depth the reasons why the mere presence of Revenge disarms providential reading.

Political economy means the relation of the ordering of the household (surplus and scarcity) to the community, city, or state (*polis*); or the consideration of household order (surplus and scarcity) from the point of view of the community, city, or state. In this way an ancient problem iterates and perpetuates itself. At the beginning of his *Politics*, Aristotle claims that to say the household and the state were the same, or that the householder and king were identical, would be false. Hence his description of how they relate seems inconsistent or even tautological:

> The state is by nature clearly prior to the family and to the individual, since the whole is of necessity prior to the part.
>
> The state is made up of households, [so] before speaking of the state we must speak of the management of the household.[95]

The apparent contradiction – as to ontological as well as chronological precedence – leads to the suggestion that the collocation or reconciliation of these units – household, village, state – could be achieved provisionally only by the jointing figure of father, husband, master, sovereign: 'The sphere of economics is a monarchy.'[96] In this way a link could be maintained between concentric social order (the topographical realisation of a hierarchy) and the distribution of things: economics – the administration of the household and estate – is according to Xenophon 'the name of a branch of knowledge', based on the appearance of 'an estate [as] *identical with the total of one's property*'.[97] The sequestration of Bel-imperia is consistent with the premise – outlined in the pseudo-Aristotelian *Economics*, for instance – that the first disposition of property in the household involved selecting and guarding a fertile wife.[98] Bel-imperia's revenge disrupts exactly that aim. The royal estate in these senses compassed everything proper to the king, the ideal outline of the kingdom figured by the perfect order within it. In searching for the origins of the Verge, one would have to go more than a long way back, pursuing an insatiable enquiry into the generative, mythic kernel of English social order – the royal *burh* and the royal palace, from which both communal boundaries (the *borough*), estate boundaries, routines of governance, and even the law itself may have derived.[99] Francis Thynne (d. 1608) suggested to his learned colleagues in the Society of Antiquaries that 'before the conquest the vierge or *friþ* being the king's peace, or the peace of the king's house, did in the tyme of king Athelstan [. . .] not extend fully to foure miles every way'. He cited the Annals of Rochester to support this claim that the 'precincte' was 'now greatly enlarged', and held that 'the word *vierge* or *virga* amongst the Latines, and the French [was] none other in effect, than *friþ* amongst the Saxons'.[100] In this way the royal house became an explanatory terminus with the appearance of a social origin. Repeatedly present within political discourse of that time is the now rather obscure assumption that, to all intents and purposes, the royal house (*qua* verge) *was* peace: the first substance of politics.

Household economy was a popular and fraught topic in English elite culture of the 1580s and 1590s. Sir Thomas Smith's version (finally printed in 1583) read the relationship as one of expansion: an overgrown family sent out its sons and daughters, in which process of 'propagation', 'a streete or village' was created, and from there thence to 'a citie or a borough' and, finally, ruled by 'that one and first father of them all', the nation or kingdom was constituted.[101] The state appeared in this way as the simple surplus of the first home.[102] Jean Bodin, whose *Six Books* were widely read and discussed in England, was more explicit:[103]

> The family [. . .] is not only the true source and origin of the commonwealth, but also its principal constituent. Xenophon and Aristotle divorced economy or household management from police or disciplinary power, without good reason [. . .] the well-ordered family is the true image of the commonwealth, and domestic comparable with sovereign authority.

For Bodin, the very notion of citizenship was anchored in a patriarchal and familial paradigm, and he assumed a deep and ongoing connection between family and commonwealth, finding the distinction between public and private itself to proceed from it:

> Nothing could properly be regarded as public if there were nothing at all to distinguish it from what was private. Nothing can be thought of as shared in common, except by contrast with what is privately owned. If all citizens were kings there would be no king.[104]

Such ideations of the household economy in the late sixteenth century tended more and more to curtail the monarch's power even as it appeared to retain its structuring force.

These were early formations of the private sphere, which, if it resembled the royal estate, also caused an exemption of its goods and persons from arbitrary or prerogative influence.[105] Thomas Kyd had translated Torquato Tasso's *The Householder's Philosophy* (*Padre di famiglia*). 'The care of a good householder is devided into two things,' wrote Kyd:

> That is his body and hys goods. In his personne he is to exercise three offices, viz. Of a *Father*, a *Husband*, and a *Maister*. In his goods two purposes are proposed, *Conservation* and *Encrease*.

His translation went on to describe how a master should administer his household, his wife and his servants, but closed with an expression of doubt that 'governments or dispensations of a house are devided into foure partes, Kingly, Lordly, Civill and Private', for

I cannot see yet how the government of a civill and a private house do differ, unlesse he call his government Civill that is busied and employed in office for the honours of Commonwealth, and that man's private that is segregat and not called to office, so that wholy hee applies him to his housholde care.[106]

Hieronimo's legal role in *The Spanish Tragedy* would seem to suggest not only an authority entirely contingent on the presence of the sovereign but – after the destruction of the Verge – the possibility or ideal availability of legal recourse beyond the scope of royal justice, in reference to a common good.[107] In this way the play seems to ruin the distinction between public law and private justice that usually co-ordinates comprehension of revenge.

The murder of Horatio is not only a felonious breach of the royal peace within the Verge, but also an attack on the marshal's family and its space. The crime simultaneously tests the quality of the justice in the royal household and the limits of the accord between family and state apparently shown by the victorious return to court with the Portuguese prisoners at the beginning of the narrative.[108] In this it reveals the paradox of the royal officer, especially one whose office is so closely related to upholding the parameters and quality of a royal household which seems to be maintained at the expense of his own house. At the end of the play, Hieronimo obliterates the sovereign's patriarchy by establishing a claim to a dutiful natural fatherhood on equal footing in 'loss' (IV.iv.114–21). Hieronimo addresses the three stunned men – the Duke of Castile, the King of Spain and the Viceroy of Portugal – as fathers, uncles and patriarchs. If he could recognise himself in Bazulto, the grieving father, he wishes now to make his enemies in his image. The complete destruction of Hieronimo's family is remade as the catastrophe of the first family. Treasonous felons like Hieronimo forfeited all their lands and chattels to the Crown, so by implication the murder of the royal 'increase' removes the wasted arbour from the private sphere and aggregates it to the royal estate. The Spanish king's final lament reverses Smith's 'one and first father of them all': 'I am the next, the neerest, last of all' (IV.iv.208).

Kyd makes the Verge, and the *oeconomia* of revenge, into an allegorical labyrinth where ends and means become uncertain. He partly effects this in and through the reception of the *locus* of Senecan tragedy, importing the Messenger's description of the palace of the Tantalids from *Thyestes*, and its realisation in Heywood's English as a doubled, sprawling place.[109] The secret inner grove of the palace in Seneca is relayed into *The Spanish Tragedy* as the violated bower or scene of irrational violence: 'The privie Palaice underlieth in secret place

[also] / With ditch ful deepe that doth enclose the wood of priviter, / And hidden parts of kyngdome olde [. . .]'[110] The tree of *The Spanish Tragedy* 'enroots a powerful fantasy of genealogy'.[111] The symbol of what Isabella calls 'this unfortunate and fatal pine' enables her destruction of the bower to foreshadow the clearance effected by her husband within the Verge, a revenge, like hers, 'upon this place'. The symmetry is created by way of reference to *Thyestes* but also with a riff on the ancient analogy of the royal house to an arboreal branching.[112] When Hieronimo is asked by visiting Portuguese the way to Lorenzo's house, he violently transposes this Senecan topography ('A hugy dale of lasting night [. . .]', *ST* III.xi.13–29). As Daniel Unruh has shown, the palace in *Thyestes* is an enforced topography that elides secret, cursed spaces with public structures. Its bounds are constantly shifting, overlapping with other spaces of thought and fields of action. It is both artificial and strangely organic.[113] Kyd uses the Tantalid palace not only to corrupt the Verge that otherwise structures the space in which Hieronimo acts, and to produce within an ancient English *topos* a distinct poetic elaboration upon a classical topography, but also to effect an opposition between sovereign space and private dwelling that mirrors the opposition between culture and nature in Seneca, so that the incursion of royal violence into his home space appears as the literally unnatural extension of a corrupt Verge.[114]

At the Verge

If it was the monarch's body which imaged and originated the Verge, if it was the master's body that imaged and originated the household, then it was the body of the common player that guaranteed and mediated mimesis of those bodies. The political disruptions presented by *The Spanish Tragedy* do not make sense unless that body is imaginatively supplied by a reader or for an audience. The inset drama of *Soliman and Perseda* produces 'lively images'. That the ghost of Andrea should find them 'sights to please the soul' enacts a bizarre defence of theatre in line with the reception of concepts of *phantasiai* and *enargeia* in Roman tragic theory.[115] But the elaborate, ostentatiously technical exploration of mimesis and allegory allowed by the inset play conceals the potential of *The Spanish Tragedy* not just to turn inward upon itself in closeted reflection, but to shape the grounds of its own theatrical occasion. The interior bifurcation of the stage-space involved in Hieronimo's production, and the splintering of the unity of the royal place it effects, works also upon the scope of performance itself.

William Rankins imagined that the theatre was a 'Laborinth', 'a place famous for filthiness', 'sen[s]ed with frawde, built by briberie, whose pathes are well beaten, as the perfect way to wickedness', 'wherein viewing manie things able to intice a pleasant eye to beholde, or an open eare to delight, by the line of grace, at length I got out'.[116] The concept of theatre suddenly possessed an interior structure quite without the concentric purity of the Vitruvian arena.[117] Its more tangled structure had instead emerged from suspicious but close observation of the new London theatres, and the presumed use made of their space by players and audiences. The image of the theatre presented by its opponents and legislators was generally that of the disorderly house. 'No person shall suffer anie plays, enterludes, Comodyes, Tragidies, or shewes to be played or shewed *in his hous, yarde, or other place whereof he then shall have rule or power*,' instructed the London authorities, in an almost explicitly oeconomic register.[118] Critics of the theatre imagined 'eavell practises of incontinenyce in greate Innes, havinge chambers and secrete places adjoyninge to their open stages and gallyries', and 'utteringe of popular busye and sedycious matters'.[119] Stephen Gosson claimed to find 'a *Gordians* knot of disorder in every play house'.[120] Edward Topsell thought them 'houses of sin'.[121] Play houses were suspected of making other houses less orderly too. John Rainald's printer claimed to have witnessed 'flocking and gadding [. . .] to these *Play-Houses* and ydle places of entercourse (many leaving their houses and sundry necessarie duties unperformed)'.[122] Anthony Munday – calling on the language of Old Testament blight – promised '*their house shalbe destroied, there shalbe none end of their plagues, their light shalbe put out*' by way of revelling in the destruction of the ancient amphitheatre in Tidena and the deaths of thousands of spectators therein.[123]

Pamphlets aimed at the theatre evince a studied commitment to the premise that theatre houses were zones of uncertain power in which words were heard and things were seen differently from anywhere else. 'Not that any filthynesses in deede, is committed within the compasse of that grounde,' Gosson clarifies, 'but that every wanton and his Paramour, every man and his Mistresse, every John and his Joan, every knave and his queane, are there first acquainted & cheapen the Merchandise in that place, which they pay for elsewhere.' Gosson argued that common players made this 'grounde' and sustained it: 'were not Players the meane, to make these assemblyes, such multitudes wold hardly be drawne in so narowe roome'. Gosson's *Schoole of Abuse* half imagines a *building*: the *subject* of his argument is the space of theatre, which is produced both by players and their critic. Thus he concludes: 'If I have beene tedious in my Lecture, or your selves be weary of your lesso[n], harken no longer for the Clock, shut up the Schoole, and get you home.'[124] This ingenious ploy confirms the reader's supposition that the titular 'schoole of abuse' refers simultaneously to the place where abuse happens (theatre) and the place where the same is diagnosed and disclosed (antitheatre). Gosson claims that his argument is comprehensive, insofar as its limits are coterminous with those of the theatre. Players both produced that space and inhabited it; the play followed them.

For the Verge to be a meaningful division of space, it had to be involved in the production and reproduction of values attached to what was beyond and outside it. To engineer a disturbance within the Verge was at the same time to reflect on how it included and excluded various qualities, things, persons. 'Her Majestie also straightly chargeth and commandeth the knight Marshal of her household,' concluded a royal proclamation of 1592 to restrain access to the court, 'that he shall cause due search to be made of all vagabonds, commonly called Rogues, that shal haunt about the Court, or in any places within the Verge, and them to apprehend.'[125] The obligation of justices to expel vagrants and 'idle persons' from the Verge had long been enforced and encouraged under Elizabeth I.[126] A particular concern was to prevent the infiltration of plague, but also involved was the desire to restrict the influence of 'private suitors' at court. Such edicts of purification necessarily bore on the common player insofar as unlicenced actors had been wrapped up in the Elizabethan vagrancy legislation of the 1570s; and insofar as the enemies of the stage, and even some of its defenders, continued to associate players with disorder, vice, idleness and vagabondage, and to insist that the theatre was itself a place where the like sort of person would congregate. Under such circumstances, theatre within the Verge acquired a deeply paradoxical aspect. The interlude arranged by Hieronimo seems to accept exactly that logic which would see shape-shifters and their disguises excluded from the Verge together with vagrants, prostitutes and the infected.

The Liberties of London were sometimes defended with reference to royal prerogative. William More guarded the liberty of Blackfriars from encroachments by the City of London around 1570 by direct appeal to the exemption of the Verge.[127] The contradictory position of the London theatres in respect of these two models of spatial authority, royal and civic, reached a crisis in June 1592, when the Mayor of London William Webbe complained to the Privy Council of 'a great disorder and tumult' in Southwark involving 'apprentices and maisterles men' who had 'assembled themselves by occasion & pretence of their meeting at a play' at the nearby Rose, 'which giveth opportunitie of committing these and & such like disorders'. The first recorded performance of *The Spanish*

Tragedy had taken place in the Rose in March of that year; more performances are recorded throughout 1592; it is probable that by then it had already been staged fairly regularly for several years in Southwark; 'Jeronymo' had been performed only three days before the riot, on 9 June, and would be performed again a week after it, on 18 June 1592.[128] Webbe's sly identification of a performance at the Rose as a proximal cause for the riot was wholly consistent with the animus with which the City pursued attempts to sever the theatres from aristocratic protection. But Webbe identified a different sort of abuse as the actual occasion of the disorder:

> I found that it began upon the serving of a warrant from my L. Chamberlein by on[e] of the Knights Mareschalls men upon a ffeltmongers servant who was committed to the Mareschallsea w*ith* certein other that wear accused to his L. by the sayed knight mareschalls men w*ith*out cause of offence (as they them selves do affirme) [...] I am infourmed by the inhabitants of Southwark men of best reputation among them that the Knight Mareschalls men in their serving of their warrants do not use themselves w*ith* that good discretion and moderate usage as wear meet to bee doon in lyke cases but after a most rough and violent manner provoking them by such hard dealing to contend w*ith* them w*hich* otherwise would obey in all duetifull sort. As I understand they did in this case whear they entred *the* house whear the warrant was to bee served w*ith* a dagger drawen affreyting the goodwife who sat by the fire w*ith* a young infant in her armes and afterwards having taken the party and certein others and committed them to prison whear they lay 5. dayes w*ith*out making their answer these mutiners apprentices assembled them selves in this disordered manner the sayed Marescharlls men being w*ith*in the Mareschalsea issued foorth w*ith* their dagers drawen & w*ith* Bastianadoes in their hands beating the people [...] The sayed inhabitants do farther complain that the sayed Mareschalls men beehave themselves very unneyborly & disdainfully among them refusing to pay scot or lot with them or any other dueties to Church or Com*m*onwealth w*hich* maketh the inhabitants more discontent w*ith* them.[129]

If the earliest audiences of *The Spanish Tragedy* included those who in 1592 were provoked to a violent riot by officers of the Verge, whose incursions into private households with naked blades belonged to a pattern of disregard for civic norms that was no doubt encouraged by the curious exemption of their jurisdiction, then it must be conjectured that the scene of Horatio's murder did not produce the affective response one might expect. The pathos of Hieronimo's discovery, one of the classic examples of tragic pathos in the English dramatic canon, suddenly seems all wrong. It is not only conceivable but fairly likely that many of the play's earliest auditors in Southwark would have been less than tearful to see the knight marshal's home violated by the forces of an arbitrary and unjust state.

The involvement of *The Spanish Tragedy* in itinerant theatre throughout the 1590s and beyond may be even more significant: 'Thou hast forgot,' Dekker taunted Jonson, 'how thou amblest (in leather pilch) by a play-wagon, in the high way, and took'st mad Ieronimoes part, to get service among the Mimickes.'[130] The Verge was an ambulatory court with an ancient power to eclipse local jurisdictions. It also worked as a temporal limit that could powerfully overlap with the travelling interlude. *The Spanish Tragedy* furnished a potent image of a *movable* court, harnessing the close association of professional theatre companies with the royal officers who patronised them. From this angle, the play seems to recover resources from the space of its theatrical actuation, and indeed works upon that space in an entirely novel manner. Far from causing the collapse of the drama back into the popular history of Southwark, for instance, the presence of the Verge could then seem to permit the tragedy to purify the space of its realisation, making it timeless and blank, as if outside history: 'All things that ever were or be, / Are closde in his concavitie.' This 'roundel' or 'compasse' is introduced by George Puttenham as the very model of Elizabethan sovereignty: 'So is the Queene of Briton ground, / Beame, circle, center of all my round.'[131] If the Verge prospects that allegedly benevolent space of English absolutism and contains its principal hopes, the 'endless tragedy' of Kyd's play makes it into a hell of uncertainty and pain which can only be truthfully presented as foreign. The contradictions exposed within that ancient circuit by the revenge of its 'author' (authority) and 'actor' (agent) threaten, at every turn, the unity and sovereignty of the dramatic work in which 'Hieronimo' is compassed.

Notes

1. Paul L. Hughes (ed.), *Tudor Royal Proclamations*, 3 vols (New Haven, 1969), 3: 39.
2. See R. B. Wernham, *After the Armada* (Oxford, 1984), 126–30.
3. In general, see J. Horace Round, *The King's Serjeants & Officers of State with their Coronation Services* (London, 1911), 82–98.
4. Lukas Erne, *Beyond the Spanish Tragedy. A Study of the Works of Thomas Kyd* (Manchester, 2001), 89.
5. Frank Whigham, *Seizures of the Will* (Cambridge, 2009), 22; Thomas Kyd, *The Spanish Tragedy*, ed. J. R. Mulryne, with introduction and notes by Andrew Gurr, 3rd edn (London, 2009), 8.
6. Cf. Katharine Eisaman Maus (ed.), *Four Revenge Tragedies* (Oxford, 1995), xiv: 'As knight-marshal [. . .] his zeal for 'equity' is entirely consistent with his meritocratic values.'

7. Derek Dunne, *Vindictive Justice. Shakespeare, Revenge Tragedy and Early Modern Law* (Basingstoke, 2016), 35; 41–4.
8. Anon., *The Spanish Tragedy, Containing the Lamentable Murders of* Horatio *and* Bellimperia: *With the Pitifull Death of Old Hieronimo. To the Tune of* Queene Dido (London, 1620). This chapter contains some reference to the first extant edition of the play, but generally the in-text references are to *ST*, and include that denotation.
9. See Timothy A. Turner, 'Torture and Summary Justice in *The Spanish Tragedy*', *SEL 1500–1900* 53:2 (Spring, 2013), 277–92, esp. 282–3.
10. John M. Collins, *Martial Law and English Laws, c.1500–1700* (Cambridge, 2016), 14–15; 92; 157.
11. Lorna Hutson, *The Invention of Suspicion* (Oxford, 2007), 279–84; John Kerrigan, *Revenge Tragedy. From Aeschylus to Armageddon* (Oxford, 1996), 177.
12. James Shapiro, '"Tragedies naturally performed": Kyd's Representation of Violence. *The Spanish Tragedy* (c.1587)', in David Scott Kastan and Peter Stallybrass (eds), *Staging the Renaissance. Reinterpretations of Elizabethan and Jacobean Drama* (Abingdon, 1991), 99–113, at 107.
13. Kerrigan, *Revenge Tragedy*, 26.
14. Maus (ed.), *Four Revenge Tragedies*, 331.
15. Emma Smith, 'Author v. Character in Early Modern Dramatic Authorship: The Example of Thomas Kyd and *The Spanish Tragedy*', *Medieval & Renaissance Drama in England* 11 (1999), 129–42, at 129.
16. *Articuli super Cartas* (28 E I), in *The Statutes: Revised Edition*, 18 vols (London, 1870–84), 1: 103–7.
17. William Shakespeare, *King Henry IV, Part 2*, ed. A. R. Humphreys, Arden 2nd ser. (London, 1981), V.v.63–5: 'Till then, I banish thee, on pain of death, / As I have done the rest of my misleaders, / Not to come near our person by ten mile.' Cf. Antonio de Guevara, *The Dial of Princes*, trans. Thomas North (London, 1568), Sig. E1: 'to be exyled and banished the verge of the court'.
18. Edward Coke, *The Second Part of the Institutes of the Laws of England, containing the exposition of many ancient and other statutes* (London, 1797), 546.
19. Anthony Fitzherbert, *The Offices of shyriffes, bayliffes of lybertyes, escheatours, constables, and coroners* (London, 1579), Sig. G4.
20. See also: Marjorie M. McIntosh, 'Immediate Royal Justice: The Marshalsea Court in Havering, 1358', *Speculum* 54:4 (October, 1979), 727–33; W. R. Jones, 'The Court of the Verge: The Jurisdiction of the Steward and Marshal of the Household in Later Medieval England', *Journal of British Studies* 10:1 (Nov., 1970), 1–29; J. H. Johnson, 'The King's Wardrobe and Household', in James F. Willard and William A. Morris (eds), *The English Government at Work: 1327–1336*, 3 vols (Cambridge, MA, 1940), 1: 243–5.
21. Anthony Fitzherbert, *Diversite de courtz, lour jurisdictions et alia necessaria et utilia* (London, 1535), 1–2.
22. John Baker, *The Reinvention of Magna Carta, 1215–1616* (Cambridge, 2017), 207. The decision in *Slade v. Morley* (1602), together with its dramatic confirmation of the ascendancy of the King's Bench, underpinned

the arguments made to decide *The Case of the Marshalsea* (1612), i.e. *Hall v. Stanley et al.*, which gave rise to the lengthiest and most detailed judicial pronouncement upon the Marshalsea Court in its history. See John Henry Thomas and John Farquhar Fraser (eds), *The Reports of Sir Edward Coke, Knt., in Thirteen Parts*, 6 vols (London, 1826), 5: 369–87; David Ibbetson, 'Sixteenth Century Contract Law: *Slade's Case* in Context', *Oxford Journal of Legal Studies* 4:3 (1 December 1984), 295–317, at 316–17; and below.

23. Douglas G. Greene, 'The Court of the Marshalsea in Late Tudor and Stuart England', *The American Journal of Legal History* 20:4 (Oct., 1976), 267–81, at 268. Also see David Chan Smith, *Sir Edward Coke and the Reformation of the Laws. Religion, Politics and Jurisprudence, 1578–1616* (Cambridge, 2014), 37–40.
24. See Jones, 'Court of the Verge', 4; Paul Brand, 'Henry II and the Creation of the English Common Law', in Christopher Harper-Bill and Nicholas Vincent (eds), *Henry II: New Interpretations* (Woodbridge, 2007), 215–41, at 216.
25. *Cox v. Gray* (1612), in John Bulstrode, *The Reports of Edward Bulstrode of the Inner Temple, Esquire in Three Parts* (London, 1688), [I]: 208.
26. Jones, 'Court of the Verge', 29.
27. 33 Hen. VIII. c.12, 'An Act for Murder and Malicious Bloodshed, within the Court', in John Raithby (ed.), *The Statutes at Large, of England and of Great Britain*, 20 vols (London, 1811), 3: 351–8.
28. John Stow, *The Chronicles of England from Brute unto this Present Yeare of Christ, 1580* (London, 1580), 1021: 'Thus every man in hys Office readye to do the execution, there was called forth Sir *William Pickering* knight Marshall, to bring in the sayde *Edmonde Knevet*, and when he was broughte to the Barre, the chiefe Justice declared to hym his trespasse.'
29. John Baker, *The Oxford History of the Laws of England. Volume VI. 1483–1558* (Oxford, 2003), 216.
30. Charles Wriothesley, *A Chronicle of England during the Reigns of the Tudors, from A.D. 1485 to 1559*, 2 vols (London, 1877), 2: 15–16.
31. James Heath, *Torture and English Law. An Administrative and Legal History from the Plantagenets to the Stuarts* (London, 1982), 78–9; 206, No. 17, '15th March 1559': 'A Letter to the Lyeutenant of the Tower that [...] he is requyred to call the Knight Marshall unto him in this matter'; 213, No. 34, '30th July, 1581': 'Mr Lieutenant is required to sende [them] to the Knight Marshall, to remaine under his charge, for which purpose he shall receave Their Lordships' warrant unto him to receave them.'
32. John Bellamy, *The Tudor Law of Treason* (Abingdon, 2013), 87.
33. Frederic Pollock and Frederic William Maitland, *The History of English Law before the Time of Edward I*, 2 vols (Cambridge, 1898), 2: 503.
34. See John Baker, 'The Tudor Law of Treason', *American Journal of Legal History* 24:3 (July, 1980), 275–6.
35. See Richard Crompton, *L'Authoritie et jurisdiction des courts de la Majestie de la Roygne* (London, 1594), 102–5, at 103: 'Pur ceo que le Marshal de le Marshalsie de court l'hostel nostre Seignior le Roy, soloit prender les fees que ensuont, de chescun que vient per *Capias* al dit Court [...]'. The Marshalsea Court was a court of record, but rolls for the

period in question are not extant. Some examples from 1316 to 1359 exist: TNA E37, Court of the Marshalsea and Court of the Verge: Plea Rolls, for which see Johnson, 'The King's Wardrobe'. For an early seventeenth-century defence of the court's jurisdiction over trespass outside that defined strictly as the royal household, see Anon., 'Reasons that the Court of Marshalsy may be fittly enabled [. . .]', in Thomas Hearne (ed.), *A Collection of Curious Discourses written by eminent antiquaries upon several heads in our English antiquities*, 2 vols (London, 1771–3), 2: 146–52, at 146: 'This court is more necessary for the publick weale of this state than any inferiour court, for herein the resiants within the verge have a most speedy triall for their causes in foure court days.'

36. McIntosh, 'Immediate Royal Justice', 727ff.
37. William Holdsworth, *A History of English Law*, ed. A. L. Goodhart and H. G. Hanbury, 16 vols (London, 1936–72), 1: 219.
38. Jones, 'Court of the Verge', 2.
39. Anon., *A New Ballad Declaring the Dangerous Shooting of the Gun at Court* (London, 1579), whence Stow, *The Chronicles of England*, 1196–204. On the sixteenth-century dialectic of hanging and salvation, punishment and mercy, see George Oppitz-Trotman, '"Into that geere the rope": Notes on the Early Modern Halter', *Sixteenth-Century Journal* 47:1 (Spring, 2016), 53–73.
40. 'The Privy Council to the Earl of Essex, Earl Marshal of England. 1598, Sept. 6'; and 'The Earl of Essex to the Privy Council. 1598, [about 6 Sept.]', in *Calendar of the Manuscripts of the Most Hon. The Marquis of Salisbury, K. G., [. . .] preserved at Hatfield House, Part VIII* (London, 1899), 334–5. On the use of provost marshals to quell riot and rebellion, see Roger B. Manning, 'The Origins of the Doctrine of Sedition', *Albion* 12:2 (Summer, 1980), 99–121, at 107–8.
41. H. G. Richardson and G. O. Sayles (ed. and trans.), *Fleta*, 3 vols (London, 1954–84), 2: 114–15; Hearne (ed.), *Collection of Curious Discourses*, 2: 90–129 (cf. BL Cotton MS Titus C. I), at 100.
42. *Reports of Edward Bulstrode*, [I]: 207–13, at 208.
43. Coke, *The Second Part of the Institutes*, 548.
44. *Reports of Edward Bulstrode*, [I]: 210.
45. Coke, *The Second Part of the Institutes*, 549.
46. John Baker, 'The Changing Concept of a Court', in *Collected Papers on English Legal History* (Cambridge, 2013), 413–41, at 416.
47. Robert Zaller, *The Discourse of Legitimacy in Early Modern England* (Stanford, 2007), 20.
48. Baker, 'Concept of a Court', 416. See Rita Costa Gomes, *The Making of a Court Society: Kings and Nobles in Late Medieval Portugal*, trans. Alison Aiken (Cambridge, 2003), Chap. 1, for an excellent enlargement of this difficulty.
49. Francis Bacon, *A Charge given by the most eminent and learned Sr. Francis Bacon, Kt., late Lord Chancellor of England, at a sessions holden for the verge* (London, 1662), 3.
50. Andrew Thrush, 'EGERTON, Sir John (c.1551–1614)', in Andrew Thrush and John P. Ferris (eds), *The House of Commons 1604–1629*, 6 vols (Cambridge, 2010), 4: 178–81, at 179.

51. See John Trusler, *The London Advisor and Guide* (London, 1790), 169–70. This, one of its decidedly later functions, was erroneously described as current in Shakespeare's time by Edward Sugden: Edward H. Sugden, *A Topographical Dictionary to the Works of Shakespeare and his Fellow Dramatists* (London, 1925), 546.
52. See Doug Eskew, '"Soldiers, Prisoners, Patrimony": *King Lear* and the Place of the Sovereign', *Cahiers Élisabéthains* 78 (2010), 29–38.
53. See W. Buckley, *The Jurisdiction and Practice of the Marshalsea & Palace Courts* (London, 1827), 18.
54. Bacon, *A Charge*, 13.
55. Erne, *Beyond the Spanish Tragedy*, 20; and Chap. 1 generally.
56. Anon., *The First Part of Ieronimo*, in Frederick Boas (ed.), *The Works of Thomas Kyd* (Oxford, 1951), I.i.
57. Cf. *ST* I.ii.96: 'knight marshal, frolic with thy king'.
58. See John Rastell, *Les Termes de la ley* (London, 1527), whence the description here: John Cowell, *The Interpreter* (London, 1607), Sig. Yyy2. Cf. Samuel Carter, *Lex Custumaria, or, A treatise of copy-hold estates* (London, 1696), 15: 'As for Tenants by the Verge, they are but Copyholders, and have no other Evidence but by Copy of Court Roll; but they are so called, because when they Surrender, they deliver a little Rod into the Stewards Hand [. . .].'
59. Thomas and Fraser (eds) *Reports of Sir Edward Coke*, 5: 378. Cf. Richardson and Sayles (ed. and trans.), *Fleta* 2: 114.
60. Antonio de Guevara, *The Familiar Epistles of Sir Anthony of Guevara*, trans. Edward Hellowes (London, 1575), 160.
61. Thomas Stocker, *A Tragicall Historie of the troubles and civile warres of the lowe Countries, otherwise called Flanders* (London, 1583), 68; Adam Henricpetri, *Histoire des troubles et guerres civiles des Pays-Bas* (s. l., 1582), 177; Adam Henricpetri, *Niderlendischer Ersten Kriegen, Empörungen, Zweitrachten, Ursprung, Anfang und End* (Basel, 1575), Sig. T3^v.
62. Curtis Perry, 'The Uneasy Republicanism of Thomas Kyd's *Cornelia*', *Criticism* 48:4 (Autumn, 2006), 534–55; Eugene D. Hill, 'Senecan and Vergilian Perspectives in *The Spanish Tragedy*', *English Literary Renaissance* 15 (1985), 143–65, at 144.
63. Cicero, *De Inventione*, trans. H. M. Hubbell (Cambridge, MA, 1949), I.xxvii.38. See Lorna Hutson, *Circumstantial Shakespeare* (Oxford, 2015), 58–60.
64. Francis Bacon, 'Of Revenge', in Michael Kiernan (ed.), *The Essays or Counsels, Civill and Morall* (Oxford, 1985), 16.
65. Compare Thomas Kyd[?], *The Tragedye of Soliman and Perseda* (1599), in Boas (ed.), *Works of Thomas Kyd*, I.iii.59: 'Even to the verge of golde abounding Spaine'.
66. Editors have commonly interpolated 'hold' to make the line scan, i.e. 'hold exempt'. This emendation has made it significantly more difficult for readers to see that 'exempt' does not mean 'keep vacant'. The quotation supplied here is an exact transcription of the play's earliest extant edition, of 1592.

67. W. Carew Hazlitt (ed.), *A Select Collection of Old English Plays*, 4th edn, 15 vols (London, 1874–6), 5: 112.
68. Thomas Kyd, *The Spanish Tragedy*, ed. Michael Neill (New York, 2014), 73n.
69. The play's printer Edward Allde, on the frontispiece of the earliest extant edition of *The Spanish Tragedy*, claimed that it was 'newly corrected and amended of such grosse faults as passed in the first impression': the imputed mistake in question seems glaring.
70. In the combined senses of 'relinquishment' and 'dispossession'. For the latter, see Jean d'Albin de Valsergues, *A Notable Discourse, plainelye and truely discussing, who are the right ministers of the Catholike Church*, trans. Edward Rishton (London, 1575), fol. 37^v: 'to exempt, that is to saye, to drive us out of our possession'.
71. Anon., *The Trueth of the most wicked and secret murthering of Iohn Brewen* (London, 1592), 6.
72. James Shirley, *The Cardinal*, ed. E. M. Yearling (Manchester, 1986), I.i.71–2.
73. *RT*, I.iii.8.
74. Mark Fortier, *The Culture of Equity in Early Modern England* (London, 2005), esp. Chap. 2. Cf. Dunne, *Vindictive Justice*, 37–8.
75. *Pace* Arthur Lindley, *Hyperion and the Hobbyhorse: Studies in Carnivalesque Subversion* (Newark, 1996), Chap. 5.
76. William Baldwin et al., *A Myrrour for Magistrates* (London, 1563), Sig. A3.
77. See Gillian Rose, *Hegel contra Sociology* (London, 2009), 201: 'The boundary is a quality'; Bradin Cormack, *A Power to do Justice. Jurisdiction, English Literature, and the Rise of Common Law, 1509–1625* (Chicago, 2007), 9: 'Jurisdiction […] [is] the substance of the limit.'
78. 'Extravagant' gained its meaning of 'beyond bounds' in the sixteenth century, albeit well before *Hamlet* Q2, which is given by the *OED* as the first instance. Cf. Edward Hall, *The Union of the Two Noble and Illustre Famelies of Lancastre & Yorke* (London, 1548), fol. 205: 'the extravagant fooes, lyngeryng beyonde the sea'.
79. Abraham Fraunce, *The Lawiers Logicke* (London, 1588), fol. 38.
80. Ibid. fol. 39, quoting Edmund Plowden, *Les Comentaries, ou les reports de Edmonde Plowden* (London, 1571), fol. 37^v: 'Et en ceo realme sont diverz autorites, et nul poit exceder ces limits et boundes, et pur ceo si le marshall teigne plee de choce fait hors del vierge, ou le admiral de choce fait en corps le countrie, ceo serra voide, car lour authoritie extende al lieu certein, et deins certeine precinct, et nemy aylours [. . .]'
81. On Kyd as a scrivener, and his education, see James R. Siemon, 'Sporting Kyd', *English Literary Renaissance* 24:3 (Autumn, 1994), 553–82, at 573–8. It is faintly possible that Fraunce and Kyd moved in the same intellectual spheres; it has sometimes been suggested that Kyd was part of the Sidney circle and shared in its republicanism. See Iris Oberth, 'Appropriating France in Elizabethan Drama', in Gabriela Schmidt (ed.), *Elizabethan Translation and Literary Culture* (Berlin, 2013), 275–98, esp. 293–5.
82. The phrase is Bradin Cormack's. Cf. Cormack, *A Power to Do Justice*, 220: 'The Chorus [in *Henry V*] asserts that the play's own making depends

on its reconfiguration of jurisdictional space, the very space that generates the crisis represented in the play.'
83. See Hutson, *Circumstantial Shakespeare* generally.
84. William Shakespeare, *King Richard II*, ed. Charles R. Forker, Arden 3rd ser. (London, 2002), II.i.100–3. Gaunt uses the word as part of his general critique of Richard as 'Landlord of England' (13).
85. See Abbott Payson Usher, *A History of Mechanical Inventions: Revised Edition* (New York, 1988), 197–208.
86. Lucas Janszoon Waghenaer, *The Mariners Mirrour* (London, 1588), Sig. B3^v.
87. Thomas Blundeville, *M. Blundeville his exercises containing sixe treatises* (London, 1594), fol. 349^v.
88. E.g. Wolfgang Clemen, *English Tragedy before Shakespeare. The Development of Dramatic Speech* (London, 1961), 107.
89. Henry Porter, *The Pleasant History of the Two Angry Women of Abington* (London, 1599), Sig. A4^v; Ben Jonson, *Every Man out of his humor*, ed. Helen Ostovich (Manchester, 2001), V.30; Henry Chettle, *Englands Mourning Garment* (London, 1603), Sig. C3; Thomas Middleton, *The Blacke Booke* (London, 1604), Sig. F; William Shakespeare, *King Lear*, ed. R. A. Foakes, 3rd series (London, 1997), II.ii.336 [F: 1623]; BL Egerton MS 3876, fol. 3^v, cited in Aysha Pollnitz, *Princely Education in Early Modern Britain* (Cambridge, 2015), 352.
90. Walter Benjamin, *Ursprung des deutschen Trauerspiels*, in Benjamin, GS I/i: 270–8.
91. On the illustration, see Diane K. Jakacki, '"Canst paint a doleful cry?": Promotion and Performance in the *Spanish Tragedy* Title-Page Illustration', *Early Theatre* 13:1 (2010), 13–36.
92. Kathy Eden, *Hermeneutics and the Rhetorical Tradition. Chapters in the Ancient Legacy and its Humanist Reception* (New Haven, 1997), 20–40; 28.
93. For which there is a very extensive literature: see John Reumann, 'οικονομια as "Ethical Accommodation" in the Fathers and its Pagan Backgrounds', *Studia Patristica* 3 (1961), 370–9; Gerhard Richter, *Oikonomia. Der Gebrauch des Wortes Oikonomia im Neuen Testament, bei den Kirchenvätern und in der theologischen Literatur bis ins 20. Jahrhundert* (Berlin, 2005); Giorgio Agamben, *The Kingdom and the Glory. For a Theological Genealogy of Economy and Government* (Homo Sacer II, 2) (Stanford, 2011).
94. Richard Cosin, *An Apologie for Sundrie Proceedings by Jurisdiction Ecclesiasticall* (London, 1593), 125. Cf. Agamben's discussion of 1 Cor. 9:17 ('For if I do this thing willingly, I have a reward: but if against my will, a dispensation of the gospel is committed unto me [*oikonomian pepisteumai*]'): Agamben, *The Kingdom and the Glory*, 21–2.
95. Aristotle, *Politics*, trans. Benjamin Jowett, in Aristotle, *Works*, 2: 1988 [§1253].
96. Aristotle(?), *Economics*, trans. E. S. Forster, in Aristotle, *Works*, 2: 2130 [§1343]. The attribution of this composite work to Aristotle is very uncertain, but forms part of an 'Aristotelian' tradition. Cf. *Politics*, in Aristotle, *Works*, 2: 1998–9 [§12–13], whence: 'Of household management we have

seen that there are three parts – one is the rule of a master over slaves [. . .] another of father, and the third of husband.'
97. Xenophon, *Oeconomicus*, in E. C. Marchant (ed. and trans.), *Xenophon*, 7 vols (London, 1968), 4: [VI] 409, my emphases.
98. Aristotle(?), *Economics*, in Aristotle, *Works*, 2: 2131–2 [§1343–4].
99. Fredric William Maitland, *Domesday Book and Beyond. Three Essays in the Early History of England* (Cambridge, 1907), 185:

> Has not the sanctity of the king's house extended itself over a group of houses? The term *burh* seems to spread outwards from the defensible house of the king and with it the sphere of his *burh-bryce* is amplified [. . .] If [. . .] we doubt how to translate *burh*, whether by *house* or by *borough*, we are admitting that the language of the law does not distinguish between the two [. . .] the king's borough is the king's house, for his house-peace prevails in its streets.

100. Francis Thynne, 'Of the same', in Hearne (ed.), *Curious Discourses*, 2: 113–16, at 114.
101. Thomas Smith, *De Republica Anglorum* (London, 1583), 14–15.
102. Cf. Norbert Elias, *Die Höfische Gesellschaft. Untersuchungen zur Soziologie des Königtums und der höfischen Aristokratie mit einer Einleitung: Soziologie und Geschichtswissenschaft* (Berlin, 1969), Chap. 3.
103. See George L. Mosse, 'The Influence of Jean Bodin's *République* on English Political Thought', *Medievalia et Humanistica* 5 (1948), 73–83.
104. Jean Bodin, *The Six Books of the Commonwealth*, ed. and trans. M. J. Tooley (Oxford, 1967), 6; 8.
105. See Zaller, *Discourse of Legitimacy*, 305–6.
106. Torquato Tasso, *The Housholders Philosophie*, trans. Thomas Kyd (London, 1588), in Boas (ed.), *Works of Thomas Kyd*, 252; 284.
107. See Alan Harding, *Medieval Law and the Foundation of the State* (Oxford, 2002), 299:

> The displacement of 'state of the realm' by 'commonwealth' in the rolls of parliament accompanies the increased importance given the representatives of the shires and towns by the magnates' use of them in political struggles with the king, and the measure of initiative the Commons gained for themselves in those matters 'called common', that is the granting of taxes and the making of statutes which guarded 'common right', the 'common law', 'the good of your said Commons', and 'the state and integrity of your Crown [*l'estat et droiture de vostre Coroune*]'.

108. See Siemon, 'Sporting Kyd', esp. 556, on the smallness of Hieronimo's house; Christopher Crosbie, '*Oeconomia* and the Vegetative Soul: Rethinking Revenge in *The Spanish Tragedy*', *English Literary Renaissance* 38:1 (2008), 3–33.
109. On the uncertain relationship of the *domus* in *Thyestes* to stage-space, see Dana Ferrin Sutton, *Seneca on the Stage* (Leiden, 1986), 313–14.
110. Thomas Newton et al., *Seneca his tenne tragedies* (London, 1581), 32.
111. Vin Nardizzi, *Wooden Os: Shakespeare's Theatres and England's Trees* (Toronto, 2013), 95.

112. See Riemer A. Faber, 'The Description of the Palace in Seneca *Thyestes* 641–82 and the Literary Unity of the Play', *Mnemosyne* 60 (2007), 427–42, at 433–5, and generally; 439: 'The analogy between the palace and the tyrannical dynasty (641–56), the portrayal of the grove as place of family history (657–64), and the mingling of the upper and lower realms (665–82) show that the ekphrasis is not a mere *tour de force*, but the *locus* for the interaction of human, natural, and cosmic activities.'
113. Daniel B. Unruh, 'The Predatory Palace: Seneca's *Thyestes* and the Architecture of Tyranny', in Adam M. Kemezis (ed.), *Urban Dreams and Realities in Antiquity* (Leiden, 2014), 246–72.
114. On that opposition, see Unruh, 'Predatory Palace', 251ff.
115. See Gregory A. Staley, *Seneca and the Idea of Tragedy* (Oxford, 2009), Chap. 3.
116. William Rankins, *A Mirrour of Monsters* (London, 1587), Sig. B3^v.
117. On which, see the annotated diagrams in Frank B. Sear, 'Vitruvius and Roman Theater Design', *American Journal of Archaeology* 94:2 (Apr., 1990), 249–58.
118. 1574, 6 Dec. Act of Common Council of London, repr. *MSC* 1: 175; Chambers, *ES* 4: 273–6, my emphasis. A letter of early 1592 from the Lord Mayor to the Archbishop of Canterbury referred to 'the daily and disorderlie exercise of a number of players & playeng houses erected within this Citie': Chambers, *ES* 4: 307. For further evidence and discussion of the connections between the theatre and delinquency and riot, see Charles Whitney, '"Usually in the Werking Daies": Playgoing Journeymen, Apprentices, and Servants in Guild Records, 1582–92', *Shakespeare Quarterly* 50:4 (Winter, 1999), 433–58.
119. Ibid. This seems to associate the tiring-space with seditious plotting.
120. Stephen Gosson, *Plays confuted in five actions* (London, 1582), Sig. B.
121. Edward Topsell, *Times Lamentation* (London, 1599), 60.
122. John Rainalds, *Th'overthrow of stage-playes* (London, 1599), Sig. A2.
123. Anthony Munday, *A Second and Third Blast of retraite from plaies and theaters* (London, 1580), 123.
124. Stephen Gosson, *The Schoole of Abuse* (London, 1579), sigs C2; C4; C5.
125. *By the Queene. A proclamation to restraine accesse to the court, of all such as are not bound to ordinarie attendance, or that shall not be otherwise licenced by her Majestie* (London, 1592).
126. Surrey History Centre 6729/10, *More Molyneux Family of Loseley Park, Historical Correspondence*, Vol. XII, 'Copy of a letter from the Privy Council' [Dec. 1563].
127. Anthony Paul House, 'The City of London and the Problem of the Liberties, c.1540–c.1640', DPhil thesis, Oxford, 2006, 134.
128. R. A. Foakes and R. T. Rickert (eds), *Henslowe's Diary*, 2nd edn (Cambridge, 2002), 17–19.
129. The Lord Mayor to Lord Burghley, 12 June 1592, in *MSC* 1: 70–2. Cf. Carol Chillington Rutter (ed.), *Documents of the Rose Playhouse* (Manchester, 1999), 61–2.

130. Thomas Dekker, *Satiromastix*, in Fredson Bowers (ed.), *The Dramatic Works of Thomas Dekker* (Cambridge, 1953), IV.i.129–32.
131. George Puttenham, *The Arte of Englishe Poesie* (London, 1589), sigs N3–4.

Chapter 2

Points

The way to freedom is opened with a scalpel.

Seneca, *Epistle* 70

Little things are not to be despised [. . .] a little pricke of a rapier, may make a deadly wound.

Thomas Blague, 'A sermon preached at the Charterhouse before the Kings Majestie' (May, 1603)

What is the point of *Hamlet*? Titus Andronicus had sealed his revenge with a point: "'Tis true, 'tis true! Witness my knife's sharp point.'[1] Hieronimo had with a pen-knife ended his testimony. Physical pointiness appears throughout *Hamlet*.[2] The Prince is associated repeatedly with acuity.[3] He promises to 'speak daggers' to his mother (III.ii.386). As if 'feeling an edge of witte' set upon her, Gertrude repeats the image:[4] 'These words like daggers enter in mine ears' (III.iv.93). Gertrude's assimilation of Hamlet's own imagery converts it into the language of slander: sharp words; wounded feelings. But *Hamlet* calls on a hard distinction between the metaphorical and the material, even as (and perhaps because) Hamlet's language seems to contain an optimism that it might itself prove somehow sufficient. Connotations of verbal and mental accuracy, sharp efficacy, have a more general importance in that they contrast ironically with the notorious inability of Hamlet to effect that which appears most important. The Ghost arrives to 'whet [the Prince's] almost blunted purpose' [F: III.iv.99–100]. Hamlet has just stabbed Polonius, and his words work like daggers – but he is not the deadly instrument required: he is missing the point.

Hamlet's intent – and therefore his person – is mediated by sharp objects. These objects are not simply metaphorical or symbolic, and the mediation they effect does not obtain within a purely fictional or critical space. The sharp objects in question were actual and historical; and the epistemological difficulties created by their presence are contingent upon their complicated material reality and the histories in which that reality was implicated. The presence of the rapier in the final scene of *Hamlet* extends and confounds the play's discourses of intention, hesitation and accident, because the details of the fight are not just 'indefinite business', separable from the script's 'obligatory actions':[5] *how* Hamlet achieves his revenge seems precisely the most important thing about it. This chapter will show that *Hamlet* relates its prospective literary autonomy to its myriad theatrical realisations via sharp objects.

Scratches

The final scene of *Hamlet* draws the revenge debt into a complex of issues around the status of the duel in early modern England. Participation in the match seems to turn Hamlet's homicidal intentions into pure reaction, absolving him of the sin of revenge as indicted within Christian ethics. Hamlet's committed assertion that 'the readiness is all' may indeed echo scripture (Matt. 24: 34; Luke 12: 40), or (possibly by extension) Stoical preparedness, but it also alluded to a pressing social demand, to courage, and to instant defence of honour.[6] '*You must fight*,' wrote the author of the anti-duelling tract 'Duello foiled' (1613); 'that is, you must kill or be killed, *or at leastwise make it understood, that you dare it to the point.*'[7] The complex legal status of the duel, its connection to private honour and the departure from the State it implies, the way it purports to disclose the moral or social equivalence of participants, and its transformation of particular grievances into displays of skill and accident, all conspire to create insoluble epistemological problems for readers of the play. The close relation of sword-fighting to theatre and the investment of Hamlet's character in physical action make the resolution of the tragedy invisible to the reader of *Hamlet*. At the same time, the duel proper is not clearly represented by the play. Hamlet and Laertes agree to a non-lethal fencing match, a game and courtly spectacle through which debts may be improbably refigured and forgiven. This prospect is subverted by plots which inject lethality into the game. By these means, the duel begins to appear in it. Actual duels were often very far removed from the pure chivalric forms lionised by the masters of rapier who were in such high demand during the 1590s. The messiness of the final struggle in *Hamlet* in fact makes it more like a duel rather than less. The play retrieves important resources from this confusion of action, accident, mimesis and skill.

In the final act, Laertes is freshly returned from France, where, around 1600, numberless young men were meeting their deaths in duels.[8] To

Osric, Laertes is the 'card and calendar of gentry' (V.ii.95). He seems to be one of those who, as Ralegh put it, 'present[ed] death on the point of their swords' to any that dishonoured them:[9]

> I dare damnation. To this point I stand –
> That both the worlds I give to negligence.
> Let come what comes, only I'll be revenged
> Most thoroughly for my father.
>
> (IV.v.132–5)

As Laertes and Claudius plan out their mischief, the honour of Laertes is materially envenomed: 'I'll touch my point / With this contagion, that if I gall him slightly, / It may be death' (IV.vii.144–6). Hamlet does not at first dare it to the point, or cannot. For him, the 'point' seems to be more of an abstract affair, and certainly not the 'point' around which popular fencing manuals constructed their violent science;[10] a phenomenon of argument rather than of bloody quarrel, as in 'you make a good point' or 'what is the point of it all?'. Q1 gives us 'To be or not to be; ay, there's the point' (7: 114), momentarily using the word to refer simultaneously to an argumentative crux and the movement from life to death. As in *Julius Caesar*, a precursor to this *Hamlet*, the rhetorical point hovers about dead bodies.[11] Standing over Ophelia's grave, the Gravedigger mulls upon the legal and soteriological interpretation of her intentions: 'For here lies the point: if I drown myself wittingly, it argues an act, and an act hath three branches – it is to act, to do, to perform. Argal, she drowned herself wittingly' (V.i.10–13).

Already the play is providing occasions for Hamlet to announce a growing weariness with argumentation without action. As he asks of what he playfully holds up as a lawyer's skull a few lines later: 'Where be his quiddities now?' (V.i.94). Ophelia's funeral is also the burial of legal-theological theory and argument, connecting the 'point' simultaneously to death (the grave) and the clownish (the Gravedigger). Laertes and Hamlet fight like clowns in the grave, a sinking of honour that the chivalric rematch promises to correct. The humanist concern is that Hamlet's intellect will be compromised by such melee, sacrificed to the 'satanicall illusion and apparition of honour' or to the bathos of clownish 'action'.[12] Hamlet himself seems to know that the presence of blades will blunt even the sharpest intellect. At the beginning of the third act, he is found using a blade as a metonym both for suicide and revenge, and as a final relief from the labour of reflection:

> For who would bear the whips and scorns of time,
> Th'oppressor's wrong, the proud man's contumely.
> The pangs of despised love, the law's delay,

The insolence of office and the spurns
That patient merit of th'unworthy takes,
When he himself might his quietus make
With a bare bodkin.

(III.i.69–75)

A Bare Bodkin

How or why is the bodkin *bare*? The word stands in for the more common 'naked', carrying the sense of 'unsheathed'. Suicide with a sheathed dagger would be too upsetting or too funny to attempt, so 'bare' in this sense seems superfluous, that is, not appropriate to bareness. Aside from any prosodic consideration, it is being used chiefly to emphasise intent. The bare or naked blade is a blade that is being used for some purpose, and is the extension of someone's will, indicating imminent expression of that will – whence Iago to Roderigo in *Othello*: 'Wear thy good rapier bare, and put it home; / Quick, quick, fear nothing' (V.i.2–3). The bare blade indicated vengeful intent in ancient drama, wearing a sacrificial meaning. Orestes, atop the palace itself at the end of the Euripidean play, threatens Hermione with his sword. Both Menelaus and Apollo command: 'Orestes: remove the threat of your sword.'[13] In *Hamlet*, the Player's account of Priam's death articulates the ritualistic, propitious quality of such moments, as Pyrrhus' 'sword / Which was declining on the milky head / Of reverend Priam seemed i'th' air to stick' (II.ii.415–17). The delay is an addition to the Virgilian scene, but nevertheless seems to recall the very end of the *Aeneid*, as Aeneas hesitates before spying Pallas' belt on Turnus: the infliction of the vengeful sword-thrust closes the epic.

Hamlet's strike against the King is also suspended:

Up sword, and know thou a more horrid hent
When he is drunk, asleep or in his rage,
Or in th' incestuous pleasure of his bed,
At game a-swearing, or about some act
That has no relish of salvation in't.

(III.iv.88–92)

One way of reading 'hent' is as a substantive participle, meaning 'that which has been/will have been seized or caught', with reference to Claudius's soul; this was Dr Johnson's gloss, routinely given since.[14] Its chief meaning combines catching with violent removal. It may in this refer obliquely to the later exchange of rapiers (of which more below). 'Hent' was often inflected with 'intent', as in the February Eclogue of Spenser's *The Shepheardes Calender*: 'His harmefull Hatchet he hent in hand.'[15] It seems to shade into 'opportunity' or 'chance', combining in 'strike' or 'hit'. The astonishing compression achieved in 'horrid hent' occurs under the larger sense of 'having arrived at or reached', a sense felt by the mental ear in the apparent finality of 'hent', even as it points forward in time to something yet to be achieved, the fatal sword-strike itself.[16] In one of Robert Southwell's most memorable poems, the poet asks death, 'What doth withholde thy dint from fatall stroke?'[17] With a plausibly unlyrical force to compare with 'dint', 'hent' airs the uncertainty of a lifelike interim even as it implies a dramatic teleology. 'Bare bodkin' and 'horrid hent' are both promissory and potentially fateful. Even at this moment where Hamlet's logic seems most pitilessly his, it is the blade that will know a hent, not he. In seeming contrast, Hamlet's killing of Polonius appears to emphasise an over-quickness with his weapon, attributing a further meaning to 'bare' of 'unconsidered', 'rash' or 'hasty': Hamlet 'whips out his rapier' in a 'lawless fit' (IV.i.8–10). The fatal injury Polonius sustains through the arras, a strike both covered (hidden; cloaked) and bare (lacking full intent), may seem antithetical to the strong intention invested in 'horrid hent', but seems nearer, in its blind commitment, to the duel; and undermines the logic of the 'horrid hent' by representing the potentially equal horror of a careless murder.

'Bare' also carries the sense of 'mere': a 'mere' bodkin. That invitation to contemplate the dagger not only as a rather simple object but also as a rather common one probably seems counterintuitive. Few contemporary readers of *Hamlet* would be likely to refer to a 'mere gun'. Blades were ubiquitous in early modern England. 'Seldom shall you see one of my countrymen above eighteen or twenty years old to go without a dagger at the least at his back or by his side,' wrote Ralph Holinshed in 1586;[18] and one historian of early modern duels memorably suggests that 'in any sudden fracas swords or daggers would come out like claws'.[19] But 'bare', insofar as it might be taken to mean 'mere', could imply that the dagger is symbolic not just of intent, but of simple necessity, or even, given Hamlet's suicidal ruminations, desperate need. The word operates as such in *King Lear*, for example, working on several occasions within that play's complex handling of destitution.[20] If one allows that the 'bare bodkin' metamorphoses into the poisoned rapier of the final scene, a contradiction appears between the sharp weapon as something essential (physical), and the sharp weapon as something decorative (semiotic). The rapier was frequently included among the appurtenances of the gallant, with 'his short Cloake, and his Rapier hanging as if he were entering the List to a desperate Combate'.[21] The disapproval of foreign fashions such as the rapier and the rapier fight popularised by Vincentio Saviolo, widespread in satirical literature of the time, should not distract from the fact that the rapier was an aspirational possession.[22] Wearing a rapier implied an entitlement to use one: Giacomo di Grassi's 1594 *Arte of Defence*, which advocated 'strikinge with the point' whether one was using sword or rapier, stated that the rapier was 'a weapon more usuall for a Gentlemens wearing'.[23] Fencing masters also taught students how to fight with rapier and dagger. The deadly sharpness of the bodkin metonymically foreshadows the match at the end of the play. However, a bare blade is not the same as a naked one in implying purpose, because 'bare' implies an obscure valuation as well as an intention to act.

Hamlet's later decision to participate in the fateful contest against Laertes might be called a turn to a 'bare bodkin' – to an act that displaces thought. The bodkin is introduced by Hamlet's ruminations as something extraneous to them. It lies beyond argument; it stands in for the end of reflection: death. At the same time, the bodkin registers something anti-tragic. The word referred not only to a kind of sharp dagger but also to a woman's hairpin;[24] to a tool used by bookbinders to punch holes in stacks of quires for stitching or stapling;[25] to a sort of needle for threading ribbon; and to a small tool used for punching holes in fabrics like leather. If Hamlet does not directly compare suicide or murder to the transformation of a play into a book, he does seem to compare it to looping a ribbon or making a small puncture in a garment: he stabs Polonius through a weave. In Philip Sidney's *Arcadia*, Dido attacks Pamphilus with a bodkin: 'the little instrument of her great spight'.[26] *Hamlet* carries over the pettiness of the bodkin into the lethality of the rapier, a move that develops the cultural status of the weapon as something both trivial and dangerous:

> Aphobus: A rapier's but a bodkin.
> Deilus: And a bodkin
> Is a most dangerous weapon; since I read
> Of *Iulius Cesars* death, I durst not venture
> Into a Tailors shop for fear of Bodkins.[27]

In some quarters, the rapier was already regarded as an agent of social bathos – an emblem of dishonour and immaturity:

> I see by this dearth of good swords, that dearth of sword and Buckler fight, begins to grow out, I am sorry for it, I shall never see good manhood againe, if it be once gone, this poking fight of rapier and dagger will come up then, then a man, a tall man, & a good sword and buckler man, will be spitted like a Cat or a cunney, then a boy will be as good as a man [. . .][28]

The publication of this, Henry Porter's play *The Two Angry Women of Abington* (1599), may have been prompted by Porter's own death – stabbed through the heart by a rapier.[29] Here the last phrase, 'a boy will be as good as a man', directly relates rapier fighting to theatrical novelty, controversy, and (most importantly) fluidity, since the play was being acted by boys.[30] The Folio of *Hamlet* contains a joke that 'many wearing rapiers' feared the sharp satire – the 'goose-quills' – of the playwrights writing for the child companies (F: II.ii.335–60), again effecting this symbolic diminution. The bodkin may indeed stand for death, but it is altogether too common and too mean for it to become an effective emblem of the potential honour or pathos of tragic death.

The distinction between a bare blade and a covered one is very stark in the final scene of *Hamlet*, so that the superficial redundancy or tautology of the adjective 'bare' becomes retrospectively ironic. Claudius is confident that Hamlet 'will not peruse the foils' (IV.vii.134) and thereby discover the unbated blade which Laertes will use to effect the king's plan. 'Unbated' may here mean 'sharpened', or 'unblunted'. John Dover Wilson argued (possibly wrongly) that the soldered 'button' on later rapiers was unknown at the time of *Hamlet*.[31] In any case, the upshot of the plot is that Laertes, effecting his revenge with a sharp sword, stands against Hamlet, anticipating his own revenge with a blunt one. Hamlet unknowingly alludes to this in his pun on 'foil': 'I'll be your foil, Laertes' (V.ii.231). Hamlet seems to mean that he will be the lesser man against whom Laertes' skill might shine; but also that he will 'foil' Laertes, that is, be his 'stop', his 'lessening', or 'downfall'. The word also refers necessarily to the foil Hamlet is holding as the match gets under way, a symbol of his apparent ineffectiveness in the face of sharp practice. In this, as in so many other ways, Hamlet retains the aspect of Brutus, foiled by conscience. In 1599, the year before, audiences at the Globe would have been able to hear Hamlet's first actor, Richard Burbage, playing Brutus, appease his enemy with the words: 'To you our swords have leaden points, Mark Antony' (*Julius Caesar*, III.i.173).

This little formulation 'bare bodkin' not only foreshadows the play's final, rapiered scene, but seems to promise it, anticipating its possible disappointment as a tragic resolution. Despite its impoverishment of tragedy, the bodkin/rapier – the 'point' – cannot be relegated to the sidelines: it is not inessential, but a thematic and narratological crux. The sharp point of the blade proves resistant to assimilation into the logic of the fiction where it appears, because its lethality is never entirely symbolic.[32] The bareness becomes ineliminable.

The Civilisation of Death

The final scene of *Hamlet* begins as a rigged fencing match, a simulacrum of a duel. Once the intrigue becomes public, the ruined match seems to resemble an actual duel in at least some of its tension and lethality. At the same time, the resemblance of the match or game to the fatal duel seems ephemeral and deeply compromised. The play calls upon us to unravel this unravelling of the duel, because the question of Hamlet's intent is at stake. Hamlet's participation in the match seems to concede his own interests to the circumstances and contingencies of the match; the final scene becomes an inquest into the limits of intent in general, and into the relation of this ethical difficulty to the possibilities and ambitions of theatre.

In its resemblance to a duel, as well as in its differences from it, the climactic scene brings the relation between early modern civility and the archaism of the source material to a crisis. The sword fight reveals some of the epistemological difficulties in relating intent to honour. Norbert Elias's description of the civilising process and the work of Mervyn James on English honour politics both propose that changing social and religious expectations curbed aristocratic violence during the sixteenth century; the Elizabethan and Jacobean duel has often been described as a kind of distilled version of what used to be widespread violence.[33] V. G. Kiernan, in his history of the European duel, considered the phenomenon 'a vestigial survival of the early feudal right of private warfare'.[34] In another sense, the duel could be seen as a passing effect of the move away from chivalry towards 'civility', as the resource of a new individualism.

Markku Peltonen borrows Frank Henderson Stewart's differentiation between 'vertical' and 'horizontal' honour to embed the practice of duelling within 'the rise of civil courtesy', increasingly connected with the formation of a middling-sort ideology in recent early modern English historiography.[35] Stewart identifies horizontal honour as 'negative honour' because, unlike vertical honour, it cannot be increased.[36] As the work of Peltonen and others reveals, duels 'reached their peak long after the virtues of restraint and public service were internalised – and at the very moment when the notion of politeness gained sway'.[37] Duelling thus appears to have provided a reconciliation of the ancient honour economy with an emerging post-Reformation emphasis on virtue and civility, but an emphasis upon the displacement of the one by the other would be simplistic. One still killed for honour, and one still died for honour, but not with arms or heads hacked off, but by discreet little punctures to the chest or neck.[38] Chivalric violence lived on, transmuted as a graceful activity through which new values of civility and discretion could be articulated. The connections to older versions of chivalric form were retained, because the emerging 'middling sort' aspired to the emulation of noble ideals inhering in traditions of feud. Fear, wrote

Nicholas Breton, was 'the badge of a Coward, that cannot abide the sight of a sword'.³⁹ In Shakespeare's *Richard II*, Fitzwater vows to 'turn [Aumerle]'s falsehood to [his] heart / Where it was forged, with my rapier's point'. The conceit would simply not work were the rapier substituted for an axe or a greatsword.⁴⁰

Hamlet makes oaths over the sword of his father but brings about his revenge with a rapier: a qualitative shift. The fencing match offers the prospect of restored honour, but the anachronism of the rapiers interferes with what would otherwise begin as an archaic chivalric display. Hamlet's grace, not his strength, will register moral victory. But this promise falls victim to the play's revenge materials, since it can only appear as a reproduction of something ancient:

> Amleth, with his remarkable perception, saw that two choices surged around him, one of which was shameful and the other dangerous. He was aware that if he accepted the challenge, he would be putting his life in danger, but if he refused he would dishonour himself as a warrior.⁴¹

Unfortunately for the early modern Amleth, the honourableness of rapier fights was highly contentious. Civil or not, early modern rapier fights tended to be far deadlier than combats with sword or axe, and many traditionalists lamented the rise of duelling as an attenuation, not a demonstration, of honourable practice or nobility:

> In the olde world when swords of one length and heartes of equal courage did meet, some in difference debated the matter, and fewe were put to foile, and many were wortheley esteemed for their value. And now when the rapier and dagger dispatcheth a man quickly, neither he lives to heare his owne fame, nor no man living can let fall a good word of the quarrell, begun of such trifles, maintaind with such terror, and ended with such madnes [. . .]⁴²

Thomas Churchyard here associates the duel with petty causes and quick anger – hardly amenable to the articulation of tragic grace or the defence of reputation (and this from the author who had written the Dedication to the English translation of di Grassi's revolutionary guide to fighting with rapier).⁴³

The duel, Peltonen and others argue, was necessitated by a kind of pinprick in social courtesy: 'Even a small rupture in courtesy or civil conversation could prompt a duel.'⁴⁴ It was precisely this that the Jacobean movement against duelling planned to address, once the Earl of Northampton briefly took the matter in hand in 1613/14. The Court of Chivalry was to acquire a monopoly of response to rude, insulting and provocative words; the state was to avenge everyone's dishonour.⁴⁵ Duelling did not offer the prospect of honour's increase. It was fundamentally defensive. To refuse a duel could have social consequences, but to take up the duel and win it would not necessarily lead to any increase in standing. Duelling was about defending the claim one had made to a particular social identity. The success of Hamlet in the match might be interpreted as a restoration of civility, but that restoration is dependent on his ability to embody civility through skill and gesture. This facility of the character is indistinguishable from that of the actor playing him: the player of Hamlet finds in the duel a way to defend his claim to Hamlet's identity.

Hamlet voices a worry for his 'name' (V.ii.328), implying an awareness that the accidents of the final scene leave many questions of honour and reputation hanging. The completion of Hamlet's revenge takes place at the collapse of the duelling scene, so that whilst participation in its ritual has lent the character a certain conventional aspect in relation to the defence of honour, the moment of revenge cannot fully belong to this realm of conventional response:

HAMLET	The point envenomed too! Then venom to thy work! *Hurts the King.*
LORDS	Treason, treason!
KING	O, yet defend me, friends. I am but hurt.
HAMLET	Here, thou incestuous, murd'rous, damned Dane, Drink off this potion. Is thy union here? Follow my mother. *King dies.*

(V.ii.304–8)

There is an element of atavism when Hamlet finally effects his revenge upon the king. This might be interpreted either as a disclosure of the barbarism present in the ideal duel's ostensibly civil ritual of mutual recognition, or as an indication that the ancient right structuring Hamlet's revenge has been unhappily reconciled with modish swordplay. Hamlet's 'delight in freaks and twists of thought', the 'strange lightning of the mind', as A. C. Bradley put it, is still apparent in the complex pun on 'union': this refers to the poisonous pearl Claudius drops in the cup, to the 'incestuous' marriage, to the sacrament of the Eucharist, and to death.[46] Hamlet therefore carries through his characteristic interest in little things, fine distinctions, slight shifts in meaning, minute manipulations of words and ideas, quiddities and quibbles. His pedantic wit is caught between frailty and grace. The rapier, heavy though it might have been in these its early forms, seems a natural enough objective correlative for that wit:

The Arte and exercise of the Rapier and Dagger is much more rare and excellent than anie other Militarie exercise of the bodie, because [. . .] in particular combats, & many other accidents, where a man having the perfect knowledge and practise of this arte, although but small of stature and weake of strength, may with *a little removing of his foot, a sodain turning of his hand, a slight declining of his bodie*, subdue and overcome the fierce braving pride of tall and strong bodies.⁴⁷

The rapier was frequently imagined by its advocates as the proper extension of the noble body. Satirists drew attention to the opposite, showing how the rapier could appear an alien object, even an object with a will of its own, when worn pretentiously by those not trained in its subtle application. In Ben Jonson's *Every Man out of his Humour* (1599), the pseudo-soldier Shift is observed 'expostulating with his rapier'. 'I wonder the blade can contain itself, being so provoked,' remarks one of the onlookers; the other quipping that 'the rapier, it seems, is in the nature of a hanger-on'.⁴⁸ A character asks for rapier and dagger from a cutler in Greene's *The Scottish History of James IV* (1598), but the rapier 'must have a verie faire edge', 'because it may cut by himselfe, [and] trulie [. . .] I am a man of peace, and weare weapons but for facion'.⁴⁹ The way Hamlet holds and relates to the rapier governs the appearance of conscience, honour and intention. Hamlet's name resides somewhere between his hand and the tip of the blade it wields.

Whether a given rapier fight really protected reputation and honour was therefore highly uncertain. Often it was difficult to appreciate where the brawl ended, and the duel began. In practice, indignity could intercede against ethical formalism anywhere from the challenge to the fight itself.⁵⁰ Before the match, Laertes offers a more stereotypical declaration of injured honour, as if to argue that the duel could indeed provide a restoration of form.

> I am satisfied in nature,
> Whose motive in this case should stir me most
> To my revenge. But in my terms of honour
> I stand aloof and will no reconcilement
> Till by some elder masters of known honour
> I have a voice and precedent of peace
> To keep my name ungored.
>
> (V.ii.221-7)

Laertes declares the natural law motive resolved but craves a formal resolution to protect his honour. Except, Laertes' invitation to fence is a ruse. The honour of the match is formal in a totally different sense, that is, 'merely formal'. The scheme of the match threatens to become a joke: 'These foils have all a length?', asks Hamlet (V.ii.265). The 'duel' must operate to create the semblance of order and equality; instead it provides an intensely bathetic case of going through the motions. The threat of bathos has long been found to haunt theatrical fights, but here it intersects with a broader social anxiety concerning honour, that 'buble, which is raysed with one winde and broken with another'.[51] The descent of the match into a tumult of accidental death, misfiring plots and murder prompts its dying participants to voice anxious desire to return to the security of its solemn ritual. Laertes' reconciliation, with death impending ('Exchange forgiveness with me, noble Hamlet,' 313), suggests that if the game's formality had previously been a joke, its loss is catastrophic. At this point of reconciliation, an 'inimical intimacy', or even a 'moral tradition' of fraternity among opponents, might be discerned. In Webster and Rowley's *A Cure for a Cuckold* (c.1624), the duel is abandoned only when its participants *really* become enemies.[52] *Hamlet* likewise registers the idea that private honour in duelling could contribute less to the violent pulling-apart of the commonwealth so much as the maintenance of those communities that made it up.[53]

The contest advertised as a fencing-match can only be considered a depiction of a *duel* in an extremely qualified sense. The final scene refuses to coalesce into a straightforward mimesis of a duel. The Player's version of Pyrrhus makes 'malicious sport / In mincing with his sword [Priam's] limbs' (II.ii.451–2). In one sense, the fencing-match at the end of *Hamlet* seems to invite subtle manoeuvres, in contrast to Pyrrhus' rough-hewing of ends. Yet the match between Hamlet and Laertes is hewn roughly in other senses: epistemological, temporal, narratological, aesthetic – and political.

A Subtle Exchange

What does the rapier do to the king's name? The defeat of Claudius in the breakdown of the fencing-match alludes to the broader political implications of duelling for the relation between honour and citizenship. The author of 'Duello foiled' would argue that the duel revealed no truth, and that it was by its very nature self-defeating as a means of effecting justice. The duel was founded in the 'law', that is, the lawlessness, of revenge: 'no man ought to be a judge and a witness in his own case'.[54] In Chapman's *Bussy D'Ambois* (1607), the hero's rhetoric goes to the worry that underlay Stuart ambivalence towards the duel: 'Let me be King my selfe (as man was made) / And doe a justice that exceeds the law.'[55] Clearly, the duel could be used to assert a kind of autonomy irreconcilable with an autocracy in which the sovereign was the fount of law.[56] The echo of the duel in *Hamlet* is appropriate to the act of regicide which the contest brings about. Hamlet wins sovereignty through fencing; Claudius loses his. Hamlet's skill with a sword, and not his lineage, expresses his moral claim.

Claudius has armed Laertes with an executive sword, but by an accident of the scene the weapon turns on him. In this it recalls Priam's 'antique sword, / Rebellious to his arm [...] / Repugnant to command' (II.ii.407–8). *Der Bestrafte Brudermord*, a German version of *Hamlet* arguably derived from the ur-*Hamlet* or a 1590s Shakespearean play, mediates this idea of the disobedient blade in an interesting way, indeed resolves it into an ambiguity of grammar. This version adds a more distinctly clownish Osric (named Phantasmo) as accomplice in the poisoned-blade-and-cup plot – the scene calls for Phantasmo to hide the poisoned rapier somewhere on the stage for retrieval by Leonhardus (Laertes). Upon discovery of this treachery, Hamlet menaces the clown, perhaps even stabs him, with the poisoned blade, and as response gets the cry: 'Stecht, dass euch die Klinge verlahme!'.[57] This line has proven difficult to translate, partly because translators have been unwilling to consider the paradox of the blade injuring its wielder.[58] Possibly the sense is that in stabbing Phantasmo, Hamlet's hand will slip off the weapon's handle and down along the blade. A literal translation might read: 'Thrust, so that the blade makes you lame!' The phrase does carry this less peculiar meaning of a blade being blunted by blood or usage, as in 'Thrust, so that you make your blade lame!' That may seem a strange thing to say to someone stabbing you, but alludes to Pyrrhic victory. Whether by accident or design, the phrase distils the ambiguity at work in the Shakespearean versions. Claudius wrongly assumes that props are subject to absolute control, when, like Heywood's Thyestes, he should have learned his 'selfe same swoorde to feare / That hanged by [his] owne syde'.[59] This is what some opponents of fencing argued, that 'they whette their Swoords against themselues' who practise it.[60] The martial prowess involved in the duel carries over into a revenge against a disarmed king, divested of his executive power that is now, in the shape of the sword, turned against him.

Hamlet develops its source material into a practical critique of early modern sovereignty. Comparable to the growing power of legalism that would reach its most important milestones only a decade or so later in the *Case of Proclamations* and *Dr Bonham's Case* was the system of honour which, as Mervyn James has argued, developed a kind of moral orientation to central authority that assisted in the construction of a state consciousness, even as it imposed new limits on the sovereignty of the monarch.[61] Defiance of the Crown relied on the 'tradition of a moralized history' that had been appropriated by the economy of honour, so that even seditious disobedience could imply a reinforcement of the idea of commonwealth.[62] Many of the rebels of the previous century had fought under its banner.[63] If the 'duel' in *Hamlet* is used in one sense to excuse Hamlet from premeditated regicide, in another sense the 'duel' in general is invested with moral and political value. In a deeply obscure and indirect way, the climax of *Hamlet* anticipates the coming historical victory of civility and private honour, as expressed in the interim by the duel, over the king and his sovereign rights.[64] The play is, as John Kerrigan suggests of *Macbeth*, 'informed enough about its moment to generate prophetic insights,' but attains this power not so much through topicality as through a singular commitment to the contemporary materials of revenge.[65]

The royal plan is undone by Hamlet's skill at fencing. The plots fail, and Hamlet's revenge is achieved, because Hamlet is simply a better fencer than Laertes, defeating him twice before the exchange of rapiers. The duel works as advertised for Hamlet: his 'practice' pays off, he has shown himself to be more civil in it than anyone else. His apparently coincidental reward is to be able to administer spontaneous public justice, instead of revenge *ex malicia precogitata*, to the tyrannical king ('The king, the king's to blame', V.ii.305). But 'plot' of a different sort interferes with this bounty. The death of the king is in a literal sense an accident of the scene of duelling, indeed an 'accident' in an Aristotelian sense, that is, a probable improbability.[66] The appearance of a relation between Hamlet's revenge and the rapier fight – and the perceptibility of probable accident – is falsified by the decisive exchange of rapiers. This moment may seem an achievement of great skill – or fall out as luck. This uncertainty obscures the political content of the final passages. The exchange of rapiers, the poisoned blade for the harmless, clouds the relation of the tragedy to sovereign agency. Accident and purpose were potentially nullified by fate in ancient tragedy. In *Hamlet* they depend on the physical dynamics of actual and prospective performances. The relation of these dynamics to the appearance of providential design is likewise very uncertain.

The question of Hamlet's murderous intent hinges almost entirely on this moment of exchange, caught between skill and accident, in 'catching' (Q2) and 'scuffling' (F). The apparently crucial question as to whether Hamlet *deliberately* orchestrates the exchange of foils has led to some very technical speculation, the best of which rests on the fact that such manoeuvres of disarming, like the 'left-hand seizure', were recommended in contemporary fencing manuals and may well have been compassed by early modern actors.[67] Henry de Sainct Didier's *Les Secrets du premier livre sur l'espée seule* (1573) takes account of the possibility

Figure 2.1 'A prinse faut faire contreprinse, comme est icy monstré par ce Lieutenant au Prevost.' Henry de Sainct Didier, Traicté contenant les secrets du premier livre sur l'espée seule (Paris, 1573), fol.64ᵛ. © The British Library Board: General Reference Collection 63.a.18.

that equally matched opponents might disarm one another simultaneously (Figure 2.1). It is extremely likely that such techniques were taught at English fencing schools, since Sainct Didier cropped many of his ideas from di Grassi, whose methods were well-known in London. Q2 indicates that the fight was to be acted not with single rapiers, but with rapier and dagger (V.ii.128), making the 'left-hand seizure' less practicable.[68] It is also possible that the rapiers were exchanged not in a technical demonstration but in the midst of a brawl – in a scuffle, not a catch. George Silver, who held the rapier for an 'unperfect instrument', noted the tendency of fights with long rapiers to come quickly to 'the Close [...] wherby it commeth to passe [...] that the strongest man or best Wrastler, ouercommeth'.[69] Such a tussle would also provide opportunities for an accidental or at the least ambiguously intentional exchange. Given that *Hamlet* has a foot both in the 'barbaric' past and in the 'civil' present, it is not clear that such a staging would be less germane to the ethos of the play than a technically adept manoeuvre. A degenerate match would be consistent with the many other failed rituals shown in *Hamlet*. More importantly, purely technical explanations suppress the essential difficulty. Hamlet's intentionality in this instance cannot be represented except by the gestural activity of the actor playing him, so that this crucial moment in the play's inquisition of the ethics of intention is invisible to the reader of *Hamlet*, and untragically provisional for a given audience. Even for one confident that the play calls for a 'left-hand seizure', there can never be confidence about the way this was or is to be achieved onstage, nor the extent to which it might evidence a particular purpose or knowledge on the part of Hamlet the 'person'.

Far from being a purely technical or dramaturgical question, the moment of exchange reaches back into, and reconfigures, the play's ancient materials. In legends of Hamlet, the king tries to defend himself from his own sword being wielded against him by vainly attempting to draw a different blade that has been nailed into its scabbard. In Belleforest's version, such cunning is the salient feature of revenge:

> [Hamlet] went thither, and entring into the chamber, layd hand upon the sword of his fathers murtherer, leaving his owne in the place, which while he was at the banket some of the courtiers had nailed fast into the scaberd, and going to Fengon said: I wonder, disloyal king, how thou canst sleep [. . .] Fengon [. . .] perceived a sword naked in his hand, which he already lifted up to deprive him of his life, leaped quickly out of the bed, taking holde of Hamlet's sworde, that was nayled into the scaberd, which as hee sought to pull out, Hamlet gave him such a blowe upon the chine of the necke, that hee cut his head cleane from his shoulders.[70]

In the *Gesta Danorum* of Saxo Grammaticus, the equivalent events are split:

> Since [Amleth] kept drawing the sword and purposely cutting his fingers with its point, some of the bystanders had an iron nail struck through his sword and sheath [. . .] From the hall [Amleth] went to Fengi's bedroom [. . .] where he took the sword that hung by Fengi's bed and replaced it with his own. Then he awakened his uncle [. . .] Fengi leapt out of bed and was cut down while in the absence of his own sword he was trying in vain to draw another's.[71]

In Shakespeare's extant versions – mediated in unknown ways by the ur-*Hamlet* – the crucial symbolic clarity of Fengon/Fengi's vain attempt to wield Hamlet's sheathed weapon has been transformed into the muddle of the exchange of rapiers, and into the symbolism of Hamlet forcing Claudius to drink his own poison. The play invites us to consider whether the same macabre wit can be at work in the exchange of weapons as it clearly is in the substitution of letters that kills Rosencrantz and Guildenstern. Hamlet sees his old friends as 'baser' natures that did come 'between the pass and fell incensèd points / Of mighty opposites' (V.ii.59–61), strongly encouraging the comparison. The exchange is not just of lethal weapons, but of authority in the scene. The sword stolen from Fengon/Claudius is used narratologically as the instrument of authentic *royal* justice: Hamlet not only acquires the poisoned point in the exchange, but also a symbol of the royal will.

Removed from any intelligible scheme of cunning intent, the exchange of rapiers in *Hamlet* is pivotally difficult. In ruining the king's orchestration of the scene, and in scotching the intent of Laertes, the hero of the king's plot, the exchanged rapier acquires power as the material embodiment of theatrical uncertainty. Everything Hamlet does after the exchange of rapiers appears as extemporisation, a deviation from the royal script. Imagined as a prop with a well-defined and limited use, the rapier becomes an accident of availability, because only one is poisoned. Hieronimo, in *The Spanish Tragedy*, wins revenge by getting everyone to read from his script; Hamlet gets his by improvising on another's theme. This is the reverse side to Lorna Hutson's discovery of an emergent forensics of suspicion in early modern revenge plays. For Hutson, the delay comprises, in *Hamlet* and *The Spanish Tragedy*, 'a series of processes of enquiry into the circumstances of the wrong, seeking evidence [. . .] and corroboration'.[72] The fight at the end of Hamlet seems to abandon that procedural care entirely. All Hamlet needs is 'readiness'.

The 'duel' relocates revenge beyond the scope of intention as envisaged, for example, by Brutus and the conspirators in Caesar's death. *Hamlet* furnishes no clear causal relationship between 'the acting of a dreadful thing' – revenge against a king – and its 'first motion' (*Julius Caesar*, II.i.63–4). It is impossible to specify which motion in the fencing match is the first motion of revenge. Casca's cry 'Speak hands for me!' (III.i.76) might be contrasted with Hamlet's exclamation: 'The point envenomed too? Then venom, to thy work! *[Hurts the king]*' (V.ii.306). Q1 emphasises Hamlet's surprised recognition by allowing his speech to modulate Laertes' sudden 'The fatal instrument is in thy hand' into Hamlet's question: 'The poisoned instrument within my hand? / Then venom to thy venom, die, damned villain!' (17: 85–7). The conspirators of *Julius Caesar* orchestrate the scene, and are themselves 'mortal instruments' (II.i.66); Hamlet discovers the tyrannicidal potential of a scene organised for some other purpose entirely. In other words, the uncertainty created by the exchange gives way to a series of questions about improvisation and the legal implications of extemporised violence.

Deadly ex Tempore

Critics of the duel often emphasised its lack of any grounds that might authorise or license its action. The author of a mid-seventeenth century

'Declaration against duelling', extant as a manuscript in Trinity College, Cambridge, observed that defenders of the practice could not 'vouch other groundes then their owne conceites, to support the point'; and condemned the duellists themselves for 'revenging their supposed wronges accordinge to the Sense of their owne Smarte without any graunte by *Charter* or by dispensation, any such supposed privilege from *God* or man'.[73] The duel was, then, a deplorable improvisation of justice. It was also, in a surprising and separate sense, an actual legal improvisation, or rather a set of improvisations that were breaking open new ground in the common law.

Improvisation with sharp objects played an increasingly important role in broader legal definitions of intent. Whilst social historians of the duel have tended to assume the 'illegality' of extra-judicial duels, some legal historians have observed the more complex relationship between the rise of the duel in the sixteenth century and the more or less parallel process through which the parameters of modern homicide were defined.[74] Jeremy Horder argues that the late sixteenth-century concept of the duel encompassed not only premeditated combat but also spontaneous violent encounters (or so-called 'rencounters'), suggesting that the distinction between premeditated murder and manslaughter emerged from attempts to rationalise this bifurcation within the category of 'duel'. Specifically, in dealing with killings and injuries associated with duels, early modern lawyers began to give greater definition to the idea of 'provocation'.[75] Luke Wilson also notes how the misuse of objects constituted legally applicable evidence of suddenness: this valuation of *ex tempore* use of nearby objects played a formative role in the 'rise of manslaughter as a category of homicide intermediate between (felony) murder [. . .] and exculpable forms'.[76]

In 1581, William Lambarde offered the following recommendations to Justices of the Peace concerning the legal ambiguity of duelling, in what would become a standard and oft-reprinted handbook: 'For, if two [men] do sodainly fall out, and therupon draw their weapons, and one killeth the other, this is *Manslaughter* apparantly within the compasse of this Lawe.' Lambarde expands:

> Nowe if one doe suddenly (without anye occasion of present quarrell offered) drawe his sworde, and therewithall killeth an other, that standeth by him, this cannot bee thought but to haue bene done of a pretended purpose, and therefore hath bene taken to bee Murder.
>
> So is it taken if two fall out, and doe appoint a place to fight together, and there the one of them killeth the other, *ibid*.[77]

John Day was charged with the murder of Henry Porter in 1599, but the phrases 'murder' and 'malice aforethought' were struck out after the case: Day's claim that he had sought to avoid the fight was believed, and a verdict of manslaughter recorded.[78] Hamlet and Laertes do kill one another, but in a premeditated game of fencing. That this game becomes deadly means it momentarily acquires the aspect of a duel which seems neither entirely premeditated nor entirely unforeseen. Meeting by arrangement could be used, paradoxically, to signal both the honourableness and the illegality of a fight. From a legal perspective, the brandishing of the naked blade could indicate intent, and in fact does so as soon as Hamlet is told by Laertes that the blade he holds is doubly lethal, with the guilty king nearby.

That the king bears legal responsibility for Hamlet's death was always certain: 'If a man commaund one to poyson an other, and he killeth him with a sword, yet the Commander is *Accessorie* to this *Murder*.'[79] Hamlet's responsibility is less sure. The rapier's point does not act to confirm Hamlet's intention to avenge, but seems to supplement his subjective incapacity to do so. Its presence converts intent into an automatic response to the demands of the event, and hence halfway into manslaughter. The ruination of the honourable fencing-match seems to excuse Hamlet from any moral dilemma, as many have observed.[80] This effect results from abstraction from a practical historical struggle, through which the concept of malice aforethought was being refined in respect of equally fluid categories: accident, negligence and passion. The killing of Claudius is an entirely premeditated act (the play is indeed grounded in pre-meditation). But it is also a spontaneous reaction amidst what early modern lawyers, at least since Thomas Marowe's *De Pace Terre et Ecclesie* (1503), would have termed the 'chance-medley' produced by the duel's degeneration into an uncertain but deadly scuffle, 'a sudden brawl, shuffling, or contention'. As Coke later saw it, the phrase 'chance medley' was itself ambiguous, since to him 'medley' appeared an English compound of the Old French *mesle* (shuffling, meddling, mixture, commotion, whence mêlée) and the Latin *medletum* (death; manner of dying).[81] Others derived it from *chaud* ('hot'), with the sense of 'a hasty mixing […] of two combatants'.[82] 'Chance' was – of course – a deeply fraught concept in 1600, not least because probability (separate from simple contingency, and from what Aristotle had thought of as 'that which happens for the most part' with reference to dramatic plausibility) was an emergent idea without any mathematical underpinning at all.[83] The rapiers, intended as instruments of conspiracy, are transformed into the props of incalculable danger.

One of the problems for lawyers was defining where the duel ended and the common brawl began, or vice versa. Whilst contemporary honour books insisted on the necessary premeditation and formality of the duel proper, in practice violent single combat might yet be considered a duel if there were a challenge and an acceptance, and if it were fought with the weapons of the gentleman. In other words, using a rapier instead of some other weapon could itself change how the fight was perceived. Hamlet's 'revenge', therefore, bestrode the emerging legal distinction between manslaughter ('malicious strikings' and so-called 'chance medley'), excusable homicides, and the premeditated murder of the fully organised duel. The generic ambiguity of the play derived from a social and legal ambiguity surrounding the definition of intent in particular instances of combat. The device of the fencing-match, a duel phantasmagorical but all too concrete, provides the occasion for a confusion of *generic* law organised around problems of *social* and *moral* law. The issue of intent in the play can therefore be linked to its test of the theatre's capacity to elicit fine judgements.

The legal aporia around the duel were not simply *represented* on the early modern stage. They were figured in the movement of bodies. Early modern actors and playwrights were often duellists or brawlers: there are the well-known cases of Jonson v. Spencer (1598), and Day v. Porter (1599). In late 1597, Gabriel Spencer had stabbed James Feake through the eye with a sheathed rapier, after Feake had menaced him with a copper candlestick during an altercation.[84] The proximity of early professional acting to sword-fighting changes how intent and improvisation appear in *Hamlet*. A lesser known case will help to show why the connection drawn in *Hamlet* between martial and theatrical extemporisation is more than merely metaphorical. In 1608, the travelling English actor John Green was in the Austrian city of Graz to perform plays. The repertoire and performances of his company are detailed in a letter to a relative written by Maria Maddalena of Austria. In a postscript to her epistle, she describes a duel between a Frenchman and a red-haired fiddle-player whom it seems probable was Green:

> They went off together as far as the square near the butcher's stalls [. . .] There the Frenchman drew rapier and dagger from his leather and the Englishman had only his rapier, so he said, 'Brother, if you want to fence with rapier and dagger, then give me a dagger too.' The Frenchman gave him his own dagger and took the valet's dagger, and so they began to fight. The Frenchman was continuously lunging, while the other merely warded the thrusts, but in one of his parries he cut off the Frenchman's thumb so that he dropped his sword. The Englishman, however, was honourable, and lowering his sword stuck its point in the ground, and said, 'Brother, get a good grip of your weapon.' This the Frenchman did, rushing forward with a typically French thrust, as if he wanted to run the Englishman through. At that the Englishman finally saw red and stuck his dagger through the Frenchman's right eye into his brain, and he immediately fell. Thereupon the Englishman quickly put away

his rapier and dagger, knelt down by the Frenchman and said, 'forgive me, Brother, but you made an attempt.'

At this point, however, the duel's function as a theatre in which to measure out honour and skill was rudely disrupted by intrigue:

> He was about to lift him up and take him to the barber-surgeon, but as he turned around, there was the villain Lorenz, who ran him through about four inches above the left nipple and right out through the back under the shoulder-blade, leaving the sword sticking in him. The scoundrel had been waiting with three horses ready, and he jumped on one, Eggenberg's valet on another, and they made off together.

Green, who survived, pulled out the sword himself and made his own way to the barber-surgeon. Unlike the Frenchman, who died without regaining consciousness, Green could make uncertain expiation, confessing to one Father Ignatius.[85]

Many features present in the climax of *Hamlet* recur uncannily in this account: the fact that the Frenchman is stabbed with his own dagger; the sense of fluctuating boundaries between game of honour and lethal struggle; the provocation; the honour and effectiveness of reaction; the ideal of brotherhood imposed by the Englishman to make the fight

Figure 2.2 'Es kompt aber manchmal, das ihr zwene zusammen kommen, die da geschwinde im Rappier sind.' Michael Hundt, *Ein new künstliches Fechtbuch im Rappier* (Leipzig, 1611), Sig. R3. © Herzog August Bibliothek Wolfenbüttel: A: 31 Bell. (2).

appear a contest of equals; the destruction of the contest's appearance of honour by extraneous treachery; the Frenchman dying, like Claudius, without confession; et cetera. There is a distant possibility that some version of *Hamlet* was already in foreign repertories by 1608, but this is not the principal consideration. If *Hamlet* does not provide spectators with a duel in an absolute sense, this in fact makes it more not less like actual early modern duels such as the one involving Green, where things rarely matched up to the ideal propagated by fencing masters and theorists of civility. It is precisely through the failure of the match to resemble the ideal scene of duelling that this social history is able to enter on the side of the Prince's conscience in such a powerful way. Yet historians of early modern duelling cases have had reason to infer that apparently chance encounters or brawls were sometimes planned in advance by both parties so as to pre-empt charges of murder.[86]

Green's apparent agility and skill as a fencer went hand in hand with his considerable fame as an actor and clown. Perhaps the most bizarre feature of this narrative is the comparison it invites between the duel and theatrical show, both of which involve planning and improvisation, intent and accident. Fencing and theatre were congruent and sometimes co-extensive. In England, early theatres like The Curtain combined strong associations with fencing and duelling with unique traditions of clowning.[87] On the continent, travelling English actors like Green inhabited the same performing space as fencers. In Nuremberg and Gdańsk, to take examples hundreds of miles apart, two new theatres were opened to accommodate travelling actors: both buildings were called 'Fencing Houses' when they were founded, and city authorities throughout central and northern Europe often made little practical distinction between what they regarded as species of physical display. In Frankfurt am Main, the performances of the English Comedians in the 1590s took place immediately after fencing schools, and in the same place.[88] To a Dutch adaptation of *The Revenger's Tragedy* is appended a prefatory dialogue between Horatio (Horace, in person of the aspiring literary author) and one 'Mr Adolf, swordmaster'. Horace wishes to avenge himself upon his literary enemies by learning to fight with rapier and bringing them to a death-match. Adolf insists that rapier skill is self-defensive, and takes him in to watch a play that will show him the moral horror of revenge: *Wraeck-gieriges Treur-spel*, the translation from Middleton's English original.[89] In early modern Europe, there was a blurry line between martial competence and theatre lessons.

This struggle to make distinctions which are sometimes presented, in our age, as self-evident was not totally without foundation. Fencing instruction and honour economies both involved public demonstration;

and the combat skill of many professional actors sustained these overlapping fields of activity and skill. Green, whose lethal facility with rapier and dagger is gruesomely evidenced by Maria Maddalena's report, was one of the trailblazers of a new form of professional clown that was coming to dominate continental theatre. The founder in England of this professional tradition of aggressive extemporisation, Richard Tarlton, was himself an expert fencer, becoming a Master of Fence in 1587. This was an important feature of his posthumous legend. One story has Tarlton humiliate an absurdly dressed gallant he spied on Fleet Street:

> Tarlton seeing such a wonder comming, trips before him, and, meeting this gallant, tooke the wall of him, knowing that one so proud at least looked for the prerogative. The gallant, scorning that a player should take the wall, or so much indignifie him, turnes himselfe, and presently drew his rapier. Tarlton drew likewise. The gentleman fell to it roundly; but Tarlton, in his owne defence, compassing and traversing the ground, gaped with a wide mouth, whereat the people laughed. The gentleman, pausing, enquired why he gaped so. O, sir, saies he, in hope to swallow you; for, by my troth, you seeme to me like a prune in a messe of white broth. At this the people parted them. The gentleman noting his mad humour, went his way well contented; for he knew not how to amend it.[90]

Tarlton's reputed expertise as a swordsman went hand-in-hand with his reputation for aggressive wit – verbal parries, mocking thrusts.

Andrew Gurr has suggested that the first version of an early modern *Hamlet* was produced by the Queen's Men at the end of the 1580s (shortly after Tarlton's death). This play was – the conjecture goes – subsequently taken over and performed by the Chamberlain's Men in the 1590s (the so-called ur-*Hamlet*), and was rewritten by Shakespeare around the end of the century as the version with which we are familiar.[91] This murky history of association between *Hamlet* and the Queen's Men brings on the next example: the Norwich affray of 1583. In June of that year, Tarlton himself leapt from the stage at the Red Lion in Norwich to defend a fellow actor being assaulted at the door by two gatecrashers. Two other players and a spectator pursued the intruders. Catching up with one of them, they assailed him with the very swords that a short time before had been but props in a tragedy. He was stabbed and killed outside on the street.[92] Here, too, the law emphasised the intent shown by the 'naked Rap[i]er':

> Two of the players did Runne after the man with their wepons drawn and [Edmunde] kerrie tooke one of the players in his armes & woold have Stayed hym but one ran at hym with his sworde and he feering some daunger to hym selfe lett thother goe and ffled.[93]

All three of the involved players – Tarlton, John Singer and John Bentley – were known for their accomplishment in fencing. But the Queen's Men were recognised above all for their skill in *ex tempore* acting: as the fight developed, some amongst the audience at the Red Lion found it difficult to distinguish the violence from the improvisational high jinks that had made the troupe famous. One of the questions asked of the witnesses was whether the actors had stopped performing; and the tragedian Bentley's acrobatic leap from the stage has been interpreted by some historians as a conscious attempt to add extra drama to the events.[94] In other words, this violent brawl can be – and was – brought into an uncertain relationship with digressions from form associated with the clowning extemporisation of the company.

At first sight, *Hamlet* seems impatient with clownish digression. Hamlet himself instructs the players to 'reform' their theatre 'altogether, and let those that play your clowns speak no more than is set down for them' (III.ii.36–7). In the context of a play that seems to place special value on Hamlet's extemporisation, every version of this speech sounds incongruous. The experienced early modern playgoer may well have laughed at Hamlet's injunction, incoherent as it was given that the very essence and ethos of Tarltonesque clowning was departure from the script. The Q1 version of this speech is still more contradictory. There Hamlet will not recognise the work of the clown as improvisation at all: rather, it consisted in the introduction of prepared material. Although the Chamberlain's Men lacked a clown when the extant *Hamlet* was produced, the end of the play is hedged about by clownish figures: the Gravedigger and his assistant, Yorick, Osric and, most significantly, Hamlet himself. Hamlet needs the discipline of a script to catch the King's conscience, but he himself is the play's true extemporiser, constantly disordering prepared scenes – leaping into Ophelia's grave like Bentley from the stage, or, more credibly, like a rough-and-tumble clown.

Some have suggested that Hamlet's discourse upon Yorick was a tribute to Tarlton, the fellow of infinite jest, being conjured somewhere between Hamlet and the Gravedigger. Perhaps the ghost of Tarlton is also invoked earlier in the play, when Hamlet borrows a pipe from one of the players. Tarlton's pipe was one of his trademarks. The word 'instrument' is used on only two occasions in *Hamlet*: once in Hamlet's play upon the pipe when bamboozling Rosencrantz and Guildenstern – 'call me what instrument you will' (III.ii.362) – and again in the final scene – 'The treacherous instrument is in thy hand!' (V.ii.301). In Marlowe's (and maybe Nashe's) *Dido, Queen of Carthage*, an apparent source for the Player's speech in *Hamlet*, 'fatal instrument' is how Aeneas describes the Trojan horse.⁹⁵ Marlowe's horse is so ironically massive that it contains thousands of Greeks and will not pass through Troy's gates: parts of the city's impenetrable walls are destroyed by the Trojans in order to admit the gift. But in Shakespeare's play there is something much smaller at work: an economy not of sublime and enormous things, but one of handy props that likewise resist tragic accommodation. The instrument metamorphoses: foolish pipe becomes tragic rapier.

In this the play seems to develop an idea proposed some years earlier, in *Richard II*, where death is made an antic clown who keeps his court and 'at the last, with a little pin / Bores through [the] castle wall' (III.ii.160–70). The connection between clowning and death in Shakespeare's work seems to find its most startling culmination in one of the most extraordinary moments in all of his theatre: the entrance of the clown in Act V, scene ii of *Antony and Cleopatra* (c.1607). The clown bears a basket of sharp little things, but it is he who is recognised as the 'instrument' of death: 'What poor an instrument / May do a noble deed!' (V.ii.235–6). The 'pen' given to Hieronimo for his confession is dropped for a fatal knife (*ST* IV.iv). John Manningham depicts William Cecil, when Secretary of State, being told 'sharply' to lay aside his 'long pen-knife' – his rapier – upon entering the Court of Common Pleas.⁹⁶ Tragi-comic instruments all: pipe; pin; pen; knife; bodkin; rapier. Sometimes players will mishandle them; at other times, the player's skill will remove these objects from a purely representational or symbolic plane. Sharp objects make room for mishap and physical accomplishment.

Sharp Practice

The rapier was thought by some not simply to signify nobility, but to effect it. Swordplay offered chances of passing ennoblement to professional players, otherwise regarded with a high degree of condescension and suspicion by early modern culture at large. In *Hamlet* the issue of mimesis, and the mimesis of feeling or intent in particular, is a prominent concern for the avenger. The status of mimesis in *Hamlet* is ultimately challenged with swordplay.

Jennifer Low constructively aggregates the emphasis on grace and posture in the duel to a model of what she calls a 'sense of masculine space'. In particular, Low proposes that the duelling concept of the 'ward', which denotes both the process of deflecting a thrust and a space produced and inhabited by the dueller (see Green and Tarlton, warding above), may have carried over into more general attitudes towards deportment that complemented the ideology of civil courtesy: 'readiness' coincided with gentlemanly bearing.⁹⁷ Something of this can be seen in the way Green is reported to have handled himself, but in fact contemporary guidebooks to defence, even those specialising in the teaching of fighting with rapier and dagger, insisted that such specialisation would cultivate a more general improvisational skill:

> Which knowledge, because it is naturally graffed in the mynde, is something the rather holpen and quallified by Arte, and maketh a man so assured and bolde, that he dares to enter on any great daunger, and judgeth (when he seeth the qualitie of the weapon, and the syte wherein it is placed) what it maye do, or in how many waies it may either strike or defend. From which his judgement springs the knowledge of all that he hath to do, and how he hath to handle himselfe to encounter any danger.⁹⁸

The duel was an act designed both to restore or maintain reputation and to provide opportunities for the display of 'evenesse of Carriage', through which courage was expressed.⁹⁹ The more effectively the actor presented the duel, the less it became acting, for the required athleticism could create a field of activity in which the player could, like Laertes, or an anonymous Edgar, whose 'very gait did prophesy / A royal nobleness' (V.iii.173–4), demonstrate an equality with his betters. The actor usurped identity not simply by wearing what gentlemen wore, but doing what gentlemen did.

Many of these possibilities inhere in the handling of a single ambiguous word: practice. As some editors have noted, Hamlet's assurance – presumably concerning fencing – that 'since [Laertes] went to France I have been in continual practice' jolts hard against Claudius's reference to the duel as 'a pass of practice' (IV.vii.136), which takes the meaning of agile exercise and forces it to mean intrigue and cozenage. This subtle semantic shift expands into full-blown epistemological crisis when one considers the work of the player as a third meaning for 'practice'.¹⁰⁰ For if the grace of the citizen dueller could be appropriated by the actor at the non-representational level of agile, dextrous practice, such activity remained susceptible to association with the histrionic intriguer, practising upon the court as the actor practised upon his audience. The final scene of *Hamlet* brings all these meanings of practice to bear on the play's exploration of mimesis and its operations, which are very early on linked to the prospect of the fight. Old Hamlet is introduced to us explicitly in the guise of 'readiness'. Horatio recognises Old Hamlet because the Ghost wears 'the very armour he had on / When he the ambitious Norway combated' (Q2, I.i.59–60) – the Ghost is, we are told, 'armed at point' (I.ii.199), just as he was when, living, he faced Fortinbras in single combat. So, in the Ghost of Old Hamlet, an image of readiness is conjured. Hamlet himself experiences the revenge obligation as the encounter with emulable models later in the play, on the verge of leaving for England, as he reflects on the wars of young Fortinbras: 'Examples gross as earth exhort me,' he says, reflecting that, 'rightly to be great / Is not to stir without great argument / But greatly to find quarrel in a straw / When honour's at the stake' (Q2, IV.iv.45–58). Laertes joins this parade of examples exhorting the Prince to action. Hamlet's readiness is prompted by images he is required to imitate.

Such is the emphasis placed by the play on the connection between 'daring it to the point' and emulation that *Hamlet* may here echo the duelling scene in Robert Greene's *Friar Bacon*. This popular play, tentatively dated to around 1589, would in fact have been a near contemporary of either Thomas Kyd's ur-*Hamlet* or an earlier Shakespearean *Hamlet* of the 1590s. The scene in question shows two scholars using Friar Bacon's 'glass prospective' (l.1809) to catch up on their fathers in the country. Amazed, they find their fathers duelling, apparently over some slanderous, 'piercing taunts' (l.1826) which passed between them. In a variant on the play-within-the-play, their lethal reciprocal stabbing is shown in Bacon's 'mirror'. The watching scholars, previously friends, instantly take up rapiers and likewise kill one another.[101] It is possible that in performance the rapiers the scholars wield against each other are the very same weapons used by their fathers shown fighting in the magical mirror, suggesting the relative ease with which such props could cross epistemological barriers to appear the most 'actual' things on the stage – just as the Norwich affray seemed to confirm.

Following the macabre play-within-a-play in *Friar Bacon*, the repentant magician shatters his glass with the same 'poniard that did end the fatall lives' (l.1865). That the rapier should be used to break the very instrument used by Bacon to divine the future is a conceit that *Hamlet* seems to develop into an antinomy of philosophy and play, as Hamlet puts away reflection and commits himself to total uncertainty by agreeing to fight Laertes. Bacon's mirror is also a commonplace emblem of mimesis, to which the duels in that play are connected. The rapier game in *Hamlet* can also be conceived as an attempt to explore uncertainties relating to mimetic intention and mimetic effect. These uncertainties include Hamlet's struggle to live up to the image of his father. A concrete social anxiety underpins Hamlet's frustration at his inability to show his being moved by a sense of damaged honour with the same credibility as the Player (*Hamlet*, II.ii.485–506). As one handbook of civility had it, '[h]ee manifesteth vilitie ['baseness'] who easile swalloweth injurie, without by his owne proper valor, *shewing himself therewith moved*'.[102] Hamlet equates his cowardice implicitly with a failure of gentility:

'O what a *rogue* and *peasant slave* am I!'; 'a dull and muddy-mettled *rascal*'; 'villain'; 'ass'; 'whore'; 'a very drab' (485–522, my emphases). That soliloquy is braced by an obvious tension: if a show of gentility is a requirement for identification as a gentleman, then, as Hamlet finds, the Player proves more gentlemanly than anyone. This movement of thought pits the performance offered by Hamlet's actor against that of the Player, who appears, as it were, in a shape nearer himself. Hamlet's actor must therefore dramatise a failure of acting: a speculative emulation of emulation's limits.

Rapier fights were sometimes associated with outsized emulations of honour. In *Romeo and Juliet*, Mercutio accuses Benvolio in Act III, scene i of an over-readiness: 'Thou hast quarrelled with a man for coughing in the street' (III.i.24–5). Hamlet has shown a similar tendency towards indiscretion and what Saviolo himself called 'mad brained conceits':[103] a 'brainish apprehension' combined with a rapier has already proved deadly to Polonius, a victim we are not sure Hamlet wished to make. *Romeo and Juliet* explores the affinity between social and theatrical cues. In that play, the question of being 'moved' – both emotionally, in defence of honour; and theatrically, in response to a cue – had been thematic, announced at the beginning of the play (I.i.6–20), and developed particularly through the contests between Tybalt and Mercutio (III.i.1–75). The actor playing Mercutio is given his cue when Tybalt describes Romeo as 'my man', and the character Mercutio hears in that word, his actor's cue, provocation of a kind relating not to theatrical identity but to honour and reputation.[104] The skill of the actor in responding appropriately to theatrical cues is momentarily aligned with Mercutio's emerging sense that violence is necessary.[105] In a similar vein, Hamlet threatens to 'make nature monstrous' – a phrase John Webster used later in opposition to the measure necessary for good acting.[106]

In the final scene, however, Hamlet's over-commitment culminates in a change to the meaning of commitment itself. Recalling Bertolt Brecht's cunning use of the word 'Spannweite' ('wingspan') to describe the 'range' of character, it is possible to perceive how, in the exertion of the duel, Hamlet's 'character' is made identical with his 'arm-span', the measure of a dueller's ward, allowing a speculative identification of Hamlet and his actor.[107] The actor becomes more like Hamlet by fencing, and Hamlet as a character becomes more like the Player who could 'show himself moved'. Hamlet at the end of the play seems not only to find a way of showing what it is necessary to show. He commits to the unpredictability of the stage, that is, to all the difficulties that attend showing. In the final scene, Hamlet's committedness is no longer a character trait, or a problem of psychology, but accomplice to a daring theatrical experiment that probes the limits of intention itself. As these limits are reached in the text, the player becomes more apparent, his textual absence more conspicuous.

Critical Misadventure

Walter Benjamin thought that Hamlet's acceptance of the fencing wager represented an intentional step towards a realm of fateful objects where intention would lose meaning. For Benjamin, the end of the play asserts 'a vehement externality'. Hamlet wants to die by accident, and for this reason all the fateful props of the final scene gather around him as if he were their master.[108] That Hamlet can perceive the necessity of this submission distinguishes him from Claudius and his agents, still possessed by the assumption that these objects will do what they are told. In order to show all this, the play requires that the actors demonstrate complete mastery over the materials of the scene. Because this idea of formal degeneration seems to inhere in the play itself, it is possible to suggest that the most coherent performance of the end of *Hamlet* would be one that came closest to incoherence. The final scene interrogates its materials so closely that the prospect of its failure as a theatrical event becomes a criterion of its success.

Everything seems to resolve from an 'interim' into a 'point'. This point, as an object, a moment in time, and a formal device, is so deeply qualified as to puncture judgement. In *The Winter's Tale* (c.1611), the 'bodkin's point' becomes a metaphor both for the acutest possible power of discrimination, and the incapacity of that power to make proper formal sense of plays: 'betwixt [tragedy and comedy] you cannot thrust a bodkin's point'.[109] Just as Hamlet's 'bodkin' seems an inadequate attempt to socialise something outside society – death – so any critical description of the resources at work in the final scene of *Hamlet* must in the last instance accept that they work towards something which no act of criticism can ever put a pin through: the accidents of any given performance. These accidents – invisible, particular – contribute neither to the transformation of the stage into a prototype of the empty laboratory, as Ross Hamilton has implied, nor to an elaborate game of knowledge played between a hypothetical Elizabethan spectator and the hidden playwright supposed to have effected theatrical providence, as Michael Witmore has proposed.[110] The results of the scene-as-experiment are not verifiable, because they are deferred until the next performance; and the objectivity and externality of the scene resist incorporation into a dialogical scheme of author and spectator. Further, philosophical or theoretical enquiries must come to terms with the fact that the truth-content of the play cannot be plucked like a rose from its grounds in performance. The play explores the ethics of political and private action, and the questionable distinction between them, in and through acting. By addressing itself speculatively to all its future performances, and to the changeable material grounds of its own possibility, *Hamlet* refuses to subserve theoretical elaborations and historical definitions of accident and intent, freedom and fate, subject and state.

At the very end of the play, the State is reconstituted. Intent becomes the subject of prospective forensic enquiry. Fortinbras enters. With the King's wish to view the dismal sight of the tragedy, a new kind of evaluative sight is in prospect, overlapping with the judgement of the bewildered audience. Those assembled are left to make sense of the fencing match and what occurred within its scope, to make sense

> Of accidental judgements, casual slaughters,
> Of deaths put on by cunning, and for no cause,
> And in this upshot purposes mistook
> Fallen on th'inventors' heads.
> (V.i.365–8; F: 'forc'd cause')

'Casual' here means 'chance'. In the new legal sense introduced by the arrival of the monarch, the rapiers lying next to the bodies now appear as deodands, from the Latin *deo dandum*, 'given unto God'. Deodands were objects that had been implicated in human death where responsibility was uncertain: *omnia quae movent ad mortem, sunt Deodanda* ['all things which move to/cause death, are deodands'].[111] The valuation of the deodand in cases of manslaughter or accident was both straightforward and deeply obscure. Objects involved in cases of misadventure (horses; cartwheels; ships; candlesticks; rapiers) could be seized by the Crown – Spencer's lethal rapier was valued at five shillings; Jonson's at three; Day's at two.[112] Deodands had originated as *precium sanguinis*, a blood price taken by the Church to expiate sin, but even in the seventeenth century they could still be considered a forfeit 'to God for the pacification of his wrath in a case of misadventure'.[113] Strictly speaking, such goods were given over to the State so as to be distributed as alms for the appeasement of God. While retaining this ancient quality of propitiation, deodand law had also become a means of punitive expropriation, slight boon to Crown revenue, revenge upon human negligence, and, one suspects, a palliative quantification of chaotic nature. As *Hamlet* in its dying moments seems to breathe the pure air of an unrotten State, judgement begins of ends, means, intents and the action entire; and its players retrieve the blades.

Notes

1. William Shakespeare, *Titus Andronicus*, ed. Jonathan Bate, Arden 3rd ser. (London, 1995), V.iii.62.
2. For a list of penetrative objects in the play, see David Hillman, *Shakespeare's Entrails. Belief, Scepticism and the Interior of the Body* (Basingstoke, 2007), 213 n104.
3. For example: *Hamlet*, I.v.19–20; III.ii.241–2; III.iv.34–6; 116–18; etc.
4. William Shakespeare, *Troilus and Cressida*, ed. David Bevington, Arden 3rd ser. (London, 1998), 'Prefatory Epistle to Q2', 2.
5. Dale Anthony Girard, *Actors on Guard: A Practical Guide for the Use of Rapier and Dagger for Stage and Screen* (London, 1997), 426.
6. Michael Neill, *Issues of Death: Mortality and Identity in English Renaissance Tragedy* (Oxford, 1997), 239.
7. Henry Howard[?], 'Duello foiled, or the whole Proceedings for single Fight, by occasion whereof the Unlawfulness and Wickedness of a Duello is preparatively disputed, according to the rules of Honour and right reason, by Mr Edward Cook [Coke]', in Thomas Hearne (ed.), *A Collection of Curious Discourses written by eminent antiquaries upon several heads in our English antiquities*, 2 vols (London, 1771–3), 2: 225; 232–3.
8. Stuart Carroll, *Blood and Violence in Early Modern France* (Oxford, 2006), generally.
9. Walter Ralegh, *The History of the World*, in William Oldys and Thomas Birch (eds), *The Works of Sir Walter Ralegh*, 8 vols (Oxford, 1829), 4: 459–60.
10. Giacomo di Grassi, *Arte of Defence*, trans. I. G. (London, 1594), Sig. B3: 'the arme when it striketh with the point, striketh circulerlie'.
11. William Shakespeare, *Julius Caesar*, ed. David Daniell, Arden 3rd ser. (London, 2011), III.i.218–19. Compare: I.ii.102–11.
12. Francis Bacon, *The Charge of Sir Francis Bacon Knight, His Maiesties Attovrney Generall, Touching Duells* (London, 1614), Sig. B2ᵛ.
13. Euripides, *Orestes*, ed. and trans. M. L. West (Warminster, 1987), l.1519.
14. Isaac Reed, Samuel Johnson, George Steevens (eds), *The Dramatic Works of William Shakespeare*, 10 vols (New York, 1818), 10: 71 n2.
15. Edmund Spenser, *The Shepheardes Calender*, in Ernest De Sélincourt (ed.), *The Poetical Works of Edmund Spenser*, 3 vols (Oxford, 1910), 1: l.195.
16. Robert Nares, *A Glossary; or collection of words, phrases, names [...]* (London, 1822), 229. For 'intended': Richard Hakluyt, *The Principal Navigations, voyages, traffiques and discoveries of the English nation [...] within the compass of these 1600 yeres*, 3 vols (London, 1599–1600), 1: 190: 'Then wext he wroth, and to the Duke he sent, / And complained that such harme was hent.' For 'hit' or 'strike', observe *henten* in the works of Chaucer: Akio Oizumi, *A Complete Concordance to the Works of Geoffrey Chaucer*, 15 vols in 21 books (Hildesheim, 1991–2008), 2: 1135. For the sense of 'reach' and 'arrive': William Shakespeare, *Measure*

for Measure, ed. J. W. Lever, Arden 3rd ser. (London, 1967), IV.vi.13–14: 'The generous, and gravest citizens / Have hent the gates.'
17. Robert Southwell, 'Life is but Losse', in James H. McDonald and Nancy Pollard Brown (eds), *The Poems of Robert Southwell, S. J.* (Oxford, 1967), 50–1, l.20.
18. Ralph Holinshed et al., *Chronicles* (London, 1587), 227.
19. V. G. Kiernan, *The Duel in European History: Honour and the Reign of Aristocracy* (Oxford, 1988), 61.
20. William Shakespeare, *King Lear*, ed. R. A. Foakes, Arden 3rd ser. (London, 1997), III.iv.106–7.
21. Robert Greene, *The Defence of Conny Catching* (London, 1592), Sig. C2.
22. See, for example, Robert Greene, *A Quip for an Upstart Courtier: or, A quaint dispute betvveen veluet breeches and cloth-breeches* (London, 1592), sigs B1–2.
23. di Grassi, *Arte*, Sig.B3; 'Advertisement to the curteous reader'.
24. Thomas Dekker and Thomas Middleton, *The Honest Whore*, in Fredson Bowers (ed.), *The Dramatic Works of Thomas Dekker*, 4 vols (Cambridge, 1955), 2: II.i.12.
25. Peter W. M. Blayney, 'The Publication of Playbooks', in John D. Cox and David Scott Kastan (eds), *A New History of Early English Drama* (New York, 1997), 383–422, at 413.
26. Philip Sidney, *The Countess of Pembroke's Arcadia (The New Arcadia)*, ed. Victor Skretkowicz (Oxford, 1987), 237 (Book I, §18).
27. Thomas Randolph, *The Muse's Looking-Glasse*, in *Poems with the Muses Looking-Glasse; and Amyntas* (Oxford, 1638), 25.
28. Henry Porter, *The Pleasant Historie of the Two Angry Women of Abington* (London, 1599), Sig. E3.
29. Leslie Hotson, 'The Adventure of the Single Rapier', *Atlantic Monthly* 148 (July 1931), 26–31.
30. Andrew Crow, 'Mediating Boys: *Two Angry Women* and the Boy Actor's Shaping of 1590s Theatrical Culture', *Shakespeare Quarterly* 65:2 (Summer, 2014), 180–98.
31. John Dover Wilson, *What Happens in Hamlet* (Cambridge, 1937), 276–9; see Charles Edelman, *Brawl Ridiculous: Swordfighting in Shakespeare's Plays* (Manchester, 1992), 211 n19.
32. A perceptive modern elaboration of this theme is to be found, perhaps surprisingly, in Frank Herbert's science fiction novel *Dune*. Its protagonist Paul Atreides, whose nearly absolute prescience has brought him to the verge of being able to rewrite universal history, finds this ability thwarted during a climactic fight with poisoned blades directly inspired by *Hamlet*: 'It occurred to Paul then that he had seen his own dead body along countless reaches of the time web, but never once had he seen his moment of death [. . .] The tiny point missed Paul's flesh by the barest fraction [. . .].' Frank Herbert, *Dune* (London, 1986), 554–9, generally.
33. Norbert Elias, *The Civilizing Process*, trans. Edmund Jephcott (Oxford, 1994); Mervyn James, 'English Politics and the Concept of Honour', in Paul Slack (ed.), *Society, Politics and Culture: Studies in Early Modern England* (Cambridge, 1986), 308–415.
34. Kiernan, *The Duel*, 53.

35. Markku Peltonen, *The Duel in Early Modern England: Civility, Politeness and Honour* (Cambridge, 2003), 35–58, and generally.
36. Frank Henderson Stewart, *Honor* (Chicago, 1994), 54–63.
37. Linda A. Pollock, 'Honor, Gender, and Reconciliation in Elite Culture, 1570–1700', *Journal of British Studies* 46 (2007), 3–29, at 6, in reference to Peltonen, *The Duel*.
38. Ben Jonson, *Every Man in his Humour*, ed. Robert S. Miola (Manchester, 2000), III.iv.154–5: 'by my Hand, I will / pink your Flesh full of holes with my Rapier for this'. See Maik Goth, '"Killing, Hewing, Stabbing, Dagger-Drawing, Fighting, Butchery": Skin Penetration in Renaissance Tragedy and its Bearing on Dramatic Theory', *Comparative Drama* 46:2 (2012), 139–62.
39. Nicholas Breton, *Characters upon essaies morall, and divine* (London, 1615), 43–4.
40. William Shakespeare, *The Tragedy of King Richard II*, ed. Peter Ure, Arden 2nd ser. (London, 1956), IV.i.39–41.
41. William F. Hansen (ed. and trans.), *Saxo Grammaticus and the Life of Hamlet* (Lincoln, NE, 1983), 117.
42. Thomas Churchyard, *Churchyards Challenge* (London, 1593), 60.
43. di Grassi, 'Dedication': 'Where knowledge & courage meetes in one person, there is ods in that match [. . .] This booke of Fencing will save many mens lyves, or put comon quarrels out of u[s]e, because the danger is death if ignorant people procure a combate.'
44. Peltonen, *The Duel*, 39; 44.
45. Alan Stewart, 'Purging Troubled Humours: Bacon, Northampton and the Anti-Duelling Campaign of 1613–1614', in Stephen Clucas and Rosalind Davies (eds), *The Crisis of 1614 and the Addled Parliament: Literary and Historical Perspectives* (Aldershot, 2003), 84–97.
46. A. C. Bradley, *Shakespearean Tragedy: Lectures on* Hamlet, Othello, King Lear, Macbeth, 3rd edn (New York, 1992), 128.
47. Vincent Saviolo, *Vincentio Saviolo his practise, In two bookes. The first intreating of the use of the rapier and dagger. The second, of honor and honorable quarrel* (London, 1595), Sig. B1, my emphasis.
48. Ben Jonson, *Every Man out of his Humour*, ed. Helen Ostovich (Manchester, 2001), III.i.325–425.
49. Robert Greene, *The Scottish historie of Iames the fourth, slaine at Flodden Entermixed with a pleasant comedie, presented by Oboram King of Fayeries* (London, 1598), Sig. G4.
50. Anthony Fletcher, 'Honour, Reputation and Local Officeholding in Elizabethan and Stuart England', in Anthony Fletcher and John Stevenson (eds), *Order and Disorder in Early Modern England* (Cambridge, 1985), 92–115.
51. August Wilhelm Schlegel, *Über dramatische Kunst und Litteratur: Vorlesungen*, 2 vols (Heidelberg, 1809–11), 2: 208–10; John Bruce (ed.), *The Diary of John Manningham of the Middle Temple, and of Bradbourne, Kent, Barrister-at-Law, 1602–1603*, Camden Society 99 (London, 1868), 8, citing a sermon given by Thomas Mountford.
52. John Webster and William Rowley, *A Cure for a Cuckold* (London, 1661), III.i.

53. Hillay Zmora, *The Feud in Early Modern Germany* (Cambridge, 2011), 50; John Bossy, *Peace in the Post-Reformation. The Birkbeck Lectures 1995* (Cambridge, 1998), 34, and generally.
54. Howard[?], 'Duello foiled', in *A Collection of Curious Discourses*, 2: 225; 232–3.
55. George Chapman, *Bussy D'Ambois*, in John H. Smith (ed.), *The Plays of George Chapman: The Tragedies with 'Sir Gyles Goosecappe'* (Cambridge, 1987), Q2, II.i.198–9. Compare II.i.165–74:

> it would make Cowards feare
> To touch the reputations of true men
> When only they are left to impe the law,
> Justice will soone distinguish murtherous minds
> From just revengers
> [. . .]
> My friend only sav'd his fames deare life.

56. Almost every European sovereign implemented anti-duelling policies. See Ute Frevert, *Men of Honour: A Social and Cultural History of the Duel*, trans. Anthony Williams (Cambridge, 2007), 14:

> This was due to the fact that the centralization of political power in the person of the monarch, and the gradual dissolution of particularist feudal powers in the wake of the establishment of internal statehood, were accompanied by a vested interest in ensuring that the monopoly on the exercise of power rested with the ruling prince.

57. Anon., *Tragoedia der bestrafte Brudermord oder Prinz Hamlet aus Dännemark* (Berlin, 1781), in Albert Cohn (ed.), *Shakespeare in Germany [. . .]* (Berlin, 1865), 237–304.
58. See A. H. J. Knight, '*Der bestrafte Brudermord* and *Hamlet*, Act V', *Modern Language Review* 31:3 (July, 1936), 385–91, at 386 n1.
59. Jasper Heywood, *Thyestes*, in Henrik de Vocht (ed.), *Jasper Heywood and his Translations of Seneca's* Troas, Thyestes, *and* Hercules furens (Louvain, 1913), ll. 1565–6.
60. Stephen Gosson, *The Schoole of Abuse* (London, 1579), 29.
61. Mervyn James, 'Concept of Honour', 363–73.
62. Ibid. 373.
63. Andy Wood, *The 1549 Rebellions and the Making of Early Modern England* (Cambridge, 2007), 143–51.
64. With reference to the controversial thesis of Franco Moretti, *Signs Taken as Wonders: On the Sociology of Literary Forms* (London, 2005), 42–82.
65. John Kerrigan, *Archipelagic English. Literature, History, and Politics 1603–1707* (Oxford, 2008), 100.
66. Aristotle, *Poetics*, trans. Ingram Bywater, in Aristotle, *Works*, 2: 2322 [§1451].
67. James L. Jackson, '"They Catch One Another's Rapiers": The Exchange of Weapons in *Hamlet*', *Shakespeare Quarterly* 41:3 (Autumn, 1990), 281–98; Edelman, *Brawl Ridiculous*, esp. 191.
68. Precisely this issue was contested in a flurry of letters in the *TLS* in 1934: E. B. Goodacre, 'The Duel in *Hamlet*', *Times Literary Supplement*, 11

January 1934, 28; John Dover Wilson, 'The Duel in *Hamlet*', *TLS*, 18 January 1934, 44; Evan John, 'The Duel in *Hamlet*', *TLS*, 25 January 1934, 60; E. B. Goodacre, 'The Duel Scene in *Hamlet*', *TLS*, 8 February 1934, 38.
69. George Silver, *Paradoxes of defence wherein is proved the true grounds of fight to be in the short aunciant weapons* (London, 1599), 51.
70. François de Belleforest, *The Hystorie of Hamblet*, trans. Thomas Pavier (London, 1608), in Israel Gollancz (ed.), *The Sources of Hamlet, with an Essay on the Legend* (London, 1967), 166–311, at 254–7 (Pavier's translation is adequate).
71. Hansen, *Saxo Grammaticus*, 106–7.
72. Lorna Hutson, *The Invention of Suspicion: Law and Mimesis in Shakespeare and Renaissance Drama* (Oxford, 2007), 269.
73. Anon., 'Declaration against duelling', Trinity College, Cambridge, R.16.28, fols 4^v-5.
74. See especially Jeremy Horder's criticism of Frank McLynn's *Crime and Punishment in Eighteenth-Century England* (London, 1989): Jeremy Horder, 'The Duel and the English Law of Homicide', *Oxford Journal of Legal Studies* 12 (1992), 419–30; Jeremy Horder, *Provocation and Responsibility* (Oxford, 1992), esp. 23–42. Also see Thomas A. Green, 'The Jury and the English Law of Homicide, 1200–1600', *Michigan Law Review* 74 (1976), 413–99; and, for a recent and comprehensive overview of the legal evolution, Graham McBain, 'Modernising the Law of Murder and Manslaughter: Part 1', *Journal of Politics and Law* 8:4 (2015), 9–97.
75. The principle of 'provocation' has only recently (2009) been replaced with the term 'loss of control'.
76. Luke Wilson, 'Renaissance Tool Abuse and the Legal History of the Sudden', in Erica Sheen and Lorna Hutson (eds), *Literature, Politics and Law in Renaissance England* (Basingstoke, 2005), 121–45; 122; 125.
77. William Lambarde, *Eirenarcka; or of the Office of the Justices of the Peace* (London, 1581), 217; 255. Cf. Anon., *The Boke of Justices of Peas* (London, 1506?), 'The fourme and the maner of the charge of the Justyces of peas', Sig. A3:

> [M]urdre is [. . .] where a man by malice purpēsed lieth in a Wayte to [slay] a man and accordynge to that malycyous entent and purpose he sl[ay]eth hym so that he Whyche is slayne maketh no defence a[g]ynst hym[. F]or yf he doo it is manslaughter and no murdre [. . .] And ma[n]slaughter is [also] Where two men or mo[re] mete and by chaunce medely they fall at affray so that one of them sl[ay]th an other[. This] is but felonie in hym selfe and therfore if ony persone be defectyf in this Wyse make your presentement accordynge[ly].

78. Hotson, 'Single Rapier', 28–9 (apparently referring to TNA Assizes 351 41, Surrey, 1599, bundle 2).
79. Lambarde, *Eirenarcka*, 258–9.
80. For example: Eleanor Prosser, *Hamlet and Revenge* (Stanford, 1971), 237; Michael Neill, *Issues of Death*, 239–40.
81. Edward Coke, *The Third Part of the Institutes of the Laws of England* (London, 1644), 57 (§8).

82. Wilson, 'Tool Abuse', 140 n15.
83. See Ian Hacking, *The Emergence of Probability. A Philosophical Study of Early Ideas about Probability, Induction, and Statistical Inference* (Cambridge, 1975). On Aristotle's concept of probability, see Neil O'Sullivan, 'Aristotle on Dramatic Probability', *The Classical Journal*, 91:1 (Oct.–Nov. 1995), 47–63.
84. John Cordy Jeaffreson (ed.), *Middlesex County Records*, 4 vols (London, 1886–92), 1: xlv-xlvii.
85. The translation is mine. Compare Irene Morris, 'A Hapsburg Letter', *MLR* 69:1 (Jan., 1974), 12–22, at 20–2. The entire letter is transcribed both there and in Willem Schrickx, *Foreign Envoys and Travelling Players in the Age of Shakespeare* (Gent, 1986), 332–5. Morris, whose translation is adopted by Schrickx, mistakenly gives 'sword' for 'rapier'.
86. Roger Burrow Manning, *Swordsmen: The Martial Ethos in the Three Kingdoms* (Oxford, 2003), 196.
87. Tiffany Stern, '"The Curtain is Yours!" The Lord Chamberlain's Men at the Curtain', in Helen Ostovich, Holger Schott Syme and Andrew Griffin (eds), *Locating the Queen's Men, 1583–1603: Material Practices and Conditions of Playing* (Aldershot, 2009), 77–96.
88. Marx Mangoldt [pseud.], *Marckschiffs Nachen* (Frankfurt, 1597), in Ernst Kelchner (ed.), 'Sechs Gedichte über die Frankfurter Messe', *Mittheilungen des Vereins für Geschichte und Alterthumskunde* 6 (1881), 350–67.
89. Theodor van Rodenburgh, *Wraeck-Gieriges Treur-spel* (Amsterdam, 1618), 'Voor-spel'. See Wouter Abrahamse, *Het toneel van Theodore Rodenburgh (1574–1644)* (Amsterdam, 1997), 107–13.
90. Anon., *Tarlton's Jests* (1611), in James Orchard Halliwell (ed.), *Tarlton's Jests and News out of Purgatory, with notes, and some account of the life of Tarlton* (London, 1844): 'A sudden and dangerous fray twixt a gentleman and Tarlton, which he put off with a jest', 13.
91. Andrew Gurr, *The Shakespearian Playing Companies* (Cambridge, 1996), 76; 279–80; Thomas Lodge, *Wits Miserie and the Worlds Madnesse* (London, 1596), 56.
92. David Galloway (ed.), *Norwich: 1540–1642* (Toronto, 1984), 70–6; 73: 'one Bentley he wich played the duke came off the Stage and wyth his hiltes of his Sworde he Strooke wynsdon upon the heade [. . .] he in the blacke dublet wich kept the gate ran up into the stayge and brought An Armynge Sworde and as he was goinge out at the gate he drew the Sworde [. . .]'
93. Ibid. 72.
94. Siobhan Keenan, *Travelling Players in Shakespeare's England* (New York, 2002), 100; Kara Northway, '"[H]urt in that service": The Norwich Affray and Early Modern Reactions to Injuries during Dramatic Performances', *Shakespeare Bulletin* 26:4 (Winter, 2008), 25–46, at 36–46.
95. Christopher Marlowe, *Dido, Queen of Carthage*, ed. H. J. Oliver (London, 1968), II.i.176.
96. Bruce (ed.), *The Diary of John Manningham*, 36.
97. Jennifer A. Low, *Manhood and the Duel: Masculinity in Early Modern Drama* (Basingstoke, 2003), 47–51; 60–70.

98. di Grassi, *True Arte*, Sig. D1ᵛ.
99. Henry Peacham, *The Compleat Gentleman* (London, 1622), 185.
100. Stephen Gosson, *Playes confuted in five actions proving that they are not to be suffred in a Christian common weale* (London, 1582), Sig. B2: 'the abhominable *practises* of playes in London have bene by godly preachers, both at Paules crosse, and elsewhere, so zealously, so learnedly, so loudly cried out upon to small redresse'.
101. All reference is to Robert Greene, *Friar Bacon and Friar Bungay*, ed. W. W. Greg (Oxford, 1926).
102. Annibale Romei, *The Courtier's Academie*, trans. John Kepers (London, 1598), 81–2.
103. Saviolo, *Saviolo his practise*, Sig. P3.
104. Simon Palfrey and Tiffany Stern, *Shakespeare in Parts* (Oxford, 2007), 214–18; 453–6.
105. William Shakespeare, *Romeo and Juliet*, ed. Brian Gibbons, Arden 2nd ser. (London, 1980).
106. John Webster, *New Characters (drawne to the life) of severall Persons, in severall qualities* (1615), in Webster, *Works*, 3: 483.
107. Bertolt Brecht, 'Bemerkungen zu einem Aufsatz', in *Gesammelte Werke*, 20 vols (Frankfurt a.M., 1967), 19: 308–12, at 310.
108. Walter Benjamin, *Ursprung des deutschen Trauerspiels*, in *GS*, 1/i: 317.
109. William Shakespeare, *The Winter's Tale*, ed. J. H. P. Pafford, Arden 2nd ser. (London, 1999), III.iii.82–5.
110. Ross Hamilton, *Accident: A Philosophical and Literary History* (Chicago, 2007), 69–91; Michael Witmore, *Culture of Accidents: Unexpected Knowledges in Early Modern England* (Stanford, 2001), 82–110.
111. Ferdinando Pulton, *De pace Regis et regni viz. A treatise declaring vvhich be the great and generall offences of the realme* (London, 1609), fol. 127ᵛ. See R. F. Hunniset, *The Medieval Coroner* (Cambridge, 1962), 32–3; Anna Pervukhin, 'Deodands: A Study in the Creation of Common Law Rules', *The American Journal of Legal History* 47:3 (July, 2005), 237–56; Wilson, 'Tool Abuse'. Deodands were abolished in 1846.
112. Jeaffreson, *Middlesex County Records* 1: xlvi; Ibid. 2: 39; Hotson, 'Single Rapier', 28. If deodands were worth more than twelvepence, the death was deemed a felony.
113. John Cowell, *The Interpreter* (London, 1607), Sig. Y3; Frederick Pollock and Frederic William Maitland, *The History of English Law before the Time of Edward I*, 2 vols (Cambridge, 1898), 2: 473: 'The deodand may warn us that in ancient criminal law there was a sacral element which Christianity could not wholly suppress, especially when what might otherwise have been esteemed a heathenry was in harmony with some of those strange old dooms that lie embedded in the holy books of the Christian.'

Chapter 3

A Brief Interlude of Vice

Therefore, to worke my feate I will my name disguise.
Nicholas Udall, *Respublica* (1553)

Bridging from the dialectic of action explored in the previous chapters to the dialectic of figuration and appearance considered in those which follow, this chapter sketches a triangular historical relationship between plays of revenge, the professionalisation of theatre, and the figure known as the 'Vice'. It is no coincidence that the tradition of English revenge tragedy originated as the Vice began taking the stage under its own name. Neither is it a coincidence that the dramatic Vice disappeared from the stage just as the common player emerged on it as a novel and salient element in English culture. The Vice had acquired fame as a theatrical producer. He likely collected fees from the audience into which he often blended. He was increasingly represented as an autonomous and extra-dramatic social agent. The common player became the Vice when that figure disappeared in the 1570s and 1580s. In this way the appearance of the actor and his agency within the fictional scene acquired a specific and complex moral value. For revenge tragedy this was significant because the Vice had been the origin and impetus of the revenge narrative since English playwrights had first shown interest in the theme of extra-judicial vengeance. To ask whether revenge was a moral deviation or devilish concoction was to question the agency of the player and his interest in producing dubious illusions.

The Vice – a *name* which refers to myriad disguised strangers, temptors, corrupters and tricksters in Tudor drama – occupies a curious place in literary history. He or she often appears on the margin of the historian's scene, ready to act as an explanatory tool when the transition from medieval to modern culture is at stake.[1] Despite its status as a mere stage convention, the Vice enjoys an afterlife in academic writing as a virtually autonomous historical person, owing to the long history of attributing to it particular characteristics and dimensions. In the Vice, religious history becomes a sort of physiognomy, because that identity is taken to stand for an allegorical scheme that became impossible or undesirable in the course of the sixteenth century. Paradoxically, it was the very nomination of 'Vice' in the interludes of the middle of that century that curtailed its real participation in that allegorical structure. Consideration of the Vice unavoidably documents the translation of origin into appearance within literary historiography, as well as changing cultural attitudes towards disguise and semblance during the period in question. One of the many paradoxes of the Vice is that its unitary identity comprises manifold personas. 'Byholde [th]e dyvercyté of my dysgysyd varyauns,' boasts the Devil at the beginning of the first N-Town *Passion Play*.[2] The Prologue to *Respublica*, welcoming Mary's accession in 1553, accepted that 'All commen weales Ruin and decaye / from tyme to tyme', 'whan Insolence, Flaterie, Opression, / And Avarice have the Rewle' – in calmer times it would be shown how 'these vices bycloked collusyon / and by counterfaicte Names, hidden theire abusion'.[3] In John Bale's *Three Laws* (1538; 1562), the Vices of Idolatry, Sodomy, Ambition, Covetousness, False Doctrine and Hypocrisy were dressed as 'an olde wytche', 'a monke of all sectes', 'a byshop', 'a spyrytual lawer', 'a popysh doctour' and 'a graye friar', respectively.[4] In his *King Johan*, the Vice 'Sedition' boasts that, 'in every estate of the claegye I playe a part: / Sumtyme I can be a monke in a long syd cowle, / Sumtyme a channon in a syrplus fayer and whyght [. . .]' (ll.194–6; see ll.194–210).[5] 'Though the divell cannot alter his forme substantially,' agreed John Deacon in 1601, 'yet he may change the same in shape or figure.'[6]

The point is that Sedition remained seditious, whatever human shape he took; the Devil remained the Devil in whatever form; Vice, vicious. John Foxe, with whom Bale collaborated, supplies a telling marginal note to describe a 'counterfayted' bishop described by Steven Gratwicke at his trial in 1557: 'Here commeth in the vice in the play.'[7] Foxe relied for this upon a shared recollection of the appearance of the dramatic Vice, layering the trial with a morality play structure. But the note is not simply metaphorical or analogous. The bishop had the appearance of a Vice because his vice was apparent, just as Archbishop Stephen Langton really *was* Sedition according to the figural logic of Bale's *King Johan*. For their part, the Reformers really *were* shown, with time, to have been 'Insolence, Flaterie, Opression, / And Avarice', according to *Respublica*.[8] Foxe and Bale held that priests really *were* but false images of a false Church. Just as sixteenth-century thought knew no 'anachronism' as it is now understood, neither did it construe these identificatory claims as trivial or merely conjectural, but as potentially true. The affection for Cicero in English history-writing of that time is probably as much symptom as cause.[9] Moral principles were not derived from history; history displayed examples of virtue and vice that were contemporaneous, and therefore identifiable if one knew how to see them.[10] To write or to stage history was to engage in revelatory social criticism which *unmasked* humans to reveal the *real* forces they represented. Such reasoning naturally underpinned suspicions of sixteenth-century theatre. Reformed sight was thought to involve discrimination between the authentic Church and the spectra of Satanic unbelief, but social and political distinctions shared that same framework of expectations. Although virulent anti-theatre was shaped in the public sphere by a relatively small group of writers, the professional theatre posed an inherent threat to widespread assumptions about the interplay of human figures and historical truth. The role-playing of the commercial theatres involved a practical demonstration that the connection between essence and appearance was not logically necessary.

David Hawkes and others have framed the resulting suspicion in terms of 'anti-idolatry', a reaction to 'the displacement of *telos* by "the works of men's hands"'.[11] This could refer to the disruptions to dramatic form produced by the Vice – a sinking into the mechanisms and pleasurable fictions of theatre ('the works of men's hands'). But the evidence from the drama of the time suggests a more complex entertainment of fetishistic ideas than such accounts will sometimes admit. The Vice invited an objectification or fetishisation by making himself attractive: his didactic function was precisely to prompt fetishisation so as to bring its moral disasters into the light. His emergence in the theatre was attended initially by no consequential valuation of the player's work. With the rise of a profitable commercial theatre and with it the appearance of the common player as an autonomous social agent, this distinction between the Vice and his actor could not be sustained in the same way. The idolatrous manoeuvres which the Vice had revealed in amateur, semi-professional, or university theatre could no longer be separated from his performer. On the contrary, the Vice now seemed to furnish a model of how to understand theatrical work properly. Unlike the performer in a miracle play, the common player was not typologically implicated: his performance involved no claim that the player and his role were connected by universal history and its common fate.[12] More provisional imaginative connections had to be artificially generated by the ingenuity of the playwright, the skill of the actor and the indulgence of the audience; the common player could be anyone he wanted from one day to the next, drowning the stage with tears 'for nothing', as Hamlet says (*Hamlet* II.ii.492). Attending this disposability were a series of fetishes: the character; the player's skill; his body. Work of men's hands.

Certain players might acquire fame in certain roles to the point that their identities were entwined: Hieronimo, Hamlet, Lear and Othello were said to have 'for ever died' with Richard Burbage, for example.[13] Burbage and others had sufficient fame to appear as themselves in prologues. Despite the new possibilities of celebrity, however, from the late 1580s theatre on the public stages had begun to stress the disposability of identity and the confusions of disguise. In rejecting that, the anti-theatricalists sought a different rationale that was more consistent with what they thought they knew about essences. They assumed that identities were not really disposed of in the theatre because that was impossible. Therefore acting was less a combination of technical skill and mimetic invention, than it was the persistence of a malignant essence into other shapes:

> Are [players] not as variable in heart, as they are in their parts? Are they not as good practicers of bawdry, as enactors? [. . .] Doth not their talk on the stage declare the nature of their disposition? [. . .] Are they not notoriously known to be those men in their life abroad as they are on the stage: roisters, brawlers, ill-dealers, boasters, lovers, loiterers, ruffians?[14]

William Rankins indicted 'players, who [. . .] present before [the audience's] eyes, *as well in life as continual exercise*, such enchanting charms, and bewitched wiles, to alienate their minds from virtue [. . .] Abandon their presence, then ceaseth their power'.[15] John Cocke's 'Character of a Common Player' commended the standing legislation prohibiting and constraining the actor, 'for his chief essence is a daily counterfeit'.[16] Phillip Stubbes implored the player to leave off 'that cursed kind of life'.[17]

Stephen Gosson, quoting Lactantius, only clips the underlying idea: 'The expressing of vice by imitation brings us by the shadow, to the substance of the same.'[18] Actually it was the substance of the actor and his action, his vicious personation of vice, which was thought by these men to propagate moral failure.[19] Phillip Stubbes translates a different part of Lactantius which goes more directly to the salient notion: 'the shameless gestures of players [. . .] move the flesh to lust and uncleanness'.[20] If the player were essentially vicious, then it followed that every one of his simulations of vice concealed a vicious efficacy which could never teach virtue. Whence William Prynne, in the most copious version of the argument:

> If there were any [. . .] virtue in Stage-playes, as to alienate mens affections from the vices which they personate, they would then no doubt, not onely have reclaimed the ancient play-admiring Pagans and Comedians, but like-

wise our moderne Play-Poets, Players, and Play-haunters from all those lewd and filthy Vices which come most frequently on the stage [...] Stage-playes are so farre from working an abhorring [of vice], *that they produce, not only a loue and liking, but also an imitation of those pernicious vices that are acted in them*, which are commonly set forth with such *flexanimous rhetoricall pleasing, (or rather poysoning) streines; with such patheticall, liuely and sublime expressions, with such insinuating gestures* [...] This practise therefore of acting Vices, doth onely propagate them, not restraine them.[21]

If, as its often disappointing defenders argued, the theatre had been teaching virtue through the personation of vice, there would no longer be a need for it. Prynne's argument is that the very antiquity of theatre proved its triviality.

As tautological as that claim might be, it is now less common to assume that the early modern theatre was a place where virtue was taught, or even that this was what its plays intend. As Jeffrey Knapp observes, it was probably the anti-theatricalists who founded the extremely hardy assumption that the public theatres were instruments of secularisation.[22] Many of the very qualities now prized in the durable drama of this Golden Age – polysemy, ambiguity, marginality, the subversion of hierarchy and identity – are those first identified by contemporary anti-theatrical observers as shocking and new. Although its enemies appear to have been virtually alone amongst their peers in appreciating the confounding transgressions of the public theatres, those same qualities of ambiguity had a more widely acknowledged representative in sixteenth-century culture, called 'the Vice'.

Genealogies of Vice

The late fifteenth-century East Anglian morality play *Mankind* is often used to backstop a set of assumptions about the Vice's inheritable traits. The language of the Vice figures in that complex work builds itself parasitically around the pronouncements of Mercy, the Virtue, transforming and inverting their sentiments, logic, associations and tone.[23] When one of the Vices, Nought, converts the principles of papal indulgences into lewd rhyme (ll.143–6), Mercy threatens retribution for 'thys ydyll language' and bids them leave the space of performance – 'Out of [th]is place I wolde [the]e went' (ll.147–8). But as Mercy offers words of encouragement and advice to Mankind, the Vices call mockingly from off-stage, possibly from amongst the audience (ll.237–44). In this way the Vices mount an attack both semantic and gestural not just on the forces of good but on the coherence of the drama.

This basic function of reversal or undoing was reiterated in later uses of the Vice. A stage direction in the 1578 play *All for Money* simply ordered appropriate extemporisation for the Vice: '*here the vyce shal turne the proclamation to some contrarie sence at euery time [. . .]*'[24] Robert Persons, writing from exile in 1602, remembered 'a certayne commedy which once I saw in *Venice* [. . .] wherin the Vice of the play had taken for his invention to contradict every thing that his fellow should say'. This had the appearance of vitiation ('Vice' from the Latin *vitiare*, meaning 'spoil, corrupt, blemish'), such that 'the people being wearyed, cryed out that the foole should be thrust downe for he marred the play'.[25] The Vice was identified as a force of negation that deviated from and opposed the development of the drama in which he appeared. This is often how the Vice was recognised and it may remain the only reliable basis for comparison to figures who are deemed relatives of the Vice but are not named as such. To the extent that one can specify a person, identity, or character, it consists largely in mutability. The Vice was a shape-shifter. This basic property of what is known as the 'Vice' has not discouraged genealogical studies of his ancestors and progeny; quite the opposite. The genealogy of this 'stage convention' and fictional person continues to obtain only via a confusing network of comparisons, the terms of which are often unexamined.

The Vice has been an object of scholarly enquiry for a long time. Perhaps it may even seem a familiar face. Anglophone study of the figure can be said to have begun in earnest with L. W. Cushman's *The Devil and the Vice in English Dramatic Literature before Shakespeare* (1900), although by then it had been addressed by a handful of Anglo-American scholars and enjoyed a modest notoriety among German philologists. Cushman's seminal work observed that, with the problematic exception of Heywood's *Playe of the Weather* (1533), Pykering's *Newe Enterlude of Vice, conteyninge the historye of Horestes* (1567) was the first extant play in which the Vice ('Revenge') received a definite appellation as such in the cast-list (and indeed in the title).[26] Peter Happé, who has published extensively on aspects of the Vice over a number of decades, dates its popularity to the period 1547–79.[27] Heedless of such evidence, the common assumption survives that the Vice bears with it the didactic scheme and tradition of the allegorical morality play of the late fifteenth and early sixteenth centuries.[28] The Vice, writes Leah Scragg, was 'the figure which emerged after 1500 from the group of vices engaged in the psychomachia of the early Morality plays'.[29] Cushman established this tradition of assuming that the Vice derived from the morality play, and he distinguished the Vice from the Devil, arguing that the Vice had its more specific origins in the seven deadly sins of earlier and larger scale community drama. He also supposed that the Vice barely survived the decline of the morality play and was remembered only in its buffoonish guise in the secular tragedies.

By contrast, E. K. Chambers contended that the Vice's connection with pre-Tudor morality plays was much less certain, preferring to locate the Vice as a distinct dramatic person only in the later fashion of Marian and Elizabethan interludes.[30] It was this basic judgement that Happé and others sought to confirm and extend. Powerful evidence was marshalled for the Vice's derivation from an ongoing folk tradition distinguishable from the moralities.[31] These arguments involved a direct attack on the assumed etymological relation of the term 'Vice' to *vitium*. Frances Mares expanded on Karl Friedrich Flögel's eighteenth-century proposition that, since the character often wore a mask, or a blacked-out or reddened face in the manner of some folk fools, 'Vice' could just as easily derive from the word *vis*, meaning 'face' or 'visage' not only in Old French but also in fourteenth-century English vernacular.[32] Conjecture such as this is no stranger to the Vice – on the contrary, he seems to provoke it. The Vice continually tempts us into the marshes as we struggle to ascertain his origin.

Bernard Spivack showed how the emergence and mutability of the Vice was linked to changes in opportunities of dramaturgy – smaller companies, enclosed spaces – that prompted the allegorical *psychomachia* to develop from 'warfare to intrigue'.[33] His analysis yields startling but possibly unparsable sentences: Falstaff 'walks like a man, but his innards are allegorical'.[34] Spivack restated Cushman's distinction between Devil and Vice;[35] rejected Chambers's insistence that the Vice's initial naming in Heywood's secular work suggested a dislocation from allegorical or morality tradition; and persuasively argued that the figure emerged through a process of 'homiletic emphasis and theatrical exploitation'.[36] Chief amongst the insights of Spivack was his recognition of the growing autonomy of the Vice, or rather its outgrowing of the scheme through which it appeared to emerge:

> Having produced the figure of the Vice, the Tudor stage submitted to his spell [...] The Vice's role, much older than his histrionic title, came into its key position as soon as the martial allegory of the Psychomachia was transformed by the stage into a plot of intrigue.[37]

David Bevington and Robert Weimann took up this emphasis on the Vice's relation to the circumstances of dramatic production. Weimann especially situates the emergence of the figure within much broader contexts of dramatic and social reform.[38] The Vice transcended its limited role in the traditional *Psychomachia* and emerged in later drama not only as an expert intriguer and theatrical deceiver, but as the main attraction of the Tudor play. The Vice became emblematic of the theatre, rather than a mere convention within it.

The concept of the Vice is now secured by Weimann's most popular and widely disseminated idea – that of the *locus* and *platea* – and it has become next to impossible to invoke the Vice without entertaining that provocative elaboration of Richard Southern's terms. Although it is rarely observed by his many English-speaking readers, Weimann's *Shakespeare and the Popular Tradition* owed much to an idea that became significant in early twentieth-century German philology, namely the *mimus*, which refers both to a person and a genre or mode.[39] The first and most influential sections of Weimann's book – concerning the figures of *platea* – can be read as a variation and refinement of chapters of Hermann Reich's *Der Mimus* (1903).[40] Reich began his study by establishing a virtually unlimited antiquity for the *Mimus*:

> As far as we know, the name Mimus first appears in the fifth century B. C., in the writings of Sophron. But mimes certainly existed long before Sophron. For he had done no more than dress the folk Mimus in a cloth suitable for literature, thereby securing for him a place in contemporary literature.[41]

This is an excellent example of the problem of theatre-historical origins, which more recent scholars regard as nothing more than mythic.[42] The *mimus* continued to be a formative concept in the tradition of theatre-historical writing that acquired an independent disciplinary footing in the 1920s and 1930s. It was to this tradition that Weimann's earliest work contributed, seeking to reconcile the problem of origin in German philology to orthodox socialist realism in the GDR.[43] The antique origins of the *mimus* or μῖμος – in the coarsely comic interlude, *exordia*, dance, prose drama – and the persistence of these elements in Western dramatic culture are creatively reimagined by Weimann as plebeian eruptions:

> The oral and mimetic heritage of the popular culture has sunk beneath the surface of literary history. This is true of the ancient *mimus*, which has been transmitted in meager fragments and through polemical witness, as well as of the folk drama [...] But [...] the nonliterary nature of folk entertainment was a source of great strength to the popular tradition itself [...] The little that is left of the older mimic culture suggests a process of change that included important continuities [...] Shakespeare's drama is unthinkable without the popular tradition.[44]

Reich had emphasised the uninterrupted persistence of the *mimus* from the Greeks to Shakespeare and beyond, but at the same time used the figure of the mime as the medium of the argument that the structure of classical thought persists into modernity. To expand this thesis, Reich identifies a number of transhistorical and transnational types:

> The comic, realistic-humorous types and figures [...] imprint themselves on the popular memory forever [...] These types display in particular as in general a remarkable similarity. In Spanish, as in German, in Italian as in French and English, in Greek and Roman, peasants form the target of satire, as do ecclesiasts [...] Among these medieval and modern types [...] there is hardly one that could not be replaced with another from the Greek, Roman, and Byzantine Mimus.[45]

Likewise, Weimann implies that the popular tradition he identifies in Shakespeare is as old as theatre itself, since the basic contradiction in dramatic form reflects class antagonism yet unresolved in history. This is the implicit reason for assuming that dramaturgical patterns repeat or remain continuous. The various figures and types described by Weimann – Fool, Devil, Vice, Clown, Tarlton, Mephistopheles, Puck – are by no means interchangeable as Reich would have it, but are involved in a continuing and developing social antagonism: 'It is clear that links exist between the early ritual origins of the fool and his social functions in the late Middle Ages.'[46] Despite his scruples about the documentary basis for Reich's characterisation of the *mimus*, Weimann's argument is still forced to represent comic characters as figures of the same basic form, just as the many different faces of the Vice were taken to be aspects of a single malignance by many Elizabethans.

His reader can never be sure whether Weimann introduces such figures with the claim that they themselves were historically real in some conventional sense, or whether they are introduced as expedient allegorical devices for the explication of some other, underlying reality. This is most noticeable when historical individuals like Tarlton or Kemp are at hand. The records relating to these clown specialists are often complicit in the construction of post mortem myths; and those actors sometimes appeared in plays as *themselves* or as something close. Nevertheless, those figures have a markedly different relationship to their society than does the 'Vice' or the 'Fool'. Unlike them, they were real people, known less for magical facility than for professional skill. By arraying them alongside more imaginary figures, Weimann makes historical individuals into figures of a single, transhistorical mimetic impulse, variations upon one form:

> None of these types has a 'pure' genealogy [...] But Shakespeare's fools and clowns are nonetheless steeped in a tradition that is not primarily one of character but of social and dramatic functions. In the *mimus*, the miming fool already appears to have existed in a number of forms.[47]

Weimann notes that Tarlton and his successors supplanted the Vice.[48] In this way the common player could be (and perhaps has to be) made abstract ('individual talents in Shakespeare's troupe merged with countless other elements of clowning') at a point prior to his appearance in plays, rather than in and through their performance and their textual transmission.[49] This move bears a striking affinity to the chief claim of the anti-theatricalists, who by this argumentation seem to acquire a greater measure of historical reality than the actors they condemned. It plays too into the logic of Vice, which it extends – especially in the genealogical or demonological terms 'descendant' or 'ancestor'. Iago is the descendant of the Vice, the Vice the descendant of the Mimus, the Mimus the ancestor of the common player.

In attempting to specify the social content of his figures, Weimann has to re-create his object as a single body. An essential, unchanging body – which like Reich, Weimann continues to sustain – is seemingly required if the uninterrupted continuance of the popular tradition is to be shown. The flesh of this body is nothing less than the substance of popular tradition. The sociology of dramatic form that Weimann and his collaborators went on to explore – its expression of a 'bifold authority' reflective of a basic social antagonism – would remain involved in this curious metaphysics. The common identity of apparently separate theatrical figures was a prerequisite of a specific argument about dramatic con-figuration:

> In the speech and action of the Tudor Vice, such contrariety, therefore, informs the vibrant use of *gestus* where scripted language and performing body intersect. Beneath the discourse of role-playing, the élan and buoyancy, the sheer resilience and presence of visible, audible performers shine through. Their unyielding physicality and unconcealed earthiness exude a 'power and corrigible authority' (*Othello*, 1.3.325–6) that can seep into the texture of the play. The phrase, revealingly, is said by Iago, who, as a descendant of the Vice, foregrounds the act of counterfeiting in honest reference to 'the blood and baseness of our natures'.[50]

The basic intent of this assessment has had its formative influence on the present work, but I argue that the key sentence here conceals a set of controversial claims about literary form that stem from a naïve metaphysics and do not bear scrutiny. 'Physicality' and 'earthiness' cannot 'exude' something which 'seeps' into the 'texture' of a play, for it is in those plays that the qualities and values 'physicality' and 'earthiness' are specifically determined and imbued with new meaning. There intercedes the problem of what is variously termed appearance, semblance, constellation, or manifestation.

Local Habitations

The Vice had for a long time been as such innominate: the inclination towards sin, an inducement to evil, but not its manifestation. Vice was, in the words of Abelard, the inclination; sin the realisation or manifestation.[51] In the 1567 play *The Triall of Treasure*, the Vice is called merely 'Inclination'. While the concept of a dramatic Vice seems certainly to have crystallised by the mid-sixteenth century, the nomination of the 'Vice' in plays and their paratexts, that is, the identification provisionally justifying theatre-historical description of the type, may itself have been an innovation in the way such forces were imagined.

Efforts of theological specification notwithstanding, the number of demonic characters surfacing in late medieval European culture reveals something of the difficulty in specifying the Vice's mythic-folkloric ancestry: Apollo, Cerberus, Charon, Diana, Jupiter, Neptune, Orcus, Pluto, Proserpine, Tantalus, Venus, Vulcan, Ammon, Moloch, Berith, Tenebrifer, Cocornifer, Spigelglantz or Schonspigel, Robber, Murderer, Ragamuffin, Ribald, Cacodemon, Krumnase, Hörnli, Slange, Gobli, Barbarin, Hellhindt, Aggrapart, Annaball, Herodias, Muhammad, Pharos, Pilate, Abisme, Desperance, Inferus, Aversier, Maufé, Jrtum, Nyd, Intrew, Fals, Frauenzorn, Fergalus, Jack, Robin, Greedigut, Rumpelstiltskin, Gorgorant, et cetera.[52] The problem of naming goes to the Vice's challenge to interpretation. In John Heywood's *Playe of the Weather* (1533), the mischievous 'Mery reporte' was given the epithet of 'Vice' in the cast-list, and it was apparently last used as such less than fifty years later, in Garter's *Susanna* of 1578.[53] In the Tudor interludes through which it was developed, the Vice – such as 'Hypocrisy' in Richard Wever's *Lusty Juventus* – tended to serve only as a rather banal administrator of temptation, in no sense posing even a notional threat to the representative aims or moral message of the play, only (provisionally) to the moral fibre of the personated human at its heart.[54] The threat was made at once interior to the play – somewhat dissociated from the crucial spatial position as intermediary and boundary marker performed in previous drama – and yet more intense as a representation of human vice. As Leonard Tennenhouse suggests, the typical interlude is 'formally unified to the point of impenetrability', which strongly distinguishes it from the extant morality plays in which allegorical evil causes dismemberment of the scene.[55] The less abstracted the Vice's dramatic function, the less it could refer to anything beyond the immediate moral message of the play; and the more effective a conduit of specific moral lessons it seemed to become in tedious interludes like *Wealth and Health* (c.1557) and *Impatient Poverty* (c.1560).

On church exteriors, the gargoyles seem to localise moral threat, but the consistency of their placement hints at 'the idea of the external walls of an edifice being associated with sin'.[56] The particularisation of vice – its location in historical agents – isolated the systemic excess it threatened to govern in such manifestations, allowing at once a more careful identification of the threat and a mitigation of its interaction with the circumstances of performance. The apparent autonomy of the Tudor villain may have reflected this relocation of the origins of mischief into a human being, which permitted both an attentuation of the Vice's dramatic function and an intensification of the appearance of recognisable threat. To speak of the 'Vice' would then be to describe a fundamental change in cultural attitudes to causation and human agency, rather than the history of a stage convention. Sometimes this development is treated in terms of the Vice and the Machiavel, his more realistic cousin, which likewise attempts ineffectually to deal with this momentous historical change in terms of the approximate resemblance of figures.[57]

The anonymous *Enterlude of the Godly Queene Hester* acquires a specific importance in this context. First published in 1561 as a handbook for virtuous womanhood as the reign of Elizabeth I began, but written during the confessional turmoil of the 1530s, it was the play's chief villain and inheritor of the Vice's function, the royal advisor Aman, who spearheaded its satirical attack on Cardinal Wolsey as a corrupt advisor. Crucially, this inheritance or transferral of function is not an engrafted scholarly fiction, but a scene in the play. A trio of Vices – Adulation, Ambition and Pride – appear together on stage to bemoan their lack of employment – the counsellor Aman has done them all out of work.[58] In fact, he has bought up all the 'good clothe' (ll.373–5) and taken control of the mnemonic social symbolism of clothes ('the statute of apparell', 378). The role of the Catholic Vice has here been socialised. Vice suddenly appears to be something like a position of employment. The old Vices resolve as they head off to the tavern to 'make merye, even tyll [they] dye' (500), bequeathing their mischievous exploration of theatrical representation to Aman. But the move from allegorical Vice to historical Vice is fake: a trick to make the figment of Aman seem more dangerously real.

The Appearance of Conscience

Morton Bloomfield, in his influential study *The Seven Deadly Sins*, wrote that these notional grandfathers of the Vice figure '[were] the remnant of some Gnostic Soul Journey [...] [of] the early Christian centuries'.[59] That is, they were occasioned by sublime or metaphysical journeys. In the soul's departure from the body, it would encounter devils or perhaps angels. Imagining the vices of the mind, Bernard of Clairvaux had described what one of his modern translators wonderfully renders as vice's 'crazy labor'[60] – an evocative phrase describing how human vice was understood as misspent time, misspent work, energy wasted in self-defeating activity, wandering St Augustine's 'trackless wastes'.[61] Shooting forward in time, the connection of vicious deviation to the triviality of theatre can be found upheld in seminal English constructions of the dramatic. Charles Lamb wrote that 'there is so much in [the plays of Shakespeare], which comes not under the province of acting, with which eye, and tone, and gesture, have nothing to do'.[62] The province of acting was what Hazlitt would call 'the *pantomime* part of tragedy', antithetical to 'profounder feelings, to reflection and imagination'.[63] If one were to maintain this distinction between the 'matter' of tragedy as against its 'common things', as Hieronimo puts it in reference to his deadly production (*ST*, IV.i.161), then revenge, with its constitutional emphasis on that which is 'pertinent' to the structure of the protagonist's search for vengeance, ought to have applied new kinds of value to the impertinence and deflections of the Vice.

Yet the Vice enters early English revenge tragedy not as a cause of distraction or deviation, but as the first apparent origin of the revenge narrative.[64] He appears as an obscurer of conscience; a false prompt to action that takes a human form. John Pykering's *Newe Enterlude of Vice, conteyning the historye of Horestes*, arguably the first English revenge play, is also the first extant play to use the term 'Vice' with any paratextual consistency (noting the complex exceptions of *The Playe of the Weather* and Udall's *Respublica*).[65] *Horestes* is a hybrid text: sources as diverse as John Lydgate's *Troy Book*, Caxton's *Recuyell of the Historyes of Troye*, and Gower's *Confessio Amantis* have been proposed, and it was naturally subject to the important influence of Senecan translations that became available after around 1559.[66] The play appears from certain angles to sanction the ends of revenge even as it casts doubt over the impulse.[67] Horestes receives the pledges of allegiance from his subjects toward the end (*Horestes*, ll.970–1037). This conclusion in political harmony seems especially provocative given the possibility that the play was performed at Christmas revels, for it seems to mark the failure of the Vice's mission ('I would I were ded and layde in my grave,' l.1038) despite it being he, like a spurious angel, who brought a false missive from heaven itself in the first instance of revenge justification (ll.197–200). The play exerts a worrisome distinction between the means and motive (revenge/Revenge) and the presented ends (the political settlement depicted once revenge has been exhausted).

The political *catharsis* seems to set the righteousness of Horestes's revenge firmly in the context of political expedience. The nobles declare to Horestes: 'Most regall prynce, we now are voyd of mortall wars vexation / And through your grace we ar joyned in love with every nation' (ll.1138–9). By using the Vice as 'the messenger of godes' (in a play otherwise preoccupied with political reason), *Horestes* seems to leave the significant question of divinely sanctioned revenge unanswered, despite its hints at the potential for this idea to be abused as a way of redescribing or manipulating the representation of historical outcomes. *Horestes* entangles the idea of revenge in the internal struggles of royal households and courts. That Horestes starts the play in an antagonism with the court and at its bounds seemingly exposes him to association with the Vice, a figure of the margins. Revenge supplies a (false) obligation pertaining to the son's duty to a dead father, while representing himself merely as the shape of providential design:

Therefore, Horestes, marke me well, and forward do procede
For to reveng thy fathers death, for this [the godes] all have ment;
Which thing for to demonstrate, lo, to the[e] they have me sent.

(ll.194–6)

Revenge insists parenthetically that he is born of the protagonist's mind – 'And I as gyde with you shall go to gyde you on the way. / By me (thy mind) ther wrathful dome shalbe performd in dede' (ll.192–3). But the reference to *psychomachic* incarnation appears simply tactical. Pykering's 'Revenge' appears conscious of the probability that he will seem an allegory of an immoral tendency in the character of Horestes, and uses this knowledge of the Vice to destroy the ability of Horestes to assign him an entirely external origin: his body becomes less real even as his trickery seems to express the deviousness of a physically present human. If the Vice is at his most transgressive when 'his dramatic identity *is* the mischief he sets in motion', in 'Revenge' issues of corporeality and causation blend together.[68]

In *The Spanish Tragedy*, 'Revenge' seems to serve, with his guest the ghostly Andrea, only as audience and chorus (*ST* I.i.90–1). His position has been one of the central debates about the play since the time of Bowers.[69] By the end of the first act Revenge has begun to boast of his influence: 'I'll turn their friendship into fell despite, / Their love to mortal hate, their day to night' (I.v.6–7). This effort of negation seems to be realised in the elaborate language of transformation that increasingly characterises Hieronimo's rhetoric – most famously, in his soliloquy 'O eyes, no eyes, but fountains' (III.ii.1–21).⁷⁰ That Revenge is both abstract and affecting is the reassurance he gives Andrea: 'Though I sleep, / Yet is my mood soliciting their souls' (III.xv.18–19). Hieronimo is incapable of forgetting Horatio: this is sufficient 'destiny'. In this way Revenge can be marginal and idle; a revealer of meaning; and a guarantor of dramatic ends. As his influence appears to grow, the figure Revenge becomes visibly less active – until the play concludes and, with specific reference to the vices and demons of the moralities, he promises to 'hale [all] down to deepest hell' (IV.v.27). Even as the Vice here continues to play many of the functions for which he was known, Kyd has brilliantly formalised the Vice's position: Revenge is simultaneously an actual presence and a figment of the *topos hyperuranios*; a person, a convention and the idea of the play. The academic elevation of the Vice into a transcendent form is the legacy of this late sixteenth-century project of figural citation.

As Kyd's ingenious deployment and Ben Jonson's later satires indicated, the Vice was a custom 'to be quoted and recalled'.⁷¹ In other words, *recognition* of the Vice was part of its appeal, with his dagger of lath, the habit of exiting on the Devil's back, various kinds of masking, and possibly the symbol of the halter all forming mnemonic devices with which to invoke a popular tradition. In *Hamlet*, recognition of the Vice is transformed more uncertainly into the misrecognition of Old Hamlet. The Vice not only informs Hamlet's speech and the villainy of the King, but is received negatively in the confusion of recognition and conscience provoked by the Ghost.⁷² Bradley observed long ago that the usual consideration of Hamlet's use of the word 'conscience' was mistaken in assuming it meant 'a moral scruple'. Hamlet's 'conscience' is instead split between this and the blood duty of a son to avenge his family.⁷³ In reference to the phrase 'conscience doth make cowards' (*Hamlet*, III.i.82), Catherine Belsey suggests along similar lines that the play pits the incentive to revenge against the 'conscience' of its protagonist, but that the phrase can be traced back to the manipulations of previous Vice figures.⁷⁴ In *Horestes*, the Vice is also named 'Courage' – a Vice name found elsewhere, such as in *The Tide Tarrieth No Man* (1576). The dubiousness of the Ghost seems to track into the final scene of *Hamlet*, as if all that rapier play were provoked not by courage but by Courage and his confederates.

The Prince's injunction that his mother 'Confess [herself] to heaven' (*Hamlet*, III.iv.147) conjures the scene of Claudius's failed penitence. Hamlet's presence behind Claudius in that famous tableau evokes the stage devil, or Vice (III.iii.73–96), which may have the strange effect of imaging Everyman in Claudius. Margreta de Grazia situates Hamlet's 'diabolical determination to damn Claudius' within 'the histrionics of salvational drama', but also within the scope of the play as an impersonation of his enemy: 'Hamlet out-vilifies all the play's villains.'[75] The issue here is not one of absolute identification: *Hamlet* ruins genealogies of the dramatic Vice. The play supplies allusions to the Vice here and there so as to call into question the human dimensions of multiple characters, and therefore the scope of causation within the drama. Hamlet's hesitance in his response to the prompts of the Ghost is usually interpreted as the appearance of a mental scruple peculiar to him: an attribute of character. But his doubts also express a problem of dramatic structure, since the prompt and cause of action are implicated in conundrums of theatrical figuration.

The play's most direct reference to the Vice comes in the Prince's description of Claudius as a 'vice of kings':

> A murderer and a villain
> A slave that is not twentieth part the kith
> Of your precedent lord, a vice of kings,
> A cutpurse of the empire and the rule,
> That from a shelf the precious diadem stole
> And put it in his pocket, –
> QUEEN   No more!
> HAMLET   – a king of shreds and patches –
> *Enter* GHOST.
> Save me and hover o'er me with your wings,
> You heavenly guards! What would your gracious figure?
> QUEEN Alas, he's mad.
>
> (III.iv.94–102)

The excoriation comes reasonably fresh on the heels of the performance of the Player engaged by Hamlet, who has just imaged a false king, 'unpregnant' of 'cause' (II.ii.503), presented in a shred and a patch of a play (III.ii.129–253). It is interrupted directly by the entrance of the ghost of Hamlet's father, a 'gracious figure' to dispel the image of 'a king of shreds and patches'. Old Hamlet's 'visitation / Is but to whet [Hamlet's] almost blunted purpose' (106–7). At the height, then, of Hamlet's description of his father as the very antithesis of Claudius's Vice role, Old Hamlet again appears as exactly that vicious prompter familiar from Pykering's *Revenge*.

This was how Thomas Lodge remembered an earlier incarnation of Old Hamlet. In the course of his fanciful genealogy of Beelzebub, Lodge describes the demon's first son *Hate-Vertue* a.k.a. *Sorrow*, who, having 'wandered for a while in France, Germanie, & Italy, to learn languages and fashions', had stolen into England. He could be recognised for his 'tongue tipt with lying', and for how he 'walks for the most part in black under colour of gravity, & looks as pale as the Visard of [the] ghost which cried so [miserably] at [the] Theator like an oister wife, *Hamlet, revenge*'.[76] Because it could mean both 'mask' and 'face', the word 'Visard' throws up several unanswerable questions, such as whether Old Hamlet was equipped with a white mask when he appeared in the London theatres.[77] That which has attracted less attention is the way Lodge's genealogical game – Satan begat Beelzebub, who with Jealousy begat Sorrow – is implicitly tracked into the ur-*Hamlet*. If Sorrow walks 'in black under colour of gravity', we are minded to think not of the phantasmagoric father in the extant versions of the play but of the son, his 'inky cloak', 'customary suits of solemn black', and then the 'dejected haviour of [his] visage', which echoes in (or repeats) Lodge's pale visage. Read next to Lodge, Hamlet's claim that he has 'that within which passes show / These but the trappings and the suits of woe' seems suddenly to refer not to essence or subjectivity, but to the obscure agency of demons and Vices (*Hamlet* I.ii.76–86). '[Sorrow] is always devising of Epigrams or scoffes, and grumbles, murmures continually,' continues Lodge, stoking the intertextual embers.[78] The temptation to pursue Lodge's figuration of the melancholic as a Vice into Claudius's suggestion that Hamlet's clothes and sullenness betoken an 'impious stubbornness' can be resisted. The salient consideration here is that familial resemblance or connection in *Hamlet*, and thus the revenge motive itself, runs not only into the doubtfulness of the prompting apparition, but thereby into a secondary problem of a potentially vicious genealogy. In this way the origin of revenge in *Hamlet* becomes a theatre origin, because it was in the theatre that the Vice was truly present.

'This is the very coinage of your brain,' cries Gertrude; 'This bodiless creation ecstasy / Is very cunning in' (III.iv.136–7). Perhaps a little like Lorenzo, who 'marcht in a net, and thought himselfe unseene' (*ST* IV.iv.118), Old Hamlet is furnished with all the disturbing theatrical uncertainty of semi-corporeality or invisibility from Titivillus's kin. Such likenesses are both tenuous and negligible, however, for the doubtfulness of the apparition has more to do with his proximity to acting than with any particular resemblance. The apparent moral and regal authenticity provided by Old Hamlet's 'gostes sewt' may have been undermined by its seeming cheaply prop-like given the resources of the contemporary stage;[79] that is, the potential of the Ghost to resemble the Vice may have relied on the strikingly over-determined 'authenticity' provided by his armour. This is not to say that the Ghost would have threatened to seem what he was not, but rather that his seeming itself could be a kind of truer identity than that which it purported to represent. '*I am what I seeme*,' reflected the actor Richard

Perkins in his dedication to Heywood's *Apology*.[80] If, as Michael Camille suggests, 'evil was not an idea to medieval people [but] was real and had bodies', the Vice's threat had traditionally coincided precisely with its non-representational dimension, that is, its apparently real presence on stage.[81] There were few signs of Vice more credible than a fleshy ghost.

Many later productions of *Hamlet* recognised how Claudius and the Ghost enter a mutual doubtfulness if doubled by the same player, which is justified by the Prince's reference to 'uncle-father' (II.ii.313), as Ann Thompson and Neil Taylor note.[82] Despite the increasing prominence of the Vice making doubling difficult in some plays (like Nichol Newfangle in *Like Wil to Like*), Ambidexter and Triall in Preston's *Cambises* were played by a single actor, as were Revenge and Nature in *Horestes*, and the demon-vice Titivillus and Mercy in *Mankind*. Hamlet sublimates this ambiguity into an understanding of Gertrude's guilt: the 'rank corruption, mining all within' her, that 'infects unseen', seems reapplicable to the Ghost, the 'mole' whose influence on Hamlet is invisible to his mother. As Jones and Stallybrass have observed, Hamlet's demand that Gertrude 'assume a vertue if [she] haue it not' represents 'Virtue [...] as a garment that can be put on', like his father's armour.[83] Thus the challenge to Hamlet's conscience offered by the theatrical problem of the Ghost modulates into the avenger's insistent challenge to the conscience of Gertrude:

> Forgive me this my virtue,
> For in the fatness of these pursy times
> Virtue itself of Vice must pardon beg.
> Yea, curb and woo for leave to do him good.
> QUEEN O Hamlet, thou hast cleft my heart in twain.
>
> (III.iv.150–4)

Hamlet's riff on disturbed nature – 'Virtue itself of Vice must pardon beg' (the editors capitalise 'vice') – encloses an ambivalence related to his apologetic reception of the Ghost, and by extension the involvement of his conscience in the failure to fill the revenge debt. The haunting semantic possibility here seems to undo Hamlet's identification of Claudius as the Vice, reapplying it to the disturbing apparition of the King's more king-like brother. The Vice is present less as an entire allegorical figure than as a tradition of misrecognition through which to structure a whole nest of problems, encompassing Hamlet's mental landscape of revenge and conscience, action and inaction, acting and not-acting.[84]

The Player Appears

Usually the conclusion of a play occludes the Vice's power: the 'interlude of Vice' has ended. Robert Knapp has astutely read the discharge of the Vice at the end of *Horestes* as the final stage of the play's sublimation of anything vicious in the actions of the avenger. His misdeeds stowed away in the mobile abstraction of 'Revenge', Horestes needs no further scruple: 'By locating this Janus-faced passion in an allegorical figure, Pykering partially frees his hero from the moral ambiguity that both interests and puzzles us in later revengers.'[85] Pykering's exploitation of the doubleness of the traditional Vice reveals that the dramatic potential of the Vice no longer derived from its structural relationship to the rest of the play, but precisely from an imagined integration of this potential within the body of a man, an antagonistic social agent, the unemployed player: 'Well, syeth from them I am bannyshyd so, / I wyll seke a new master, yf I can him finde' (ll.1080–1). This Vice persists at the moment when he and the threat he poses should dissolve, and he acquires a sinister grip on the world outside the theatre: 'Parhappes you all mervayll of this sodayne mutation?' (l.1059) Similar evocations of freedom can be found in *Gammer Gurton's Needle*, *Like Wil to Like*, *Cambises* and a host of other plays from the second half of the sixteenth century, in which the placeless Vice is transformed either implicitly or explicitly into the concrete social figure of the vagrant or illegal itinerant.[86]

In the next chapter, exactly this figure turns up on the edge of the modern scene, ready to serve. In the first phase of Reformation in England, the theatricality of the Vice had furnished a striking resource for satire and criticism of lived Catholic faith. After the 1570s it was the plays themselves, in which the Vice had become a chief attraction, that could be derided as Vice-ridden. *Mutatis mutandis*, the actor himself could seem identical with the danger figured by the Vice. Popular association of the common player with vagrancy and criminal disorder, emphasised by legislation of that decade, informed new inventions of vicehood.[87] The actor who played the Vice became himself the very image or rather body of Vice, distorting appearances for worldly profits and returning an unquantifiable effect on those who paid. The effect was the involvement of the theatre's potentially moral purpose in a deeply fraught dialectic of social appearance through which the distance between origination and configuration often collapsed. That dialectic attracted the ingenuity of playwrights because although it was shaped by anti-theatrical attitudes to the theatre, it also promised a dramatic art which could free itself of a discernible social origin. The material difficulties produced by that sixteenth-century crisis of origin constrain and inform the experience of reading and watching revenge tragedy.

Notes

1. For a subtle example, see Helen Cooper, 'The Afterlife of Personification', in Ruth Morse, Helen Cooper and Peter Holland (eds), *Medieval Shakespeare: Pasts and Presents* (Cambridge, 2013), 98–116.
2. Peter Meredith (ed.), *The Passion Play from the N-Town Manuscript* (London, 1990), 'Passion Play I', 65.
3. Nicholas Udall, *Respublica*, ed. W. W. Greg (Oxford, 1952), 'Prologue', ll.19–24.
4. John Bale, *Three Laws*, in Peter Happé (ed.), *The Complete Plays of John Bale*, 2 vols (Cambridge, 1986), 2: 64–121, at 121 (Sig. G1^v).
5. John Bale, *King Johan*, in *Complete Plays*, ed. Happé, 1: 29–99, ll.90–1; ll.182–4.
6. John Deacon, *Dialogicall Discourses of Spirits and Divels* (London, 1601), 155.
7. John Foxe, *Acts and Monuments* (London, 1583), 1977; cf. 1767.
8. See Dermot Cavanagh, *Language and Politics in the Sixteenth-Century History Play* (Basingstoke, 2003), Chap. 1.
9. See William Nelson, *Fact or Fiction: The Dilemma of the Renaissance Storyteller* (Cambridge, MA, 1973).
10. See J. H. M. Salmon, 'Precept, Example, and Truth: Degory Wheare and the *Ars Historica*', in Donald R. Kelley and David Harris Sacks (eds), *The Historical Imagination in Early Modern Britain. History, Rhetoric, and Fiction, 1500–1800* (Cambridge, 1997), 11–36.
11. David Hawkes, *Idols of the Marketplace. Idolatry and Commodity Fetishism in English Literature, 1580–1680* (Basingstoke, 2001), 7.
12. See Sarah Beckwith, *Signifying God: Social Relation and Symbolic Act in York's Play of Corpus Christi* (Chicago, 2001).
13. Anon., 'A Funerall Elegye on the Death of the Famous Actor Richard Burbage who Died on Saturday in Lent the 13 of March 1619', in Glynne Wickham, Herbert Berry and William Ingram (eds), *English Professional Theatre, 1530–1660* (Cambridge, 2000), 182.
14. Anthony Munday, *A Second and Third Blast of retrait from plaies and theaters* (London, 1580), 112; 115.
15. William Rankins, *A Mirrour of Monsters* (London, 1587), sigs 2^v and 13^v, my italics.
16. John Cocke, 'The Character of a Common Player', in John Stevens, *Satirical Essays Characters and Others* (London, 1615), 295.
17. Phillip Stubbes, *The Anatomie of Abuses* (London, 1583), Sig. M.
18. Stephen Gosson, *Plays confuted in five actions* (London, 1582), Sig. G4^v.
19. Such a collocation of ends and means is noted by the apologist Richard Baker, writing quite soon after the publication of Prynne's *Histriomastix*: 'the *evil* of *Hypocrisie* is not in the *Act*, but in the *End*: and though *Players* may be guilty of the *Act*; yet certainly of the *End* they are not': Richard

Baker, *Theatrum Redivivum, or the Theatre Vindicated* (London, 1662), 21.
20. Stubbes, *Anatomie*, Sig. L6ᵛ. For the context of the original, see Lactantius, *Divine Institutes*, ed. and trans. Anthony Bowen and Peter Garnsey (Liverpool, 2003), Book VI, 20.29, 376.
21. William Prynne, *Histriomastix, the players scovrge or actors tragedie [. . .]* (London, 1633), 102–3.
22. Jeffrey Knapp, *Shakespeare's Tribe. Church, Nation, and Theater in Renaissance England* (Chicago, 2002), 1.
23. Anon., *Mankind*, in Greg Walker (ed.), *Medieval Drama: An Anthology* (Oxford, 2000), ll.118–21. All further reference is to this edition.
24. Thomas Lupton, *All for Money*, ed. Ernst Vogel, *Shakespeare Jahrbuch* 40 (1904), II.1008–9.
25. N.D. (*pseu.* Robert Persons), *The Warn-Word to Sir Francis Hastinges wast-word* (Antwerp, 1602), Sig. Q4.
26. L. W. Cushman, *The Devil and the Vice in English Dramatic Literature before Shakespeare* (Halle a. S., 1900), 54–145. Also see: Adolphus William Ward, *History of English Dramatic Literature, to the Death of Queen Anne*, 3 vols (London, 1899), 1: 109–12; Wilhelm Creizenach, *Geschichte des Neueren Dramas*, 5 vols (Halle a. S., 1893–1916), 1: 463–70; 3: 504–48, esp. 504–6; Katherine Lee Bates, *The English Religious Drama* (London, 1893), 206–9. Cushman may have overlooked *Respublica* in asserting the originality of the Vice's nomination in *Horestes*.
27. Peter Happé, 'The Vice: A Checklist and an Annotated Bibliography', *Research Opportunities in Renaissance Drama* 22 (1979), 17–35, at 17. See Peter Happé, 'The Vice, 1350–1605: An Examination of the Nature and Development of a Stage Convention', PhD thesis, University of London, 2006; Peter Happé, 'Laughter in Court: Four Tudor Comedies (1518–1585), from Skelton to Lyly', *Tudor Theatre* 6 (2002), 111–27; Peter Happé, 'Deceptions: "The Vice" of the Interludes and Iago', *Theta* 8 (2009), 105–24.
28. See John D. Cox, *The Devil and the Sacred in English Drama, 1350–1642* (Cambridge, 2000), 77–81; 101–6; 146–9. David Bevington also assumed a morality play origin: David Bevington, *From 'Mankind' to Marlowe: Growth of Structure in the Popular Drama of Tudor England* (Cambridge, MA, 1962), 122–3, and generally. Also see Alan C. Dessen, *Shakespeare and the Late Moral Play* (Lincoln, NE, 1986), 17–37.
29. Leah Scragg, 'Iago – Vice or Devil?', *Shakespeare Survey* 21 (2002), 53–66, at 53.
30. E. K. Chambers, *The Mediaeval Stage*, 2 vols (Oxford, 1903), 2: 204.
31. See Peter Happé, 'The Vice and the Folk-Drama', *Folklore* 75 (1964), 161–93; Frances Hugh Mares, 'The Origin of the Figure Called "The Vice" in Tudor Drama', *Huntingdon Library Quarterly* 22:1 (1958), 11–29, based on a dissertation: F. H. Mares, 'The Origin and Development of the Figure Called the "Vice" in Tudor Drama', B.Litt. thesis, University of Oxford, 1954; Robert Withington, 'The Ancestry of the "Vice"', *Speculum* 7 (1932), 525–9. Withington withdrew from this position slightly in 'Braggart, Devil, and "Vice"', *Speculum* 11 (1936), 124–9. See also his earlier essay: Robert Withington, 'The Development of the "Vice"', in

Essays in Memory of Barrett Wendell (New York, 1926; repr. 1967), 155–67. For one of the most recent and thorough reassessments of the Vice, see Charlotte Steenbrugge, *Staging Vice. A Study of Dramatic Traditions in Medieval and Sixteenth-Century England and the Low Countries* (Amsterdam, 2014).

32. Mares, 'Origin of the Figure Called "The Vice"', 28–9, based on a philological tradition dating from the end of the eighteenth century: see Karl Friedrich Flögel, *Geschichte der Hofnarren* (Leipzig, 1789), 57–8. Flögel's speculations as to the etymology of 'Vice' are not given in their entirety by Mares, but link the Vice's name also to the '*Vis d'ane*' – the donkey mask or part-mask with which the fool has long been associated. Mares also considered the possible derivation from the Latin *vice*, meaning literally 'in the place of'.
33. Bernard Spivack, *Shakespeare and the Allegory of Evil: The History of a Metaphor in Relation to his Major Villains* (New York, 1958), especially Chap. 5; 135.
34. Ibid. 458.
35. Disputed by Cox, *Devil and Sacred*, 101–6.
36. Spivack, *Allegory of Evil*, 138.
37. Ibid. 151.
38. Bevington, '*Mankind' to Marlowe*, generally; Robert Weimann, *Shakespeare and the Popular Tradition in the Theater*, ed. Robert Schwartz (Baltimore, 1978), esp. 112–60, and generally.
39. Weimann, *Popular Tradition*, 6: 'It would be difficult to support Hermann Reich's claim of an "unparalleled continuity" down to Shakespeare. But even so the *mimus* deserves more attention within the framework of the popular tradition than it has generally received'; and 6–11, generally.
40. See Hermann Reich, *Der Mimus. Ein litteratur-entwicklungsgeschichtlicher Versuch*, 2 vols (Berlin, 1903), 1/ii: esp. 820–900.
41. Ibid. 1/i: 12.
42. See '"Geschichtliches Wissen muss einfach gesichert und tradiert werden" Interview mit Christopher Balme [. . .]', in Jens Ilg and Thomas Bitterlich (eds), *Theatergeschichtsschreibung. Interviews mit Theaterhistorikern* (Marburg, 2006), 116–24, at 118: 'Es gibt keinen Ursprung. Das ist eine metaphysische Frage'; R. Schoch, 'Inventing the Origin of Theatre History: The Modern Uses of Juba II's "teatriké historia"', *Journal of Dramatic Theory and Criticism* 27:1 (2012), 5–23.
43. Stefan Corssen, 'Die Anfänge der deutschsprachigen Theaterwissenschaft', in Gesellschaft für Theatergeschichte (ed.), *Max Hermann und die Anfänge der deutschsprachigen Theaterwissenschaft* (Berlin, 1992), 20–8, at 26–7.
44. Weimann, *Popular Tradition*, 15.
45. Reich, *Der Mimus*, I/i: 41–2.
46. Weimann, *Popular Tradition*, 31.
47. Ibid. 12.
48. Ibid. 155.
49. Ibid. 12.
50. Robert Weimann and Douglas Bruster, *Shakespeare and the Power of Performance* (Cambridge, 2008), 27–8.
51. Peter Abelard, *Ethics*, ed. and trans. D. E. Luscombe (Oxford, 1971), 2–5;

4–5: 'vice is that by which we are made prone to sin, that is, are inclined to consent to what is not fitting so that we either do it or forsake it'. Cf. Thomas Aquinas, *Summa Theologica*, ed. and trans. Fathers of the English Dominican Province (London, 1920–9), 1642: 'the vice of any thing consists in its being disposed in a manner not befitting its nature'.
52. Jeffrey Burton Russell, *Lucifer: The Devil in the Middle Ages* (Ithaca, NY, 1984), 249–50. Cf. Meinolf Schumacher, 'Catalogues of Demons as Catalogues of Vices in Medieval German Literature: *Des Teufels Netz* and the Alexander Romance by Ulrich von Etzenbach', trans. Edward Potter, in Richard Newhauser (ed.)rt, *In the Garden of Evil: The Vices and Culture in the Middle Ages* (Toronto, 2005), 277–90, esp. 281–3. For an excellent description of this necessary ambiguity, see Michael Camille, *Image on the Edge: The Margins of Medieval Art* (London, 1992). For an insistence on the theological genealogy, see Withington, 'Braggart, Devil, and "Vice"', 124–9.
53. For an objection to the importance of Heywood's drama in the history of the Vice, see Spivack, *Allegory of Evil*, 137. Mares, 'The Origin of the Figure Called "the Vice" in Tudor Drama', 12: Mares here provides a convenient list of plays where the Vice is explicitly named.
54. Richard[?] Wever, *An Enterlude Called Lusty Iuventus, liuely describing the frailtie of youth: Of nature, prone to vyce: By grace and good councell traynable to virtue*, ed. Helen Scarborough Thomas (New York, 1982).
55. Leonard Tennenhouse (ed.), *The Tudor Interludes 'Nice Wanton' and 'Impatient Poverty'* (London, 1984), 9.
56. Camille, *Image on the Edge*, 91.
57. For an outline of that literature, see Katherine Eisaman Maus, *Inwardness and Theater in the English Renaissance* (Chicago, 1995), 35 n1.
58. Anon., *The Enterlude of Godly Queene Hester*, in *Medieval Drama*, ed. Walker, ll.372–580.
59. Morton W. Bloomfield, *The Seven Deadly Sins: An Introduction to the History of a Religious Concept, with Special Reference to Medieval English Literature* (East Lansing, 1967), 20.
60. Bernard of Clairvaux, *Sermons on Conversion*, ed. and trans. Marie-Bernard Said (Kalamazoo, 1981), 50.
61. St Augustine, *Confessions*, ed. R. S. Pine-Coffin (Baltimore, 1961), Book 7: 21.
62. Charles Lamb, 'On the Tragedies of Shakespeare, Considered with Reference to their Fitness for Stage Representation' [1818], in E. V. Lucas (ed.), *The Works of Charles and Mary Lamb*, 7 vols (London, 1903–5), 1: 97–111, at 99.
63. William Hazlitt, *A Review of the English Stage; or, A Series of Dramatic Criticisms* [1818; 1821], in P. Howe, ed., *The Complete Works of William Hazlitt* 21 vols (London, 1930–34), 5: 169–424, at 222.
64. See Ronald Broude, '*Vindicta Filia Temporis*: Three English Forerunners of the Elizabethan Revenge Play', *Journal of English and Germanic Philology* 72:4 (Oct., 1973), 489–502.
65. Cushman, *Devil and Vice*, 66–7.
66. Karen Maxwell Merritt, 'The Source of John Pikeryng's *Horestes*', *Review of English Studies* 23 (1972), 255–66; Friederich Brie, '*Horestes*', *Englische*

Studien 46 (1912), 68–71; Robert Knapp, 'Horestes: The Uses of Revenge', *ELH* 40 (1973), 205–20.
67. Cf. Robert Potter, *The English Morality Play: Origins, History, and Influence of a Dramatic Tradition* (London, 1975), 119–20. But for the 'mainstream' reading of *Horestes*, see Eleanor Prosser, *Hamlet and Revenge* (Stanford, 1971), 41–4.
68. Maura Giles-Watson, 'The Singing "Vice": Music and Mischief in Early English Drama', *Early Theatre* 12:2 (2009), 57–90, at 61.
69. Fredson Bowers, *Elizabethan Revenge Tragedy* (Princeton, 1940), 68–71.
70. See Wolfgang Clemen, *English Tragedy before Shakespeare* (London, 1961), 271–2.
71. Weimann, *Popular Tradition*, 150–1.
72. Cf. Michael E. Mooney, *Shakespeare's Dramatic Transactions* (Durham, NC, 1990), 77–81; 93.
73. A. C. Bradley, *Shakespearean Tragedy: Lectures on* Hamlet, Othello, King Lear *and* Macbeth, 3rd edn (New York, 1992), 80.
74. Catherine Belsey, 'The Case of Hamlet's Conscience', *SP* 76:2 (Spring, 1979), 127–48.
75. Margreta de Grazia, 'Hamlet's Smile', in Peter Holland and Stephen Orgel (eds), *From Performance to Print in Shakespeare's England* (Basingstoke, 2006), 231–42, at 241.
76. Thomas Lodge, *Wits Miserie and the Worlds Madnesse* (London, 1596), 55–6.
77. See Simon Palfrey and Tiffany Stern, *Shakespeare in Parts* (Oxford, 2007), 54–6; Stanley Wells, 'Staging Shakespeare's Ghosts', in *Shakespeare on Page and Stage. Selected Essays* (Oxford, 2016), 255–70.
78. Lodge, *Wits Miserie*, 56.
79. R. A. Foakes and R. T. Rickert (eds), *Henslowe's Diary*, 2nd edn (Cambridge, 2002), 318.
80. Richard Perkins, 'To my loving friend and fellow, Thomas Heywood', in Thomas Heywood, *An Apology for Actors* (London, 1612), 10.
81. Michael Camille, *The Gothic Idol: Ideology and Image-Making in Medieval Art* (Cambridge, 1989), 63.
82. Ann Thompson and Neil Taylor (eds), 'Appendix 5: Casting', in *The Tragical History of Hamlet, Prince of Denmark* (London, 2006), 553–65, at 560.
83. Ann Rosalind Jones and Peter Stallybrass, *Renaissance Clothing and the Materials of Memory* (Cambridge, 2000), 266.
84. Thompson and Taylor, 'Casting', 560.
85. Robert S. Knapp, 'Uses of Revenge', 211.
86. Mr S., Master of Art [William Stevenson?], *Gammer Gurton's Needle* [1553?], ed. Charles Whitworth (London, 1997), I.i.1–2, where 'the Bedlem' Diccon declares: 'Many a mile have I walked, diverse and sundry ways, / And many a good man's house have I been at in my days'; Ulpian Fulwell, *An Enterlude intituled Like wil to like quod the Deuil to the Colier* (London, 1568), in Peter Happé (ed.), *Two Moral Interludes* (Oxford, 1991), ll.96–9: 'Nichol newfangle was and is, and euer shallbe: / And there are but few that are not acquainted with me. / For so soon as my prentishod was once come about: / I went by and by the whole world about'; Thomas

Preston, *The Life of Cambises, King of Percia* (London, 1569), in Robert Carl Johnson (ed.), *A Critical Edition of Thomas Preston's 'Cambises'* (Salzburg, 1975), ll.1175–80. Cf. Jonson, *Devil is an Ass*, I.i.55–7, where Iniquity proclaims he 'will fetch thee a leap / From the top of Paul's steeple to the Standard in Cheap: / And lead thee a dance through the streets without fail'.
87. On criminal dissimulation, see for example Robert Greene, *A Disputation, between a He-Cony-Catcher, and a She-Cony-Catcher* (London, 1592), Sig. B: 'tush wee dissemble in show, we goe so neat in apparrell, so orderly in outward appearance, some like Lawyers Clarkes, others lyke Servingmen [. . .]'

Chapter 4

Servants

> He that worketh deceit shall not dwell within my house:
> he that telleth lies shall not tarry in my sight.
>
> Psalm 101:7

Before Gloucester suffers the extrusion of his second eye, someone emerges from the background to call a halt to the terror:

> 1 SERVANT Hold your hand, my lord.
> I have served you ever since I was a child,
> But better service have I never done you
> Than now to bid you hold.
> REGAN How now, you dog?[1]

The servant's sudden appearance is the entrance of an ethical presence onto a scene of devastated ethics, giving a body and a voice to the desire of the audience for it all to stop. The anonymity of the servant is barely diminished by his importance: before he is allowed any more of a name than 'dog' and 'peasant', he is cut down by Regan (III.vii.79) – but not before he has visited a 'hurt' upon his master. Kent and Edgar essay 'better service' through disguise, but '1 Servant', as some editors make him out of 'serv.' (F) and 'Servant' (Q), lacks any such afterlife. The contrast between the servant who lends Regan his sword and the servant who wields one against his master shows that the servant can emerge as a represented subject only against his position of service: nobody remembers the acquiescent servant.

The intervention of the servant against Cornwall and Regan is a problem of theatrical *appearance* before it is one of ethics; or more accurately, the ethical question is inseparable from that of recognition. Stephen Greenblatt suggests that the servant acts 'not out of political motives [. . . or] personal ambition', but because 'he has an ethically adequate object' (the phrase adapted from an evasive remark President Bill Clinton once made). He serves his master by preventing him from performing 'an unworthy action': good service is ethically adequate to him.[2] But evaluating the servant as an ethical person is governed by the arduousness of recognising him. The difficulty in accounting for his presence in the theatre when we read of him is tantamount to rethinking the difficulty in recognising him politically. Little is available to the reader's intuition of him. He never acquires a name, let alone a character. The nearly objective need to which his step forward responds – the necessity that someone do or say something before Gloucester loses both his eyes – means that abhorrence of his master's actions is not in itself sufficient for the attribution of personhood or character. He certainly knows 'the purpose what he is to speak to', has found his moral cue, and improvises upon it with a sword – but this is all.[3] He is not yet a fictional person but a figure whose figuration is partial.

Tones and gestures that relate the stark simplicity of the appearance of conscience in the blinding scene to the subjectivity of a particular human are unavailable to the reader of the play. If these would allow a recognition of the servant in the theatre where his response takes shape, recognition becomes doubly abstract in reading *King Lear*. This scene shows the violent reduction of a man's capacity for recognition, the removal of sight: how does the 'good' servant interact with that theme of diminished vision? With his dying words, as he passes from the light, he inadvertently reminds Cornwall of this task, the bringing of darkness ('You have one eye left / To see some mischief on him', 80–1). He thereby cancels by accident any possible effect his intervention might have had.[4] That may appear a rather callow infliction of irony on Shakespeare's part, but I think he had something else in sight, for the result is an encounter with a servant figure which cannot be understood in narratological or instrumental terms. Instead we are prompted to confront an issue of figuration. Asking what '1 Servant' actually *is* prompts enquiries not only into the terms on which persons are produced in theatre and drama, but into the possible relation of those phenomenological questions to the role of misrecognition in the maintenance of social relations – in the past and across, into the present.

In *King Lear* the bonds of feudal service, sometimes imagined to involve 'the outspokenness of an open relationship', have disintegrated.[5] Lear's retinue dwindles, while servants who tell the truth are put out of doors or murdered. Of the three followers in whom Lear places his greatest trust, two serve in disguise and the third is hired to extemporise. None is a servant in any bare sense, even as all other comforts are stripped away: the superfluities of disguise survive, because these servants can serve only when misrecognised. And yet in the *True Chronicle History of King Lear* (1608) – but not in the *Tragedy of King Lear*

(1623) – the fellows of the disobedient servant linger behind following the atrocity wrought upon Gloucester, to voice condemnation and prepare salves ('flax and whites of eggs') for him. This ad hoc chorus is given shape and power by its momentary disclosure of an otherwise silent community of servants, given air to speak almost as themselves, to claim a space in which they might indeed be recognised without disguise or punishment.

But Bosola was waiting in the wings. In the hands of the servant-villain, the functionality of the servant graduates to a devious theatrical energy, a kind of dextrous stage competence, an 'agilitie' or nimbleness that habitually threatens the very bounds of the service in which it appears. As the bleak hinterland of *The Duchess of Malfi* draws into view following the strangulation of its heroine, Bosola shows the murdered children to his master Ferdinand, as he had shown the Duchess wax effigies earlier: 'Doe you not weepe?', he asks.[6] Ferdinand returns the query: 'Why didst not thou pitty her?' (IV.ii.260). In asking this, Ferdinand accords his servant a post facto ethical independence governed by the access of Bosola to the work of killing. Ferdinand wishes for a disobedient servant such as Regan had to kill: 'what an excellent / Honest man, might'st thou have bin' (260–1). In this he recalls his brother's lament at the opening of the play, as Bosola haunts him for payment owed to murderous service in the past: 'Would you could become honest' (I.i.39); and the contrast of Bosola to the servant Antonio, whose 'nature is too honest for such businesse' (16).

Ferdinand collocates service and role-playing or dishonesty, predicating his criticism of Bosola on the non-identity of Bosola the man and Bosola the servant:

> For thee, (as we observe in Tragedies
> That a good Actor many times is curss'd
> For playing a villaines part) I hate thee for't;
> And (for my sake) say thou hast done much ill, well.
>
> BOSOLA Let me quicken your memory: for I perceive
> You are falling into ingratitude: I challenge
> The reward due to my service.
>
> (IV.ii.275–81)

The period between the imprisonment of the Duchess and her death is characterised by an interest in mimetic efforts and effects. The waxen figures of her murdered family, the hideous realism of which is meant to provoke mental breakdown, typify this interest (IV.i.55ff.). Concentration on the organisation of mimetic representation seems to bring about the failure of the service contract which brought it into effect. The 'tragedy', like the blinding of Gloucester, is a spectacle to undo oaths and contracts. Both Bosola and Ferdinand seem to apprehend the catastrophe of the play as a nadir of the service bond agreed in the opening scene ('What's my place? / [...] / I am your creature', I.i.272–4):

> BOSOLA   Let me know
> Wherefore I should be thus neglected? Sir,
> I serv'd your tyranny: and rather strove,
> To satisfie your selfe, th[a]n all the world;
> And though I loath'd the evill, yet I lov'd
> You, that did councell it: and rather *sought*
> *To appeare a true servant, th[a]n an honest man.*
> (IV.ii.314–20, my emphasis)

Bosola, like his actor, pursues recognition through misrecognition, 'appearing a true servant'. Both he and his actor appear and disappear in and through acts of service.

The player – 'a good actor' in a 'villaines part' – was able to show this servant with an accuracy peculiar to his profession. Playing not only made a virtue of adopting and relinquishing positions within the theatre house, of mastery over coming and goings, substitutions and reversals, tricks of disguise and anonymity, but was itself actuated by a particular legal half-fiction: that the player himself was fundamentally a servant, and acting a service. It was in (and out of) the guise of the servant that professional actors staked a claim to be heard in the commonwealth. The theatre offered a house in which the activity of the actor acquired the relative security of service, for the interval of the play. The theatre, as Russell West has shown, must be examined as a 'phenomenon tied up in demographic mobility'.[7] And as Patricia Fumerton suggests, the economy of early modern 'unsettledness [...] involved not only the legally vagrant, but also the "respectable" yet unstable servant and apprentice classes; it even touched poor householders [...] the housed poor were increasingly forced to mobilise their labor in a makeshift, grab-bag fashion – resulting in a kind of "at-home" unsettledness'.[8] This historical unsettledness was translated bodily into the new theatres.

This chapter shows how revenge tragedy manifests this vacillation between service and non-service, occupation and idleness, contract and non-identity. It argues that the relation between service and playing cannot be discerned without first acknowledging the legal and historical problems involved in the category of 'servant'. As an object of consideration, 'the servant' is a mélange of abstractions both historical and contemporary, nullibiquitous. The theatrical representation of service and servants in England was mediated by the player's presence – because each performance was itself a deeply ambiguous *act of service*. Through the dialectic of recognition and service in revenge tragedy, theatre disclosed the incoherence of service as a category of identity. An interplay of theatrical identities – actor – servant – avenger – is expressed in and through intrigue. In exploring this dialectic, I articulate its special challenge to historicist reading. As I show, it works a serious mischief on some of the most important and ubiquitous categories used to explain the relation of early modern tragic plays to their society.

The Servant Abstract

Servants occur so frequently that they are not included in the *Index of Characters in Early Modern English Drama* unless the play gives them either a name or a specific function.[9] This is unsurprising: when positions of apprenticeship are counted, as many as two-thirds of people might have occupied positions of service at some point in their lives.[10] Servants were necessary to the dramaturgical re-creation of domestic and courtly spaces, their interiors and the routes connecting them; as well as to the practical dimension of tragic scenes. Letters need to be delivered; messages, arrivals or news announced; weapons and bodies carried off. Characterisation tends to rely on deviations from this functionality: letters are misplaced, intercepted, opened or manipulated; messages are garbled, misheard, or altered; bodies are multiplied, hidden, or otherwise employed. Characters who serve others emerge from and against the pure functionalism of the service idealised by masters.

The historical contradictions involved in the terms 'servant' and 'service' obstruct discussion of the relation of theatre to the social history of service. Michael Neill suggests that in early modern England, 'it was almost impossible to conceive of a properly human existence outside the hierarchy of masters and servants that made up the "society of orders"'.[11] This is one way of saying that the word 'servant' is an abstraction produced through and for particular social constellations. It can never be sufficient as a denotation of actual people who lived in service, bearing in mind (with James C. Scott) that subordinates could reinforce their 'servant' identity, perform humility, to regain a measure of control over their own lives.[12] Just as often, they were coerced into those representations, the autonomy of their self-designations illusory.[13] Neill shows how idealisations of feudal duty and universal service were articulated with ever greater urgency against the increasing mobility of people seeking employment and the implicit revaluation of loyalty produced by the cash-nexus into which they entered. Kent experiences service to Lear as an ontological condition, a self-perficient identity, whereas for other figures, like Iago, service is a more deeply conditional and temporary state, a part. To the latter, acts of service do not proceed from a self-perception as a servant, but express the agency of an individual voluntarily entering into contingent and temporary states of service, from which the individual itself appears to remain separate. This separation is what the servant retrieves from employment that makes unlimited claims upon him.

In a commentary on contradictions between the experience and definition of law, Hegel explains the distinction between particular acts of service and general, indentured service:

> By alienating the *whole* of my time, as made concrete through work and the totality of my production, I would be making the substantial quality of the latter, i.e. my *universal* activity and actuality or my personality itself, into someone else's property.[14]

Neill tries to show that the crisis of service at the turn of the seventeenth century was experienced and realised as the progressive demystification of hierarchical relationships. At hand is the reduction of relations of love, duty and sacred obedience to a cash transaction.[15] Archaic service relations in *Lear* and *Othello* acquire, in this acount, something like a new virtue which is endangered at every turn by the self-interested and the mercenary. To suggest such a transition, to argue that it bespeaks a historical shift, can imply that the cash transaction is not itself mystifying, which is uncritically to assimilate (among many other things) the simple image of waged labour as it was presented by early modern reactionaries for defacement. Whether hierarchy has been demystified or not, what motivates Iago, who seems more 'modern' in his disobedience and thus in his service, is neither more clearly nor more richly presented than what motivates Kent. The early modern crisis of service remystified the subject who entered into wage transactions, because the transaction itself presumed – and showed – an autonomy in its parties that did not exist except in a purely formal, i.e. legal sense. In discussing the sixteenth-century discontinuity in realisations of service, Neill and others tend to fall into an identitarian trap, adopting the legal definition of the individual as if it were the subject itself, and therefore an ethical rather than a merely legal foundation in the process of alteration.[16]

This assumption underpins many recent attempts to describe early modern configurations of service that seem irreducible to cash. As Mark Thornton Burnett has observed, there has been a shift of emphasis in literary scholarship, from service considered in terms of authority, subordination, deferential speech and economic dependency to service considered as a fundamentally ethical relation.[17] Following Neill, much of this work recommends we approach dramatic representations of service as if they were chiefly ethical inquisitions depicting variety and depth in actual lived relationships out in the world. David Evett and David Schalkwyk both argue that Shakespearean versions of the master–servant relationship expose 'a degree of theoretically induced myopia in prevailing assumptions and critical practice', due to their complex and often affectionate character. Relations between servants and masters could comprise 'intimate, multifaceted, affective, and playful forms that cannot be reduced to mere relations of power and subordination or resentful resistance'.[18] Criticising the over-emphasis of materialist critics on 'impersonality' as the new marker of waged service, but neglecting most of the considerable scholarship in English economic and social history that is directly relevant to any critique of cultural materialism, Schalkwyk suggests that 'the diachronic thesis of the inexorable "rise of capitalism"' produces an inattention to 'local nuances'. Without mentioning that in addition to its 'intimate [...], affective, and playful forms', relations between servants and masters could also include extortion, defraudment and all kinds of violence, Schalkwyk invokes Raymond Williams to propose 'the complicated interrelation and coexistence of residual, dominant, and emergent forces by which service continued to be practiced and experienced'.[19] Judith Weil likewise chooses to avoid what she calls 'narrow, utopian [sic] prejudices against subordination in general and work in particular'.[20]

Weil, Schalkwyk and others who have worked on the ethics of service in early modern literature were influenced by Peter Laslett's *The World We Have Lost* (1965).[21] Laslett's concept of 'the life-cycle servant' underpins departures from materialist interpretations of early modern service and is often represented as a creative break in English historiography of the servant. Laslett argued that the master-servant relationship formed the crux of a patriarchy in which 'every relationship could be seen as a love-relationship'.[22] In this the influence of his work, despite its original demographic and quantitative focus, blended appealingly with growing, subcutaneous interest in the Pauline transformation of service into brotherhood (Phlm 1:15–16).[23] Laslett tried to show that service was simply a stage of life that came to an expected end in marriage and the creation of a new family. That is, it was a kind of temporary, almost natural state before the establishment of an independent household.[24] The pervasive association of service with forms of youth or juvenility during the early modern period has been well-documented and is important.[25] However, service can be imagined as a form of transition only to the extent that other, more stable forms of occupational or social identity are posited. In this case the key construct is the household itself.[26]

One indirect consequence of Laslett's research was that the assumptions of Elizabethan political discourse could be reproduced and implicitly bulwarked through ethical interpretations of service: as if the servant did indeed *belong* to the household somehow prior to *possessing* it for him or herself.[27] Ethical criticism of early modern service and its dramatic representation reinstates a political and economic argument that often gels unexpectedly with the paternalism of the late sixteenth century. 'In that world,' writes Michael Neill in a review of Schalkwyk's book, 'the relationship between masters and servants in many respects resembled that between parents and children'.[28] Given that this could only be what Neill actually calls 'literal truth' from the perspective of the property-owners ('householders'; 'fathers'; 'masters'), it is unsurprising that such accounts of early modern service retrieve so many resources from contemporary documents and plays, for such sources were often involved in the reproduction and dissemination of exactly that perspective.

Clearly, Kent's service is not that of the domestic servant or rural labourer, but much effort was invested during the sixteenth century to extend the sacral meaning of service to relations throughout the social hierarchy of England. The word 'service' could encompass all the relations that made up the commonwealth, whence Cheke 'to the rebel' of 1549, for imprisoning of the king's subjects: 'For neither can the king be served, nor families kept, nor the common-wealth looked unto, where freedome of libertie is stopped, and diligence of service is hindered; and the helpe of strength and health abated'.[29] It is not always clear in contemporary sources whether the author – writer, court, or speaker – applies 'service' in the sense used to describe relations of power within the ancient hierarchy of orders, or with more explicit reference to legal and financial covenants. Frequently, the words 'servant' and 'service' are caught between this older meaning and the newer senses they acquired in the course of the sixteenth century. This first definition, paternalistic, is found in most texts describing and proscribing social order. The second meaning of 'servant', which could reach to include 'journeyman' and 'apprentice', generally referred to a 'wage-labourer': one considered to have forsaken his English birthright by becoming dependent upon others following the loss of land.[30] The common law began, around 1600, to justify its hegemony with reference to English 'birthright', cementing the lasting connection between property ownership and legal freedom.[31] The acquisition of an estate was expected to coincide with the acquisition of political rights.[32] Sixteenth-century land enclosures had compelled more and more people to leave behind older relations and concepts of service – local, customary – and enter into new relations and concepts of service – mobile, waged. Consequently there emerged an increasingly visible landless population just at that moment in English history when legal-political freedoms were being tangled more tightly into the possession of land, through which the citizen's part in the commonwealth was actualised and presumed.[33] Courts ruled naturally enough that a landholder's servant had 'no interest' in the land of his master.[34] These changing economic relations created a crisis in the paternalism and Christian pastoralism that continued to inform descriptions of the duties owed to each other by master and servant.

The capacity of servants to forsake and remake familial ties anew enabled them to become uncertain, provisional members of a household. The virtue of servants arose from their identity in relation to the household, but 'servants' increasingly needed to skip between houses in order to advance, or were beholden to temporally-bounded contracts through which their servant-identities were legally constituted. Servants were disposed to erode the ideology of the household, usually imagined as consistent and enclosed, whilst continuing to constitute and maintain it institutionally and practically. Within the scope of this capacity to undermine the central political imaginary of the time, servants, journeymen and apprentices could use the terms of the service contract itself to lodge complaint against the masters to whom they were otherwise subjugated.[35] In one famous case of petty treason from 1583, a servant induced by his mistress to murder his master sought to find grounds to commit manslaughter by provoking an argument about wages.[36] A servant might find ways to assert him- or herself as a servant, but outside the specific legal identity forged for them by the contract of service, he or she was largely excluded from the realm of recognised social discourse and identity: without estate but within the estate of another.

Discourse on *representation* of servants and service in early modern theatre denies the difficulty involved in relating theatrical acts of service to real people whose experiences were shaped by this insecurity. Although the observation that the common player was a servant with a vagrant aspect has been made often enough for it to sound routine, it has not prompted the engagement with the many intricate issues of dramatic personation and figuration that seem to snap at its heels.[37] Every attempt to draw a direct relation between actual servants and servants as they appear in tragedy, if it neglects the mediation of the actor-servant and depends instead on the representations of character, is, as Thomas Nashe suggested of *prosopopoeia*, a rhetorical sleight of hand: 'the supposing or faining of a person'.[38] The dramatic servant is used to create and sustain the figure of the actual servant which it is taken to represent. Despite the difficulty in identifying common economic features among servants; the pitfalls of identifying servants without reference to the fluidity of the legal, economic and social structures that enforced or encouraged that identity; and the controversy surrounding their relation to class, it is clear enough that their position between house-holding and vagrancy could entertain its own milieu, opening up possibilities of shared experience.[39] Despite the reservations I have sketched above, the attempt to describe this 'servant' experience cannot simply be abandoned.

Revenge tragedy provides unlikely resources for this continuing project. The rest of the chapter pursues a speculative prosopography of serving figures in revenge tragedy. It shows how subtleties of theatrical epistemology and dramatic character derived to some extent from lived paradoxes in the economic and moral category of service. I abandon the presumption that servant characters are simply repositories of lived experience in the past, focusing instead on the way dramatic figurations and disfigurations respond to early modern stage mimeses of the social scenarios through which service was construed and undone. This new approach to the tragic 'servant', and to the origins of the intriguer, is pursued in three sections, mirroring the three chief stages of service: procurement; performance; and dismissal.

Procurement

The appearance on stage of men seeking positions of service, and in turn the appearance on the page of these same figures, relates to the appearance in the city of rural migrants seeking employment; and to the appearance on the edge of the State of men seeking recognition within it. In John Fit's *A Diamonde most precious* (1577), a citizen of London, master of his own servants but formerly a servant himself, instructs a young man who has come from the country to seek work as a servingman. The dialogical form presents the paternalist ethos of the work, which shows the receptive mind of the young itinerant being imprinted with the entire moral and legal edifice that governed expectations of service in early modern London. Masters could be fined if their servants did not attend church (but almost never were). Sometimes when vagrants were identified and punished, they were put to work under particular masters, each master 'bound [. . .] to keep his servant for an entire year, and at the expiration of the term to produce him, or sufficient proof of his death, at General Session of the Peace'.[40] 'A christian Householder ought to have ouer his children and servants, a much more christian care,' wrote Robert Cleaver in 1598, 'then he hath over his dumbe & insensible beasts, that so he may take a singular comfort from the daylie contemplation of their encrease in spirituall graces.'[41] 'Take such as are of mean and poor estate and know not how to maintain themselves but by service,' advised William Gouge.⁴² The description of proper service in *A Diamonde most precious* conforms to this paternalist tradition, in which the ignorant were to be taught the ethos of the commonwealth, but it is produced on the occasion of an encounter with a wandering labourer who is in danger of being mistaken for a rogue and vagabond. 'The Lawes of this Realme are verye straightly looked upon now a dayes, concerning such matters,' the labourer is informed, 'especially if they have not a Pasport from whence they come.' The Citizen enquires into the traveller's family and background, and warns him that, 'the Citizens that lack servants, and especialy those that are men of great welth, will seeke to have some sufficient Sureties for those that they wil entertayn into their service'.⁴³

Suspicion of servants ran deep, and deeper still when their origins – the land they came from, their family, their previous employment, their reasons for leaving all of this – were obscure. In 1604, Sir William Wentworth advised his son never to trust any servant, except 'some auncyennt servants of your fathers whose welth and creditt depend most upon our hous and are seated on your ground', for 'allmost all trecheries have bene wrought by servantes and the finale ende of their service is gaine and advancement'.⁴⁴ Cleaver implies that mastery required close attention to what servants were up to, when urging citizens to ascertain that their serving-men attended church:

> For in the sixe daies, when their servants are in their owne busines, [masters] will not let them come and goe at their owne pleasure, and content themselves with a bare imagination, that they bee at their workes, but will bee sure of it, and therefore set them to it, look upon them in the doing of it, and call them to an account for it.⁴⁵

The procurement of a servant was assumed to be fraught with risk. Bad servants were a threat not just to the households in which they were employed, but to the very commonwealth which the orderly household signified and produced: 'An house in which good servants live, prospers,' reflected William Whateley, 'but idle and untrusty servants quickly bring it to nought.'⁴⁶ In attempting to distinguish the 'godly' serving-man from the ever more numerous and apparently ever more mercenary servants arriving in London, Walter Darell began with the observation that

> we see daily by experience, howe circumspecte eache Gentleman is, in receiving a servaunt, doubtfull to take him without greate warrantize: and this is, by reason that youth having their libertie, & nouzeled so long in idlenesse, are prone and apt to vice and wickednesse, utterly undoing them selves thorough their owne wilfulnesse.⁴⁷

The hiring of incompetent or unsympathetic serving-men became a staple of comic narrative even before the heyday of the theatrical servant. In Humphrey Gifford's translation of Straparola's *La piacevoli notti* (c.1555), likely known to later playwrights, Pandolfus, a gentleman of Padua, 'chaunced to meete with one' whom he thought to make a servant, but unluckily demands that 'hee would at no time doe him any other service, but looke to his horses and ride with him': 'Héereon they concluded, and there were Indentures of covenants [*L'instrumento*] drawn, sealed, and delivered for the performance of the premises.' The technical legal terms 'indentures of covenants' and 'performance of the premises', substantial elaborations upon the somewhat simpler document mentioned in the original story, indicate that Gifford has adapted the tale with great attentiveness to the English legal situation. Pandolfus falls under his horse into a ditch, and cries for his servant to help.

> His servaunt standing still, gave him the looking on, saying that he was not bound to doe it, and that there was no such thing contained in his Indenture of covenaunt, and taking the copie thereof out of his pocket, beganne from poynt to point to reade the conditions of it.

When the servant was badly chosen, the covenant became a potentially comic liability.[48]

The election of servants, and the contract through which their service was formalised, were each of them difficult moments. Much of this difficulty stemmed from the struggle to reconcile wages to duty. Sir Thomas Smith had supposed that those serving-men who 'ser[ved] for the time' did so 'as *servi* and *ancillae* did in the time of gentilitie, and [were] for other matters in libertie as ful free men and women'.[49] John Day averred that the contemporary servant was unlike the servitor of the ancient world, that he or she was instead the product of Christian mildness, which had tempered and loosened the terms of 'Bondage': '*Serving Men*, are such as having no Revenewes to maintain themselves, betake themselues to serve Others, & are hired for wages to serve by the yeare.'[50] The obedience and loyalty of the waged servant, if it were to exist, would necessarily hark back to older kinds of bond, since the ideal relationship could not be produced by even the most exacting contract of annual indenture. Darell distrusted any servant who professed to be a serving-man 'uppon [...] extremitie', for these '*Sucklinges*, or otherwise *Caterpillars*' that lived only from the meagre wages of service and had not practised 'some trade in [their] youth', would surely 'want reliefs [...] by unlawfull meanes'.[51]

This difficulty in placing the waged servant in the imaginary commonwealth made the employment of new servants a persistent anxiety in a society still coming to terms with a service that was temporally limited and pecuniarily expressed, hence the ubiquity of approving reference to 'ancient' servants. New relations were founded upon suspicion, not trust. 'Where's the Maister among a many,' Day wondered, 'that either consults with his owne eies, as king *David* here said hee would doe, or if his *Servants* be not as they should be, rids his hands of them presently[?].'[52] Likewise, Gouge advised:

> The first thing that a man, who taketh vpon him to be a master, must take care of, is to entertaine good servants into his service. *Mine eies* (saith Dauid) *shall be upon the faithfull of the land, that they may dwell with me: he that walketh in a perfect way he shall serve me.* What doth this phrase (*mine eies shall be upon the faithfull*) imply, but that he will diligently and carefully inquire after such: yea *mine eies* (saith he) not another mans eies: he would not put all the trust upon others.[53]

The capacity of the master to judge character with his eyes was frequently represented as the only measure of good election. In the absence of a perceptive master, the servant was unreliable. Myriad cases involve the fear that any servant was capable of petty treason, through which the affinity of State and household had been set in law.[54] The formative relationship thought to obtain between household and State magnified every crime committed by a servant against his household:

> When a servant raigneth, that is despiseth his maisters gouernment, and followeth his owne will, and his owne wayes, it is a thing so evill, and disorderly, that it maketh the earth to be mooved, the whole house, yea somtimes the whole towne, or citty to be disquieted

fulminated Thomas Fossett.[55] 'What deadly *poyson* may wicked servants be to our children?' echoed Matthew Griffith decades later; 'What *moathes* to our *ward-robes*? What *Theeves* to our *Store*?' 'Let us,' he concluded, 'be circumspect in the choice of our servants.'[56]

Each time an actor makes an entrance in the theatre-house, a complex process of re-cognition is called for. Whether the audience identifies the actor or the character first cannot be determined: before any of the particularities of the entrance and the way the actor makes it can be considered, there is an uneasy identity of actor with character, for the actor has entered a space in which recognition of who he is proceeds to a sense that a given character has arrived. The sense that 'the entrance of the actor [. . .] had the performative power to create [. . .] the very location that would give that entrance a fictional significance' is of course vital to how the early modern theatre worked.[57] But there is also a converse and less frequently adduced problem of figuration: the suspension of this new figure between its fictional identity and its appearance as a mere outline of a person, a suspension that dynamically relates to the space its entrance has assisted in producing. When it is at issue, this moment tends to be called 'liminal' ('of the threshold'), which is almost completely undescriptive. In revenge tragedy, the re-cognition of theatre entrance (and with it, the initial appearance of person in drama) is often conflated with the recognition and judgement of servants. Pedringano is summoned into dramatic being by Lorenzo's 'Ho Pedringano' and '*Vien qui presto*' ('come here at once'), interpellations which in the first extant edition *precede* the stage direction indicating the servant's nominal entrance. 'Hath your Lordship any service to command me,' speaks this new figure which has suddenly and indistinctly emerged on the verge of his master's sight. The effect, for the reader at least, is a momentary identity of the scope of the mental scene with the master's range of vision.[58]

In Henry Chettle's *Hoffmann* (c.1602), the masterless man Lorrique simply appears in response to the need of the avenger. His entrance is impeded by possibly invisible undergrowth:

> Yet this is somewhat like, but brambles, you are too busy: were I at luningberg, and you catch me thus, I should go near to ask you at whose suit – but now I am out of scent and fear no serjeants, for I think these woods and waters are commonwealths that need no such subjects; nay they keep not a constable at sea, but a man's overwhelmed without order.

Lorrique compares catching brambles to arrests effected by sergeants and constables of the commonwealth, half-voicing a fear he may be taken for a vagrant. The corrupted text of the play will reveal Lorrique to be the valet of the Duke's son, Otho. In entering as he does, Lorrique appears outside service. While Otho is 'ayring himself' in Hoffmann's cell, Hoffmann usurps his position as master of Lorrique. Identification of Lorrique as Otho's man is delayed, because storm and shipwreck have disrupted that relation. Nature has disordered the bond of servant to master. Before he can be reunited with his master and take up his position as valet, Lorrique encounters Hoffmann, and enters into a new kind of service contract. This will eventually allow Hoffmann to impersonate the dead Otho; the impersonation begins with the acquisition of his servant. In the common law, 'if a man find an other man's servant wandring abroad, and reteyne him, this is lawfull, if he knew nothing of the first reteiner' – but Hoffmann commits his first trespass against Otho's sovereignty in purposely contracting his valet.[59]

After a brief description of his vengeful intentions, Hoffman demands Lorrique's loyalty: 'Therefore without protraction, sighing, or excuses / Sweare to be true.' Lorrique vows instantly, assuring his new master that he has no inheritance – no land, no possessions, no history – other than 'villainy': 'Villany is my onely patrimony.' In this he appears in contradistinction to Hoffmann himself, whose own patrimony, forcefully and bizarrely emblematised by the preserved skeleton of his father, gives substantial motive for revenge. When Otho indicts Lorrique for his 'turn', Lorrique replies, 'Ile turne anything sir rather than nothing.' His deceptively simple answer collocates survival and shifts of service with theatrical metamorphoses, the changing or 'turning' of livery. Lorrique's nominal position remains the same, however, since his new master assumes the identity of the old.[60] Ithamore in *The Jew of Malta* (1589?) appears similarly ready for imprinting, 'tractable and obedient', but not 'to good order and godly government'.[61] Barabas initially assumes the role of a master judging a prospective servant for his virtues: 'Now let me know thy name, and therewithal / Thy birth, condition, and profession.' In fact it is a capacity for deceit – exactly that characteristic thought most often to be found in 'bad' servants – that Barabas seeks.[62] Ithamore's 'readiness', his pliability, is a distortion of innocence, a satire of the juvenile itinerant seeking education and employment in a godly household. The uses to which Barabas puts him make up the antithesis of a Christian education.

Daniel de Bosola appears on the edge of court, out of service, haunting his former master, the Cardinal, for whom he has already committed murder. The Cardinal now shuns him for the sake of his own reputation. 'Who wold relie upon these miserable dependances,' Bosola asks Antonio, 'in expectation to be advanc'd to morrow?' He bitterly reimagines social hierarchy, infusing it with torpor and death: 'Places in the Court, are but like beds in the hospital, where this mans head lies at that mans foote, and so lower, and lower' (I.i.52–64). This note of vulnerability is echoed when he next enters to a complex scene in which he is persuaded to enter Ferdinand's service and infiltrate the Duchess's household: 'I was lur'd to you' (I.i.218). The word 'lure' makes Bosola into a fish caught on a hook; or a hawk recalled from exercise. The conversation begins with a discussion of the Cardinal's distrust of Bosola:

> FERDINAND. My brother, here, (the Cardinall), could never
>   Abide you.
> BOSOLA. Never since he was in my debt.
> FERDINAND. May be some oblique character in your face,
>   Made him suspect you.
> BOSOLA. Doth he study Phisiognomie?
>   There 's no more credit to be given to th' face,
>   Than to a sicke mans uryn.
>   (I.i.219–24)

Bosola challenges the grounds for a *particular* suspicion based upon appearances – of the prospective servant – by voicing a *general* distrust of appearance – germane to the theatre. Throughout the play, Bosola will be obsessed with the interpretation and misinterpretation of faces.

Physiognomy was a controversial art in early modern England, but was numbered among the techniques counted proper to the perception necessary for politic enlistment: 'It is a great discoverie of dissimulations, and a great direction in Businesse,' wrote Francis Bacon.[63] Others were less impressed: Thomas Dekker mocked the wealthy nobleman who hoped to find a good servant by this art:

He calls forth one by one, to note their graces,
Whilest they make legs he copies out their faces,
Examines their eye-browe, consters their beard,
Singles their nose out, still he rests afeard.[64]

Beatrice cannot stand Deflores in Middleton and Rowley's *The Changeling* (1622), suspicious of his forward service and 'ominous, ill-faced' looks.[65] Deflores observes however that 'there's daily precedents of bad faces / Beloved beyond all reason' (II.i.84–5). He is proved somewhat correct. In the midst of scorning Alsemero for proposing to challenge Alonzo, her betrothed, Beatrice remembers this foul visage that has haunted her: 'Blood-guiltiness becomes a fouler visage, / And now I think on one – ' (II.ii.40–1). So she will utter his name, thereby recognising Deflores and removing him from neglect: 'Ha, I shall run mad with joy! / She called me fairly by my name, De Flores, / And neither "rogue" nor "rascal"!' (II.ii.71–3). Suddenly his face, which first bespoke obscure villainy in the servant, signifies opportunity, and Beatrice mends her language: 'What ha' you done / To your face o' late? You've met with some good physician' (II.ii.73–4). The mistress then touches the face of her prospective servant: judgement of the servant's physiognomy is twisted into the semblance of a love scene, foreshadowing the play's later development of the words *service* and *performance* into fluid co-ordinators of erotic and contractual confusion.[66] 'Hardness becomes the visage of a man well,' declares Beatrice; 'It argues service, resolution, manhood / If cause were of employment' (II.ii.93–5). Deflores enters into service.

Meanwhile, Ferdinand answers Bosola with reference to the axioms of the prudent householder: 'You must give great men leave to take their times: / Distrust doth cause us seldome be deceiv'd' (I.i.226–7). In this way, the audience is sensitised to Bosola's dishonesty, but also to the facial expressions and gestures of his actor.[67] Against this universal suspicion of servants, Bosola insists on the reciprocality of the master–servant relationship. He predicts the reciprocation and reproduction of distrust:

> BOSOLA. Yet take heed:
> For to suspect a friend unworthily
> Instructs him the next way to suspect you,
> And prompts him to deceive you.
> (I.i.230–2)

Bosola had a point: suspicion or censure of servants could itself produce or prompt disobedience. In 1585 a servant named Lawrence Medoppe, alias Grimshawe, accompanying one John Barrowe, was reproved by his master for carrying his money 'so losely one or other maye snatche yt'. So Grimshawe made off with the money himself.[68] The subtlety of Bosola's answer, his reference to the dynamics of actual, non-idealised contract such as this, its capacity to change the contractees, is met by Ferdinand only with money: 'There's gold.'

The contract is obscurely rendered in mutual metaphor by both parties: Bosola is to be a 'familiar', 'a very quaint invisible devil in flesh', 'an intelligencer', 'a thriving thing'; he fears he will be 'a villain'; 'a politic dormouse', a 'creature'. The word 'familiar' probably incarnates Bosola as a Satanic pet. The Belvoir witches of 1618 were servants bearing grudges against the family which had turned them out of service; it was against them that they sent forth their familiars.[69] That later case attributed to those servants a magical language of command. As John Kerrigan has noted, the oath to do service reduced the credit of further oaths, because servants were accorded less credit.[70] The fear of the deceitful servant gave words spoken in service less grip. In revenge tragedy, this diminution of the relation between the serving man's language and his intentions is translated into a sort of advantageous changeability. The alienation of Bosola from his many guises, Ferdinand thinks, will suit the purpose (infiltration), without his falling under that same suspicion with which Ferdinand and the Cardinal have regarded him:

> FERDINAND. Be your selfe;
> Keepe your old garbe of melancholly: 'twill expresse
> You envy those that stand above your reach,
> Yet strive not to come neere 'em.
> (I.i.265–8)

Bosola's self is reduced to garb, even as Hamlet appears in him ('Good Hamlet, cast thy nighted color off' [*Hamlet*, I.ii.68]). Richard Burbage, Hamlet some years before, played Ferdinand in the first runs of *The*

Duchess of Malfi in 1613 and 1614;[71] here he addresses a fresh iteration of himself. In and through this economy of shifting roles, of positions in the (theatre) house taken up, and dropped, and swapped, remembered, and undone, acting is found pertinent to service; and service to tragic intrigue. The beginnings of service in the plot appear obscurely, for the act of service has already begun.

When Vindice appears onstage as the servant Piato, he and Hippolito immediately begin reflecting on the terms of that appearance. The production of the servant's demeanour is staged explicitly:

VINDICE   What brother, am I far enough from myself?
HIPPOLITO As if another man had been sent whole
           Into the world, and none wist how he came.

Vindice announces an intention to become an entirely inscrutable servant: the nightmare of the commonwealth. He wishes that he may be struck 'into dauntless marble', that his 'visage' may be 'turned', and that he may 'blush inward'.[72] Within the scope of a play that has long been held to respond to 'the disintegration of a whole social order', the scene in which Lussurioso procures Piato goes once more to the lord's inability to discern truly.[73] He makes no 'Diligent, and wise search' by which 'to finde out the disposition and abilitie' of Piato, but has relied on 'another mans eies':[74] 'My lord, after long searches, wary enquiries, / And politic siftings, I made choice of yon fellow, / Whom I guess rare for many deep employments' (I.iii.20–2). Having received gold ('though it be dumb, [it] does utter the best thanks', 28), Hippolito retires. His introduction of Ferdinand to the prospective servant Piato invites us to imagine the staging thus: Vindice, having withdrawn to one side (17–18), waits slightly apart ('yon fellow'). Like 1 Servant from *King Lear*, he stands on the verge of a new identity. Anticipating Bosola, the figuration of Vindice's alias relies on the curiously oscillating relation between the murky depths of his past 'employment' and his silent haunting of the scene's edges – his face, like marble, registering nothing. The initial surprise of Lussurioso at the forwardness of Piato gives way to the (mistaken) belief that his very form has been tailored to the intentions of the lecher. He believes that his new servant's blankness is a sign he is receptive to imprint and not, as it is, the very appearance of deceit: 'Fit, fit for me, e'en trained up to my hand' (I.iii.46); 'He's e'en shaped for my purpose' (57).

Vindice lays on a vision of a suggestible servant impressed with the vice of the master. Lussurioso's asides attribute to the formation of Piato a kind of syntax: 'trained up', 'shaped' for 'my hand', 'my purpose'. The sense here of Piato as a kind of prosthesis to the master, or his tool, recalls the Hamlet of Q1 ('the poisoned instrument within my hand?' (Q1 17.95); and, obversely, 1 Servant's sudden interjection during Gloucester's blinding: 'Hold your hand, my Lord' (*King Lear*, III.vii.71).[75] Such moments allude to the co-dependence of 'good action' and the exercise of authority by proxy. Paul Griffiths notes that the phrase 'at [one's] own hand' referred to working alone outside regulatory instititions, without master, likely improperly.[76] Piato appears ready to act as the hand of his master, to perform for him upon 'a lady'. The name of Vindice's sister is withheld awhile from Piato, its reception (located within the co-ordinates of giving/taking that structures the speech of both master and servant) thus emphasised as a kind of finalisation in the contract between the two men. Lussurioso piatos Castiza: Lord (subject), Servant (verb), Woman (object). This is Lussurioso's

Figure 4.1 Frontispiece, '*A Horrible Cruel and Bloudy Murther*, committed at Putney in Surrey on the 21 of Aprill last, 1614, being Thursday, upon the body of Edward Hall *a Miller of the same parish*, Done by the hands of *John Selling, Peeter Pet* and *Edward Streater*, his servants' (London, 1614). © Bodleian Library: 4° G 29(5) Art.

version. It misunderstands what Piato is. Although Vindice takes the opportunity to test the virtue of his own family, Piato will do nothing for his lord. Lussurioso holds this contract to be the means to the end (Castiza). Instead this encounter between the lord and his new servant works not on Vindice's house but on Lussurioso, making his lust appear pointless. Revenge is shown as an accomplishment of service: an autonomy of action won in a contract to deceive. The acting of service appears as an undoing of that contract under the rubric of which it is notionally achieved.

Performance

In the nineteenth century, Hegel could describe the following difficulty in the concept of contract: 'The distinction between *property* and *possession*, the substantial and external aspect [of ownership] becomes, in contract, the distinction between the common will as *agreement* and its actualization through *performance*.'[77] At the beginning of the seventeenth century, the distinction between agreement and performance was influencing common law. *Assumpsit* – which refers both to a promise as well as to the action taken by one party against the other in the event they fail to perform it – gained ground over debt as a means of judging contract disputes. As Luke Wilson has shown, the victory of Coke in *Slade's Case* (1597–1602) suggested that contracts were necessarily incomplete at the time of bargaining, their completion contingent on 'bilateral performance'. The *assumpsit* invested the interval between promise and performance with a new value, determined retroactively by the (fictional) promise said to have attended the entrance into contract.[78] *Assumpsit* was used increasingly to settle matters where, by departing service or otherwise misbehaving, the servant broke covenant with his master.[79] This was because the law of debt that had been used to understand failures of contracts covered under the durable Statute of Labourers (1351) was difficult to apply to agreements of general service. The latter were obviously distinct from the provision of particular goods or actions (those transactions being more readily understood in terms of debt).

Typical contracts of waged service had the servant commit to 'dwell, tarrie, serve, and abide [. . .] unto the full end and terme', while he 'well, faithfully, and obediently serve[d]' his lord.[80] In order for the largely oral contracts involved in the procurement of servants to be binding, the master had to offer 'consideration': food, clothes, shelter and other provisions such as to support their servant. Although consideration, like the promise, was a complex legal fiction, in this context it dovetailed with paternalist expectations. Didactic works espoused the virtues of a master who treated his servants fairly. Although servants deserting their service were entitled to nothing, and were vulnerable to prosecution under trespass and *assumpsit*, masters frequently put their servants out of doors on spurious grounds before their time was up. The gap between *consideratio* or promise and performance has been shown to be important to comic confusion in early modern farce.[81] In revenge tragedy, the service contract appears manipulable, disposable and obscure – because it was.

Although the servant was not obliged to obey illegal commands such as those received by Piato or Bosola, the covenant of waged service included an array of possible services. The servant entering contracts bounded by time rather than skill sold their labour power in the abstract. This distinction, between concrete and abstract labour, is familiar from Marx; but the abstract formalisation of service, the subsidence of godly obedience into a problem of appearance, was already of serious concern to the religious and political writers of early modern England. Neither is this difficulty readily understood as a distinction between essence and appearance, translated into obedience and deceit. John Ford's *'Tis Pity She's a Whore* (1633) explores the premise that loyalty itself might needs involve a disturbing manipulation of appearances. When Hippolita engages Vasques as an intriguer in her service, actual loyalty is performed as a lament for the suffering of old trusty servants:

HIPPOLITA	Wilt thou feed always upon hopes? Well, I know thou art wise, and seest the reward of an old servant daily what it is.
VASQUES	Beggary and neglect.
HIPPOLITA	True; but *Vasques*, wert thou mine, and would bee private to me and my designs, I here protest myself, and all what I can else call mine, should be at thy dispose.[82]

Like Hoffmann, Hippolita trespasses against Soranzo in seeking to co-opt his servant, but the false contract into which Vasques enters himself involves the very model of generous consideration. In return for 'rest and security', he vows to be 'a special actor' in the designs of his mistress, whatsoever they be, and never to disclose them until they be 'effected'. The insistence of Hippolita upon his discreet possession of those things 'private to me and my designs', on his 'silence' (761) and 'secrecy' (768; 1517), ironically produces the inwardness so often associated with the avenger as the discretion of the servant under contract.

In the fourth Act, Vasques finally confirms that he has tricked Hippolita in order to serve Soranzo the better, but this does not simply close the (sub-)plot. Whilst the character of Vasques is 'loyal', his characterisation relies upon repeated switches between loyalty and betrayal, or rather upon the impression of his movement in and out of a consistent term of service before his loyalties can be laid bare. Vasques achieves recognition as an *exorbitantly, ferociously* loyal agent. Having just finished presenting himself falsely to Giovanni as his trusty servant, he proudly declares his success to his master: 'Sir, I am made a man, I have plied my cue with cunning and success' (IV.iii. 250–1). Vasques is 'made a man' because he has performed his contract of obedience to his master: he is made a [serving]man. He is also 'made a man' in the general sense seemingly excluded by the first: he is self-possessed. The word 'ply', so proximate acoustically if not etymologically to 'play', refers to several actions at once. Vasques has plied Giovanni: he has given him a false cue. He has plied his cue as a tradesman would his trade: Vasques has dissembled like an experienced player, a professional. For an actor to ply his cue was a kind of straining obedience, the work of his peculiar service. For all its nearness to 'play', 'ply' registers diligence. To ply cues was to produce the actor's part, which was not a mere fiction but also, as Stern and Palfrey suggest, 'self-revealing, self-describing, and [. . .] self-fulfilling', with 'self-worth and part [. . .] intertwined'.[83] Vasques has taken his chances; steered a course. He has turned, folded, bent, braided or intertwined his cue as if it were cloth (Latin: *plicare*).

Livery denoted a servant in performance of service, and indicated that the wearer was not himself. That villains and thieves went about impersonating servants was a common concern, but many citizens took the connection between livery and identity entirely at face value. A serving-man, joked Thomas Overbury, 'tels without asking who ownes him, by the superscription of his Livery'.[84] Samuel Rowlands was more circumspect, claiming that there were many delinquent and idle rogues 'about the Citie and the suburbs', 'that under the habit of a Gentleman or serving man, think themselves free from the whip, although they can give no honest account of their life'.[85] In the hearings for the Norwich affray involving the Queen's Men in 1583, some deponents expressed naive confusion that the actors should not have been in the livery of their service as the affair spilled over into the street. Margery Bloom, for instance, found it hard to reconcile what she had witnessed with allegations against the 'redcoats' (the name for Queen's servants), because 'no of them had [on] there cotes at that tyme'.[86] A philosophical dialogue of 1602 uses cognition of livery as an example of false syllogism:

> You say he is a serving-man, because he weares a blue coate; this *because*, signifieth here in this speech a Probable co[n]sequution [*sic*], because few weare

a blue coate but serving men. A blue coate makes not a serving man, no more than a hood a Monck. For if it shoulde be the cause of a serving man, then if a woman put it on, she were a serving man.[87]

Livery could be stolen.[88] Robert Persons, reporting on Edward Coke's inappropriate 'levity of speech', puts an anti-Catholic slander in his mouth involving a dastardly abbot who 'tooke on a serving mans apparrel' so that he could brawl with a hedge-breaker.[89] Professional actors left their livery at home. On the stage it was only invisibly present, licensing the very activity which most undermined the stable relationship between identity and clothing that livery was thought to guarantee. Every other year, each member of the King's Men received a little over three yards of crimson cloth.[90] One of the few liberties accorded to players was exemption from sumptuary law, which among other things forbade serving-men from wearing 'any Shert, or Shert band, under or upper Cappe, Bonet, or Hat garnished, mixt, made, or wrought with silke, golde, or siluer'.[91] The same exemption exposed the player to double suspicion, appearing always with the aspect of the 'slovenly servingman' who had 'exceed[ed] the boundes of his calling, and [crept] into acquaintance with velvet, sattin, and such costly stuffe'.[92]

When, at the beginning of *'Tis Pity*, Vasques challenges the braggart Grimaldi to a duel, he is accused of seeking a performance to which his livery does not entitle him: 'think'st thou I'll balance my reputation with a cast-suit?' Vasques tells him that his master 'keeps servants thy betters in quality and performance' (I.ii.8–12). Service is expanded to take in the elevations, or apparent elevations, of competent swordplay: Vasques has been sent in place of his master as part of a calculated insult. But Vasques himself stresses that he is indeed Grimaldi's better, in quality and performance. Grimaldi's harping is a performance fit for a coquean – a mannish woman – and Vasques makes that performance into a profession, so that Grimaldi sounding like a coquean not only announces but creates and confirms his social identity. By contrast, Grimaldi clings to the ideology of noble essentiality or blood, like Peacham:

> we [must not] Honor or esteeme those ennobled, or made Gentle in blood, who by Mechanicke and base meanes, have raked up a masse of wealth, or because they follow some great man, weare the Cloath of a Noble Personage, or have purchased an ill Coat at a good rate; no more than a player upon the Stage, for wearing a Lords cast suit: since nobilitie hangeth not upon the aiery esteeme of vulgar opinion, but is indeed of it selfe essentiall and absolute.[93]

By this time, the language of blood was opposed by an ascendant ideology of deeds and manners.

Tirades against waged service and its implications insisted on the performances that would mark out the noble serving-man from the common servant, since livery or household identity was no longer any guarantee of probity or godliness. A 1598 tract entitled *A Health to the gentlemanly profession of serving-men*, authored by 'I.M.', described these true serving-men as 'men of [...] courage, not fearing to fight in the maintenaunce of their Maisters credite'; 'Men of strength, of activitie'; 'Men fine, neate, and nimble'. I.M. added that 'the Clowne, the Sloven, and Tom althummes, are as farre unfit for this profession, as Tarltetons toyes for Paules Pulpit'.[94] Here noble agency is imputed to the activity of service ('gentlemanly serving-men'), but the possible claims of the player to this nobility are pre-empted instantly. Anxiety hovers here, and occasions the pre-emption. If nimble and active performances could glean some of this magic stuff, nobility, then players, like Vasques, were well-positioned to discover in their own profession some reprieve from dishonour. I.M. insists instead on the inherent idleness and slovenliness of the professional player: however graceful, active, neat, or nimble the player's performance, it was an expression of an undeletable and incorrigible idleness. The claims of Vasques to performance are therefore deeply ambiguous in an actor's mouth.

The player in particular was incarnated the idle servant, producing more idle servants. The legal imperative for the Tudor actor, 'mighty of body' and 'able to labour', was to become a patronised servant as a validation of his physical capacity for work, but the city anti-theatricalists complained that the theatres were 'the ordinary places for vagrant persons, Maisterles men [...] and other idele and daungerous persons', and that plays and theatres 'maintaine[d] idlenes in such persons as haue no vocation & draw apprentices and other servantes from theire ordinary workes'.[95] From this perspective, playing was an animate idleness. Revenge tragedy frequently discovers this in the intriguing, active servant whose performances of service are opaque, misdirected or bewildering. In *The Duchess of Malfi*, the scene in which the Duchess is murdered is a travesty of the household. Undone by her love for one household servant (Antonio) and the deceit of another (Bosola), the Duchess ends her life with a series of commands to servants: 'Pull, and pull strongly, for your able strength / Must pull downe heaven upon me. *They strangle her*' (IV.ii.217–24). 'Able strength' recalls the statutes that defined productive capacity as being 'myghtie in body and able to laboure'. Bosola's hideous exploitation of a capacity for ruthless action makes him irredeemable, the 'bloudy beaste' and 'pestilent manqueller' of Painter's moralising original:[96] 'Some other strangle the children' is the order he speaks a moment later (226), recalling the Duchess's use of the word 'other' as a reference to Bosola beneath his mask. It is precisely this irredeemability, and its association with self-alienation ('Never in my own shape, / That's forfeited', IV.i.131–2), that permits a delineation of character, and a redemption from merely formal duty, even at that very moment in the play when the agency of Bosola is most wholly suborned to the instructions of another, Ferdinand. It is from this point that the servant Bosola begins to possess the play, the chief concern of which is now the performance of good service: revenge.

Possession in *The Changeling* is more disturbingly concrete. It features a servant whose performances appear spurious from the start (I.i.95–6). The servant, Deflores, has already distorted and expanded his role as a messenger so as to serve his own ends, forcing errands and framing ways to come into the sight of his desire's object, Beatrice (II.i.29–2). This misuse of position is linked to a claim that his fundamental nobility can be disconnected from his actual performances as a servant: 'Though my hard fate has thrust me out to servitude, / I tumbled into th'world a gentleman' (II.i.48–9). His incomprehension that Beatrice should receive him so coldly arises from this esteem in his own performance, echoed later when his reward for murder is disgust: 'Offended? Could you think so? That were much / For one of my performance, and so warm / Yet in my service' (III.iv.55–9).

The essential problem of their relationship can be understood in terms of consideration. Beatrice thinks she has employed Deflores in the murder in return for gold, but the contract is improperly delineated and closed:

BEATRICE	When the deed's done,
	I'll furnish thee with all things for thy flight;
	Thou mayest live bravely in another country.
DEFLORES	Ay, ay: we'll talk of that hereafter.

(II.ii.143–6)

The deed performed, Deflores considers it 'light and cheap / For the sweet recompense that I set down for't' (III.iv.19–20). The recompense is to be set down subsequent to the act. Beatrice, baffled ('I'm in a labyrinth!', 74), offers Deflores money, but finds this will not answer: 'Do you place me in the rank of verminous fellows / To destroy things for wages?' (66–7). Even still, a note of sudden vulnerability is sounded at the apex of a contract dissolved into outright sexual blackmail: 'You see I have thrown contempt upon your gold: / Not that I want it not, for I do – *piteously*' (14–15, my emphasis). Unlike desire, service must be implicitly 'answerable' (22) when steeped in contractual language. What Deflores performs cannot be legitimately contracted, but his performance raises him from servitude so that he may appear like himself in insisting upon a right to any consideration he might choose to receive. The performance of a service, agreed upon but uncertainly defined, alters the situation of both parties, their reciprocity placed on an entirely different footing: 'Fly not to your birth,' instructs Deflores, 'but settle you / In what the act has made you' (137–8).

Dismissal

In *Horestes* (1567), the Vice tradition is married to the tradition of the insouciant servant that one can trace back past the A and B figures of *Fulgens and Lucrece* (1497), to *The Castle of Perseverance* (c.1440), and most probably to a much more general and nebulous tradition of serving folk fool. Following the execution of Horestes's mother, Revenge is put out of service:

> *Enter the Vyce singing this songe.*
> A newe master, a newe,
> No lenger I maye:
> A byde by this daye
> horestes now doth rew.
> A new master a new
> And was it not yll?
> his mother to kyll?
> I pray you how saye you?
> A new master a new,
> Nowe ites to late
> So shut the gate
> horestes gines to rew.[97]

Later, the Vice reappears in the guise of a beggar, 'trymley promoted': 'A begginge, a begginge, nay now I must go.' But then he abandons that appearance, resolving to seek a new service position: 'What shall I begge: nay thates to bad / Is their neare a man, that a saruant doth lacke?' He takes off his beggar's coat '& all [his] thynges', and addresses the audience: 'What thinke you scorne, me your servaunt to make, / A nother wyll haue me, yf you me for sake' (ll.1247–53). The end of the play ends the service of Revenge, and this is how he appears, but in putting off his beggar's coat he is reduced to the player, speaking as Revenge. The threat – 'A nother wyll have me' – voices an expectation that such servants as he are in demand, but also an assurance that the deceitful facility of the actor will guarantee future employment. Revenge was itself a form of justice inimical to the commonwealth, and the 'bad' servant, in committing petty treasons within the household, inflicted harm upon the state. The actor of Revenge appears here as the social perception of himself in abstract: as the shape-shifting enemy of godly society and its laws.

Many service contracts involved bonds of a year, sometimes several years, that constrained both servant and master. Beier notes that 'living-in servants who stayed more than a year were exceptional.'[98] In *The Tempest* (c.1610), this period of indenture is subtly related to the time of performance. Almost the entire plot – sometimes deemed 'entirely typical of an Elizabethan revenge tragedy' – is shown to occur between the expiry of Ariel's contract of indenture and his actual freedom:[99]

> ARIEL   I prithee,
> Remember I have done thee worthy service,
> Told thee no lies, made thee no mistakings, served
> Without or grudge or grumblings. Thou did promise
> To bate me a full year.[100]

Prospero reminds Ariel that he found him trapped in a cloven pine tree for refusing the 'grand hests' of the witch Sycorax, for being 'a spirit too delicate / to act her earthy and abhorred commands' (I.ii.272–4). Faced with Prospero's threat of a second round of imprisonment, Ariel promises to be 'correspondent to command / And do [his] spriting gently' (297–8); and in turn, Prospero creates a new contract: 'Do so, and after two days / I will discharge thee'. Immediately prior to the Epilogue, Prospero keeps his promise, giving Ariel his last 'charge', the ships to be delivered safely home: 'Then to the elements / Be free, and fare thou well' (V.i.319–20). As in *Horestes*, the Epilogue responds to the difficulty of determining exactly what sort of contract is coming to an end. The dismissal of Ariel lends the Epilogue its central theme: Prospero's want of ready hands. Prospero suddenly acquires the aspect of Ariel, trapped on 'a bare island' by a 'spell': 'Let your indulgence set me free' (*Epilogue* l.20). Prospero is bound by the dissolution of Ariel's bond. He sets Ariel free; now, lacking 'Spirits to enforce' (l.14), he must plead for the same indulgence from the audience. With barely conceivable subtlety, this wandering 'free' reinstates the confusing relation between the term of Ariel's service and the time of the play, so that with applause all its actors will be put out of service.

The word 'free' seems to register comic bounty, the sighing dispersal of players and play-goers in the wake of a happy conclusion. It is better understood as the prospect of tragic destitution. For with the end of the play and his act of service, represented as the nullification of contractual duty and identity, the actor becomes masterless. A servant released from service was usually 'free' in the worst of all senses. This anxiety can be isolated in Prospero's words to Ariel: 'Then to the elements / Be free.' The phrase contains the threat of physical exposure and material lack: Lear put out of doors, 'contending with the fretful elements' (III.i.4); or the creatures keeping Timon of Athens company in 'the spite / Of wreakful heaven, whose bare unhoused trunks, / To the conflicting elements exposed, / Answer mere nature'.[101] A common social history links the epilogue of *Horestes* to the epilogue of *The Tempest*, the beggar's suit to the magician's robe. The putting on and putting off of clothes, and the destruction and remaking of clothing for new theatrical purposes, lent all theatrical garments a 'vagrant' aspect.[102] At the end of *The Tempest*, as at the end of *Horestes*, the vagrant appears flickering in Ariel and Prospero as they are each put differently out of service. The end of each of these plays is about undressing as service ends: 'Noble men [. . .] upon the ill behaviour of their servants, first pull off their livery before they turne them out of service.'[103]

Jean-Christophe Agnew suggests that the ideological expectation that the itinerant actor was 'virtually indistinguishable' from 'the casual labourer and the wandering rogue' underwrote the inclusion of players in the 1572 Vagabonds Act.[104] David Mann has shown that representations of players in plays frequently emphasised their itinerancy.[105] Their touring did not cease with the success of the theatres in London: seasonal considerations and plague restrictions prompted trips across the country and even abroad. The theoretical antinomy of servant and vagabond may be inadequate. The typical travelling player bestrode the line between the two states, apparent structure (service) and its apparent lack (vagabondage). Players were sometimes in the theatre house and sometimes on the road. Actual vagrancy was often impermanent; but so were positions of service. For most of the large numbers of people moving in and out of employment, as Griffiths has suggested, vagrancy was but 'a brief interval', and for many service could be picked up and dropped with some degree of liberty.[106]

The widespread fear of masterless men in early modern societies has been well-documented. At that time, as now, it was not appreciated that a wage economy must needs produce and artificially sustain a surplus of labour in order to suppress wages and disempower subordinates.[107] Even then, however, some writers recognised that criminality could be produced by the imposition of need. John Day, misquoting Thomas More, wrote that 'our *Country first makes Theeves, and then hangs them up*':

> Such [waged servants], while they are in Service, are for the most part exceeding well, but when they are once cashird, and put out of Service, or put

themselves out, and have not wherewithall to maintaine themselues, then are they forced a many of them to steale, and then you knowe what followes.[108]

William Westerman, again citing More's Stranger in a sermon from 1600 entitled 'A prohibition of revenge', wrote that his countrymen 'suffered such a multitude of servingmen, to bee trained up in idlenesse and pride: which after being thrust out of service, must needes be driven to theeverie'.[109] To be a vagrant was to live within the everyday compass of a cultural tautology. Thomas Harman himself described the 'Ruflars' – vagrant, villainous ex-soldiers – as 'out-casts of serving-men', lieutenants of vice who, after an underground apprenticeship of 'a yeare or two at the furthest become upright men', chief and incorrigible rogues – 'unlesse they bee prevented by twinde hemp'.[110] At the same time, military men could lament the enlistment of 'roges, or masterles men, or inhabitants of prisons, such as if they had their deserts, they were to be sent rather to [the] gallowes, then to the warres'.[111] The homeless have been trapped on this ideological merry-go-round for a long time.

Vagrancy was not just a condition of actual poverty, nor merely a legal status, but a social imaginary or fictive identity with real consequences for those who fell under its banner. Falling 'out of service' was widely observed to have terrible consequences:

> Many idle persons drop of Gentlemens houses, who with a frowne of their maister, are turned out of all preferment, not able to get their owne livelyhood, but constrained through want to follow bad courses, & being out of service, fall into offence of lawe, and are many times eaten up by Tyborne.[112]

Dismissal could come on many pretexts, and instantly: here a mere 'frowne' is adequate to inflict poverty, criminality and execution. 'The Servant, that wasteth his masters goods wilfully, shall sodenly be called to an account of his Lord & master, and beeing founde faultie and culpable, shalbe utterly thrust out of service,' wrote the lawyer Thomas Bentley in 1582, pitilessly:

> [Then he will] bee forced to make this or the like pitifull mone, and woeful lamentation: & say, alas, alas what shal I doe, for my master hath put me away: I can neither digge nor labour with my handes to get mine owne lyving, and to begge I am ashamed, to steale I dare not, alas what shal I now do, what shall I most wretched caitiffe doe: and who will now receive me into their house and service. &c [?][113]

The worry that discharged servants could bear enmity towards their former masters was a mainstay of discourse about service. A crime committed by the dismissed servant fell under the law of petty treason, extending this term beyond the scope of the contract itself: 'for the execution of the fact doth respect and looke backe to the original cause, which was the malice the servant conceived against his Master when he was a servant'.[114] Service relations could persist beyond the contract at other times too: Alex Shepard records that witnesses could be deemed unreliable when testifying in defence of former masters.[115]

In *The Duchess of Malfi*, the revenge of Bosola against his former masters is perceived by him as a kind of service to himself, as he breaks from the almost orbital dependence on the Cardinal and Ferdinand that is witnessed early in the play: 'The last part of my life / Hath done me best service,' he exclaims, having killed Ferdinand (V.v.63–4). With the death of his master, service to himself can be announced. It is when Ferdinand and Bosola part company and dissolve their strange contract that both shed their 'nobility'. Ferdinand loses the imputed sanity of governance, Bosola the disguise he wore at murder: 'He's much distracted: Off, my painted honour' (323). Bosola emerges from vicious service and from the disguises of acting at the same moment, which forces a momentary identity of the two. His suddenly empathic character – witness especially the tenderness with which he consoles the Duchess at her revival (IV.ii.328–41) – rises from the ruins not only of his functional theatrical status as villainous servant, but from the disguises it entailed. The shedding of disguise is to Bosola a sort of death, for flesh itself is deemed by him a kind of camouflage: 'And though continually we bear about us / A rotten and dead body, we delight / To hide it in rich tissue.' Bosola repossesses his will from the moral calamity to which his service has brought him. Bosola's growing sensitivity to the Duchess as the human 'object' of his service sustains the independence of his revenge-work. It is here that he begins his service to the dead, and it is in the moral duty of burial that he assumes the guise of the avenger proper, finally blending his elective service with the ancient tragic emphasis on ceremonial propriety: 'I'll beare thee hence, / And execute thy last will' (IV.ii.366–7).

Near the beginning of the final Act, Bosola assumes his original stage-position on the margins of the court. Now he stands for the gnawing guilt of his former master, and the baleful reciprocity of this master–servant relationship. Finally, Bosola's *melancholia* is made substantial in service, and his tragic laments express not only a general scepticism but the perspective of a servant exempted from service. His compassion is tempered by the uncertainty of future accommodation: 'I must looke to my footing; / In such slippery yce-pavements, men had neede / To be frost-nayld well: they may breake their neckes else.' And his revenge is mediated by the need to find and to serve a master, even a dead one (V.ii.322–33). The affinity between service and revenge is articulated with most force at this moment: the play makes little room for the precept that 'there is one common Master of us all, who if Masters doe abuse their servants and the power which they have over them, hee will require, repay, and revenge it'.[116] Broken service calls for Bosola to find a way to serve himself, and pursue an ethical life – 'a most just revenge' – no longer guaranteed by the relative justice of a higher authority. Elsewhere, the prospect of such autonomy is entirely snuffed out. Lorrique in Chettle's *Hoffmann* is driven by a sequence of discoveries from master to master, and back again, until Hoffman stabs him: 'Yet as thou wert my servant just and true, / Ile hide thee in the ditch: give dogs their due' (ll.2426–7).

In *The Revenger's Tragedy*, the actor-servant can be understood as a mediator that vanishes. The action reveals that Lussurioso's syntax of power was illusory. The encounter of the avenger and his victim is mediated by this disappearing prospect of the ideal servant, Piato. Personation shorn of character, he is merely the form through which revenge can be realised, actualised within the court from which the avenger is excluded. Once the 'structure' of revenge 'content' has been realised, Piato vanishes; the 'form' of service is relinquished: a disguise. Curiously, Lussurioso does not mention the instigations of his traitorous servant as he attempts in vain to save himself (II.iii.46–56). His recognition of the treachery is made clear only in an aside, so that the actual existence of Piato is detained as it were from open acknowledgement within the scope of the scene's 'official' and 'legal' narrative (that is, Lussurioso's assault on the bedded Duke and Duchess; his arrest). Piato's mediation vanishes into the scene of his master's undoing. Even as it accomplishes something entirely different, this disappearance conforms to the final perfection in the logic of service itself, which is precisely the self-exemption of the servant from the effects of his service, his invisibility at his own act, the man 'who heareth much and medleth least'.[117] The vanishing mediation of service in the completion of revenge is revealed, through Middleton's play at least, as an allegory of playing that vanishes in the completion of the play, producing a sequence of identities, each of which mediates the others: actor; servant; avenger.

Unmasking

The career of the servant-avenger has thus been traced through its different stages: procurement; performance; dismissal. A prosopography such as has been outlined in this chapter – an essay towards the science of *prosopopeia* rather than a merely rhetorical settlement with 'fained' or 'supposed' persons whom we find convenient to call 'servants' – discovers that the arduousness involved in describing service and servants in social historical terms, and the difficulty of describing particular phenomena in the theatre, such as dramatic type or genre, have a common origin: the misrecognition of human beings involved in the production of social and hermeneutic order. The misrecognition of the actor-servant travels into the poetics of dramatic character, and so into the historical imagination, where it forms a shadow side to the mythology of character. Perhaps every reading of an early modern play includes a desire to resurrect, to rediscover and recognise the human with whom some of us think to share a 'modernity'. In revenge tragedy, the servant is repeatedly dehumanised: he is a dog, a dormouse, a caterpillar, a moth, a creature, a thing. It pays to take such invective seriously, because the servant, as a social imaginary, could not be fully human.

Revenge tragedy relates service to deception and disguise. Disguise often strengthens the apparent reality of a character, because it cunningly replaces one relation – that of actor to *character* – with another – that of *character* to the *persona* it adopts. The difficulty here is that the word 'actor' in this constellation cannot actually denote anything concrete, real, or particular: it is a generalisation that adopts the particularity of historical performances as its most urgent and at the same time its most absent predicate of comprehension. The moment when disguise is removed is frequently the moment when a character seems most transcendentally real, and this is because unmasking invests *character* with the player's physical and social being. In reading play-texts, this unmasking is too easily recruited to a generalised role-playing, the imputed theatricality of society at large. To argue that actual early modern service was itself a 'performance' is not an uncomplicated business. The chief struggle of this chapter has been to hold in view a service acted by servants playing as servants: the specific theatricalities of the new professional theatre houses. In the attempt, it has shown how the category of 'servant' was vulnerable to the epistemological complexity of its treatment in that theatre; and that the drama originating there retains at least some of that potential for epistemic disruption. Several of these plays possess an ability to undo the very terms on which we understand them and their relation to lived history. An explanation for that might include some sort of admission that the structure of our thought still partakes in early modern origins. Revenge tragedy resists that unmasking of the 'actual' servant through which the human is made unrecognisable.

Notes

1. William Shakespeare, *King Lear*, ed. R. A. Foakes, Arden 3rd ser. (Walton-on-Thames, 1997), III.vii.71–4.
2. Stephen Greenblatt, 'Shakespeare and the Ethics of Authority', in David Armitage, Conal Condren and Andrew Fitzmaurice (eds), *Shakespeare and Early Modern Political Thought* (Cambridge, 2009), 64–79, at 76.
3. Richard Brome, *The Antipodes* (London, 1640), Sig. D2^v; Peter Thomson, *On Actors and Acting* (Exeter, 2000), 5.
4. Stanley Cavell, *Disowning Knowledge in Seven Plays of Shakespeare* (Cambridge, 2003), 45–7.
5. M. M. Mahood, *Bit Parts in Shakespeare's Plays* (Cambridge, 1992), 160.
6. John Webster, *The Duchess of Malfi*, in Webster, *Works*, 1: IV.ii.247.
7. Russell West, *Spatial Representations on the Jacobean Stage: From Shakespeare to Webster* (Basingstoke, 2002), 158; Barry Taylor, *Vagrant Writing: Social and Semiotic Disorders in the English Renaissance* (Hemel Hempstead, 1991).
8. Patricia Fumerton, *Unsettled: The Culture of Mobility and the Working Poor in Early Modern England* (Chicago, 2006), 11.
9. Thomas L. Berger, William C. Bradford and Sidney L. Sondergard (eds), *An Index of Characters in Early Modern English Drama: Printed Plays, 1500–1660* (Cambridge, 1998), 7.
10. Ann Kussmaul, *Servants in Husbandry in Early Modern England* (Cambridge, 1981), 3.
11. Recent scholarship of dramatic service includes: Michael Neill, *Putting History to the Question. Power, Politics, and Society in English Renaissance Drama* (New York, 2000), 20–48; Michael Neill, '"He that knowest thine": Friendship and Service in *Hamlet*', in Richard Dutton and Jean E. Howard (eds), *A Companion to Shakespeare's Works*, 4 vols (Oxford, 2003), 1: 319–38; Linda Anderson, *A Place in the Story: Servants and Service in Shakespeare's Plays* (Newark, 2005); David Evett, *The Discourses of Service in Shakespeare's England* (Basingstoke, 2005); Judith Weil, *Service and Dependency in Shakespeare's Plays* (Cambridge, 2005); David Schalkwyk, *Shakespeare, Love and Service* (Cambridge, 2008); David Schalkwyk, '"Love's Transgression": Service, Romeo, Juliet, and the Finality of the *You*', in Graham Bradshaw et al. (eds), *Placing Michael Neill: Issues of Place in Shakespeare and Early Modern Culture*, Shakespearean International Yearbook 11: Special Issue (Farnham, 2011), 111–48; Michelle M. Dowd, 'Desiring Subjects: Staging the Female Servant in Early Modern Tragedy', in Michelle M. Dowd and Natasha Korda (eds), *Working Subjects in Early Modern English Drama* (London, 2011), 131–44; Elizabeth Rivlin, *The Aesthetics of Service in Early Modern England* (Evanston, 2012).
12. See James C. Scott, *Weapons of the Weak: Everyday Forms of Peasant Resistance* (New Haven, 1985); Andy Wood, 'Deference, Paternalism and Popular Memory in Early Modern England', in Steve Hindle, Alexandra Shepard and John Walter (eds), *Remaking English Society: Social Relations*

and Social Change in Early Modern England (Woodbridge, 2013), 233–53; Liam J. Meyer, '"Humblewise": Deference and Complaint in the Court of Requests', *Journal of Early Modern Studies* 4 (2015), 261–85.
13. See Hillary Taylor, 'The Price of the Poor's Words: Social Relations and the Economics of Deposing for One's "Betters" in Early Modern England', *Economic History Review* (forthcoming).
14. G. W. F. Hegel, *Elements of the Philosophy of Right*, ed. Allen W. Wood, trans. H. B. Nisbet (Cambridge, 1991), 97 (§67).
15. Neill, *Putting History to the Question*, 33.
16. On this, see Gillian Rose, *Hegel contra Sociology* (London, 2009), esp. 90–6.
17. Mark Thornton Burnett, 'Review of *Shakespeare, Love and Service*, by David Schalkwyk', *Shakespeare Quarterly* 60:2 (Summer, 2009), 230. See also: Mark Thornton Burnett, *Masters and Servants in English Renaissance Drama and Culture* (London, 1997).
18. Schalkwyk, *Shakespeare, Love and Service*, 4; cf. Evett, *Discourses of Service*.
19. Schalkwyk, *Love and Service*, 28–9; Chap. 1, generally. In Kent in the 1590s, 10 per cent of all murders were committed against servants and apprentices by their masters: J. S. Cockburn, 'Patterns of Violence in English Society: Homicide in Kent 1560–1985', *Past & Present* 130:1 (Feb., 1991), 70–106, at 94. The author's reading of their own data is telling: 'Most deaths of servants seem to have been the result of sudden impatience or loss of temper rather than the culmination of a long period of systemic violence', 97. On abuse of servants and its concealment from the record, see Kussmaul's terse summary: *Servants in Husbandry*, 47–8; and Taylor, 'Economics of Deposing'.
20. Weil, *Service and Dependency*, 1.
21. See Schalkwyk, *Love and Service*, ix; Weil, *Service and Dependency*, 2–4. The influence is less obvious, but still important, in Evett's *Discourses*: see 217 n.7; and Neill is most attentive to some of the paradoxes Laslett's account introduces: Neill, *Putting History to the Question*, 21.
22. Peter Laslett, *The World We Have Lost: Further Explored* (London, 1988), 5. See 1–21 on master–servant relations. Cf A. L. Beier, *Masterless Men: The Vagrancy Problem in England, 1560–1640* (London, 1985), 22–8.
23. See John S. Coolidge, *The Pauline Renaissance in England: Puritanism and the Bible* (Oxford, 1970); Julia Reinhard Lupton, 'The Pauline Renaissance: A Shakespearean Reassessment', *The European Legacy: Towards New Paradigms* 15:2, Special Issue: Shakespeare and the Ethics of Interpretation (2010), 215–20.
24. Peter Laslett, *Family Life and Illicit Love in Earlier Generations* (Cambridge, 1977); Peter Laslett, 'Family and Household as Work Group and Kin Group: Areas of Traditional Europe Compared', in Richard Wall et al. (eds), *Family Forms in Historic Europe* (Cambridge, 1983), 513–63.
25. See Keith Wrightson, *Earthly Necessities: Economic Lives in Early Modern Britain* (New Haven, 2000), 58–9; Michael Mitterauer, 'Servants and Youth', *Continuity and Change* 5 (1990), 11–38; Michael Mitterauer, *Sozialgeschichte der Jugend* (Frankfurt a.M., 1986).

26. On its often bitter reality, see Michelle M. Dowd, *Women's Work in Early Modern Literature and Culture* (Basingstoke, 2009), Chap. 1; Susan Amussen, 'Punishment, Discipline, and Power: The Social Meanings of Violence in Early Modern England', *Journal of British Studies* 34:1 (1995), 1–34; Martin Ingram, *Church Courts, Sex and Marriage in England, 1570–1640* (Cambridge, 1987), 259–81.
27. See Christopher Hill, *Society and Puritanism in Pre-Revolutionary England* (London, 1966), 443–81; Thomas Heywood, *An Apology for Actors* (London, 1612), 44.
28. Michael Neill, 'Ich Dien', *London Review of Books* 31:20 (22 October 2009), 11–16.
29. John Cheke, *The Hurt of Sedition* (London, 1549), sigs C2-3.
30. Christopher Hill, *Change and Continuity in Seventeenth-Century England* (New Haven, 1991), 224–6. For a reactionary view from the time, see Thomas Smith, *De Republica Anglorum* (London, 1583), 33: 'the fourth sort or class [. . .] which have no free lande [. . .]'.
31. Paul Halliday, 'Birthrights and the Due Course of Law', in Lorna Hutson (ed.), *The Oxford Handbook of Law and Literature, 1500–1700* (Oxford, 2017), 587–603.
32. 'Estate' was of specific political consequence: see Steve Rappaport, *Worlds within Worlds: Structures of Life in Sixteenth-Century London* (Cambridge, 1989), 218–19.
33. Karl Marx, *Das Kapital*, in *Marx-Engels-Werke*, 43 vols (Berlin, 1956–90), 23: 741–92.
34. Richard Brownlow, *Reports of diverse choice cases in law taken by those late and most judicious prothonotaries of the Common Pleas, Richard Brownlow & John Goldesborough* (London, 1651), 133.
35. Keith Wrightson, '"These which be participant of the common wealth": Class, Governance, and Social Identities in Early Modern England', unpublished working paper.
36. Anon., *A briefe discourse of two most cruell and bloudie murthers* (London, 1583), Sig. B2^v.
37. Schalkwyk, *Love and Service*, 9–12; Meredith Anne Skura, *Shakespeare the Actor and the Purposes of Playing* (Chicago, 1993), 29–63; Paola Pugliatti, *Beggary and Theatre in Early Modern England* (London, 2003).
38. Thomas Nashe, *Have with you to Saffron-Walden* (London, 1596), Sig. S4.
39. Paul Griffiths, *Youth and Authority: Formative Experiences in England, 1560–1640* (Oxford, 1996), 113–75; Burnett, *Masters and Servants*, 14–53.
40. John Cordy Jeaffreson (ed.), *Middlesex County Records*, 4 vols (London, 1886–92), 1: 81.
41. Robert Cleaver, *A Godlie Forme of householde government for the ordering of private families* (London, 1598), Sig. A3^v.
42. William Gouge, *Of Domesticall Duties* (London, 1622), 649.
43. John Fit, *A Diamond most precious* (London, 1577), Sig. B1.
44. J. P. Cooper (ed.), *The Wentworth Papers, 1597–1628* (London, 1973), 15.

45. Cleaver, *Godlie Form*, 29.
46. William Whately, *Prototypes* (London, 1640), 65.
47. Walter Darell, *A Short Discourse of the life of servingmen* (London, 1578), Sig. A4.
48. Humphrey Gifford, *A Posie of Gilloflowers* (London, 1580), Sig. H1.
49. Thomas Smith, *De Republica Anglorum*, 114.
50. John Day, *Day's Festivals* (Oxford, 1615), 251–2.
51. Darell, *Short Discourse*, Sig. B1.
52. Day, *Day's Festivals*, 262.
53. Gouge, *Of Domesticall Duties*, 647.
54. Frances E. Dolan, 'The Subordinate('s) Plot: Petty Treason and the Forms of Domestic Rebellion', *Shakespeare Quarterly* 43:3 (Autumn, 1992), 317–40.
55. Thomas Fosset, *The Servants Dutie* (London, 1613), 46.
56. Matthew Griffith, *Bethel: Or, A forme for families* (London, 1633), 379–80.
57. Henry S. Turner, *The English Renaissance Stage. Geometry, Poetics, and the Practical Spatial Arts, 1580–1630* (Oxford, 2006), 173.
58. Thomas Kyd, *The Spanish Tragedie* (London, 1592), Sig. C3. Modern editors generally bring the stage direction forward.
59. William Fulbeck, *A Parallele or conference of the civill law, the canon law, and the common law of England* (London, 1601), 80.
60. Henry Chettle, *The Tragedy of Hoffman; Or, A Revenge for a Father*, ed. Harold Jenkins and Charles Sisson (Oxford, 1961), ll.63–93.
61. Cleaver, *Godlie Forme*, 384.
62. Christopher Marlowe, *The Jew of Malta*, ed. James R. Siemon (London, 2001), II.iii.165–9.
63. Francis Bacon, *The Twoo Bookes of Francis Bacon. Of the proficience and advancement of learning, divine and humane* (London, 1605), 37.
64. Thomas Dekker, *The Wonderful Yeare 1603* (London, 1603), Sig. B3^v.
65. Thomas Middleton, *The Changeling*, ed. Douglas Bruster, in Middleton, *Works*, II.i.51.
66. Christopher Ricks, 'The Moral and Poetic Structure of *The Changeling*', *Essays in Criticism* 10 (1960), 290–306, at 295–9.
67. Sibylle Baumbach, *Shakespeare and the Art of Physiognomy* (Leicester, 2008), 78.
68. Jeaffreson (ed.), *Middlesex County Records* 1: 160–1.
69. Anon., *The Wonderful Discoverie of the witchcrafts of Margaret and Phillip Flower* (London, 1619).
70. John Kerrigan, *Shakespeare's Binding Language* (Oxford, 2016), 28.
71. Webster, *Works*, 1: 468.
72. *RT*, I.iii.1–10.
73. Leo G. Salingar, '*The Revenger's Tragedy* and the Morality Tradition', *Scrutiny* 6 (1937–8), 402–22.
74. Gouge, *Of Domesticall Duties*, 649; 647.
75. Simon Palfrey and Tiffany Stern, *Shakespeare in Parts* (Oxford, 2007), 325.
76. Griffiths, *Youth and Authority*, 357.
77. Hegel, *Philosophy of Right*, trans. Nisbet, 108 (§78).

78. Luke Wilson, *Theaters of Intention: Drama and the Law in Early Modern England* (Stanford, 2000), 79–80.
79. A. W. Brian Simpson, *A History of the Common Law of Contract: The Rise of the Action of Assumpsit* (Oxford, 1975), 262.
80. William West, *The first part of Simboleography* (London, 1615), §175: 'A Condition for a Servant, or Apprentice', Sig. L4^v.
81. See for example Andrew Zurcher, 'Consideration, Contract, and the End of *The Comedy of Errors*', *Law and Humanities* 1:2 (2007), 145–65.
82. John Ford, *'Tis Pity She's a Whore*, ed. Martin Wiggins (London, 2003), II.ii.135–40.
83. Palfrey and Stern, *Shakespeare in Parts*, 45–6.
84. Thomas Overbury, *Sir Thomas Overburie his wife with new elegies upon his (now knowne) untimely death* (London, 1616), Sig. E1.
85. Samuel Rowlands, *Greenes Ghost haunting conie-catchers* (London, 1602), Sig. A3.
86. David Galloway (ed.), *Norwich: 1540–1642*, Records of Early English Drama (Toronto, 1984), 74.
87. Jeremy Corderoy, *A Short Dialogue, wherein is proved, that no man can be saved without good workes* (London, 1604), 75.
88. Jeaffreson (ed.), *Middlesex County Records* 1: 74–5; Robert Greene, *The Second Part of conny-catching* (London, 1591), Sig. B7; Robert Greene, *The Third and last part of conny-catching* (London, 1592), sigs D1–2.
89. Robert Persons, *A quiet and sober reckoning with M. Thomas Morton [...] also adjoyned a peece of a reckoning with Syr Edward Cooke* (London, 1609), Sig. I3.
90. Ann Rosalind Jones and Peter Stallybrass, *Renaissance Clothing and the Materials of Memory* (Cambridge, 2000), 175.
91. *A Declaration of the Queenes Maiesties will and commaundement, to have certaine lawes and orders put in execution against the excesses of apparell* (London, 1588), [fol. 2].
92. Henry Crosse, *Vertues Commonwealth* (London, 1603), Sig. L1.
93. Henry Peacham, *The Compleat Gentleman* (London, 1622), 3.
94. I.M. [?Gervase Markham], *A Health to the gentlemanly profession of serving-men* (London, 1598), sigs B2^v-B3.
95. 22 Hen. VIII, c. 12, *An Acte concernyng punysshement of Beggers & Vacabundes*, in Alexander Luders et al. (eds), *The Statutes of the Realm, printed [...] from original records and authentic manuscripts*, 12 vols (London, 1810–28), 3: 328, whence 14 Eliz. c. 5, *An Acte for the punishment of Vacabondes and for Relief of the Poore & Impotent*, in Luders et al. (eds), *Statutes*, 4: 590; repr. Chambers, *ES* 4: 269–7: 'All and everye persone and persones beynge whole and mightye in Body and able to labour, havinge not Land or Maister [...]'; The Lord Mayor and Aldermen to the Privy Council, 28 July 1597, repr. *MSC* 1: 78; and Chambers, *ES* 4: 321–2.
96. William Painter, *The Palace of Pleasure*, ed. Joseph Jacobs, 3 vols (London, 1890), 3: 42.
97. John Pykering, *A Newe Enterlude of Vice*, in Marie Axton (ed.), *Three Tudor Classical Interludes* (Cambridge, 1982), ll.1019–30.

98. Beier, *Masterless Men*, 24.
99. E. M. W. Tillyard, *Shakespeare's Last Plays* (London, 1938), 49.
100. William Shakespeare, *The Tempest*, ed. Virginia Mason Vaughan and Alden T. Vaughan, Arden 4th ser. (London, 1999), I.ii.246–50.
101. William Shakespeare [and Thomas Middleton], *Timon of Athens*, ed. H. J. Oliver, Arden 2nd ser. (London, 1984), IV.iii.230–4.
102. Jones and Stallybrass, *Renaissance Clothing*, 175–206.
103. John Downame, *Lectures upon the foure first chapters of the prophecie of Hosea* (London, 1608), 89.
104. Jean-Christophe Agnew, *Worlds Apart: The Market and the Theater in Anglo-American Thought, 1550–1770* (Cambridge, 1986), 66.
105. David Mann, *The Elizabethan Player: Contemporary Stage Representation* (London, 1991), 14.
106. Griffiths, *Youth and Authority*, 334; 167.
107. The baseless assumption that the servant's wage would be supplemented by income from smallholding kept wages low and most servants in poverty, just as in the twenty-first century zero-hour contracts are often informally predicated on the assumption of secondary employment: Beier, *Masterless Men*, 26; Hill, *Change and Continuity*, 220.
108. Day, *Day's Festivals*, 252.
109. William Westerman, *Two Sermons of Assise the one intituled A prohibition of revenge, the other, A sword of maintenance* (London, 1600), 24.
110. Thomas Harman, *The Groundworke of Conny-Catching* (London, 1592), Sig. B1.
111. Matthew Sutcliffe, *The Practice, proceedings, and lawes of armes* (London, 1593), 62.
112. Henry Crosse, *The Schoole of Pollicie* (London, 1605), Sig. S3^v.
113. Thomas Bentley, *The Sixt Lampe of Virginitie* (London, 1582), 68. One of the fictitious petitions included in Anthony Nixon's *The Foot-Post of Dover* (1616) was another such lament, of 'an old Servingman, a young beggar': 'So long as I was strong, I was backt with something: so long as I could perform all serviceable duties, I wanted for no promises. But Time which turneth all things, hath turned me out of service [. . .] Thus have I bene served for all my serving [. . .] A man were better serve hogges than some men, many wives, most widdowes.': Anthony Nixon, *The Foot-Post of Dover* (London, 1616), sigs C4–C4^v.
114. Ferdinando Pulton, *De pace Regis et regni viz. A treatise declaring which be the great and generall offences of the realme* (London, 1609), 111.
115. Alexandra Shepard, *Accounting for Oneself: Worth, Status, and the Social Order in Early Modern England* (Oxford, 2015), 183. Also see Taylor, 'Economics of Deposing'.
116. Thomas Fosset, *The Servants Dutie*, 46.
117. Darell, *A Short Discourse*, Sig. A1^v.

Chapter 5

Figures

> The corpse was the first object for men.
> Posed before them like a problem and an obstacle, lying.
>
> Michel Serres, *Statues*

'But are you sure they are dead?' Here, in the Additions to *The Spanish Tragedy* of 1602 that may have been written in around 1597, Hieronimo voices a new and surprising uncertainty as to the reality of his theatre trick (*ST* IV.iv.[1]). Such a question is impossible to Greek tragedy, but death in Elizabethan and Jacobean drama generally happens in the light.[1] Its tragic catastrophes often include specific injunctions for the disposal of bodies: 'Go, bear those bodies to a place more comely'; 'bear up those tragic bodies'; 'bear them from hence'; 'take up the bodies'; 'take up these slaughtered bodies, see them buried'; 'remove the bodies'; 'go bear his body hence'; 'take up our hapless son'; 'remove the bloodless body'; 'remove these ruin'd bodies from our eyes'. Such notices are eminently pragmatic, and it is part of the playwright's competence to furnish them, but the actions they provoke are involved in a strange conjunction of stage management and the representation of political or ethical renewal. Perhaps because the need for an efficient disposal of tragic bodies is so often conspicuous, tragic ends become inconclusive. Although John Webster was not an incompetent playwright, *The Duchess of Malfi* supplies neither internal nor ordinary stage directions for the removal of bodies, so that the dead linger for so long that they eventually seem to get back up and look at us.[2]

The decaying or dying body has a tyrannous presence on Webster's stage.[3] After the first blow, it takes Flamineo dozens of lines in verse and prose to die in *The White Devil* (*WD* V.vi.227–70), giving him enough time to enquire into the make of the blade and observe his own quivering life: 'I recover like a spent taper, for a flash' (230; 278). This was Flamineo's second protracted 'death': he had faked an elaborate expiration not minutes before, in order to reveal a plot. 'I could kill you forty times a day,' says one of his enemies. Given Flamineo's durability, it would be dark before he spoke his last – even if the killers made an early start. Flamineo's double death is not simply funny, but experiments at the knife-edge between tragic seriousness and outright farce. The dead in the theatre concentrate and condense the difficulties associated with determining 'forms and shapes' in theatre and drama, because they introduce a dysfunctional dualism of uncertain materials and uncertain spirits.[4] When Ferdinand looks at the corpse of the Duchess and says, 'Mine eyes dazell' (IV.ii.251), we are called to envisage the tears welling in his eyes, refracting candlelight and doubling images. But that famous line also refers obliquely to specific difficulties of cognition, of saying exactly what this dead thing is and what it means to say it is dead. 'For who'er saw this duchess live and die,' wondered Thomas Middleton, 'That could get off under a bleeding eye?'[5] The Duchess has not yet died – 'She's warme, she breathes' (IV.ii.330) – but this is revealed only after Bosola and Ferdinand have fallen out over the spectacle of what they take to be her corpse.

Although such tortuousness has often appalled moral critics as the sign of an impure theatre, it in fact attenuates the fanaticism which Lionel Abel finds necessary for the infliction of tragic death.[6] Without the security of fate, death in early modern drama became less a question of 'when' than it was of 'how'. As previous chapters have argued, this interrogation of 'how' developed new problems of the 'who'. Early modern tragic drama struggles to reconcile myths, historical persons and actors whose new status expressed the separation of theatre from the *polis* in which tragic death is often assumed to have had formative power. Webster's tragedies seem moreover to show how the post-Reformation inability fully to delete the premise that there were inter-penetrating communities of living and dead resulted in a threat to the distinction between life and death insofar as it could be represented in secular tragedy. Ordinarily this dilemma is reframed in terms of an imputed delight in the macabre, or in terms of philosophical pessimism. As Joseph Morris remarked long ago, Webster seems to have seen 'the potential death-cloth clinging round every living person' – students know this from T. S. Eliot's claim that 'Webster was much possessed by death / And saw the skull beneath the skin,' intuiting that 'thought clings round dead limbs'.[7]

Whose limbs? Writing of Richard Perkins's original performance as Flamineo in *The White Devil*, Webster declared that it 'crowned' both the beginning and end.[8] This phrase recurs in the last breath of *The Duchess of Malfi*: '*Integrity of life, is fames best friend / Which nobly (beyond Death) shall crowne the end*' (V.v.119–20). Delio had predicted that fame would melt like snow, recalling Bosola's evocation of 'slippery yce-pavements' (V.ii.324). Yet the closing lines imply that the actor, a 'wretched eminent thing' in performance, can win an integrity and fame 'beyond Death': beyond the end of the performance. Or he can break his neck and never be remembered: Bosola's thought. Although he suspects a different fate, Bosola is indeed remembered, in the performance wherein his death is compassed, and in a reading that speculates upon or visualises such a performance: 'Death hath ten thousand severall doors,' laments the Duchess, 'For men, to take their Exits: and 'tis found / They go on such strange geometricall hinges, / You may open them both wayes' (IV.ii.206–9). This extraordinary deformation of the standard *theatrum mundi* trope forces the singularity of tragic death into the context of its infinitely varied figurations.

In this final substantive chapter, such provocations are taken totally seriously. This may seem perverse given the common wisdom that revenge tragedy borders continually on the laughable, and that it has become all but impossible to hear long auto-elegies without a smile ('I have lost my voice / Most irrecoverably'). In Thomas Pynchon's 1966 novel *The Crying of Lot 49*, a synopsis of the fictional seventeenth-century revenge play *The Courier's Tragedy* becomes an absurdly protracted discourse upon the violence of revenge tragedies, complete with elaborate, agonising death-scenes that include glossectomy, castration, 'a lye pit, land mines, [and] a trained falcon with envenomed talons', adding up to what one of the watching characters describes as 'a Road Runner cartoon in blank verse'.[9] A century earlier, an anonymous little tirade against Wilkie Collins cited the supposedly unmerited success of *The Spanish Tragedy* as an indication that only hindsight and the development of good taste could amend the vagaries of 'the mob': for 'sensationalism must be left to be dealt with by time, and the improvement of the public taste'.[10] William Archer's attacks on what he saw as the appeasement of 'an eagerly receptive but semi-barbarous public' were just the cutting edge of scorn for a popular stage on which 'there is scarcely any room [...] for all the corpses' (echoed in Pynchon as 'a stage dense with corpses').[11] The assertion of Fredson Bowers that revenge plays were 'linked only by a delight in blood and sensationalism' eclipsed a subtler tradition of reading that had its real spring in Elmer Edgar Stoll's erudite 1905 book on Webster, even as it set out a lasting concept of the 'revenge tragedy'.[12] Critics have continued to blanch at a record of brutality that is routinely treated in terms of taste. Peter Sacks describes a 'revoltingly grotesque series of horrors [...] [that] seem to have little function but to ironize man's inadequate expressions of pain and loss'.[13] Linda Woodbridge qualifies her discussion of the political content of the best revenge plays by stating, 'there is no point denying that England's golden age of revenge drama [...] luxuriated in sensationalism'.[14] That there is much to find disturbing in these plays might go without saying: 'some other strangle the children', speaks Bosola. Perhaps one wishes he had not said it – or finds it amusing that he does. Either way, it ought to be considered that the question of who or what Bosola is when he speaks those words is rather too vexing to sustain outrage or cynicism.

I seek to explain the preoccupation with lingering death in English revenge plays not as 'sensationalism', but as one consequence of more or less serious artistic enquiries into the altered matter of tragedy. Moral and aesthetic judgement of violent tragic extremities are undermined by exploring how those same scenes chip away at the very foundations of equitable judgement. The chapter concludes by outlining some of the paradoxes of reading and watching revealed here and in earlier pages; and turns to the *figural* as the mode of interpretation through which many of those paradoxes can be disclosed, registered and worked through. By unearthing the topic of *figura* with reference to Erich Auerbach's increasingly obscure essay on its history in Western culture, I expand some of the premises introduced in the previous chapters and cautiously broach the possibility that the issues of action and figuration they pursue might show themselves, from a new angle, as blind-spots not only in early modern knowledge but in the concept of history that informs modern historicism.

Dead Sensibilities

Webster inherited his father's carting business, which had at times involved the transportation of plague victims to large pits and at others the transportation of the frightened living out of the city.[15] He also flattered other dead people with artificial pyramids encrusted with artificial jewels, paraded through Cheapside.[16] One might say, as Webster himself did of the Black Prince in *A Monumental Column*, that it was Webster's 'trade / To fashion death-beds, and hath often made / Horror look lovely'.[17] Just as often, he dumps dead flesh in public and lets it rot there. A stage-direction instructs the actor of the Duchess of Malfi to sleep with his eyes open, like a 'madman' as Cariola suggests, but probably more like a corpse (IV.ii.16–17) – 'she's somewhat a grave look about her', as Vindice jokes elsewhere, having made his sister's skull into a person who seems so whole in the half-light as to prove kissable (*RT*,

III.v.135). 'Who do I looke like now?' asks the Duchess a few moments later.

> Like to your picture in the gallery,
> A deale of life in shew, but none in practise;
> Or rather like some reverend monument
> Whose ruines are even pittied.
>
> (IV.ii.30–4)

The first comparison threatens to reduce the Duchess to mere appearance, making her actor at once a moving picture and a corpse, having no life 'in practise' despite 'practise' describing skill at making oneself a living 'picture' in the theatre. The second simile implicitly connects 'monument' to 'show' and 'ruin' to 'practice'. Real people are monuments; their impersonators, their ruins. Whence Bosola to the Servant bearing up the body of Antonio: 'Looke thou represent, for silence, / The thing thou bear'st' (V.iv.83–4). Webster explores this confusing dialectic of mimesis and deathliness at length – by making the Duchess die slowly. Bosola constructs a 'tomb' for her before she dies, bringing her with pseudo-sacramental care 'by degrees to mortification' (IV.ii.164). 'Mortification' means several things at once: death, accomplished; a suppression of flesh and its desires; shame or humiliation. As Simon Palfrey and Tiffany Stern have recognised in their study of actors' cues, 'the dying moment was central not only to tragic teleology, but to contemporary appraising of an actor's relative mastery of his craft'.[18] At the moment of her death, the Duchess is both a husk of a person, her player's skill (or lack thereof) most apparent; and a character in its most enlarged and emancipated stage, on the verge of entering myth. The latter effect is less variable than the appearance of skill, because of the resilience of the supposition that a bodily mortification augurs a spiritual effect. As Joseph Hall remarked in a 1628 sermon to James I, 'hee that spares not to act meet and due penalties upon the flesh, gives more colour of the soules humiliation', for 'he that made both, will have us crucifyed in both'.[19] The mortification of the Duchess causes her spiritualisation: 'I am Duchesse of *Malfy* still' (IV.ii.131).

But Webster will not let her go. After her strangulation, she seems to become a voice emanating from a ruin, and suddenly an even stranger afterlife is in prospect:

> ANTONIO   I doe love these auncient ruynes:
> We never tread upon them, but we set
> Our foote upon some reverend History,
> And questionles, here in this open Court
> (Which now lies naked to the injuries

	Of stormy weather) some men lye Enterr'd	
	Love'd the Church so well, and gave so largely to't,	
	They thought it should have canopide their Bones	
	Till Doomes-day: But all things have their end:	
	Churches, and Citties (which have diseases like to men)	
	Must have like death that we have.	
ECHO	*(from the Dutchesse Grave)* Like death that we have.	
DELIO	Now the *Eccho* hath caught you.	
		(V.iii.9–20)

The Echo, and the 'Spirit' that some suppose to cause it, is older than the Duchess: Delio indicates that this 'wall / (Peece of a Cloyster)' is known for it (4–5). Delio also suggests an uncertainty and perhaps even a playful scepticism about the echo's supernatural properties. Elsewhere echoes are synonymous with flattery (V.ii.235–7). The play calls for the actor of the Duchess to give voice to the echo, or to impersonate the sonic effect. The tonal qualities of the echo cannot be read, so that it is impossible to determine whether it is natural or supernatural. Yet the reader still knows they are to inscribe the identity of the Duchess into the sound, for this is plainly the logic of the play ('*wifes-voyce*', 26): the echo is itself an echo, reciting and urging us to recall the Duchess happy, declaring, 'We now are man and wife, and 'tis the church / That must but echo this' (I.i.475–6). The distance between a *mere* echo and the voice of a ghost is itself re-experienced as the distance between the 'voice' of the echo on the printed page and the presence of a real person speaking its words in a ruined theatre. *The Duchess of Malfi* seems reflexively to anticipate this curious affinity. In describing the ancient ruin, the very stage becomes the image of a future ruin, an 'open Court / (Which now lies naked to the injuries / Of stormy weather)'. The monastic ruin is implicitly extended to encompass the whole theatrical place, the 'Court' where 'men lye Enterr'd', as if the actors themselves were formerly 'canopide [. . .] Bones' now exposed to view and animation. *The Duchess of Malfi* moved between Blackfriars and the open-aired Globe. Such a dis-canopying allowed this line to refer prefiguratively to its actors as echoic 'bones' beneath future heavens, when in Blackfriars it populated the ruin with phantoms of the past.[20] Out of time, the stage imagined for *The Duchess of Malfi* must be both a monument and a ruin; both a perfect, homogeneous space fit for universal tragedy and a series of broken rooms.[21] 'Bear her into th'next roome,' commands Bosola of Cariola's corpse (IV.ii.243).

Webster's court is always disintegrating. Amidst its fragments, a new monument is prospected: 'Let us make noble use / Of this great ruine; and joyne all our force / To establish this yong hopefull Gentleman /

In's mothers right,' urges Delio (V.v.110–12). Recollection of Antonio's complaint makes this politic establishment of his son ambiguous: 'How they fortifie / Themselves with my ruine!' (V.i.35–6). But if the echoey ruin has already been extended to encompass the stage, and if it here encompasses the matter of tragedy itself, Delio's injunction seems initially to refer neither to the play nor the stage but to Bosola's body, lying before him. This creates a contradiction or disjunction within the finality of Delio's 'ruin', for Bosola had personalised the same term with his dying testament, provoked by the question as to how Antonio had come to be killed:

> In a mist; I know not how:
> Such a mistake as I have often seene
> In a play: Oh, I am gone.
> We are onely like dead wals or vaulted graves,
> That ruin'd, yeildes no eccho. Fare you well.
>
> (V.v.93–7)

The 'meta-theatrical' moment of the first three lines invites us to read the simile ('we are like') with retroactive force: the 'we' refers simultaneously to bare humans and to a corpus of performers. The active form of the verb *ruin* seems to have become usual only from the 1580s, before which *ruin* was something that befell persons and properties, not something that might itself be effected by one person against another. It was a state into which one might fall, which one might seek, or which one might bring another to, but it remained largely intransitive and passive. Bosola uses the word in this older sense, which is carried through into Delio's noun. Now Bosola is dead, but his player lies breathing on the stage as Delio refers to 'this great ruine' (V.v.110). The mediating effect of Delio's speech is to refer *ruin* to the just-ended agency of the player that remains of Bosola. Bosola removes from his killing of Antonio and his own death the question of human agency, thereby settling the objectivity of this tableau as a scene of mischance, ahead of Delio's allusion to its ruinousness. The dislocation of moral agency from the scene seems natural because Bosola is speaking from a time in which his death has already 'happened'.

This deeply strange post-mortem speaking position – the Greeks called such devices *eidolopoeia* ('idol-making') – is contained in the images of the 'dead wall' and the 'vaulted grave'.[22] Those are spaces in which only the sequestered or the dead can hear themselves echo. Ruined, the dead wall and vaulted grave no longer resonate, for they are no longer enclosed. The interior sense perhaps tests a conceit of the soul as an escaping sound. Human consciousness, by extension, is reduced to the overlapping echoes produced within an intact body, sounds nobody hears. There is also an idea that the playhouse is itself a space in which the voices of dead people resonate and vibrate. Webster nudges at the prospect of the theatre as a corporeal hollow; the murmur of its departing audience, the escape of the soul from a ruined body which, the performance over, 'yeildes no [dialogical] eccho'. The dramatic text is also an enclosure in which echoes can be heard. In fact, the repetition of the 'echo' inhabiting the monastic ruin of an earlier scene is perhaps louder on the page than in the theatre. The key problem of moral agency in *The Duchess of Malfi* is thus shrouded by the play in obscure theatre shapes and sounds of uncertain origin. It is connected also to a blurring of animate and inanimate bodies that has been prefigured by the earlier scene in which the artificial waxen figures of Antonio and the children – soundless bodies – are presented to the Duchess as if they were their actual corpses.

Lights! Lights! Lights!

One possible objection to Descartes' consideration of wax is that in trying to supply a phenomenology of a piece of wax so as to isolate intellectual knowledge from physical sensation, the philosopher must perforce suppress the temporality of the actions involved in accomplishing the logical reduction of the wax to 'something extended which is flexible and mutable' (*quam extensum quid, flexibile, mutabile*).[23] What Descartes describes is a set of actions performed by a subject ('Descartes') in time and space. The wax was 'recently' taken from the hive (*nuperrime ex favis fuit educta*); it is brought close to the fire 'while [he] speak[s]' (*dum loquor, igni admovetur*); and the reflective mood is enforced by tense, through which the smell, sight and touch of the wax are consigned to the past (*quid* [. . .] *comprehendebatur*). This narrative is usually accepted as a 'thought experiment'. That is a pre-judgement which somewhat conspires in Descartes' exclusion of historical content – the removal of 'this wax' (*hanc ceram*) from the actual experience of a seventeenth-century philosopher with easy access to a beehive – so as to furnish a purely mental scrutiny. The smell, taste, sight and sound of wax are plainly not abstract in Descartes' account. The descriptive mode of the experiment is at least as historical and specific as it is logical and general. He smelled, he tasted, he heard – and it was *wax* at hand, not any old matter. Jacques Lezra subverts this line of thinking by pointing out that Descartes' block of wax 'is not an accidental figure for the operation of perception': it is chosen so as to enter into a tradition of waxy figurations in ancient philosophy.²⁴ 'This wax' appears to be both a piece of wax (possibly) held in the hand of René Descartes (possibly) in 1638 or 1639; and Plato's wax in *Theaetetus*; Aristotle's wax of *De Anima*; a relative of the wax-tablets and waxen images that recur in ancient thought via Zeno, Ovid, Cicero and the rest. The wax of *Meditations* is a literary substance unknown in the material world, to which it nonetheless appears proper: peculiar philosophical *stuff*. I claim that the substances of early seventeenth-century drama, likewise, cannot be grasped by analogy to the social materials they represent, nor reduced to the bare materials of theatre history. They are simultaneously proper to literary matter and to the theatres in which they were originally produced.

When Descartes turned from his lump of wax to regard humans shuttling back and forth outside his window on the street below, he discovered it had taught him scepticism: 'What do I see except hats and cloaks, which might conceal automata?'²⁵ The properties of the wax figures in *The Duchess of Malfi* create a similar crisis of recognition. They seem to hover between the definitely historical, the illusory and the speculative. Their relation to any sort of human is conspicuously uncertain. Together they make up a *tableau cadavérique* that can be compared to the highly theatrical inset dumbshows of other revenge plays, yet the whole scene seems also to be a dramaturgically impractical and recognisably literary fantasy. The scene has routinely been at the centre of criticisms of Webster's ghoulishness and sensationalism, and continues to exercise critics.²⁶ Certainly the figures are emblematic of the liturgical care with which Bosola and Ferdinand arrange the mortification of the Duchess – wax votives and effigies are proper to the religion of the villains in Webster's play and to their transformation of the scene into a travesty of a church interior.²⁷ Wax death masks were instrumental in the practical development of pictorial realism.²⁸ There were travelling exhibitions of wax effigies in England at the time Webster worked on the play;²⁹ and the sculptor Abraham van der Doort was around to supply such figures.³⁰ As Rory Loughnane persuasively suggests, however, it is overwhelmingly probable that the players themselves played the wax images of their dead characters.³¹ Bosola's description of 'faign'd statues' (IV. ii.338) then seems perfectly accurate. It becomes obvious that some sort of special theatrical substance has been manufactured. Even to denote that residue may involve epistemological difficulties inseparable from the specific terms on which that residue is encountered.

They are not immediately revealed as waxen. It is only afterwards that the audience is informed that they, like the Duchess, have been 'plag'd in art' and that the 'presentations' were 'fram'd in wax'. The reader has benefited in advance from a printed stage direction: '*Here is discover'd, (behind a Travers;) the artificiall figures of* Antonio *and his children; appearing as if they were dead*' (IV.i.54–5). In both cases, a curious sort of knowledge is supplied which the Duchess herself is shown to die without. Margaret Owens suggests that Webster's intent was antithetical to that of Shakespeare's at the end of *The Winter's Tale* – that 'where Shakespeare cultivates indeterminacy on the issue of the statue's substance', Webster guides us 'toward certainty: to the understanding that within the fictive frame of the play, the truth of the spectacle is that the bodies are inorganic'.[32] Loughnane likewise supposes that this trickery called for 'a bewildering suspension of disbelief'. Whether believed or disbelieved, knowledge of these bodies remains deeply uncertain: to some extent the usual questions of credulity and plausibility are red herrings. Loughnane's conjecture as to the effect on the audience seems natural, but it suppresses the contingencies of theatrical circumstance. Upon encountering the inanimate hand in the dark, the Duchess calls for 'light'. Exactly how much light is supplied governs how much belief the audience must suspend. 'Let her have lights enough' (IV.i.52) is an injunction reinforcing Ferdinand's sorcerous control, but also, *a fortiori*, the circumstance that the quantity and effect of the torchlight presently supplied, its adequacy, will vary with every production and with the sensible credulity expected of different audiences. To the reader, the mental scene can be envisaged in bright light or total darkness, with the same uncertainty.

Like Owens, although more explicitly, Loughnane presents his discussion of the wax figures under the rubric of 'meta-theatre' and with reference to 'a blend of Catholic and Protestant detail' in the commemorative practices said to be enacted by the play. The problem of our judgement's participation in the afterlife of the play is pre-empted in Loughnane's essay by two manoeuvres which are instructive to examine. The first is the reduction of the play's textual self-referentiality to plain examples of meta-theatre, presuming all are satisfied that such a term needs no explanation. This move protects historicism from the need to respond to the play's anticipation of its reception and rememberment in a future indeterminate enough to enclose the historicist position. The second is the wholesale relocation and confinement of the contest between text and show created by *The Duchess of Malfi* to a narrower and bifurcated field of historical response: the terms of the play's possible reception by early modern audiences and the terms of its possible reception by early modern readers. In Loughnane's essay this is accomplished through legitimate scholarly reference to the evidently literary scope of the play's first quarto. The epistemological difficulty created by the appearance of theatrical shapes in printed drama is thereby detained. It is reframed more harmlessly as a question of historicist task: with enough contextual information about wax art and theatre practices, the substance of the statues might be specified, and the scene read without difficulty. Within a similar space, Owens can argue that the 'flimsy, composite wax figures' emerge as a critique of aristocratic pretence; and Lynn Maxwell can suggest that the scene is imprinted (not unlike the proverbial wax tablet) with the history of sympathetic magic: 'it wastes me more / Than were't my picture, fashion'd out of wax, / Stucke with a magicall needle' (IV.i.61–3).[33] These and similar accounts are cogent but necessarily partial, in that they fail to confront the salient problem of apprehension or perception and so miss Webster's most important artistic contrivance.

To the reader such an issue should appear both plain, intractable and integral to the experience of reading and interpreting *The Duchess of Malfi*. The likelihood that real actors were called upon to double dead characters only exacerbates the obscurity of dramatic personhood, since Webster carefully undermines distinctions between animate and inanimate figures. That Antonio is figured by his waxen iteration is portended in an earlier scene: 'your kisse is colder / Then that I have seene an holy Anchorite / Give to a dead mans skull'. 'My heart,' he responds, 'is turned to a heavy lumpe of lead' (III.v.84–7). The Echo will later resound: '*Thou art a dead Thing*' (V.iii.39). 'What art thou?' asks Bosola in the darkness later. 'A most wretched thing, / That onely have thy benefit in death, / To appeare my selfe' (V.iv.48–50). At that moment a servant enters with a dark lantern, and the appearance of receding self is aligned with dramatic illumination. Here the player comes closest to drawing death into conjunction with the end of performance and his being able to 'appeare [his] selfe'. The play has repeatedly drawn attention to the shapes its players make: 'Never in mine owne shape,' swears Bosola as he is tasked with the executions (IV.i.131), but Antonio sees positive advantage in going 'in [his] own shape' (V.i.68) to frighten the Cardinal. 'You may discerne the shape of lovelinesse / More perfect, in her teares, then in her smiles,' Bosola tells the Duchess's brother (IV.i.7–8). The Cardinal passes off his brother's madness as a ghost story, which indeed it might be: 'None of our family dies but there is seene / The shape of an old woman' – 'Such a figure / One night (as the prince sat up late at's booke, / Appear'd to him' (V.ii.86–91).

Rupert Brooke writes perfectly accurately of Webster's theatre, that 'life there seems to flow into its forms and shapes with an irregular, abnormal and horrible volume'.[34] The artificial images of the wax tableau both commemorate and prefigure the dead, collapsing time.

They are both artificial and real in the sense that they share the flesh of those they represent, in the bodies of actors. Waxen images had gained their durable importance in funerary art not simply for their lifelikeness, but because through that mimesis they projected lasting presence. As Julius von Schlosser showed, wax effigies were not merely fairground curiosities, but had enjoyed ritual centrality for millennia. By the end of the sixteenth century they were implicated not only in emerging notions of the transcendent artwork, but in an increasingly strict antinomy of high and low culture that they modelled as a dialectic of perfect artifice and conspicuously inanimate lumpenness.[35] 'The wax figure is in fact the stage on which the semblance of humanity overturns itself,' wrote Benjamin of realistic Parisian waxworks of the nineteenth century: '[They] enact nothing so much as a horribly sly mediation of viscera and costume.'[36]

The wax likenesses of Webster's play arbitrate between the durability of printed literature and the ephemerality of a low form, art and mere flesh. The transformation of players into wax images of themselves secures them a lasting presence separate from the authorial monumentalisation in which publication of *The Duchess of Malfi* was involved. In dedication, Webster's peers introduced the play conventionally as a tomb and monument to Webster's name. It was, wrote John Ford, 'a Master-peece / In which, whiles words and matter change, and Men / Act one another', Webster had raised his own monument and secured 'lasting Fame'.[37] But in fixing players so ambiguously in wax, Webster had allowed them also to enter – not as themselves but at least as figures of themselves – into what Benjamin called 'the allegorical home'.[38] In wax they acquire a purer and more classical aspect, partly redeeming them from the discourse in which they are otherwise implicated, that of more common and insubstantial materials. Flesh in *The Duchess of Malfi* is 'a little crudded milk, phantasticall puffe-paste', bodies 'paper-prisons' filled with 'earth-worms' (IV.ii.117–18). 'Crud' meant infected matter, and here touches on 'curd' to imply a fated corruption. 'Puffe-paste' was usually a metonym for 'bombast', but really meant the 'puff pastry' incorporated in newfangled pies 'given to load the stomach very heavily'.[39] Bosola's phrase may have called to mind Atreus and Titus Andronicus, their pies indigestible. Even here there is something the matter with slight things. The corpse of this tragic drama really is phantom stuff, strongly resistant to the metaphysics which continues to underpin the distinction between the durable materials of drama and the ephemeral illusions of theatre.[40] The Duchess is given a mysterious cold hand in the dark, but its substance is unspecifiable even in the light. This is how *The Duchess of Malfi* embalms its rotting figures.

Troublesome Motes

The Watcher on the palace ramparts in the Aeschylean *Agamemnon*, waiting beneath the stars for the distant beacon to light, is replaced in the Senecan play by *Thyestis umbra*, a shadow 'departinge from the darkned dens' and passing across the threshold of his father's house, his shape indistinct as he waits for Phoebus to 'bryng day now by and by'. As this shade acquires imaginative shape, it appears not only solid but obscene material, freighted with flesh. His children whom he ate lie 'crammed [. . .] within [his] Rybs', and 'have theyr Tombe' in him. He has filled his daughter's womb with 'younge bones'.[41] Stephen Greenblatt suggests that at Hamlet's death the Prince 'incorporates' the ghost of his father via the 'reiterated expression "I am dead"': possibly the most basic eidolopoetic phrase of all.[42] Greenblatt finds that the 'Senecan revenge plot' and 'the twisted ruins of the purgatorial system' can be reconciled and transcended in Hamlet's death, even if the Ghost's travels render the stage a purgatorial space in which nothing is yet resolved.[43] Greenblatt rightly notes that the task of vengeance 'becomes mired in the flesh that will not melt away', but it is only in the brief epilogue to his book that he hints at the suspended implications of that recognition. He turns to the closing lines of *The Tempest* to note that Prospero was 'delicately poised between the imaginary world of the theater, between the princely magician and the impoverished actor': 'He is not, of course, crying out from Purgatory; he is speaking from the stage. And in place of prayers, we offer the actor's ticket to bliss: applause.'[44] The negotiation of purgatorial tradition enabled by the actor's performance is located by this analysis only in the form of Prospero's epilogue – in the apparent return to the concrete for which the epilogue provides. Here the implicit jargon of 'liminality' is at its most obstructive.[45] Through it, the ongoing and constitutive involvement of dramatic material in uncertain residues is made into a simple device to enforce the boundary between illusion and reality.

The prefatory ghosts of revenge tragedy directly trouble that boundary and have accordingly attracted a great deal of commentary, much of which deflects their confusing intervention in procedures of figuration by recasting it as a psychosocial problem of post-Reformation repression and superstition. For two decades, the dominant view of ghosts in revenge plays has been supplied by a historicist orthodoxy which holds that revenge tragedies showed 'a fantasy response to the sense of despairing impotence produced by the Protestant displacement of the dead'.[46] In fact this method of framing the Ghost is more venerable, but it is only relatively recently that such figures have been exposed to determined sociological inquisition and identified as complex emanations of religious and social upheaval.[47] I seek here not so much to supplant these interpretations, as to challenge the scope of their explanatory power by interrogating the common assumption that such a deduction is availed by play-texts without any cost. Dramatic revenants create hermeneutic crises which must be artificially reconciled so that the historical origins of those figures can be specified.[48] That is not to say that historicist accounts of the origins of the Elizabethan dramatic ghost do not possess any explanatory power, only that the Ghost's real mischief has been suppressed and that a new sort of literary-historical phenomenology may be necessary to confront it.

'English Seneca read by candlelight,' wrote Thomas Nashe, with a witty joining of bad reading and sore eyes, 'yeeldes manie good sentences.' 'And if you intreate him faire in a frostie morning, he will affoord you whole *Hamlets*,' he continues, before wryly correcting himself – 'I should say handfulls of tragical speeches.'[49] In a candlelit study, one could retrieve some questionable fragments; in daylight entire spurious Hamlets emerged. Nashe satirically exploits the distinction between *whole* dramatic persons and the handfuls of speeches that make patchwork entirety. At the start of the extant *Hamlets*, a questionable wholeness is indeed at stake. The Ghost is a provisionally complete illusion that seems to require visual impairment for its wholeness to be shaped. 'Well may it sort that this portentous figure,' says Barnardo at the start of *Hamlet*, on a cold, dark night, 'Comes armed through our watch so like the King' (I.i.108–9). 'A mote it is to trouble the mind's eye,' supplies Horatio in the second Quarto (1604). *Mote* is another word produced by Shakespeare's nearly incredible power of poetic compression. Although it appears in only one of the extant versions of the play, it interprets something into and out of the others. It carries a sense of illumination – the mote of dust suspended in the light of the watchers' torches – although this was by no means a cliché in 1604. The 'mote' is suspended too in an atomistic discourse (of which more later) through which 'vicious moles' will later encounter the science of the molecular.[50] It also refers to (pre-telescopic) astronomical observation: the passage or *motion* of celestial objects. In Latin and Middle English it meant the centre of an epicycle – an epicycle was a circle travelling the circumference of a larger circle, as familiar from diagrams of Ptolomaeic orbits.[51] The mote is something indistinct and fabulous on the verge of the scene and at the edge of vision, and also an artefact of sight.

An allusion of the astronomical sort has been reinforced in advance by earlier recollections of the sightings – 'When yond same star that's westward from the pole / Had made his course t'illume that part of heaven / When now it burns' (I.i.35–7), which has reference to ancient tragedies of vengeance.[52] And it is developed shortly afterwards: 'the moist star / Upon whose influence Neptune's empire stands / Was sick almost to doomsday with eclipse' (117–19). *Mote* is therefore echoed by the later 'motion': 'It lifted up its head and did address / Itself to motion like as it would speak' (I.ii.215–16). 'Mote' is a noun for something that can perhaps only be described as something which moves rather than stays still, minimal theatre. Through that motion (Latin: *motus*), the son is moved, and the player moves the audience by showing him moved (see Chap. 2).[53] It itself recalls 'moiety' spoken some lines before ('Against the which a moiety competent / Was gaged by our king, which had return / To the inheritance of Fortinbras' [89–91]), which means chiefly 'part' or 'small remainder' (here, 'an equal share'). Together, *moiety* and *mote* inherit a discourse of partiality that has begun with Horatio's answer to Barnado's question: 'Is Horatio there?' 'A piece of him' (17–18).

That striking answer may refer to a kind of diminution effected by cold, but it alludes chiefly to the emergence of a figure from darkness, illuminated by torches. This being Horatio's first appearance, torchlight, or the call to imagine torchlight, gains a quick meaning of disfigurement. It is bound up in the initial identification of character, still at its most perceptibly partial. The dynamic here recalls the Additions to *The Spanish Tragedy* (Q4 1602), in which Shakespeare was likely involved. There Hieronimo encounters torch-wielding servants in the dark: 'Who's there? Sprites, sprites? [...] What make you with your torches in the dark?' (III.12A.22–4). It also reimagines the visitation of Caesar's Ghost, candle-lit, to Brutus: 'How ill this taper burns! Ha! Who comes here? / I think it is the weakness of mine eyes / That shapes this monstrous apparition.'[54] His eyes are strained by the dim light of a failing candle, and perhaps by the smokiness of a taper made of tallow: without trimming, tallow candles would flicker and gutter.[55] In *Julius Caesar* the distinction between a printed ghost and a performed one is exercised by variations in theatrical light, and in the reader's situation. The indoor theatres probably used smoky tallow since beeswax candles were prohibitively expensive. The image of a Ghost could in those circumstances be linked more credibly to physical impairment.[56] Furnished with reliable electric light, a reader can now encounter Caesar's ghost as happily in the evening as in the day, but the play's first readers would have perceived this figure differently depending on whether or not they were directly experiencing Brutus' eye-strain or just recollecting it.[57] 'Electricity,' suggests Drew Milne, 'has become the holy light of indoor theatre.'[58] Motes are harder to see under the bright lights of the future.

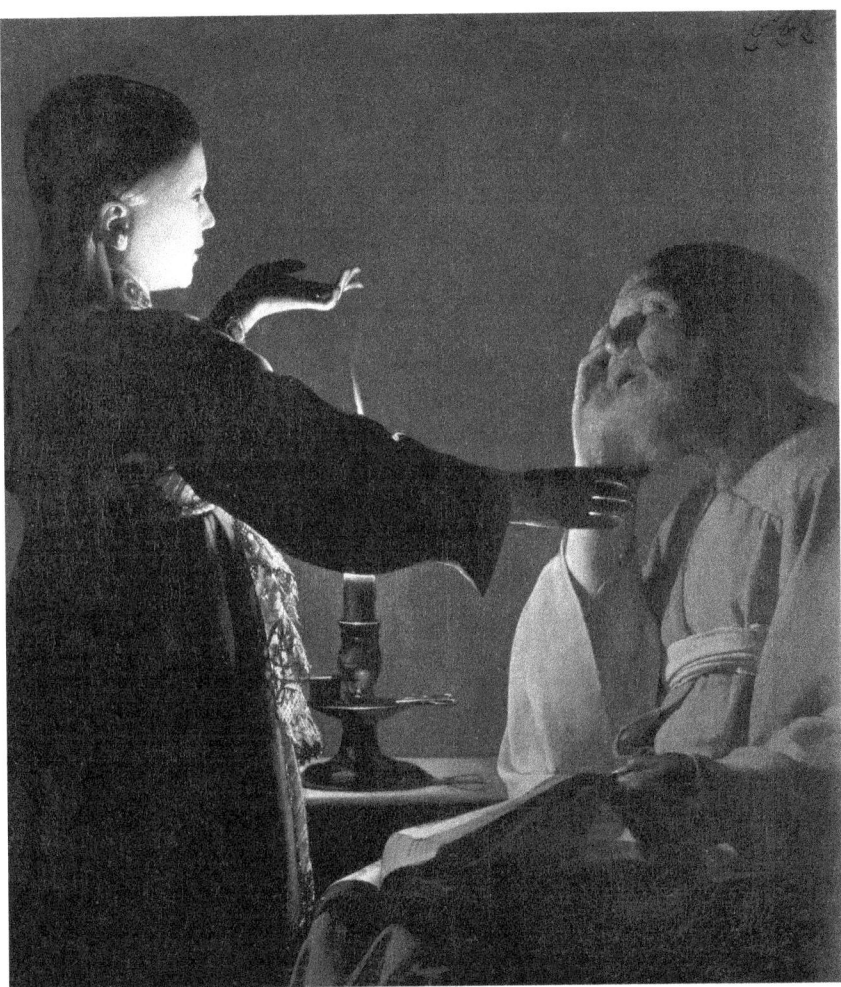

Figure 5.1 Georges de la Tour, *L'Apparition de l'Ange à Saint Joseph* (c.1643). © Nantes-Métropole, Musée d'Arts. Photography: C. Clos. Inventory Nr 642.

Recollecting Horatio's half-lit partiality ('a piece of him'), and looking forward to the synecdochic hand in *The Duchess*, *mote* suspends the Ghost in the history of stage-lighting.[59] It was common in the new theatres for games with lighting to be played explicitly with reference to the appearance of selfhood. The opening scene of *Othello*, for example, seems to take place in fictitious darkness. However, there is neither internal nor ordinary stage direction to imply such gloom until the very closing lines of Iago and Roderigo's opening dialogue, when it is enforced retroactively: implicitly, in the former's instruction to his conspirator to call out 'As when by night and negligence the fire / Is spied in populous cities'; and more concretely, when Iago calls to Brabantio: 'awake!'[60] The effect is to transform a conversation between two fully illuminated figures, a conversation which the reader has already been busy imagining as a scene, into voices in the dark. This technique works with backward force upon Iago's description of his 'shows of service', his promise to separate seeming and being, his forswearing of any 'outward action' that might 'demonstrate / The native act and figure of my heart / In complement extern' (I.i.60–2). Having already lent Iago the mind shape of a man, the reader finds it recedes abruptly into darkness, or rather finds that it was never fully in the light: 'What profane wretch art thou?' asks Brabantio (113), peering down upon the darkling stage. 'Strike on the tinder, ho! / Give me a taper,' he at last calls out. 'Light, I say, light!' (138–42). Ferdinand gives the Duchess a hand in the dark: 'Hah? Lights: oh horrible!' (IV.i.51).

Players in the private houses tended to prefer clothes that showed radiant in candlelight.[61] Light and texture were symbiotically active in the theatrical articulation and disarticulation of images. In the study, darksome images populate fully radiant pages. As it would have been in the Globe, the darkness from which Horatio and then the Ghost appear is absent to the reader of *Hamlet* – torches, candles, lanterns burning daylight. Delio intones at the last that the footprints 'these wretched, eminent things' left in the snow – their 'fame' – would vanish in the shining of the sun that melts 'both form and matter' (V.v.112–16). The allusion to prospective sunshine refers obliquely to theatrical conditions – the dark interior of a private playhouse, the sun shining on the exposed world of the public stage. Masaccio incorporated the light of chapels into the compositions he installed there:[62] perhaps *quattrocento* innovations in painterly mimesis might find an analogue in the incorporation of real light sources into dramatic compositions. That argument, beyond the present scope, would be difficult but has *prima facie* merit. It goes to key unanswered questions about the formation of a distinctive English dramatic corpus in which scene-lighting is repeatedly and emphatically connected to revelations and concealments of identity and purpose. Readers of such drama are invited to furnish imagined scenes with appropriate light sources, but not unconditionally. The fictitious illuminations which seem often to record actual ways of seeing in historical theatres make those places into *original* theatres precisely through the constraints and contradictions their textual traces impose on reading by electric light.

The question of how to see the Ghost is also, of course, a moral one – and there is no convincing reason why the distinctions and indistinctions produced by that dialectic of light should be separate from the apparition's moral challenge. All our future attempts to know the Ghost will be bedevilled by the chief allusion of 'mote' to vernacular translations of Christ's parable of 'The Mote and the Beam'.[63] Both Wycliffe and Tyndale translated κάρφος, *karphos*, meaning 'a small particle', 'twig', 'a splinter of wood or straw', with ancient reference to 'toothpick', into 'mote'. The Greek word derived from *karphó*, meaning 'to dry up, wither'. Jerome gave *festucam* – a piece of straw – but the logic of the parable requires that the mote be of the same stuff as the beam.[64] In attempting to remove the mote from Horatio's mind's eye, we neglect the beam in ours: our apprehension of the Ghost is far trickier even than the scholar's, in fact a different task entirely, for the dubiousness of the mote's substance is part of the general uncertainty at play in our imaginative construal of dramatic person. The strangeness of the Ghost is indistinguishable from the remoteness of Barnardo, Horatio, Hamlet. To attempt an understanding of dead things in the early modern theatre is to confront the epistemological difficulty of its figures and their potential to provoke us to critical examination of our own viewing instruments: 'The splinter in your eye is the best magnifying glass,' wrote Adorno.[65] Shakespeare had sounded a similar idea in *King John*. Hubert de Burgh, under the orders of the tyrant, is on the verge of gouging out the eyes of Arthur of Brittany. Arthur cries:

> O heaven, that there were but a mote in yours,
> A grain, a dust, a gnat, a wandering hair,
> Any annoyance in that precious sense!
> Then feeling what small things are boisterous there,
> Your vild intent must needs seem horrible.[66]

The mote causes an irritation that is identical with appreciation of the irritated faculty and a renewal of moral vision. Its annoyance is therefore precious.

Like Adorno's 'splinter' – implicitly prismatic as a shard of the broken optic of science – *mote* is a residue requiring light for notice. The most paranoid of the medieval demonologists had taken dust particles for myriad cunning devils, momentarily caught in sunlight before settling on the monk's manuscript or cowl.[67] Benjamin thought that the plush furniture and trained dresses of the nineteenth-century bourgeois interior were created to conjure 'the mystery of dust motes playing in the sunlight' for a less enchanted age.[68] Shakespeare possibly had the association of the scriptural mote with darkness and dim fathers from Robert Cawdry's *Treasurie or Store-house of Similies* (1600) –

> Like as a man that hath never so good eyes (yet if hee bee in a deepe darknesse) cannot for all the goodnesse of his eyes, know and discerne his owne

Father, standing directly before him; much lesse a beame or a mote in his eye, untill such time as he hath light to discerne him withall [. . .]⁶⁹

– but this he has combined with Senecan gloom and a miraculous host of other tangents which complicate the recognition of ancestors. 'It will be demanded why in the likeness of ones father or mother, or kinsfolks, [the Devil] oftentimes presents himself unto us?' anticipates Thomas Nashe in his *Terrors of the Night* (1594). 'No other reason can bee given of it but this,' he averred: 'that in those shapes which hee supposeth most familiar unto us [. . .] we will sooner harken to him.'⁷⁰

To think through *mote* is to think through a fundamental moral bind of familiarity and unfamiliarity along the other paths on which the word takes us. That Horatio should deem the Ghost a *mote* also helps, for instance, to establish the possibly Epicurean or Lucretian register developed later in *Hamlet*, as in the Prince's 'quintessence of dust', a description of bare humanity opposite to humanism's 'man [. . .] infinite in faculties, in form and moving' (II.ii.269–74). Hamlet's Epicurean reduction of the human shape to what Helkiah Crooke later disdained as 'a number of Atomies or Motes, such as we see in the Sunne', proposes the Ghost of Q2 as an analogous residue.⁷¹ While it calls to mind glimpses of a distant celestial object's passage or motion (*motus*), *mote* refers to the greatest imaginable reduction of matter, with an aspect of triviality or negligibility; to an irritating particle lodged in the body (read: state), but here, in the 'mind's eye'; and to a discovered fault, the still uncertain properties of which are carried in a final valence of *mote* – the modal verb, expressing permission or possibility.⁷²

Horatio's 'mote' is a prospectively physical irritation to non-physical sight, a check on its liberty, but in this it continues to refer to physical ghosts. Even as many possibilities leak necessarily out of the scene, Horatio outlines the Ghost as a mere image: no less consequential for it, but a stall on philosophy, which originates, as Aristotle (and possibly Plato) thought, with *thaumazein* or what is here termed the 'strange'.⁷³ Like the witches, the Ghost vanishes as Horatio begins his interrogation, leaving him to resemble Macbeth standing, 'rapt in the wonder of it'.⁷⁴ Old Hamlet does not dawdle for questions. Horatio accepts the Ghost because of 'the sensible and true avouch of [his] own eyes', but the 'image' of the dead king has merely 'appeared'. The scholar's 'belief' is attended by no certainty as to the properties of the 'thing'. 'Wonder *by its very nature* is pre-theoretical' – necessarily lost by enquiry.⁷⁵ The concept of wonder splits sight. Judgement makes it vanish, so it can refer only to pre-intellectual vision. It is therefore logical to say that the Ghost is less an object of wonder than the stuff of wonder itself.

Aristotle thought that wonder incites the very inquisition which will delete it.[76] This paradox beleaguers scholarly discourse purporting to clarify the Ghost's social and religious origins and content. Meanwhile, descriptions of the creation of wonder in the early modern theatre are caught in a special version of that paradox, because they diminish their readers' capacity to experience the very effect they claim is essential to our interaction with the plays.[77] The shadowy or ghostly wonder which appears at the start of *Hamlet* prevents the identification of *thaumazein* with the theatre's capacity or duty to elicit pre-critical emotional response – one of the chief presumptions of neo-Aristotelian theories of tragedy since at least the seventeenth century.[78] The dead thing which passes across the (mental) stage in the opening scenes of *Hamlet* blurs the ancient distinction between what Christine Hunzinger calls 'the critical spirit' and 'stupid amazement'.[79] It causes not just wonder but a mistrust of sensible perception, intuition and judgement that continues to disturb how one might wish to frame, sight, contemplate, or reflect upon the play. At the same time as prospective intuition of the apparition is exposed to a plethora of reflexive confusions, those same confusions block the dianoetic transformation of the Ghost into a figure of argument. As Quentin Skinner implicitly accepts, it is impossible to decide whether the appearance of the Ghost and its apprehension by the play's characters make up an insinuative or a prefatory construction. The 'thing' only becomes available to equitable judgement once it enters into a dialogue with Hamlet, and it is only at this point that Skinner can begin the rhetorical enquiry into its complex *prohoemium*.[80] For in the opening scenes this thing is quite alien to any question of structure and is even detained from the narrower issue of motive which it will eventually consume. Instead it provokes crises of appearance and identity that are still unresolved and call again and again for a laborious discernment.

Scott Wayland observes that apostrophe replaced medieval eidolopoeia, 'first-person address spoken by the dead', in post-Reformation elegies.[81] Figures such as the Ghost were not only incompatible with the official religious culture of late sixteenth-century England but explored new complications in the relations that might be assumed to exist between poetic expression and the human origin of that language. The emergence of the Ghost concentrates the insoluble difficulty of deciding whether the figures conjured by the play are historical substances or mere phantoms of the mind. The opening of *Hamlet* entwines the identification of narrative origins with the identification of theatrical and dramatic shapes. As Ann Rosalind Jones and Peter Stallybrass have pointed out, the materiality of the Ghost is ineliminable and becomes more troublesome the stronger the attempt to erase it with 'complex lighting' and other techniques is pursued.[82] Prologuing ghosts force narrative origins into uncertain shapes which must be discerned. 'What ill am I appoynted for?' asks the ghost of Tantalus at the beginning of *Thyestes*, like a Vice.[83] The judgement of intent and circumstances, a task proper to evaluation of character, cannot free itself from the strenuities of such figurations. This naturally extends to the moral optic through which revenge plays have been routinely seen and read. That Horatio locates the mote in his 'mind's eye' may derive from the Vulgate's *oculis cordis*, which Tyndale had given not as 'the eyes of the heart' but as 'the eyes of your mynde', but it has neo-Platonic valence too and relates obliquely and with real ambiguity to indistinct and popular concepts of spiritual sight.[84] In the Sonnets, that combination of meanings is involved by Shakespeare directly in lyric apostrophe: 'my soul's imaginary sight / Presents thy shadow to my sightless view'.[85] These meanings share reference to the figuring of absent others such that their physical shape appears partially real. They refer inchoately to a phenomenology of theatre, which bodies shadows of absent persons and thereby recalls some of the myths associated with the earliest plastic arts: the invention of drawing and sculpture in the tracing of the valedictory shadow.[86] As Harold Brooks notes, in Studley's translation of the Senecan *Medea* (1566), *incerta umbra* was given not as 'uncertain shadow' but as 'mishapt [*mis-shapen*] ghost', foreshadowing the translation, decades later, of dubious origins into vexing figures.[87]

The Ghost is the most troublesome prologue imaginable. The Prologue to *Wily Beguilde*, published in 1606 but probably watchable on the public stage earlier than 1596, implicates the appearance of players as themselves in the obscure word *spectrum*, which is presented as the title of a play that, like Nashe's Hamlet, is said to be 'nothing but patch-pannell stuffe, olde gally-mawfries and cotton-candle eloquence'. A 'Juggler' utters an incantation, and the play, the title of which is set up to be seen on stage, is replaced with *Wily Beguilde*: '*Spectrum is conveied away: and Wily beguilde, stands in the place of it*'. Only a prologue to *Spectrum* remains:

> Spectrum is a looking glasse indeede,
> Wherein a man a History may read,
> Of base conceits and damned roguerie:
> The very sinke of hell-bred villeny.[88]

The effect is to combine the body of the 'Prologue', the players and the play-text of this 'lost' play into a single mysterious *Spectrum*. *Spectrum* was an uncommon word in the sixteenth century but alluded to uncertain apparitions. Anthony Anderson had applied it to the questionable post-mortem appearance of Samuel to Saul in 1 Samuel 28: 'this was not Samuel, but the delusion of sathan, and is called in the storye Samuel, respecting therby the mind of Saule, supposing this *Spectrum* to be Samuel'.[89] That scriptural ghost seems almost invisibly present to this Prologue. Saul, having expelled all magicians from his kingdom, had nevertheless gone out in disguise to speak to a witch – the so-called Witch of Endor – who summons 'Samuel' for him. The incantation used by the 'Juggler' directly connects the vanquishing of *Spectrum* to the debates around witchcraft. Specifically, the magical phrase used to substitute the plays – *Hei fortuna furim nunquam credo* – appears to have been taken directly from Scot's *Discovery of Witchcraft* and its explication of the Old Testament story in terms of theatrical tricks. 'Now cometh in *Samuel* to play his part,' wrote Scot, 'but I am perswaded it was performed, in the person of the Witch her self, or of her confederate'.[90] The Prologue to *Wily Beguilde* adduces a strange and compelling notion of a ghost play – *Spectrum* – that has to be juggled out of sight.

In *Hamlet* Q2 the phenomenon witnessed in the opening scene – whether juggling trick or sublime encounter – is psychologised by repetition. Horatio's 'mote [. . .] to trouble the mind's eye' is refreshed in his conversation with Hamlet in the next scene: 'My father, methinks I see my father.' '*Where*, my lord?': the witnesses to the Ghost, yet unseen by Hamlet, look about them in alarm. 'In my mind's eye, Horatio' (I.ii.183–4). Then the dialogue is inverted. Horatio shows his friend his own hands to describe the resemblance of the Ghost to Old Hamlet, accidentally announcing the manifest fleshiness of the Ghost: 'I knew your father, / These hands are not more like.' 'But *where* was this?' (210, my emphasis). Now the eye of Hamlet's mind, borrowed from Horatio, is turned back out: 'My lord, upon the platform where we watch' (211–12). When the mote reappears to Hamlet in the 'closet scene', it is potentially repsychologised. The experience of the audience is perhaps 'mediated' there by 'attributed mental states', and the reader may be confused by the 'fluctuating presence' of the Ghost, effected by 'the text's fluctuating focus', as Raphael Lyne suggests.[91] But in the Ghost's initial figurations the difficulty created is not one of 'empathizing with [. . .] characters under strain', but more basically troublesome to the perception of dramatic person as such, its shapes, substances and shifts.[92] The mote, then, is still in my eye, and still in yours.

By animating all these adduced senses in a reader's painful blink, *mote* inflects the other words used to describe the Ghost: 'thing' (I.i.20), 'sight' (24), 'apparition' (27), 'figure', 'form' (46), 'fantasy' (53), 'image' (80), 'illusion' (126) and 'spirit' (170). Hamlet worries it has a suspicious 'pleasing shape' (II.ii.535). Above all, *mote* applies to all these terms a special problem of proximity. The mote is both an object observed passing at a great distance (remotely) and a particle infecting the observer's eye. Crooke would describe 'the brim of the eye-lids' as 'a wall of defence with their hayres shot out that no smal motes or other annoyances might fall into the eyes when they are open'.[93] In *Orlando Furioso*, Rogero is described, in John Harington's translation (1591), 'mounted up so hie, / He seemd to be a mote or little pricke, / For no man could distinguish him by eie'.[94] Figures, forms, fantasies, images and shapes are in *Hamlet* not only harbingers, precursors and prologues of uncertain future significance, but provoking and precious impediments to historical recognition.[95]

Figura

Erich Auerbach records how a squad of Greek words – *morphē*, *eidos*, *schēma*, *typos*, *plasis* – was reduced in Hellenised Latin to a prospectively binary distinction between *forma* and *figura*. In general, he writes, *figura* took the place of *schēma* to give the sense of 'outward shape', but that it also gradually acquired the senses of *typos* ('imprint') and *plasis* ('moulding'), and that from this *figura* began slowly 'to impinge on the domain of *statua* and even of *imago, effigies, species, simulacrum*'.[96] Lucretius seems to have originated the application of *figura* to 'ghost'.[97] Auerbach notes that Herman Diels translates *figura* with 'Atomen' ('Atoms') on several occasions, but thereby over-simplifies the conceptual genealogy.[98] David Sedley gives a more nuanced account than this, showing that *figura* in Lucretius does not quite mean 'atoms', which are described instead via an array of other terms cognate with 'first bodies' (*corpora prima*). *Figura* nonetheless relates in Luretius to *simulacrum*, *effigies, imago*, which in turn substitute for older translations of εἴδωλον (*eidolon*), the 'thin films of atoms which stream off bodies and cause vision', *spectra* and *idola*.[99] If one wished to impose a strict Lucretian interpretation of Horatio's 'mote', it would describe a confusion between a first substance and its formal appearance.

Although that is suggestive as far as the Ghost's role as image and first body in *Hamlet* goes, the questions I wish to raise here do not concern literary or philosophical influence *per se*. The key Lucretian text, *De Rerum Natura*, was available only in manuscript form in late 1590s northern Europe. Although Montaigne's incorporation of Lucretius is interesting for reading Montaigne, attempts to establish even an indirect connection to Shakespeare are always going to be uphill.[100] It is nevertheless worthwhile to observe that the appearance of Caesar's ghost in *Julius Caesar* was likely influenced by Plutarch's account of Cassius' Epicurean interpretation: 'An impression on the senses is like wax, and the soul of man, in which the plastic material and the plastic power alike exist, can very easily shape and embellish it at pleasure.'[101] That waxy imprint seems to be received in Shakespeare's play when Cinna is instructed by Cassius to 'set up with wax' a letter 'upon old Brutus' statue' (I.iii.145–6). This circumstance is not mentioned again, but the other letter is discovered by Lucius who goes looking for a taper and flint with which to light the 'study' or 'closet' of Brutus. We are invited to imagine parallel scenes: Brutus reading the letter himself, and the duplicate letter fixed with wax to the statue of Brutus. The premise that these simulacra exist on a single plane is enforced by the play, because the letter's contents are disclosed not by candlelight but by 'the exhalations whizzing in the air' (II.i.44): Brutus and his statue are exposed to the same ominous sky.

The letters aim expressly at a kind of animation ('Speak, strike, redress! / Brutus, thou sleep'st: awake!' [55–6]). They refer backwards to the statue: Brutus, inactive and inert, stirred to 'first motion' (63–4). That discourse is mirrored in the vision of bleeding statues prefiguring Caesar's death (II.ii.75–90). The play is not only about the undoing of monuments and the remaking of them. It concerns the way theatre lends old illusions and ideas corporeal, plastic liveliness; and in turn the way those ancient monuments fill out with historical matter those 'figures' and 'fantasies' drawn 'in the brains of men' (II.i.230–1). The Duchess announces: 'This is flesh and blood, (Sir,) / 'Tis not the figure cut in Allabaster / Kneeles at my husbands tombe' (*Duchess* I.i.440–1). From a figural perspective, that basic theatre phenomenology is readily transposed into an issue of solid ghostliness. Bosola adduces the metaphor of a witch's familiar, 'a very quaint invisible Divell, in flesh' (I.i.247). Ferdinand supposes flesh can leave marks. He gives the Duchess the waxy hand to kiss with the words, 'bury the print of it in your heart' (IV.i.45). This ancient premise that dead matter – the scheme – could print as it were inwardly onto spirit or life would retain its dynamic applications. 'I feare yet the iron yoke of an outward conformity hath left a slavish print upon our necks,' exclaimed John Milton in *Areopagitica*.[102] Bosola shifts the idea with typically weird brilliance: 'A Polititian is the divells quilted anvell, / He fashions all sinnes on him, and the blowes / Are never heard' (III.ii.323–5).

Perhaps, then, the phenomenological question pursued in this chapter's middle sections is really some sort of humanist question in disguise. Some of the complexities and difficulties of the modern reader's encounter with dramatic shapes might be explained in part as the consequence of the troubled reception of the structures of classical thought in baroque art. This is how Auerbach's exploration of *figura* comes to seem highly suggestive. It is nevertheless questionable whether Auerbach's essay recommends a concept of *figura* and develops it as a 'critical instrument'.[103] His essay is better grasped as an attempt to explore the contours and shapes of Western culture with reference to the plasticity of a word used to describe exactly that property.[104] If Auerbach's exposition of *figura*, both in the essay 'Figura' and in *Mimesis*, has been taken seriously at all, it has been criticised for its apparently weak explanatory and descriptive power.[105] To my knowledge, however, the implications of Auerbach's essay for theatre history and dramatic epistemology have never been properly addressed, although it is in this arena especially that it does acquire and retain genuine critical potential, especially on the scene of contemporary historicism. *Figura* stemmed from *fingo, fingere*, the combined meanings of which describe nothing so well as theatre: 'to shape, fashion, form'; 'to adorn, dress, arrange'; 'to teach, instruct'; 'to dissemble'. Despite great interest in the Ovidian dimensions of significant early modern drama, Ovid's use of *figura* to describe the 'mobile, changeable, multiform, and deceptive' has been identified there chiefly as a hermeneutic playfulness rather than as a means of representing the new substances and shapes of a professional and commercial theatre.[106]

Sixteenth-century anti-theatricalism was strongly figural in that it could abide no separation of good faith from its proper bodies. Players were like 'painted sepulchres', as Stubbes put it, but the real point was that theatre disfigured an 'infinite varietie' of persons, and that this was the same thing as disfiguring true faith.[107] The iconophobic phase of the English Reformation introduced a set of contentions about images, idols, effigies and simulacra that both enriched and threatened the commercial theatres that sprang up in just those years the phase is said to have begun.[108] Conversely, Ann Kibbey has advanced the striking thesis that seventeenth-century Calvinism was characterised by a figural mode of social recognition.[109] This proceeded from iconoclasm – 'iconoclasts needed to kill these images by disfiguring them to guarantee that they were dead' – into special forms of social prejudice, and genocide in the New World.[110] Image-making in the early modern theatre was caught up in myriad social and religious complexities, but its dramatic legacy involves not only this historical crisis of representation but a challenge to anodyne and neutral description of it, as if our own encounter with these figures in their afterlife did not itself entail efforts of historical imagination.

Thinking about *figura* in a restrained way, as a means of grasping some of the procedures and assumptions about images and words in early modern England, nevertheless possesses the accidental virtue of interdicting the usual roads along which such an intellectual tradition can be traced. When Francis Meres claims that the 'sweete wittie soule of Ovid lives in mellifluous and hony-tongued Shakespeare', he is not imputing mere resemblance.[111] Neither is it quite correct to suggest Meres is calling on the fantastic supernatural proposition of Pythagorean *metempsychosis*, which only reinforces a purely metaphorical interpretation of 'soule [. . .] lives'.[112] The comparison made by Meres of ancient poets to contemporary authors is pursuing what Auerbach would recognise as a figural relation.[113] Something of the real Ovid was figured by Shakespeare; or, Shakespeare was genuinely Ovidian. The poets of the English Renaissance were the fulfilment of their classical models. Given the weakness and suspicion attaching to notions of authenticity in our own time, such a proposition seems alien or at least disquieting. It seemed less bizarre in the late sixteenth century. Jasper Heywood prefaced his 1560 translation of *Thyestes* with an account of 'Seneca' appearing to the translator as a ghost or dream image to express his desire that his 'name' should be renewed.[114] Richard Halpern notes, 'the ghost is another figure for tradition', and suggests that in the ghosts of Elizabethan and Jacobean revenge plays 'the Senecan ghost is also always in some sense the ghost *of* Seneca'.[115]

Halpern seems to mean 'figure' metaphorically, but there is a pervading sense in much early modern thought that such figures were partially real, at least insofar as they referred to actual substances, shapes, pressures and receptions. Here one can appreciate the difference between the metaphorical or loose application of *figure* or *figural* and the flickering historical or realistic element that Auerbach shows it to possess. Just as the statues and motes of this chapter prove rather indigestible when swallowed by historicist explanation, *figura* in the strong sense cannot be assimilated to a purely 'realistic' history-writing. This is especially true of one that purports to describe tradition, influence and transmission while positioning itself in such a way as to imply that its own viewpoint stands outside or beyond those figurations and disfigurations, at an Archimedean point. At hand instead is the problematic but sure survival, against social scientific realism, of a notion of 'the "matter" of tradition', which Gerard Passannante has found to be basic to the earliest European philology, and which may inhere still in the renewed affection for the material text and its permutations.[116]

In *Mimesis*, Auerbach presents a figural account of sixteenth-century English drama. He tries to reframe the relation between the medieval

Christian theatre and 'the creatural view of man' that he finds in Elizabethan (and above all Shakespearean) tragedy:

> In the Elizabethan theatre, the superstructure of the whole is lost; the drama of Christ is no longer the general drama [...] The great order of the past – Fall, Divine Sacrifice, Last Judgment – recedes, the human drama finds its order within itself; and here the antique precedent intervenes [...][117]

By 'superstructure' and 'order', Auerbach means something like 'mould' or 'imprint'. The account of discontinuity given here reminds one of his descriptions of Democritean 'film images' and the Lucretian definition of structures that 'peel off things like membranes and float round in the air'.[118] Auerbach *figures* the emergence of secular realism. It bears the imprint of what he saw as the crisis at the heart of Christianity – the incarnational antinomy produced by its requiring both historical reality and the transcendence of that reality.[119] The 'dissolution of medieval Christianity [...] brings out [...] a will to trace the secret forces of life.' In this way Auerbach seeks to account for the appearance of spirits and ghosts in Shakespeare: 'he embraces reality but he transcends it'.[120] Here Auerbach disappointingly crowns the 'Cosmic Poet'; while 'tragic characters attain their final completion here below'. All of the quotations Auerbach gives in these now rather neglected passages on *Macbeth* and *Hamlet* feature the appearance of players as walking shadows and spirits melted into air. Not a word is expended upon the materiality of these invoked figures, nor upon the involvement of their allegorisation in the very dilemma of dramatic immanence that is at stake in Auerbach's history.

The first decades of the professional English theatre saw many practical explorations of the cultural relation thought to exist between playing and the provision of fake revenants. Before summoning Alexander the Great and his paramour for Charles V's entertainment, Faustus had admitted, 'it is not in my ability to present before your eyes the true substantial bodies of those [...] consumed to dust'.[121] That the bodies do prove substantial within the logic of the scene makes their theatrical figuration almost identical with demonic incarnation. Notwithstanding the didactic power of that elision of the theatre with its fictional shapes, it is also clear that the commercial theatres involved a practical separation of its professional class from the materials they presented. This paradox created a set of confusions and contradictions within the notion and practice of theatrical figuration. Figures were the chief materials of the professional dramatist. The most inventive among the new cadre of writers sought to test and expand their properties. The characters or myths we freely discuss as if they were real people have been separated from that basic crisis of representation only via a massive cultural effort in the intervening centuries.[122] That which was called personation in early modern English preceded characterisation: the work of figuration describes a middle ground, the historical distance one travels back between the production of psychological character and the reinvention of tragic bodies.

In the sixteenth and seventeenth centuries, nobody knew characters like we do.[123] 'Character' referred to 'charactery', which meant both the skill in delineating essential moral or social character; shorthand transcription (brachigraphy; tachygraphy; semography); and the shape and sense of letters and symbols used to express thought. In the first sense, related to the others, it can be connected to the emerging Theophrastian Renaissance represented above all by Joseph Hall and Thomas Overbury, through which the physiognomy of a specific vice was transformed into delineation of social type. The emerging seventeenth-century practice of charactery was a specific kind of figural thinking: the formation of a recognisable shape that bore on actual people with a partial realism. Overburyian characters were partially real figures. Webster himself contributed to this primitive tradition in his *New Characters (drawne to the life) of severall Persons, in severall qualities* (1615).[124] Exactly this mode is occasionally employed in *The Duchess of Malfi*, as in Antonio's description of the Cardinal ('Observe his inward Character: he is a mellancholly Church-man' et cetera, *Duchess*, I.i.147–55).

Elsewhere, 'character' refers to physiognomy, as when Ferdinand supposes that Bosola has been suspected for 'some oblique character in [his] face' (I.i.221). This seems to involve 'character' in a contradiction of essence and appearance, but in fact the antinomy is spurious. Antonio in the earlier passage is making an image of the Cardinal for Delio, hence his friend's response: 'You have given too much of him' (156). The phrase 'inward character' contains the real paradox: a physiognomy of the interior. In common with many of his contemporaries, Webster is conscious that character is caught in the partial knowledge of figure, and that charactery was the realisation, in a single outward sketch or scheme ('character'), of multiple accreted inferences. Character was both lively image and dead matter. 'We are all confounded,' speaks the poisoned Hippolito in Middleton's *Women beware Women*. 'How?' asks the Duke. 'Dead,' comes the response.[125] The dialectic of life and death through which dramatic works think together their figures and their own reception is concentrated in the tragic corpse, involving both its show and its text in a single issue of material.

In Auerbach's approximately chronological account of the history of *figura*, Quintilian's application of the word to an apparatus of rhetorical techniques appears incongruous because in such constellations the involvement of *figura* in issues of materiality and historicity is minimised, and yet this section directly precedes the description of Christian figural hermeneutics in which such elements come most to the fore.[126] With the sixteenth-century fragmentation of Christian *oikonomia* and the elevation of the textual above the visual, the more technical and linguistic elaboration of *figura* in classical rhetoric 'intervened'.[127] Indeed, *figura* has received most attention from scholars of the English literary Renaissance where it pertains to *ars rhetorica*: Cicero, Quintilian; their reception by Rainolds, Puttenham, Peacham, inter alia; the immersion of Renaissance dramatists in the rhetorical pedagogy of the grammar schools; and the oratorical structure of plays. Here *figura* acquires a sense of enforcement – firm impressions, blows, pressure, *enargeia*.[128] It was through this rich legacy that an apprehension of *figurative language* emerged, and with it the distinction between what Puttenham called 'ornament' and plain or ordinary language.[129] The largely successful struggle in recent years has been to show that rhetoric was not simply ornamental to dramatic language nor as it were ancillary to early modern drama itself, but pervasive and formative. Lorna Hutson has argued convincingly that the 'compositional techniques of inventing arguments out of topics of circumstance' (*figurae*) were the means by which English drama created the '*imagined dramatic world*', and that this achievement was separate from 'innovations in theatrical mimesis – of staging or of bodies in performance' (*figurae*).[130] Despite the contradiction which might inhere in an outright distinction between figures of speech and theatrical figures, dramatic rhetoric and tragic corpses do seem to have little in common. On the other hand, there is no 'bare' corpse in early modern tragedy, no body that can be interpreted 'literally' or is 'unmistakeable'.

'There is no "engagement with character" that is antecedent or alternative to the play's lines of poetry,' writes Hutson, who shows how, far from being a technical encampment, circumstantial arguments were and are 'image-forming' and therefore productive both of character and worlds.[131] Rhetorical figuration is nevertheless haunted by a problem of personhood, not least because Quintilian assumed that the orator must be a good man.[132] This makes the image of the common player a problem for rhetoric too. Moreover, 'the play's lines of poetry' need either to be spoken by someone, or for us to imagine them being spoken by someone, and so include suspect figures in a way that other forms of 'poetry' do not. The dead and dying in drama necessarily challenge the integrity of these 'imagined worlds' precisely because they show figures at their most suspect. Here the category of 'poetry' (as in 'lines of poetry') has proven too obliging for the way it frees dramatic speech from the human shapes that speak it, shifting the problem of *figura* into an allegorical or metaphorical domain. It is detained there only by Poetry, an effective guard only insofar as she can be identified as a form of knowledge into which dramatic speech can be (or even *should* be) dissolved – which is very doubtful.[133]

In the most well-known passages of his essay, Auerbach claims that the problem of establishing the relative validity of the Old Testament to the New Testament spawned a figural hermeneutic, opposed to a purely allegorical exegesis. The events of the Old Testament were historical and could not be transformed into merely allegorical stuff. 'Moses is no less historical and real because he is an *umbra* or *figura* of Christ,' Auerbach writes, 'and Christ, the fulfillment, is no abstract idea, but also a historical reality.'[134] Although figural hermeneutics were part of the supersessionist structure of medieval and early modern anti-Semitism, Auerbach perspicaciously shows how the figural relation involves no *necessary* diminution or cancellation of the figure in the identification of its fulfilment: 'there is no lack of examples in which the figure has the greater concreteness'.[135] As Jeffrey Librett and Kathleen Biddick suggest, 'there is nothing to guarantee the irreversibility of figural thinking *except the theological notion of supersession*. Without the fantasy of supersession the figure of the Christian is always possibly the truth of the Jew'.[136] Auerbach testifies that in the guise of biblical typology, *figura* moved to the very centre of what would later be called the philosophy of history: at hand is the ancient premise that an event was not the cause of the next one, but its prefiguration. His account and the tradition it excavates poses a curiously potent challenge to terminologies of genre and type in contemporary cultural and literary study. What is lost in the gap between those categories ('Vice', 'servant', 'revenger' and so on) and the types that were 'warrants *and* [. . .] verifications of the expected fulfilment'?[137] That question is involved in what Julia Reinhard Lupton calls 'the complicity of "typology" and "Renaissance"' and the 'necessity' of working 'through these terms to their limits'.[138]

Auerbach's essay derives its originality from exactly such an implied pursuit of a figural historical logic beyond the exegetical. It is under this gaze that statues, images and monuments become not only commemorative but anticipatory. Shadows, effigies and examples begin to point to a future that includes the observer looking back at them. The closest Auerbach comes to really considering the dead on the stage is in his book on Dante: 'Although their bodies remain hidden, the light phenomena [*Lichterscheinungen*] of Paradise possess affective gestures' which refer to their former earthly life.[139] This 'metamorphosis' of real people 'touches only [their] appearance and not [their] form' – '[their] new appearance is the continuation, elevation, and interpretation of their former appearance and thus reveals [their] true form'.[140] Adi Efal's *Figural Philology* expands on these dynamics of *figura*:

> Even when it contains reality, some part of this reality is missing or covered, that is to say not directly attainable. Indeed, figural realism is a partial realism, in the sense that only a part of the reality of the thing is maintained by the figure. The intuition that captures the figure works in retrospect, after a body has moved, and after this movement has caused something else to move; it is an anamnesic process, a mnemonic operation whose task is to discover a certain movement occurring in the past.[141]

Alluding, as I have, to Pliny's fable of the departing man's shadow being traced on the wall by his lover, Efal defines figure as 'the condensation of a transmission of a form'.[142] The projection of the shadow is made possible by a lamp (but which?), and the shadow is emphatically '*somebody's* image' (but whose?).[143] I suggest that the many awkward figures of revenge tragedy – statues, ghosts, corpses – condense the transmission of a form, that form being the player who populated both the real and imagined theatre spaces of the late sixteenth and early seventeenth centuries. That form comprised both a new social imaginary and a group of men who existed. In and through its figures, English revenge tragedy projects a vexing legacy into the future.

Revenge tragedy is heavily involved in disclosures of that originary form. Revenge narratives thematise the translation of first bodies into new constellations, and the efforts involved in remembering them. Hieronimo presents his dead son. 'Methinks I hear, / His dismal outcry echo in the air,' he states (*ST* IV.iv.107–8). That announcement is neither metaphorical nor psychotic. It enforces the figural relation the avenger seeks to create between the corpses of young men now gathered before the court. The scene of Horatio's murder is figured and fulfilled by the scene of revenge: 'Speak, Portuguese, whose loss resembles mine' (113). From the perspective this last section has attempted to recover, it is possible to see that *The Spanish Tragedy* is uninterested in the merely symbolic or allegorical. Horatio's dead shape is involved not only in commemoration, but in prefiguration. Through it Hieronimo remembers a real event in the past – Horatio's murder – and looks forward to a real event in the future – the murder of his murderers. The presentation of Horatio's corpse collapses the temporal fabric of the drama. When Hieronimo claims that 'They murdered me that made those fatal marks' (96), he is not being quaint. He is working on an apotheosis of the figural logic called forth by the teleology of revenge, which gives *The Spanish Tragedy* its expressive force.

When – as it does in a play – 'an eye for an eye' describes a temporal or historical relationship, it is not simple exchange but potentially figure and fulfilment. Fold or crease the narrative of revenge so that the first corpse almost touches the second: Horatio, Balthazar; Old Hamlet, Claudius; Thyestes, Atreus. Theatre doubling is one way in which that figuration can be enforced, but stage-work must later be reworked by a reading sensitive to the tension between its procedural encounter with printed figures and the struggle to interpret and distinguish them, as the avengers demand, by moving backwards and forward with the flick of a page through time, in search of what the Greeks called 'the mark of a blow' – but which an Elizabethan or Jacobean might have imagined as the strike of a bodkin through a stack of quires.[144] As that figural structure encountered emerging early modern notions of causality, originality and identity, it produced new complications of personhood and appearance in tragic drama. The bodied persons of those plays are incomplete and whole, fictitious and real, abstract and historical, flies in the social scientific ointment. The remains of the player belong to a stratified corpus too dazzling for any scheme of genre. That corpus is bequeathed to our time as one book leaf above another.

Notes

1. For a survey of off-stage deaths in Greek drama, see Sri Pathmanathan, 'Death in Greek Tragedy', *Greece and Rome* 12 (1965), 2–14.
2. At the end of the play, one such direction is given by the Cardinal in respect of Julia's corpse ('Take up that body', *Duchess*, V.ii.304).
3. For a very early consideration of Webster within the scope of the revenge tradition, see Clayton M. Hamilton, '*The Duchess of Malfi* Considered as a Tragedy of Blood', *Sewanee Review* 9:4 (Oct., 1901), 410–34.
4. The phrase is from Rupert Brooke, *John Webster & the Elizabethan Drama* (London, 1917), 158.
5. Thomas Middleton, [Dedicatory verses to *The Duchess of Malfi*], in Middleton, *Works*, 1894.
6. Lionel Abel, *Metatheatre. A New View of Dramatic Form* (New York, 1963), 27.
7. Joseph Morris, 'John Webster', *Fortnightly Review* 77 (June, 1902), 1064–78, at 1069; T. S. Eliot, 'Whispers of Immortality', in *Selected Poems* (London, 1954; repr. 1971), 42–3, ll.1–2; 7.
8. Webster, 'Epilogue', *The White Devil*, in Webster, *Works*, 2: 254.
9. Thomas Pynchon, *The Crying of Lot 49* (London, 2000), 43–55; 47.
10. Anon., Unsigned Review, *Westminster Review* 86, new series 30 (Oct., 1866), 269–71.

11. William Archer, *The Old Drama and the New: An Essay in Re-Valuation* (London, 1923), 29; William Archer, 'John Webster', *The Nineteenth Century* 87 (Jan., 1920), 126–32, at 126; Pynchon, *Crying*, 51.
12. Fredson Thayson Bowers, *Elizabethan Revenge Tragedy, 1587–1642* (Princeton, 1940), 62; Elmer Edgar Stoll, *John Webster: The Periods of his Work as Determined by his Relations to the Drama of his Day* (New York, 1905, repr. 1967), esp. 83–152.
13. Peter Sacks, 'Where words prevail not: Grief, Revenge and Language in Kyd and Shakespeare', *English Literary History* 3 (Autumn, 1982), 576–601, at 587.
14. Linda Woodbridge, *English Revenge Drama: Money, Resistance, Equality* (Cambridge, 2010), 167.
15. Charles R. Forker, *Skull beneath the Skin: The Achievement of John Webster* (Carbondale, 1986), 26–7.
16. See John Webster, *Monuments of Honor* (London, 1624), in Webster, *Works* 3: 253–94, at 282:

    > Vppon an Artificiall Rocke, set with mother of Pearle and such other precious stones, as are found in quarries, are placed foure curious Paramids charged with the Princes Armes, the three Fealthers, which by day yeeld a glorious shew, and by night a more goodly, for they haue lights in them, that at such time as my Lord Maior returnes from Pauls, shall make certaine ouals and squares, resemble pretious stone [. . .]

17. John Webster, *A Monumental Column*, in Webster, *Works*, 3: 373–86, ll.84–7. It is probable that Webster broke off from writing *The Duchess of Malfi* in order to compose *A Monumental Column*, commemorating the death of Prince Henry. See David Gunby, 'The Life of John Webster', in Webster, *Works*, 1: 3–17, at 10.
18. Simon Palfrey and Tiffany Stern, *Shakespeare in Parts* (Oxford, 2007), 218.
19. Joseph Hall, *One of the Sermons preacht at Westminster, on the day of the publicke fast (April 5. 1628)* (London, 1628), 90.
20. See Tiffany Stern, '"A ruinous monastery": The Second Blackfriars Playhouse as a Place of Nostalgia', in Andrew Gurr and Farah Karim-Cooper (eds), *Moving Shakespeare Indoors. Performance and Repertoire in the Jacobean Playhouse* (Cambridge, 2014), 97–114.
21. Webster praised Thomas Heywood for bringing 'to our equall view / Faire Monumental Theaters', 'whose ruines had bene ruin'd but for you': Thomas Heywood, *An Apology for Actors* (London, 1612), Sig. A2ᵛ.
22. Aphthonius the Sophist, *Progymnasmata*, in George Alexander Kennedy (ed. and trans.), *Progymnasmata. Greek Textbooks of Prose Composition and Rhetoric* (Atlanta, 2003), 89–127, at 115. Cf. Richard Rainolde, *The Foundacion of Rhetoric* (London, 1563), fol. xlix.
23. René Descartes, *Meditationes de prima philosophia* (Paris, 1641), Meditation II, §11–14.
24. Jacques Lezra, *Unspeakable Subjects: The Genealogy of the Event in Early Modern Europe* (Stanford, 1997), 103–4.
25. Descartes, *Meditationes*, §13.

26. See Ralph Berry, *The Art of John Webster* (Oxford, 1972), 20–1. Since then numerous commentaries have appeared, such as David M. Bergeron, 'The Wax Figures in *The Duchess of Malfi*', *SEL 1500–1900* 18:2 (1978), 331–9; Marion Lomax, *Stage Images and Traditions: Shakespeare to Ford* (Cambridge: 1987), 127–54; Michael Neill, *Issues of Death: Mortality and Identity in English Renaissance Tragedy* (Oxford, 1997), 328–53; Thomas Rist, *Revenge Tragedy and the Drama of Commemoration* (London, 2008); Brian Chalk, 'Webster's "Worthyest Monument": The Problem of Posterity in *The Duchess of Malfi*', *Studies in Philology* 108:3 (2011), 379–402; Margaret E. Owens, 'John Webster, Tussaud Laureate: The Waxworks in *The Duchess of Malfi*', *ELH* 79:4 (Winter, 2012), 851–77; Rory Loughnane, 'The Artificial Figures and Staging Remembrance in Webster's *Duchess of Malfi*', in Andrew Gordon and Thomas Rist (eds), *The Arts of Remembrance in Early Modern England: Memorial Cultures of the Post Reformation* (London, 2013), 211–28; Lynn Maxwell, 'Wax Magic and *The Duchess of Malfi*', *Journal for Early Modern Cultural Studies* 14:3 (Summer, 2014), 31–54; Jay Zysk, *Shadow and Substance. Eucharistic Controversy and English Drama across the Reformation Divide* (Notre Dame, 2017), Chap. 5.
27. Roberta Panzanelli, 'Compelling Presence. Wax Effigies in Renaissance Florence', in Roberta Panzanelli (ed.), *Ephemeral Bodies. Wax Sculpture and the Human Figure* (Los Angeles, 2008), 13–40; Guido Antonio Guerzoni, 'Use and Abuse of Beeswax in the Early Modern Age. Two Apologues and a Taste', in A. Daninos (ed.), *Waxing Eloquent: Italian Portraits in Wax* (Milan, 2012), 43–59.
28. Panzanelli, 'Wax Effigies', 21.
29. Owens, 'John Webster', 857–60.
30. See Michael Neill, 'Monuments and Ruins in *The Duchess of Malfi*', in James Redmond (ed.), *Drama and Symbolism* (Cambridge, 1982), 71–87.
31. Loughnane, 'The Artificial Figures'.
32. Owens, 'John Webster', 861.
33. Ibid. 871; Maxwell, 'Wax Magic and *The Duchess of Malfi*'.
34. Brooke, *John Webster*, 158.
35. Julius von Schlosser, 'Geschichte der Porträtbildnerei in Wachs', *Jahrbuch der Kunsthistorischen Sammlungen des Allerhöchsten Kaiserhauses* 29 (1910/11), 171–258, esp. 250.
36. Walter Benjamin, *Das Passagen-Werk*, in Benjamin, *GS* V/i: 516.
37. John Ford, 'To the Reader of the Authour, and his Dutchesse of *Malfy*', in Webster, *Works* 1: 471.
38. Benjamin, *Ursprung des deutschen Trauerspiels*, in Benjamin, *GS* I/i: 391–2.
39. Charles Estienne and Jean Liébault, *Maison rustique, or The Country Farme*, trans. Richard Surflet (London, 1616), 586.
40. Cf. Susan Zimmerman, *The Early Modern Corpse and Shakespeare's Theatre* (Edinburgh, 2007).
41. John Studley (trans.), *The Eyghth Tragedye of L. Annaeus Seneca, Entituled Agamemnon*, in Thomas Newton et al., *Seneca his tenne tragedies* (London, 1581), 141–2.

42. Stephen Greenblatt, *Hamlet in Purgatory* (Princeton, 2001), 229. See *Hamlet* V.ii.317; 322; F, V.ii.287; 292. The phrase appears only once in Q1 at 17.102.
43. Greenblatt, *Hamlet*, 225.
44. Ibid. 243.
45. *Contra* Douglas Bruster and Robert Weimann, *Prologues to Shakespeare's Theatre. Performance and Liminality in Early Modern Drama* (London, 2004).
46. Neill, *Issues of Death*, 246. An outline of the bibliography would include above all Greenblatt, *Purgatory*, esp. Chap. 4; but also R. N. Watson, *The Rest is Silence: Death as Annihilation in the English Renaissance* (Berkeley, 1994); Huston Diehl, *Staging Reform, Reforming the Stage* (Ithaca, 1997), 94–124; and Scott Dudley, 'Conferring with the Dead: Necrophilia and Nostalgia in the Seventeenth Century', *ELH* 66:2 (Summer, 1999), 277–94. Peter Marshall summarises in his *Beliefs and the Dead in Reformation England* (Oxford, 2002), 313: 'Literary critics have been attracted to the idea that the impulses blocked by the abolition of purgatory and intercessory prayer became sublimated in the imperatives of English Renaissance revenge tragedy.'
47. John Dover Wilson, *What Happens in* Hamlet (Cambridge, 1937), 51–86. See Kathryn A. Edwards, 'The History of Ghosts in Early Modern Europe: Recent Research and Future Trajectories', *History Compass* 10:4 (2012), 353–66.
48. This tendency is perhaps part of the anti-fetishism of the social sciences, against which see Bruno Latour, 'On Interobjectivity', trans. Geoffrey Bowker, *Mind, Culture, and Activity* 3:4 (1996), 228–45, at 236: 'Objects do *do* something, they are not merely the screens or the retroprojectors of our social life. Their sole function is not merely to "launder" the social origin of the forces that we project onto them.' However, the objecthood of the matter I will present here is complicated by its status as both the condensation and product of distinct literary and cultural afterlives.
49. Thomas Nashe, 'To the Gentlemen Students of both Universities', in Robert Greene, *Menaphon* (London, 1589), Sig. **3.
50. For this suggestion, and for a persuasive restoration of *Hamlet* and its rhetoric of infinity and division to early modern mathematical and scientific discourse, see Joseph Christopher Jarrett, 'Mathematics and Late Elizabethan Drama, 1587–1603', PhD thesis, University of Cambridge, 2017, esp. Chap. 5.
51. Hans Kurath (ed.), *Middle English Dictionary* (Ann Arbor, 2001), 722.
52. For example: Seneca, *Agamemnon*, in L. Annaeus Seneca, ed. Rudolf Peiper and Gustav Richter, *Tragoediae* (Leipzig, 1921), ll.42–3: '*post decima Phoebi lustra devicto Ilio / adest*'.
53. See Evelyn Tribble, *Early Modern Actors and Shakespeare's Theatre. Thinking with the Body* (London, 2017), 28–9, discussing Thomas Heywood, *An Apologie for Actors* (London, 1612), 20–1. On the polysemy of 'move', see further J. H. Prynne, *They that Haue Powre to Hurt: A Specimen of a Commentary on* Shake-speares Sonnets, *94* (Cambridge, 2001), 25–8.
54. William Shakespeare, *Julius Caesar*, ed. David Daniell, Arden 3rd ser.

(London, 2011), IV.iii.274–5. All further reference is to this edition. Cf. Plutarch, *The Lives of the noble Grecians and Romanes compared*, trans. Thomas North (London, 1579), 796: 'looking towards the light of the lampe that waxed very dimme, he saw a horrible vision of a man'.
55. See Emily Cockayne, *Hubbub. Filth, Noise & Stench in England* (New Haven, 2007), 146–7; John E. Crowley, *The Invention of Comfort: Sensibilities and Design in Early Modern Britain* (Baltimore, 2001), 112: 'The flame of these illumination sources was inevitably sooty and a menace to respiratory health even before they began to exhaust a room's oxygen.'
56. R. B. Graves, *Lighting the Shakespearean Stage, 1567–1642* (Carbondale, 1999), 15–16.
57. See Leah Knight, *Reading Green in Early Modern England* (London, 2014), esp. 25–8.
58. Drew Milne, 'Electra Traces: Beckett's Critique of Sophoclean Tragedy', *Didaskalia, Ancient Theatre Today* 5:3 (Summer, 2002), www.didaskalia. net/issues/vol5no3/milne.html (accessed 5 December 2018).
59. See Martin White, '"When torchlight made an artificial noon": Light and Darkness in the Indoor Jacobean Theatre', in Andrew Gurr and Farah Karim-Cooper (eds), *Moving Shakespeare Indoors* (Cambridge, 2014), 115–36; Neil Vallelly, 'Being-in-Light at the Early Modern and Reconstructed Theatres', PhD thesis, University of Otago, 2015; Gösta M. Bergman, *Lighting in the Theatre* (Stockholm, 1977).
60. William Shakespeare, *Othello*, ed. E. A. J. Honigmann, Arden 3rd ser. (London, 2006), I.i.73–8. All further reference is to this edition.
61. White, 'Light and Darkness', 129–31.
62. See Victor I. Stoichita, *A Short History of the Shadow*, trans. Anne-Marie Glasheen (London, 1997), 58.
63. Matt. 7:1–5; Luke 6:37–42; David Daniell (ed.), *Tyndale's New Testament* (New Haven, 1995), 28; 100.
64. See Philip L. Culbertson, *A Word Fitly Spoken. Context, Transmission, and Adoption of the Parables of Jesus* (Albany, 1995), 206–7.
65. Theodor W. Adorno, *Minima Moralia. Reflexionen aus dem beschädigten Leben*, in Rolf Tiedemann et al. (eds), *Gesammelte Schriften*, 20 vols (Frankfurt, 1986), 4: 55: 'Der Splitter in deinem Auge ist das beste Vergrößerungsglas.'
66. William Shakespeare, *King John*, ed. E. A. J. Honigmann, Arden 2nd ser. (London, 1967), IV.i.91–5.
67. Richalm of Schöntal, *Liber revelationum de insidiis et versutiis daemonum*, in Bernhard Pez (ed.), *Thesaurus anecdotorum vovissimus*, 6 vols (Augsburg, 1721–9), I/ii: 373–472, at 421 (§xli): 'Saepe, quando claudo oculos, video daemones tanquam pulverem densum, undique mihi circumfusos, & corpora ipsorum minutissima; sicuti pulvis vel atomi in sole; sic densos video ipsos omni homini eo modo circumfusos, & adhaerentes.'
68. Walter Benjamin, *Das Passagen-Werk*, in Benjamin, *GS* V/i: 158.
69. Robert Cawdry, *Treasurie or store-house of similies* (London, 1600), 843.
70. Thomas Nashe, *The Terrors of the night, or a discourse of apparitions* (1594), Sig. B3.
71. Helkiah Crooke, *Mikrokosmographia* (London, 1615), 8. Cf. Thomas

Robertson, *Lillies Rules Construed* (London, 1633), Sig. 3ᵛ: '*atomus* [means] a mote in the Sunne'.
72. Andrew Zurcher, 'Spenser's Studied Archaism: The Case of "Mote"', *Spenser Studies* 21 (2006), 231–40.
73. Plato, *Theaetetus*, trans. M. J. Levett and Myles Burnyeat, in John M. Cooper (ed.), *Plato. Complete Works* (Indianapolis, 1997), 173 [§155d]; Aristotle, *Metaphysics*, trans. William David Ross, in Aristotle, *Works*, 2: 1554 [§982b].
74. William Shakespeare, *Macbeth*, ed. Kenneth Muir, Arden 2nd ser. (London, 1997), I.v.5–6.
75. Mark Kingwell, 'Husserl's Sense of Wonder', *Philosophical Forum* 31:1 (Spring, 2000), 85–107, at 89.
76. See John Sallis, '"A wonder that one could never aspire to surpass"', in Kenneth Maly (ed.), *The Path of Archaic Thinking. Unfolding the Work of John Sallis* (Albany, 1995), 243–74.
77. Cf. T. G. Bishop, *Shakespeare and the Theatre of Wonder* (Cambridge, 1996).
78. In this as in other ways, neo-Aristotelianism misrepresents Aristotle: see Ryan Drake, 'Wonder, Nature, and the Ends of Tragedy', *International Philosophical Quarterly* 50:1 (197) (March, 2010), 77–91. For a brief description of how the simple identification of wonder with emotion informed seventeenth- and eighteenth-century dramatic theory, see most recently Charis Charalampous, *Rethinking the Mind–Body Relationship in Early Modern Literature, Philosophy and Medicine. The Renaissance of the Body* (London, 2016), esp. 120–3.
79. Christine Hunzinger, 'La Notion de θῶμα chez Hérodote', *Ktèma* 20 (1995), 47–70, at 56–7.
80. Quentin Skinner, *Forensic Shakespeare* (Oxford, 2014), esp. 73–85.
81. Scott Wayland, 'Religious Change and the Renaissance Elegy', *English Literary Renaissance* 39:3 (2009), 429–59, at 451.
82. Ann Rosalind Jones and Peter Stallybrass, *Renaissance Clothing and the Materials of Memory* (Cambridge, 2000), 245; and see Chap. 10, generally.
83. Seneca, *Thyestes*, trans. Jasper Heywood, in *Seneca his tenne tragedies* (London, 1581), 21.
84. See Alwin Thaler, 'In My Mind's Eye, Horatio', *Shakespeare Quarterly* 7:4 (Autumn, 1956), 351–4.
85. William Shakespeare, 'Weary with toil. I haste me to my bed' (Sonnet 27), in Katherine Duncan-Jones (ed.), *Shakespeare's Sonnets*, Arden 3rd ser. (London, 2007), 27: ll.9–10.
86. Pliny the Elder, *Naturalis Historiae Libri XXXVII*, ed. Karl Friedrich Theodor Mayhoff, 6 vols (Leipzig, 1906), 5: XXXV.43.
87. Harold F. Brooks, '*Richard III*: Antecedents of Clarence's Dream', *Shakespeare Survey* 32 (1979), 145–50, at 146.
88. Anon., *A pleasant comedie, called Wily Beguilde* (London, 1606), Sig A2ᵛ.
89. Anthony Anderson, *The Shield of our Safetie* (London, 1581), Sig. H3ᵛ. Compare William Sclater, *A Key to the Key of Scripture* (London, 1611), 21: 'onely a bare spectrum, and shadow of man, as Manichees dreamt'.
90. Reginald Scot, *The Discovery of Witchcraft* (London, 1584), 147. See

Philip Butterworth, *Magic on the Early English Stage* (Cambridge, 2005), 85; Charles Zika, 'The Witch of Endor: Transformations of a Biblical Necromancer in Early Modern Europe', in Charles Zika and F. W. Kent (eds), *Rituals, Images and Words: The Varieties of Cultural Expression in Late Medieval and Early Modern Europe* (Turnhout, 2005), 235–59.
91. Raphael Lyne, 'Shakespeare, Perception and Theory of Mind', *Paragraph* 37:1 (2014), 79–95, at 89.
92. Ibid. 90.
93. Crooke, *Mikrokosmographia*, 536.
94. John Harington, *Orlando Furioso in English Heroical Verse* (London, 1591), 28.
95. *Contra* Lyne, 'Shakespeare, Perception and Theory of Mind', 91: 'the theatre is a form in which to explore contradictory mind-states that pertain naturally to ghost stories'; and Evelyn Tribble, *Cognition in the Globe. Attention and Memory in Shakespeare's Theatre* (New York, 2011), 31: 'movement across the stage should not in general impose excessive cognitive demands'.
96. Erich Auerbach, 'Figura', *Archivum Romanicum* 22 (1938), 436–89, reprinted in *Neue Dantestudien* (Istanbul, 1944), 11–71; and in *Gesammelte Aufsätze zur romanischen Philologie* (Berlin, 1967), 55–92. For the reader's convenience I refer here and throughout to a readily available English translation: Erich Auerbach, 'Figura', trans. Ralph Manheim, in *Scenes from the Drama of European Literature: Six Essays* (Minneapolis, 1984), 11–76.
97. Auerbach, 'Figura', 17.
98. Ibid. 17; n9.
99. David Sedley, 'Lucretius' Use and Avoidance of Greek', *Proceedings of the British Academy* 93 (1999), 227–46, at 230–4.
100. David Butterfield, *The Early Textual History of Lucretius' De Rerum Natura* (Cambridge, 2013), 305–6.
101. Plutarch, *Brutus*, in Bernadotte Perrin (ed. and trans.), *Plutarch's Lives*, 11 vols (Cambridge, MA, 1961), 6: 125–247, at 206–9 (§37). In North's Plutarch, the wax becomes clay: 'therefore the imagination is resembled to claye, and the minde to the potter': Plutarch, *The Lives*, trans. North, 1072.
102. John Milton, *Areopagitica* (London, 1644), 36.
103. *Contra* Carl Landauer, '*Mimesis* and Erich Auerbach's Self-Mythologizing', *German Studies Review* 11:1 (Feb., 1988), 83–96.
104. See Christopher Lane, 'The Poverty of Context: Historicism and Nonmimetic Fiction', *PMLA* 118:3 Special Topic: Imagining History (May, 2003), 450–69, at 457–8.
105. James Porter suggests that 'the field has moved on and [. . .] Auerbach has become a part of its history rather than a part of its current working models': James I. Porter, 'Disfigurations: Erich Auerbach's Theory of *Figura*', *Critical Inquiry* 44 (Autumn, 2017), 80–113.
106. Auerbach, 'Figura', 23.
107. Phillip Stubbes, *The Anatomie of Abuses* (London, 1583), lv^v; lvii^v.
108. Patrick Collinson, *From Iconoclasm to Iconophobia. The Cultural Impact of the Second English Reformation* (Reading, 1986).

109. Here I do not mean to imply an identification of anti-theatre and Puritanism: see Margot Heinemann, *Puritanism and Theatre* (Cambridge, 1980), 18–47.
110. Ann Kibbey, *The Interpretation of Material Shapes in Puritanism* (Cambridge, 1986), 47.
111. Francis Meres, *Wits Treasury* (London, 1598), fol. 281^v.
112. *Contra* Jonathan Bate, *Shakespeare and Ovid* (Oxford, 1994), 2.
113. Hayden White persuasively argues that Auerbach's account of 'a figure-fulfillment-figure relationship [. . .] is what constitutes a tradition as such': Hayden White, *Figural Realism. Studies in the Mimesis Effect* (Baltimore, 2000), 91.
114. Jasper Heywood (trans.), *The seconde tragedie of Seneca entituled Thyestes* (London, 1560), 'The Preface'.
115. Richard Halpern, 'The Classical Inheritance', in Michael Neill and David Schalkwyk (eds), *The Oxford Handbook of Shakespearean Tragedy* (Oxford, 2016), 19–34, at 28.
116. Gerard Passannante, *The Lucretian Renaissance. Philology and the Afterlife of Tradition* (Chicago, 2011), at 122.
117. Erich Auerbach, *Mimesis. Dargestellte Wirklichkeit in der abendländischen Literatur* (Tübingen, 2001), 308–9.
118. Auerbach, 'Figura', 16–17.
119. Porter, 'Disfigurations', 89.
120. Auerbach, *Mimesis*, 312.
121. Christopher Marlowe, *Doctor Faustus*, ed. David Bevington and Eric Rasmussen (Manchester, 1993), A-Text, IV.i.47–50.
122. See Deirdre Lynch, *The Economy of Character. Novels, Market Culture, and the Business of Inner Meaning* (Chicago, 1998).
123. James Dougal Fleming, *The Mirror of Information in Early Modern England. John Wilkins and the Universal Character* (Basingstoke, 2017), 75–114.
124. John Webster, *New Characters (drawne to the life) of severall Persons, in severall qualities*, in Webster, *Works*, 3: 459–86, at 483–4.
125. Thomas Middleton, *Women Beware Women*, ed. John Jowett, in Middleton, *Works*, V.i.181–2.
126. Auerbach, 'Figura', 25–8.
127. Auerbach, *Mimesis*, 308–9; see the quotation, *supra*.
128. See J. C. Mann, 'The Orphic Physics of Early Modern Eloquence', in Howard Marchitello and Evelyn Tribble (eds), *The Palgrave Handbook of Early Modern Literature and Science* (London, 2017), 231–56, esp. 237–9.
129. Quintilian, *Institutio Oratoria*, ed. and trans. Harold Edgeworth Butler, 4 vols (Cambridge, MA, 1922), 350 [IX.i.1]: '*figura, sicut nomine ipso patet, conformatio quaedam orationis remota a communi et primum se offerente ratione*'. Cf. George Puttenham, *The Arte of English Poesie* (London, 1589), 132. See G. N. Leech, 'Linguistics and the Figures of Rhetoric', in Roger Fowler (ed.), *Essays on Style and Language: Linguistic and Critical Approaches to Literary Style* (London, 1966), 135–56; Mary E. Hazard, 'An Essay to Amplify "Ornament": Some Renaissance Theory and Practice', *SEL, 1500–1900* 16:1 (Winter, 1976), 15–32.

130. Lorna Hutson, *Circumstantial Shakespeare* (Oxford, 2015), 171.
131. Ibid. 172.
132. Quintilian, *Institutio Oratoria*, ed. and trans. Butler, 356 [XII.i.1].
133. See Raymond Geuss, 'Poetry and Knowledge', *Arion* 11:1 (3rd ser.) (Spring/ Summer, 2003), 1–31; Simon Jarvis, 'For a Poetics of Verse', *PMLA* 125:4 (Oct., 2010), 931–5, at 934: 'Let's not let everything dissolve into everything else.'
134. Auerbach, 'Figura', 34.
135. Ibid. 33; Kevin Killeen, *The Political Bible in Early Modern England* (Cambridge, 2016), 22–51.
136. Kathleen Biddick, *The Typological Imaginary: Circumcision, Technology, History* (Philadelphia, 2003), 6; Jeffrey S. Librett, *The Rhetoric of Cultural Dialogue. Jews and Germans from Moses Mendelssohn to Richard Wagner and Beyond* (Stanford, 2000), 12–18. To respond properly to Librett's detailed and persuasive critique of Auerbach would take us beyond the scope of the position reached at the end of this chapter, a position reached chiefly in an effort to cast new light on the limits of historicism as it pertains to the interpretation of early modern plays.
137. Charles Kannengiesser, *Handbook of Patristic Exegesis. The Bible in Ancient Christianity*, 2 vols (Leiden, 2006), 1: 230.
138. Julia Reinhard Lupton, *Afterlives of the Saints: Hagiography, Typology, and Renaissance Literature* (Stanford, 1996), xxii. On Auerbach, esp. 20–3.
139. Erich Auerbach, *Dante als Dichter der irdischen Welt* (Berlin, 2001), 192.
140. Ibid. 190–1.
141. Adi Efal, *Figural Philology: Panofsky and the Science of Things* (London, 2016), 66.
142. Ibid.
143. Stoichita, *History of the Shadow*, 15.
144. Kannengiesser, *Handbook of Patristic Exegesis*, 1: 228.

Chapter 6

Bare Facts, Endless Tragedies

> why here are tracks – a second proof – tracks of feet, matching each other – and like unto my own!
> *Aeschylus, Libation Bearers*

> but how could a footprint be made in such stony ground?
> *Euripides, Electra*

> beyond the adventurous and uncertain footprints of single players, there appear the marks of a collective identity
> Raimondo Guarino, *Shakespeare: La Scrittura nel Teatro*
> (trans. Paola Pugliatti)

Were one to be sunk in candlelit reverie and a light abruptly switched on, the start would be no less sudden and complete than it is to turn from the ghosts and ghastly statues of the previous chapter to the quintessential revenge play *sans* revenger: *Arden of Faversham*. Thomas Kyd wrote it some time before 1592, likely in collaboration with William Shakespeare.[1] The murderers Black Will and Shakebag lie in wait for their victim under the cloak of night, but this play's darkness is not that from which Old Hamlet emerges, or in which the Aeschylean beacon lights. It more apparently derives from actual concern about nocturnal criminal mischief.[2] An issue of Senecan reception or literary substance seems suddenly very remote in Aldersgate, St Paul's, Greenwich, Sheppey, Southwark, Rochester, Rainham Down, or the Nag's Head in Cheapside: places in the play. *Arden of Faversham* distinguishes itself in several ways. Among the many attempts on Arden's life, that involving the commission of a crucifix painted with poison seems the least proper to the setting.[3] Lorna Hutson is right to suggest that in *Arden of Faversham* the hermeneutic uncertainty of action is minimised and that it 'unfolds with a claustrophobic inevitability, as every time a character is called for, or a scheme of action is suggested, that character or action follows immediately'.[4] It is significant, then, that nothing ever comes of the poisoned crucifix plot. Arden does not suffer any fate to compare with Clois Hoffman, his father, and Prince Otho (their brains boiled with a burning crown), the Duke of *The Revenger's Tragedy* (poisoned by a skull), Julia of *The Duchess of Malfi* (poisoned by a bible), or Ithocles of John Ford's *The Broken Heart* (trapped in a mechanised throne): he is bundled into death by a couple of London cutthroats wielding daggers and a towel. His death is grisly, certainly; 'baroque', hardly. Like *Hamlet*, *Arden of Faversham* evinces a greater scepticism than *The Spanish Tragedy* when it comes to the relative lethality of plays, images and bare blades. The painter ('Clarke') threatens to 'cuff' or 'knock' the servant Michael: 'What, with a dagger made of a pencil?' comes the devastating retort (10.72–3). Perhaps some defect of the extant text explains the disappearance of the painter after he has given Michael a knock, but a possibly stronger explanation can be made with reference to its generic effect. If, as was suggested in the Introduction, a work can image a genre in its conspicuous departure from it, the non-event of the assassination by poisoned crucifix can be understood as a narrative turn which both construes *and* expels revenge tragedy. The crucifix prepared by the painter enters unused into the banal criminal repertoire of Arden's wife Alice and her confederates. As she and her lover reaffirm the dubious constancy of their love, the figure of Clarke the painter fades silently into the scene's background, never to be seen again (10.81–107). Except Hieronimo seems to encounter him in later iterations of *The Spanish Tragedy* as 'Bazardo', an indistinct figure in the darkening grove.

Arden of Faversham starts several inchoate revenge plots, and is rich in vengeful threats, but figures no avenger. The dislanded Reede, whose plot has been expropriated by Arden from him and his family ('needy and bare', 13.17), comes closest. That Arden may simultaneously have been innocent and at the same time a landlord who had it coming is implied at the end of the play: 'Arden lay murdered in that plot of ground / Which he by force and violence held from Reede' ('Epilogue', 10–11). There is a fraught social history underpinning Reede's curses – 'That plot of ground, which thou detains from me – / I speak it in an agony of spirit – / Be ruinous and fatal unto thee!' (13.34) – and their apparent efficacy.[5] But there is no revenge here except God's, in combination with his legal instruments. 'God heareth the teares of the oppressed and taketh vengeance: note an example in Arden,' wrote Holinshed in the margin of his version of the story.[6] If Arden's death is finally permitted to occur in its specific form, after numerous failures, by an obscure dispensation, it is also repaid upon those whose freedom in committing the crime is dramatised by their persistence in the face of thwarts they are incapable of perceiving as divine. A providential snowfall exposes the murderers to the law as they bear his body in: 'As we went it snowed all the way, / Which makes our footsteps will be spied.' Alice is assured that 'the snow will cover them again', but mere moments later the *polis* is at her door with warrants (14.354–8). Looking around, Arden's friend Franklin (a semi-choric addition to the story of Holinshed's *Chronicles*) detects the murder:

> I fear me he was murdered in this house
> And carried to the fields: for from that place,
> Backwards and forwards, may you see
> The print of many feet within the snow.
> And look about his chamber where we are
> And you shall find part of his guiltless blood.

'It is too manifest,' agrees the Mayor (14.386–95). The footprints are traceable only in the moment before they are covered by time; miss them, and the plot goes unperformed. This idea is strongly implicated not only in the many circumstantial mischiefs which manifest the *oeconomic* ordering of human action within time and space by God (the footprints *were* seen there in time), but also in the question of theatrical ephemerality and its relation to truth (the dialectic of 'true bodies' and 'true histories'). The footprints are implicated, that is, in the premise that the truth of Arden and his death might only appear in a play.[7] In this sense the factuality of Arden's death might indeed be *too* manifest, beyond the ken of those who have not seen it. This is why Franklin and the Mayor, standing in the room where Arden was murdered, are already acquiring the aspect of prospective deponents. The play is transforming into testimony.

Although the footprints will disappear in the snow, Arden's blood stubbornly resists all deletion. The murderers hope earlier in the play to find 'some other place / Whose earth may swallow up this Arden's blood' (3.112–13), but later find that 'the blood cleaveth to the ground and will not out' (14.247), however much they scratch and scrape. There is then a subtle interplay of the passing and the permanent within the play itself – but it is detained within its 'plot'. 'Embodying a sense of the past still focused more on space than time and more on site than dates,' writes Alexandra Walsham, providential legends manifested 'a belief that God literally inscribed his judgments in the landscape'.[8] *Arden of Faversham* presents itself as a record of that local inscription: a circumscription. In a stunning Epilogue, Franklin entrenches that boundary:

> Thus have you seen the truth of Arden's death.
> As for the ruffians, Shakebag and Black Will,

> The one took sanctuary and, being sent for out,
> Was murderèd in Southwark, as he passed
> To Greenwich, where the Lord Protector lay.
> Black Will was burnt in Flushing on a stage.
> Greene was hanged at Osbridge in Kent.
> The painter fled, and how he died we know not.
> But this above the rest is to be noted:
> Arden lay murdered in that plot of ground
> Which he by force and violence held from Reede:
> And in the grass his body's print was seen
> Two years and more after the deed was done.
> Gentlemen, we hope you'll pardon this naked tragedy
> Wherein no filèd points are foisted in
> To make it gracious to the ear or eye.
> For simple truth is gracïous enough,
> And needs no other points of glossing stuff.[9]   [*Exit*]

There is no record of *Arden of Faversham* being performed in the early modern theatres. The self-consuming Epilogue potentially transforms the play into a text which declares a truth withheld from anything but 'ear or eye'. An unwise modernisation makes 'glossing' out of the original 'glozing', which – although it certainly contains the meaning of 'exegesis' explored below – possessed a pejorative sense of 'artificial', 'specious', 'deceptive' and 'flattering'. Encountered outside its theatre plot, the text of *Arden of Faversham* simultaneously purports to describe historical fact while calling forth a suspect 'glossing' of its factuality.

In this, his oblique and possibly reluctant summons to future glossers, Franklin is clearly doing something quite distinct from Hamlet, discovered at the beginning of this book voicing a concern for his name. The literalism involved in the idea of a 'naked tragedy' is paradoxical. As James Dougal Fleming notes of the early modern development of scientific factuality in reference to 'literal' exegesis of Scripture ('glozing'), 'the literal meaning is not supposed to be a function of interpretation. Therefore, "literal interpretation" is an oxymoron'.[10] Were Arden's death really manifest, an Epilogue – which appears from one angle at least to be the very threshold or beginning of paratextual glossing – would not have been needed to say so.[11] Yet the burdened hermeneutics of an analysis of *Arden of Faversham* are of another order to those required to meet the challenge issued by revenge tragedy in its figural mode. Without an avenger, *Arden of Faversham* need not anticipate the labour of future interpretation, of ends, means, intents and person. Neither does it expose its figures to a potentially indefinite difficulty of figuration: they are presented as facts. 'Time, nor place, nor persons alter me,' speaks Arden. How is this vouched? By his 'quick return' to the scene of his murder (10.31–3). *Arden of Faversham* remains within the circle of its own history – no 'endless tragedy' (*ST* IV.v.48), but 'true report'. If Franklin's Epilogue presents an entirely different set of complications from the words with which Revenge ends *The Spanish Tragedy*, why can they be arraigned under the same concept?

An Autopsy for Metatheatre

It may be a hasty pathologist who cuts open a subject showing such concerning vitality – but it has become so pallid that it is hard to credit the signs of life, which are too many to register.[12] 'Metatheatre' echoes in seminar rooms and lecture halls everywhere. It has become common for students as well as scholars to adduce *metatheatre* in such a way as to evidence their own credibility. *Metatheatre* often functions less as a criterion of early modern knowingness than as a baseline of contemporary academic competence. *Metatheatre* is also attractive as a means of dissolving historical distance. It helps transform 'early modern' drama into something to which a prospective community of 'modern' readers can relate without much arduity. It takes a profoundly challenging dimension of the early modern dramatic legacy and represents it to an age burdened with the need to appear too knowing to be anything as passé as historical. Although *metatheatre* has been implicated in a vast range of theories about the theatre, it has, like a corpse floating near multiple shipwrecks, become separated from them. It is generally introduced as if its theorisation were complete. In this section, some of the assumptions and procedures involved in applying the term *metatheatre* to early modern tragic drama are extracted and weighed. The confusions inhering in them conspire against an explication of figuration and may dictate how this book is interpreted.

It is best to start with the skin. At its most abstract and bare, *metatheatre* presents an artificial hierarchy of *theatre* and *metatheatre* that secretes a noxious concept of *theatre*. Assuming everything proper to *metatheatre* is extruded from *theatre*, what remains is perfect fantasy; a complete, seamless illusion. Any use of *metatheatre* potentially contains a specific and rather severe argument about *theatre*, meshing with a loose set of realist and naturalist presumptions that attend dispositions to the late capitalist theatre institution. *Metatheatre* secretly works on a definition of *theatre* without ever having to defend or expound it. A distinction between *metatheatre* and *metadrama* can only be drawn if one accepts the insinuated definition of *theatre* contained in *metatheatre*: that the theatre is a place where a sustained illusion or fiction is produced and effected. Assuming that this is a good definition of early modern theatre (which it is not), *metatheatre* can have no effect upon the reader of the drama in which it appears, for the reader is not exposed to the arsenal of techniques proper to an illusionistic theatre (the reader is not in a *theatre*) so that the purported effect of *metatheatre* (to interrupt and enter into a functional tension with the fiction) cannot operate. That being the case, *metatheatre* is identified as the trace of historical conditions in the *theatre* to which the *drama* originally related. That which, *per metatheatre*, appears as an enquiry into the historicity of the play in fact allows its historical substance to be safely stowed away while *drama*, which against the operations of *metatheatre* seems to transcend the terms of its historical presentation, is appreciated and digested. This works only because occasions of *metatheatre* can apparently be identified, listed and as it were excised from the *drama*. The case is somewhat different where the insinuated concept of *theatre* is received more as the description of an intact or undisturbed fiction than as the description of a house of illusion. Then *metadrama* and *metatheatre* are simply identical, because the question of *theatre* has been displaced by the question of *drama*, so that *metatheatre* really means *metadrama*. The effect of the concept of *metadrama* on *drama* is just the same as the effect of *metatheatre* upon *theatre*. Drama was only itself before modernity, states *metadrama*, and modern authors are incapable of producing it. Another way of saying this is that *metadrama* makes *drama*, whatever that would be, into a primitive form. In this way a set of vacuous but convenient assumptions about form and history are disseminated by the concepts *metatheatre* and *metadrama*.

This blistering terminological membrane has proved surprisingly sticky. Tracy C. Davis and Thomas Postlewait try to distinguish metadrama ('a play which comments on the conventions of its genre') from metatheatre ('a performance calling attention to the presentational aspects of theatre and its conventions in the moment of its transpiring'), but thereby detain from metadrama the capacity for presentational reflection and from metatheatre the possibility of its interference in genre.[13] Richard Hornby finds that metadrama disintegrates in his hands when he tries to specify its properties: 'metadrama can be defined as drama about drama; it occurs whenever the subject of the play turns out to be, in some sense, drama itself [...] *all* drama is metadramatic, since its subject is always, willy-nilly, the drama/culture complex'.[14] Likewise, James L. Calderwood admits that metadrama may amount to 'dramatic art itself', which draws closer to the truth but remains tethered to a formalist programme.[15] In its unlikely career as an instrument of classical philology, metatheatre has been characterised as the play which shows self-awareness; the play-within-the-play; a synonym for metatext; 'theatrically self-conscious theatre'.[16] In particular, a tension has arisen between a *technical* account of metatheatre and a *generic* one. The former attempts to specify a range of technical features of plays (prologues, soliloquies, asides, inset plays, et cetera); the latter usually involves specific arguments about tragic incapability and modernity, 'definite form' rather than 'device'.[17] In short, the problem of definition has proved sufficiently attractive fodder for discussion that it has actively abetted the retention of premises which few would accept if they were pressed. One reason for the vitality of *metatheatre* is that it can be inflated and deflated with great rapidity and expediency but remains problematically definite enough for indefinite discussion of its problems. Stripped of this outer layer, a multitude of strange organs is suddenly visible. It is not at all clear how they are all connected, whether they ought to be, and if the confused pathologist was right to start at all. 'I do not want things to be here as they are in the Comedies, where everything is known to everybody,' says Pamphilus towards the end of Terence's *Hecyra*.[18] 'The play's the thing / Wherein I'll catch the conscience of the king,' speaks Hamlet (III.i.539–40), not far off two millennia later. Understanding can surely achieve no advantage in yanking these occasions under the same concept. Yet *metatheatre*, even with its guts out, just will not die.

Although the *theatrum mundi* conceit has, in various permutations, been culturally thematic for a very long time, Lionel Abel's *Metatheatre: A New View of Dramatic Form* (1963) inaugurated a new and specific way of thinking about how it appeared in Shakespeare and seems to have entered *metatheatre* into use. 'Hamlet's philosophizing about action,' wrote Abel, 'is a projection into the play of the playwright's difficulty in making his hero tragic.'[19] 'Metatheatre has replaced tragedy.'[20] Why did Shakespeare find it difficult to make Hamlet tragic? One of Abel's first answers is that Shakespeare 'desired to produce a work of a formal structure not incompatible with the presence in it of a greatly conceived character,' which would seem to make metatheatre a creative election rather than any sort of cultural incapacity.[21] Along similar lines, it is suggested that Shakespeare was able to create the character as a dramatist by experiments with the play-within-a-play, which would make metatheatre a kind of negative capability.[22] Abel suggests that in Falstaff the metatheatre of *Hamlet* is already embryonic: 'Falstaff is too large for a purely historical drama.' A revelatory footnote qualifies some of the terms on which Falstaff's 'spontaneous dramaturgy' can be described:

A witty eighteenth-century writer, [Maurice] Morgann, was led to speculate on Falstaff's birth, parentage, childhood, early associates, and adventures *before* Falstaff's appearance in Shakespeare's play. True, Morgann's essay on Falstaff, defending his character, led to a new, misleading kind of criticism. On the other hand, one cannot think Morgann completely wrong in his observations and judgments. It was objected that Morgann's mistake was to take Falstaff for a real person, instead of as a character in a play. But this character, being essentially a dramatist, can be said to have the capacity and impulse to exist apart from the playwright who created him. Falstaff, the creation of Shakespeare, is himself a creator.[23]

A few pages later, Abel supplies 'The Myth of Metatheatre', imagining Aeschylus being kidnapped by Orestes after a performance of the *Oresteia*.[24]

If one can resist Abel's coaxes, and instead stop to consult Maurice Morgann's somewhat satirical essay of 1777, the mythography involved here becomes a little clearer. 'Cowardice *is not* the *Impression*, which the *whole* character of *Falstaff* is calculated to make on the minds of an unprejudiced audience,' writes Morgann, who proceeds to develop a playful distinction between '*mental Impressions*, and the *Understanding*'.[25] 'The Understanding seems for the most part to take cognizance of *actions* only, and from these to infer *motives* and *character*,' he continues.

> But the sense we have been speaking of proceeds in a contrary course; and determines of *actions* from certain *first principles of character*, which seem wholly out of the reach of the Understanding [. . .] We often love or hate at first sight; and indeed, in general, dislike or approve by some secret reference to these *principles*; and we judge even of conduct, not from any idea of abstract good or evil in the nature of actions, but by referring those actions to a supposed original character in the man himself.[26]

Morgann's essay is generally thought, for reasons which may be evident here, to have crystallised the eighteenth-century shift away from a neo-Aristotelian problem of action to the consideration of Shakespeare's characters, what Brian Vickers calls 'the people of Shakespeare's creation'.[27] Morgann's distinction between 'the *real* character of *Falstaff*' and 'his *apparent* one' seems agenda-setting.[28] His modern editor Daniel Fineman argues, however, that Morgann does not 'extract' Falstaff from the drama but instead pursues him within it, seeking 'to pin down the impressions he conveys or those other characters convey about him'.[29] Morgann's insight is that 'Falstaff' might acquire a reality and wholeness, such that a conversation about his 'constitution' might begin, opposite to, but also through, the terms on which he *appears*, the *impressions* he leaves. This account of his character is not a million miles away from figuration in the rhetorical sense, i.e. something which is insinuated within language without its being uttered, the 'hidden allusion'.[30] In Morgann's terms, one acquires a separate *feeling* for Falstaff that stands in contradiction to what he actually does and says in the play, even as it is the play itself which produces that feeling. The impression of Falstaff's cowardice, suggests Morgann, is 'aggravated to the spectators' through 'the idle tricks of the Player, who practises [. . .] all the attitudes and wild apprehensions of fear', a 'mummery' of which there is 'no hint [. . .] in the play'.[31] In this way the prose of character begins to free itself from the dramatical and theatrical constellations through which it is produced, a move involving not only a dismissal of performance in favour of text, but a disavowal of the labour of figuration.

Within Morgann's essay, however, the foundations of Romantic character criticism are exposed in such a way that the problem of figuration is already acquiring perceptible critical potential. But Lionel Abel, introducing *metatheatre*, gets from Morgann to 'the feeling that characters can be superior to their situations', which allegedly impelled Shakespeare to write *Hamlet*, without any scruple.[32] He greets Hamlet as if he were already free of the play, in his nineteenth-century, mythic guise. Just as psychoanalytical Shakespeare criticism 'proceeds as a return to Classical structure from the vantage point of Romantic subjectivity', Abel's insertion of metatheatre seems to build upon Romantic character criticism from a formalist position.[33] It presents a solution to the difficulty of reconciling the Romantic Hamlet to the formal properties of early modern drama, and does not address the real challenge of making sense of *Hamlet* with respect to its complication of dramatic figure (in which the Romantics and the Victorians had shown little to no interest at all). That this is true can be seen firstly in how Abel frames the problem: as a tragic person responding to an injunction.[34] As I have shown, it is not so much the injunction as its origin which precipitates Hamlet's circumspection. Further, the presumption of Hamlet's personhood must indefinitely ossify the work of figuration and its various contingencies. That the Ghost is introduced as the origin and shape of law directly challenges us not to argue about why Hamlet does or does not do this or that, but who he can be and what sort of obligation that struggle for recognition inflicts upon us. Abel is unwilling or unable to address this part of Hamlet's afterlife except in the superficial terms of a shift from 'psychology' back to 'form'.[35] Morgann, whom Abel cites as an amusing curiosity, had already begun on a model of the extravagant character that, for all its many problems, implicitly challenged the logic involved in such a dichotomy.[36]

Abel's account of metatheatre (the origin of *metatheatre*) is tautological in at least one more important way. It locates *Hamlet* at a discontinuity which the play both produces and in which it participates. Abel treats *Hamlet* as his chief instantiation of *metatheatre* but presents this as something other than arbitrary. *Hamlet* marks a threshold in the history of drama, a point at which it became impossible or nearly impossible for tragedy not to be metatheatre.[37] 'Hegel thought that after *Hamlet*, all modern tragedies would be tragedies of the intellectual,' writes Abel: 'I think he should have said tragedy would be replaced by metatheatre.'[38] Can it be that a misreading of Hegel fathered *metatheatre*? 'That [revenge] which in the Greek poets [Aeschylus and Sophocles] had an ethical warrant, the death of Agamemnon, acquires in Shakespeare the solitary form of a mad crime,' the German wrote.[39] For Hegel, *Hamlet* was a tragedy of incapability only in the sense that it was art which had lost 'the vocation to present basic conflict' and was 'limited to its medium, to configuration'.[40] 'The actual collision' of the tragedy turns not on the fact that 'the son in his ethical revenge must injure ethics itself', but on 'the subjective character of Hamlet'.[41]

While never explicitly attending to Hegel's interpretation of *Hamlet*, Gillian Rose helps us to understand how this description of tragic configuration comports with his distinction between absolute and relative ethical life, and their corresponding artforms. Absolute ethical life appears in ancient Greece. Relative ethical life is 'the system of the political economy of bourgeois property relations in which law is separated from the rest of social life'.[42] Relative ethical life produces an 'ideal of freedom or unity' which 'denies real relations and hence fixes them'. Because the social unity imaged by these relations covers up the reality of those relations, violence against that unity is incapable of transforming underlying relations and can only 'injure them'. 'The ideal of law or social unity implies revenge,' precisely because it is an ideal: an illusion.[43] Art, then, 'represents the lack of unity between the abstract ideal of freedom and the abandoned concrete world; it reproduces the real lack of political and social unity', writes Rose. 'It is [itself] illusion: it represents an ethical life which has been determined as subjectivity, which knows itself infinitely free and does not know itself as infinitely unfree'.[44] With this gloss in mind, Hegel's interpretation of Hamlet becomes both clearer and vastly more complicated than Abel suspects. Hamlet is a 'figure' implicated in 'the weakness of indecision [...] the consideration of reasons according to which a decision should be made'; and the supreme example of the contradiction which often 'leaps into the eye' [*der bald genug ins Auge springt*], involving the 'formal characteristics of individuals whom we encounter as concrete, living humans'.[45] By contrast, the figures of Greek tragedy appear within a (fictitious) society 'in which there is no subjectivity and hence no representation'. There, the society 'contains conflict and injustice', but because it is substantially free, these are 'transparent and intelligible'.[46] For Hegel, it would be rank absurdity to interpret the *Oresteia* as an account of potential criminality. By contrast, the ends, means and persons of early modern revenge tragedy are continually involved in a law that severs tragic action from its potentially universal meaning. Revenge in early modern plays, but not in the originary tragedies to which they respond, can only appear as a departure from relative values. Without the possibility of transforming them, revengers become reflective and tragedy delves into its own grounds.

Endless Task

That is only a marginally fuller account of Hegel's thinking than that supplied by Abel in *Metatheatre* ('tragedies of the intellectual' indeed), but it may be sufficient to explain why *metatheatre* is not going anywhere soon. What does the attempt to dissect *metatheatre* really involve when there is no serious prospect of its dying? 'It means that the proposition which we have affirmed, or the concept we have devised of the nature of an object, fails to correspond to the state of affairs or object which we have also defined as the state of affairs or object to which it should correspond.'[47] Efforts to rescue *metatheatre* express the continuing struggle to understand why it is that a correct conceptual vocabulary cannot be found for the strange tendency of early modern plays to differentiate themselves from the world they represent. Abel implicitly identifies tragedy with theatre by inventing *metatheatre*. This certainly creates new terminological problems.[48] On the other hand, there is something accurate in the implication that early modern tragedy introduced into its own 'poetry' lasting traces of a theatre coming to terms with a new social position. As I have suggested elsewhere, the *theatrum mundi* conceit in Renaissance drama often possesses a melancholic aspect, not least in the mouth of Jacques.[49] Although *metatheatre* is often involved in the premise that the self-referentiality of Elizabethan and Jacobean plays can be taken to suggest the general theatricality of all social relations, the incorporation of theatre language into drama seems more often to allude to the specific socio-economic position of professional theatre producers.[50] That is, prologues, epilogues and any and all reference, however faint, however oblique, to the technical or social circumstances of theatre, refer to theatre producers whose work was no longer embedded in a political or religious community, but spoke back into it from a new and indefinable position. That is, moments of 'metatheatricality' announce both professional distinction and the *exclusion* of theatrical practice from social norms and experiences. They indicate and declare a knowingness that is better understood as reflection upon the new grounds created for theatre and dramatic writing in the late sixteenth century than it is as an inauguration of general scepticism regarding authentic social being.

In *The Self-Aware Image*, the art historian Victor Stoichita describes the sixteenth century as 'an epoch that had witnessed the birth of art as a problem'.[51] He pursues the elegant thesis that visual art was invented under iconoclastic pressure, forged by the 'constant tension between the absolute negation of the image and its unlimited exaltation': 'By raising the issue of art in terms of function, reception, and context, Protestant critics created, in a dialectical manner, the modern notion of art.'[52] I likewise suggested, in the Introduction to this book, that English dramatic art emerged under the pressure of a severe and multi-dimensional anti-theatricalism with roots in a suspicion of fleshly images. Here revenge tragedy comes back in as that mode in which a crisis of figures and figuration can most clearly be seen to produce dramatic art, involve it in a problem of origin, and set the terms of its continuing life by varying the injunction to remember and requite. As Donna Hamilton suggested in the 1970s, *The Spanish Tragedy* was not only England's first major tragedy, but 'one of the first defenses of the play as an art form'.[53] Stoichita's analysis of the split-level images originating in Flemish art of the mid-sixteenth century, the creation of the pictorial aperture as 'the space of *istoria*, the foreground that of the anecdote', seems perilously applicable both to the intruding 'frame' of the dialogues between Revenge and Andrea, and to Hieronimo's inset play of *Soliman and Perseda*.[54] The notorious complications of the *mise en abyme* supplied by Kyd may proceed from a more constitutive difficulty: 'In a society in which the art form has become relatively autonomous from other social institutions which it re-presents,' suggests Rose/Hegel of 'art as we understand it', 'it loses the integrity of the classical ideal and becomes contradictory'.[55] If the 'self-aware image' issues a request for 'the beholder's collaboration', *The Spanish Tragedy* seems not only to call forth infinite 'glozing stuff', but to detain it in a specific and prior difficulty of recognition.[56] The Hieronimo of the fourth quarto may have found 'it to be my son Horatio' merely by 'looking upon him by the advantage of [a] torch' (*ST* 3.xiiA.150–1), but the original bodies of the tragedy are encountered by readers in a sort of gloom – not least because the possible involvement of their hermeneutic procedures in the play's 'endless tragedy' is not accommodated by any model of reading oblivious to its own historicity.

In 1928 Walter Benjamin could suggest that the baroque *Trauerspiel*, especially in its death scenes, issued an appeal comparable to those uttered by martyrs – a supplication outside time, quite unlike the epochal decision of antique tragedy.[57] But to open an edition of *Hamlet* in 2019 is nevertheless to arrive on the scene rather late to hear it, irrespective of the play's continuing popularity. *The Origins of English Revenge Tragedy* has shown that its subject is acquiring an ever more archaic aspect, its figures becoming ever more vexing. This historical process, part of the continuing life of these plays, will conspire to cover up the traces of the early modern performers through whom the ancient motives of revenge were implicated in the contradictions of early modern English society. That the Verge – arguably the very ground of English revenge tragedy with all its corrupt courts – has proved elusive for so long is but the first index of that mounting obscurity. The presence of common players on the scene of revenge provoked and entailed the transformation of origins into semblance. Their presence was instrumental to the invention of tragic art in England. The absence of these figures from the texts which both record and perpetuate this problem of figuration cannot be reckoned in terms of any cultural binary of theatre and drama. Figuration is a medial term referring to the labour involved in making sense of figures arising from a historical dialectic (rather than a polarity) of performance and text; and to the work of historical imagination involved in speculation that the mental images we supply to plays relate to persons who lived in the past.

Holger Syme suggests that in collaboration with innovative printers, playwrights like Ben Jonson were able 'to recreate a set of effects characteristic of the stage' and make 'the book a theater'.[58] Syme's is just one attempt to overcome the vision of 'page and stage' as 'mutually exclusive territories'. It may be that such an account of the early modern book secretly informs a semiological account of theatre which one might want to think against. That is, in claiming that the book was made into a theatre, one might also be implying that there is something already potentially bookish about the theatre – stoking the old debate about chronological, ethical and ontological priority. As I have shown, procedures of figuration involve the thinking together of performance and text as well as their thinking apart. This is how they encounter and deepen the complications of human figure pursued with such startling variety and vigour in English play culture of the 1590s. It is certain that the processes of figuration described in this book are mediated by textual materiality and its historical convolutions. The last line of the previous chapter anticipates the description of that mediation, which is beyond the scope of the task I have faced here. But there is a danger that the rigour with which print mediations are observed may disable, rather than advance, the project to comprehend the process through which early modern dramatic art attained its separation from the society which produced it, and the consequences thereof. Performance (which, in all the complicated senses explored here, can and must compass the scene-shaping work of reading) may in part involve 'the doomed search for originals by continuously auditioning stand-ins', but *Hamlet* teaches us that to remember a lost figure is often the same as trying to get rid of it.[59] English revenge tragedy looks forward to a future in which the figures of history can be reliably determined, and the debts they impose cancelled. Until that time, the labour of figuration will continue.

Notes

1. *Arden of Faversham* is the centre of an ongoing and at times venomous disagreement amongst attribution experts. The argument for Kyd's authorship or part-authorship is venerable. See Walter Miksch, *Die Verfasserschaft des Arden of Feversham* (Breslau, 1907); Charles Crawford, 'The Authorship of *Arden of Faversham*', *Jahrbuch der Deutschen Shakespeare-Gesellschaft* 39 (1903), 74–86. Brian Vickers still gives the play wholly to Kyd: Brian Vickers, 'Thomas Kyd, Secret Sharer', *Times Literary Supplement*, 18 April 2008, 13–15. His interpretation of the evidence, which is mired in controversy, is likely to be represented more fully in his forthcoming edition of Thomas Kyd's oeuvre. For some of the more recent moves to draw *Arden of Faversham* into the Shakespeare canon, see MacDonald P. Jackson, *Determining the Shakespeare Canon*: Arden of Faversham *and* A Lover's Complaint (Oxford, 2014), 7–126, which updates and condenses an argument Jackson has been working on since the 1960s. Martin Wiggins is an outlier in arguing that *Arden* is not the work of any major dramatist of the 1590s, but of an enthusiastic amateur. See Martin Wiggins (ed.), *A Woman Killed with Kindness and Other Plays* (Oxford, 2008), 'Appendix I. The Unknown Author of *Arden of Faversham*', 284–7.
2. Paul Griffiths, *Lost Londons. Change, Crime, and Control in the Capital City, 1550–1660* (Cambridge, 2008), Chap. 9.
3. [Thomas Kyd and William Shakespeare], *Arden of Faversham*, in Jonathan Bate, Eric Rasmussen et al. (eds), *William Shakespeare and Others. Collaborative Plays* (Basingstoke, 2013), 1.596–634. All further reference is to this edition.
4. Lorna Hutson, *The Invention of Suspicion* (Oxford, 2007), 262.
5. See Lena Cowen Orlin, 'Man's House as his Castle in *Arden of Faversham*', *Medieval and Renaissance Drama in England* 2 (1985), 57–89; David Atwell, 'Property, Status, and the Subject in a Middle-Class Tragedy: *Arden of Faversham*', *English Literary Renaissance* 21 (1991), 328–48; Garret A. Sullivan, Jr, '"Arden lay murdered in that plot of ground": Surveying, Land, and *Arden of Faversham*', *English Literary History* 61 (1994), 231–52; Frank Whigham, *Seizures of the Will in Early Modern English*

Drama (Cambridge, 2009), Chap. 2; Randall Martin, '"Arden winketh at his wife's lewdness, & why!": A Patrilineal Crisis in *Arden of Faversham*', *Early Theatre* 4 (2001), 13–33. For something a little more to the point, see Andy Wood, 'Fear, Hatred and the Hidden Injuries of Class in Early Modern England', *Journal of Social History* 39:3 (Spring, 2006), 803–86.
6. Ralph Holinshed et al., *The Third Volume of Chronicles* (London, 1586), 1066. For the narrative at large: 1062–6; for the circumstance of the body's print in the plot, see 1066:

> This one thing séemeth verie strange and notable, touching maister Arden, that in the place where he was laid, being dead, all the proportion of his bodie might be séene two yeares after and more, so plaine as could be, for the grasse did not grow where his bodie had touched: but betwéene his legs, betweene his armes, and about the hollownesse of his necke, and round about his bodie, and where his legs, armes, head, or anie other part of his bodie had touched, no grasse growed at all of all that time. So that manie strangers came in that meane time, beside the townesmen, to see the print of his bodie there on the ground in that field. Which field he had (as some have reported) most cruellie taken from a woman, that had beene a widow to one Cooke, and after maried to one Richard Read a mariner, to the great hinderance of hir and hir husband the said Read: for they had long injoied it by a lease, which they had of it for manie yeares, not then expired: neverthelesse, he got it from them. For the which, the said Reads wife not onelie exclaimed against him, in sheading manie a salt téere, but also curssed him most bitterlie even to his face, wishing manie a vengeance to light upon him, and that all the world might woonder on him. Which was thought then to come to passe, when he was thus murdered, and laie in that field from midnight till the morning: and so all that daie, being the faire daie till night, all the which daie there were manie hundreds of people came woondering about him.

7. See Brian Walsh, *Shakespeare, the Queen's Men, and the Elizabethan Performance of History* (Cambridge, 2009).
8. Alexandra Walsham, *Providence in Early Modern England* (Oxford, 1999), at 97. See 65–115 for a compendius description of how providential belief and 'authentic' oral legends interacted with late sixteenth-century print culture.
9. I have here supplied metrical diacritics excised by the editors, viz. murderèd; filèd; gracïous. On 'glossing' for 'glozing', see the main text.
10. James Dougal Fleming, 'Making Sense of Science and the Literal: Modern Semantics and Early Modern Hermeneutics', in Kevin Killeen and Peter J. Forshaw (eds), *The Word and the World. Biblical Exegesis and Early Modern Science* (Basingstoke, 2007), 45–60, at 46.
11. See Robert Weimann and Douglas Bruster, *Prologues to Shakespeare's Theatre. Performance and Liminality in Early Modern Drama* (London, 2004), 31–2, on the interpretation of prologues and epilogues as paratexts in Gérard Genette's *Seuils* (Paris, 1987).
12. At the time of incision, a special issue of *Shakespeare Bulletin* on 'Metatheatre and Early Modern Drama' has just appeared: *Shakespeare Bulletin* 36:1 (Spring, 2018). At a paper given in Cambridge in February 2018, Ceri Sullivan described 'the theatrical elements of private prayer' and

the 'actor-character identification' necessary to its success, with explicit reference to *metatheatre* and an evident presumption that her listeners would know exactly what she meant. Ceri Sullivan, 'The Playscripts of Early Modern Prayer', paper delivered on 20 Febuary 2018 to the English Faculty Renaissance Graduate Seminar, University of Cambridge.
13. Tracy C. Davis and Thomas Postlewait, 'Theatricality: An Introduction', in Tracy C. Davis and Thomas Postlewait (eds), *Theatricality* (Cambridge, 2003), 14–15.
14. Richard Hornby, *Drama, Metadrama and Perception* (London, 1986), 31.
15. James L. Calderwood, *Shakespearean Metadrama. The Argument of the Play in* Titus Andronicus, Love's Labour's Lost, Romeo and Juliet, A Midsummer Night's Dream, *and* Richard II (Minneapolis, 1971), 5.
16. Stavros A. Frangoulidis, *Handlung und Nebenhandlung. Theater, Metatheater und Gattungsbewußtsein in der römischen Komödie* (Stuttgart, 1997), 2; Niall M. Slater, *Plautus in Performance* (Amsterdam, 2000), 10; Nikos G. Charalabopoulos, *Platonic Drama and its Ancient Reception* (Cambridge, 2012), Chap. 2.
17. Lionel Abel, *Metatheatre: A New View of Dramatic Form* (New York, 1963), 60.
18. Terence, *Hecyra*, in Edward St John Parry (ed.), *Publii Terentii Comoediae Sex* (London, 1857), V.iv.26–7: *placet non fieri hoc itidem ut in comoediis, / Omnia omnes ubi resciscunt.*
19. Abel, *Metatheatre*, 45.
20. Ibid. 72.
21. Ibid. 68.
22. Ibid. 66.
23. Ibid. 66–7.
24. Ibid. 74–6.
25. William Arthur Gill (ed.), *Morgann's Essay on the Dramatic Character of Sir John Falstaff* (London, 1912), 4–5.
26. Ibid. 6–7.
27. Brian Vickers, 'The Emergence of Character Criticism, 1774–1800', *Shakespeare Survey* 34 (1981), 11–22, at 11.
28. Gill (ed.), *Morgann's Essay*, 14.
29. Daniel Fineman (ed.), *Maurice Morgann: Shakespearian Criticism* (Oxford, 1972), 3–140, at 80.
30. Erich Auerbach, 'Figura', trans. Ralph Manheim, in *Scenes from the Drama of European Literature: Six Essays* (Minneapolis, 1984), 11–76, at 26–7.
31. Gill (ed.), *Morgann's Essay*, 24–5.
32. Abel, *Metatheatre*, 68.
33. Julia Reinhard Lupton and Kenneth Reinhard, *After Oedipus. Shakespeare in Psychoanalysis* (Ithaca, 1993), 238.
34. Abel, *Metatheatre*, 41; 45–9.
35. Ibid. 40.
36. Ibid. 68.
37. I have written about a similar problem in Adorno's deployment of Hamlet as the 'first individual': see George Oppitz-Trotman, 'Adorno's Hamlet', *New German Critique* 43:3 (Nov., 2016), 175–201.
38. Abel, *Metatheatre*, 112.

39. G. W. F. Hegel, *Vorlesungen über die Ästhetik III*, in Eva Moldenhauer and Karl Markus Michel (eds), *Werke*, 20 vols (Frankfurt a.M., 1990), 15: 559.
40. Gillian Rose, *Hegel contra Sociology* (London, 2009), 151.
41. Hegel, *Ästhetik*, in Moldenhauer and Michel (eds), *Werke*, 15: 559: 'Die eigentliche Kollision dreht sich deshalb auch nicht darum, daß der Sohn in seiner sittlichen Rache selbst die Sittlichkeit verletzen muß, sondern um den subjektiven Charakter Hamlets.'
42. Rose, *Hegel contra Sociology*, 59.
43. Ibid. 73.
44. Ibid. 145.
45. Hegel, *Ästhetik*, in Moldenhauer and Michel (eds), *Werke*, 15: 562; 560.
46. Rose, *Hegel contra Sociology*, 134.
47. Ibid. 52.
48. Thomas G. Rosenmeyer, '"Metatheater": An Essay on Overload', *Arion: A Journal of Humanities and the Classics* 10:2, 3rd ser. (Autumn, 2002), 87–119, at 91:

    > The traits Abel recognizes in his new genre clearly function within theatrical practice; it is not as if tragedy were theater in the first instance, against which metatheater were to set itself up as an enterprise raised above the theatrical experience, and exercising a superior diagnostic function, or from which paratheater would secede to form an independent domain.

49. George Oppitz-Trotman, 'Shakespeare's Abandoned Cave: Bertolt Brecht and the Dialectic of "Greatness"', in Giovanni Cianci and Caroline Patey (eds), *Will the Modernist: Shakespeare and the European Historical Avant-Gardes* (Oxford, 2014), 165–86.
50. *Contra* Erving Goffman, *The Presentation of Self in Everyday Life* (New York, 1959). Goffman's influential book forms part of *metatheatre*'s hinterland, but even he issued the qualification: 'All the world is not, of course, a stage, but the crucial ways in which it isn't are not easy to specify.'
51. Victor Stoichita, *The Self-Aware Image. An Insight into Early Modern Metapainting*, trans. Anne-Marie Glasheen (London, 2015), 301.
52. Ibid. 127.
53. Donna B. Hamilton, 'The Spanish Tragedy: A Speaking Picture', *English Literary Renaissance* 4:2 (Spring, 1974), 203–17, at 204.
54. Stoichita, *Self-Aware Image*, 57.
55. Rose, *Hegel contra Sociology*, 145.
56. Stoichita, *Self-Aware Image*, 57.
57. Walter Benjamin, *Ursprung des deutschen Trauerspiels*, in Benjamin, *GS* I/i: 315.
58. Holger Syme, 'Unediting the Margin: Jonson, Marston, and the Theatrical Page', *English Literary Renaissance* 38:1 (Feb., 2008), 142–71. Also see Julia Stone Peters, *Theatre of the Book 1480–1880. Print, Text, and Performance in Europe* (Oxford, 2003).
59. Joseph Roach, *Cities of the Dead. Circum-Atlantic Performance* (New York, 1996), 3; John Kerrigan, *Revenge Tragedy. From Aeschylus to Armageddon* (Oxford, 1996), 183.

Bibliography

Manuscript Sources

BL Cotton MS Titus C. I.
BL Egerton MS 3876.
Surrey History Centre 6729/10.
TNA Assizes 351 41, Surrey, 1599.
TNA E37, Court of the Marshalsea and Court of the Verge: Plea Rolls.
Trinity College, Cambridge, R.16.28.

Printed Sources

A Declaration of the Queenes Maiesties will and commaundement, to have certaine lawes and orders put in execution against the excesses of apparell (London, 1588).
Abelard, Peter, *Ethics*, ed. and trans. D. E. Luscombe (Oxford, 1971).
Aeschylus, *Libation Bearers*, in Alan H. Sommerstein (ed. and trans.), *Oresteia: Agamemnon. Libation Bearers. Eumenides* (Cambridge, MA, 2009), 208–351.
An Act for Murder and Malicious Bloodshed, within the Court, in John Raithby (ed.), *The Statutes at Large, of England of Great Britain*, 20 vols (London, 1811), 3: 351–8.
An Acte concernyng punysshement of Beggers & Vacabundes, in Alexander Luders et al. (eds), *The Statutes of the Realm, printed [...] from original records and authentic manuscripts*, 12 vols (London, 1810–28), 3: 328.
An Acte for the punishement of Vacabondes and for Releif of the Poore & Impotent, in Alexander Luders et al. (eds), *The Statutes of the Realm, printed [...] from original records and authentic manuscripts*, 12 vols (London, 1810–28), 4: 590.
Anderson, Anthony, *The Shield of our Safetie* (London, 1581).
Anon., 'A Funerall Elegye on the Death of the Famous Actor Richard Burbage who Died on Saturday in Lent the 13 of March 1619', in Glynne Wickham, Herbert Berry and William Ingram (eds), *English Professional Theatre, 1530–1660* (Cambridge, 2000), 181–3.

Anon., 'Reasons that the Court of Marshalsy may be fittly enabled [. . .]', in Hearne (ed.), *A Collection of Curious Discourses*, 146–52.

Anon., *A briefe discourse of two most cruell and bloudie murthers* (London, 1583).

Anon., *A New Ballad Declaring the Dangerous Shooting of the Gun at Court* (London, 1579).

Anon., *A pleasant comedie, called Wily Beguilde* (London, 1606).

Anon., *Mankind*, in Greg Walker (ed.), *Medieval Drama: An Anthology* (Oxford, 2000), 258–79.

Anon., *Tarlton's Jests* (1611), in James Orchard Halliwell (ed.), *Tarlton's Jests and News out of Purgatory, with notes, and some account of the life of Tarlton* (London, 1844), 13.

Anon., *The Boke of Justices of Peas* (London, 1506?).

Anon., *The Enterlude of Godly Queene Hester*, in Greg Walker (ed.), *Medieval Drama: An Anthology* (Oxford, 2000), 408–31.

Anon., *The First Part of Ieronimo*, in Frederick Boas (ed.), *The Works of Thomas Kyd* (Oxford, 1951), 295–337.

Anon., *The Returne from Parnassus* (London, 1606).

Anon., *The Spanish Tragedy, Containing the Lamentable Murders of* Horatio *and* Bellimperia: *With the Pitifull Death of Old Hieronimo. To the Tune of* Queene Dido (London, 1620).

Anon., *The Trueth of the most wicked and secret murthering of Iohn Brewen* (London, 1592).

Anon., *The Wonderful Discoverie of the witchcrafts of Margaret and Phillip Flower* (London, 1619).

Anon., *Tragoedia der bestrafte Brudermord oder Prinz Hamlet aus Dännemark* (Berlin, 1781), in Albert Cohn (ed.), *Shakespeare in Germany in the sixteenth and seventeenth centuries: An account of English actors in Germany and the Netherlands, and of the plays performed by them during the same period* (Berlin, 1865), 237–304.

Aphthonius the Sophist, *Progymnasmata*, in George Alexander Kennedy, ed. and trans., *Progymnasmata. Greek Textbooks of Prose Composition and Rhetoric* (Atlanta, 2003), 89–127.

Aquinas, Thomas, *Summa Theologica*, ed. and trans. Fathers of the English Dominican Province (London, 1920–9).

Aristotle, *The Complete Works of Aristotle*, Jonathan Barnes (ed.), 2 vols (Oxford, 1984).

— *Economics*, trans. E. S. Forster, in Aristotle, *Works*, 2: 2130–51.

— *Metaphysics*, trans. William David Ross, in Aristotle, *Works*, 2: 1552–728.

— *Poetics*, trans. Ingram Bywater, in Aristotle, *Works*, 2: 2316–40.

— *Politics*, trans. Benjamin Jowett, in Aristotle, *Works*, 2: 1986–2129.

— *Rhetoric*, trans. W. Rhys Roberts, in Aristotle, *Works*, 2: 2152–269.

Articuli super Cartas (28 E I), in *The Statutes: Revised Edition*, 18 vols (London, 1870–84), 1: 103–7.

Bacon, Francis, *The Twoo Bookes of Francis Bacon. Of the proficience and advancement of learning, divine and humane* (London, 1605).

— *The Charge of Sir Francis Bacon Knight, His Maiesties Attovrney Generall, Touching Duells* (London, 1614).

— *A Charge given by the most eminent and learned Sr. Francis Bacon, Kt.,*

late Lord Chancellor of England, at a sessions holden for the verge (London, 1662).
— 'Of Revenge', in Michael Kiernan (ed.), *The Essays or Counsels, Civill and Morall* (Oxford, 1985), 16–17.
— *Novum Organum*, in Graham Rees and Maria Wakely (eds), *The Oxford Francis Bacon, Vol. 11: The Instauratio Magna Part II: Novum Organum and Associated Texts* (Oxford, 2004).
Baker, Richard, *Theatrum Redivivum, or the Theatre Vindicated* (London, 1662).
Baldwin, William et al., *A Myrrour for Magistrates* (London, 1563).
Bale, John, *King Johan*, in Peter Happé (ed.), *The Complete Plays of John Bale*, 2 vols (Cambridge, 1986), 1: 29–99.
— *Three Laws*, in Peter Happé (ed.), *The Complete Plays of John Bale*, 2 vols (Cambridge, 1986), 2: 64–121.
Bekker, Immanuel (ed.), *Aristotelis Opera*, 5 vols (Berlin, 1831).
Bentley, Thomas, *The Sixt Lampe of Virginitie* (London, 1582).
Bernard of Clairvaux, *Sermons on Conversion*, ed. and trans. Marie-Bernard Said (Kalamazoo, 1981).
Blague, Thomas, 'A sermon preached at the Charterhouse before the Kings Majestie on Tuesday, the tenth of May. 1603' (London, 1603).
Blundeville, Thomas, *M. Blundeville his exercises containing sixe treatises* (London, 1594).
Boas, Frederick (ed.), *The Works of Thomas Kyd* (Oxford, 1951).
Bodin, Jean, *The Six Books of the Commonwealth*, ed. and trans. M. J. Tooley (Oxford, 1967).
Breton, Nicholas, *Characters upon essaies morall, and divine* (London, 1615).
Brome, Richard, *The Antipodes* (London, 1640).
Brownlow, Richard, *Reports of diverse choice cases in law taken by those late and most judicious prothonotaries of the Common Pleas, Richard Brownlow & John Goldesborough* (London, 1651).
Bruce, John (ed.), *The Diary of John Manningham of the Middle Temple, and of Bradbourne, Kent, Barrister-at-Law, 1602–1603*, Camden Society 99 (London, 1868).
Bulstrode, John, *The Reports of Edward Bulstrode of the Inner Temple, Esquire in Three Parts* (London, 1688).
By the Queene. A proclamation to restraine accesse to the court, of all such as are not bound to ordinarie attendance, or that shall not be otherwise licenced by her Majestie (London, 1592).
Calendar of the Manuscripts of the Most Hon. The Marquis of Salisbury, K. G., [. . .] preserved at Hatfield House, 24 vols (London, 1883–).
Carter, Samuel, *Lex Custumaria, or, A treatise of copy-hold estates* (London, 1696).
Cawdry, Robert, *Treasurie or store-house of similies* (London, 1600).
Chapman, George, *Bussy D'Ambois*, in John H. Smith (ed.), *The Plays of George Chapman: The Tragedies with 'Sir Gyles Goosecappe'* (Cambridge, 1987), 7–264.
Cheke, John, *The Hurt of Sedition* (London, 1549).
Chettle, Henry, *Englands Mourning Garment* (London, 1603).

— *The Tragedy of Hoffman; Or, A Revenge for a Father*, ed. Harold Jenkins and Charles Sisson (Oxford, 1961).
Churchyard, Thomas, *Churchyards Challenge* (London, 1593).
Cicero, *De Inventione*, trans. H. M. Hubbell (Cambridge, MA, 1949).
Cleaver, Robert, *A Godlie Forme of householde government for the ordering of private families* (London, 1598).
Cocke, John, 'The Character of a Common Player', in John Stevens, *Satirical Essays Characters and Others* (London, 1615), 295.
Coke, Edward, *The Third Part of the Institutes of the Laws of England* (London, 1644).
— *The Second Part of the Institutes of the Laws of England, containing the exposition of many ancient and other statutes* (London, 1797).
Cooper, J. P. (ed.), *The Wentworth Papers, 1597–1628* (London, 1973).
Corderoy, Jeremy, *A Short Dialogue, wherein is proved, that no man can be saved without good workes* (London, 1604).
Cosin, Richard, *An Apologie for Sundrie Proceedings by Jurisdiction Ecclesiasticall* (London, 1593).
Cowell, John, *The Interpreter* (London, 1607).
Crompton, Richard, *L'Authoritie et jurisdiction des courts de la Majestie de la Roygne* (London, 1594).
Crooke, Helkiah, *Mikrokosmographia* (London, 1615).
Crosse, Henry, *Vertues Commonwealth* (London, 1603).
— *The Schoole of Pollicie* (London, 1605).
Darell, Walter, *A Short Discourse of the life of servingmen* (London, 1578).
Day, John, *Day's Festivals* (Oxford, 1615).
de Belleforest, François, *The Hystorie of Hamblet*, trans. Thomas Pavier (London, 1608), in Israel Gollancz (ed.), *The Sources of Hamlet, with an Essay on the Legend* (London, 1967), 166–311.
de Guevara, Antonio, *The Dial of Princes*, trans. Thomas North (London, 1568).
— *The Familiar Epistles of Sir Anthony of Guevara*, trans. Edward Hellowes (London, 1575).
de Valsergues, Jean d'Albin, *A Notable Discourse, plainelye and truely discussing, who are the right ministers of the Catholike Church*, trans. Edward Rishton (London, 1575).
Deacon, John, *Dialogicall Discourses of Spirits and Divels* (London, 1601).
Dekker, Thomas, *The Wonderful Yeare 1603* (London, 1603).
— *Satiromastix*, in Fredson Bowers (ed.), *The Dramatic Works of Thomas Dekker* (Cambridge, 1953), 1: 299–396.
Dekker, Thomas and Thomas Middleton, *The Honest Whore*, in Fredson Bowers (ed.), *The Dramatic Works of Thomas Dekker*, 4 vols (Cambridge, 1955), 4: 24–132.
Descartes, René, *Meditationes de prima philosophia* (Paris, 1641).
di Grassi, Giacomo, *Arte of Defence*, trans. I. G. (London, 1594).
Digges, Thomas, *A Perfit Description of the Cælestiall Orbes*, in Leonard Digges, *A Prognostication Everlastinge* (London, 1576).
Downame, John, *Lectures upon the foure first chapters of the prophecie of Hosea* (London, 1608).
Duncan-Jones, Katherine (ed.), *Shakespeare's Sonnets*, Arden 3rd ser. (London, 2007).

Eliot, T. S., 'Whispers of Immortality', in *Collected Poems 1909–1962* (New York, 1963), 45–6.
Estienne, Charles and Jean Liébault, *Maison rustique, or The Country Farme*, trans. Richard Surflet (London, 1616).
Euripides, *Orestes*, ed. and trans. M. L. West (Warminster, 1987).
— *Electra*, in David Kovacs (ed. and trans.), *Suppliant Women. Electra. Heracles* (Cambridge, MA, 1998), 152–299.
Fit, John, *A Diamond most precious* (London, 1577).
Fitzherbert, Anthony, *Diversite de courtz, lour jurisdictions et alia necessaria et utilia* (London, 1535).
— *The Offices of shyriffes, bayliffes of lybertyes, escheatours, constables, and coroners* (London, 1579).
Foakes, R. A. and R. T. Rickert (eds), *Henslowe's Diary*, 2nd edn (Cambridge, 2002).
Ford, John, *'Tis Pity She's a Whore*, ed. Martin Wiggins (London, 2003).
— 'To the Reader of the Authour, and his Dutchesse of *Malfy*', in Webster, *Works* 1: 471.
Fosset, Thomas, *The Servants Dutie* (London, 1613).
Foxe, John, *Acts and Monuments* (London, 1583).
Fraunce, Abraham, *The Lawiers Logicke* (London, 1588).
Fulbeck, William, *A Parallele or conference of the civill law, the canon law, and the common law of England* (London, 1601).
Fulwell, Ulpian, *An Enterlude intituled Like wil to like quod the Deuil to the Colier* (London, 1568), in Peter Happé (ed.), *Two Moral Interludes* (Oxford, 1991), 79–107.
Galloway, David (ed.), *Norwich: 1540–1642*, Records of Early English Drama (Toronto, 1984).
Gifford, Humphrey, *A Posie of Gilloflowers* (London, 1580).
Gosson, Stephen, *The [Schoole] of Abuse: conteining a pleasaunt inuectiue against poets, pipers, plaiers, jesters, and such like caterpillers of a comonwelth* (London, 1579).
— *Playes confuted in five actions proving that they are not to be suffred in a Christian common weale* (London, 1582).
Gouge, William, *Of Domesticall Duties* (London, 1622).
Greene, Robert, *The Second Part of conny-catching* (London, 1591).
— *A Disputation, between a He-Cony-Catcher, and a She-Cony-Catcher* (London, 1592).
— *A Quip for an Upstart Courtier: or, A quaint dispute betvveen veluet breeches and cloth-breeches* (London, 1592).
— *The Defence of Conny Catching* (London, 1592).
— *The Third and last part of conny-catching* (London, 1592).
— *The Scottish historie of Iames the fourth, slaine at Flodden Entermixed with a pleasant comedie, presented by Oboram King of Fayeries* (London, 1598).
— *Friar Bacon and Friar Bungay*, ed. W. W. Greg (Oxford, 1926).
Griffith, Matthew, *Bethel: Or, A forme for families* (London, 1633).
Hakluyt, Richard, *The Principal Navigations, voyages, traffiques and discoveries of the English nation [. . .] within the compasse of these 1600 yeres*, 3 vols (London, 1599–1600).

Hall, Edward, *The Union of the Two Noble and Illustre Famelies of Lancastre & Yorke* (London, 1548).
Hall, Joseph, *One of the Sermons preacht at Westminster, on the day of the publicke fast (April 5. 1628)* (London, 1628).
Hansen, William F. (ed. and trans.), *Saxo Grammaticus and the Life of Hamlet* (Lincoln, NE, 1983).
Harington, John, *Orlando Furioso in English Heroical Verse* (London, 1591).
Harman, Thomas, *The Groundworke of Conny-Catching* (London, 1592).
Hazlitt, W. Carew (ed.), *A Select Collection of Old English Plays*, 4th edn, 15 vols (London, 1874–6).
Hearne, Thomas (ed.), *A Collection of Curious Discourses written by eminent antiquaries upon several heads in our English antiquities*, 2 vols (London, 1771–3).
Henricpetri, Adam, *Niderlendischer Ersten Kriegen, Empörungen, Zweitrachten, Ursprung, Anfang und End* (Basel, 1575).
— *Histoire des troubles et guerres civiles des Pays-Bas* (s. l., 1582).
Herbert, Frank, *Dune* (London, 1986).
Heywood, Jasper (trans.), *The seconde tragedie of Seneca entituled Thyestes* (London, 1560).
— *The Second tragedie of Seneca entituled Thyestes*, in Thomas Newton et al., *Seneca his tenne tragedies* (London, 1581), 21–39.
— *Thyestes*, in Henrik de Vocht (ed.), *Jasper Heywood and his Translations of Seneca's* Troas, Thyestes, *and* Hercules furens (Louvain, 1913), 87–195.
Heywood, Thomas, *An Apology for Actors* (London, 1612).
Holinshed, Ralph et al., *The Third Volume of Chronicles* (London, 1586).
— *Chronicles* (London, 1587).
Howard, Henry [?], 'Duello foiled, or the whole Proceedings for single Fight, by occasion whereof the Unlawfulness and Wickedness of a Duello is preparatively disputed, according to the rules of Honour and right reason, by Mr Edward Cook [Coke]', in Hearne (ed.), *A Collection of Curious Discourses*, 225–42.
Hughes, Paul L. (ed.), *Tudor Royal Proclamations*, 3 vols (New Haven, 1969).
I.M. [?Gervase Markham], *A Health to the gentlemanly profession of servingmen* (London, 1598).
Jeaffreson, John Cordy (ed.), *Middlesex County Records*, 4 vols (London, 1886–92).
Jonson, Ben, *The Comicall Satyre of every man out of his humor* (London, 1600).
— *Every Man in his humour*, ed. Robert S. Miola (Manchester, 2000).
— *Every Man out of his humor*, ed. Helen Ostovich (Manchester, 2001).
Kyd, Thomas [?], *The Spanish Tragedie* (London, 1592).
— *The Tragedye of Soliman and Perseda* (1599), in Frederick Boas (ed.), *The Works of Thomas Kyd* (Oxford, 1951), 161–229.
— *The Spanish Tragedy*, ed. J. R. Mulryne, with introduction and notes by Andrew Gurr, 3rd edn (London, 2009).
— *The Spanish Tragedy*, ed. Michael Neill (New York, 2014).
Kyd, Thomas and William Shakespeare, *Arden of Faversham*, in Jonathan Bate and Eric Rasmussen, with Jan Sewell, Will Sharpe, Peter Kirwan and

Sarah Stewart (eds), *William Shakespeare and Others. Collaborative Plays* (Basingstoke, 2013), 1–70.
Lactantius, *Divine Institutes*, ed. and trans. Anthony Bowen and Peter Garnsey (Liverpool, 2003).
Lambarde, William, *Eirenarcka; or of the Office of the Justices of the Peace* (London, 1581).
Lodge, Thomas, *Wits Miserie and the Worlds Madnesse* (London, 1596).
Luders, Alexander et al. (ed.), *The Statutes of the Realm, printed [. . .] from original records and authentic manuscripts*, 12 vols (London, 1810–28).
Lupton, Thomas, *All for Money*, ed. Ernst Vogel, *Shakespeare Jahrbuch* 40 (1904).
Mangoldt, Marx [*pseud.*], *Marckschiffs Nachen* (Frankfurt, 1597), in Ernst Kelchner (ed.), 'Sechs Gedichte über die Frankfurter Messe', *Mittheilungen des Vereins für Geschichte und Alterthumskunde* 6 (1881), 350–67.
Mann, David, *The Elizabethan Player: Contemporary Stage Representation* (London, 1991).
Marlowe, Christopher, *Tamburlaine the Great* (London, 1590).
— *Dido, Queen of Carthage*, ed. H. J. Oliver (London, 1968).
— *Doctor Faustus*, ed. David Bevington and Eric Rasmussen (Manchester, 1993).
— *The Jew of Malta*, ed. James R. Siemon (London, 2001).
Maus, Katherine Eisaman (ed.), *Four Revenge Tragedies* (Oxford, 1995).
Meredith, Peter (ed.), *The Passion Play from the N-Town Manuscript* (London, 1990).
Meres, Francis, *Wits Treasury* (London, 1598).
Middleton, Thomas, [Dedicatory verses to *The Duchess of Malfi*], in Middleton, *Works*, ed. Taylor et al., 1894.
— *The Blacke Booke* (London, 1604).
— *The Changeling*, ed. Douglas Bruster, in Middleton, *Works*, ed. Taylor et al., 1632–78.
— *The Revenger's Tragedy*, ed. MacDonald P. Jackson, in Middleton, *Works*, ed. Taylor et al., 543–93.
— *Women Beware Women*, ed. John Jowett, in Middleton, *Works*, ed. Taylor et al., 1488–1541.
Milton, John, *Areopagitica* (London, 1644).
Munday, Anthony, *A Second and Third Blast of retrait from plaies and theaters* (London, 1580).
Nashe, Thomas, 'To the Gentlemen Students of both Universities', in Robert Greene, *Menaphon* (London, 1589), sigs **1–A3.
— *Pierce Penilesse his supplication to the divell* (London, 1592).
— *The Terrors of the night, or a discourse of apparitions* (1594).
— *Have with you to Saffron-Walden* (London, 1596).
Newton, Thomas et al., *Seneca his tenne tragedies* (London, 1581).
Nixon, Anthony, *The Foot-Post of Dover* (London, 1616).
Overbury, Thomas, *Sir Thomas Overburie his wife with new elegies upon his (now knowne) untimely death* (London, 1616).
Painter, William, *The Palace of Pleasure*, ed. Joseph Jacobs, 3 vols (London, 1890).
Peacham, Henry, *The Compleat Gentleman* (London, 1622).

Perkins, Richard, 'To my loving friend and fellow, Thomas Heywood', in Thomas Heywood, *An Apology for Actors* (London, 1612), fols 22ᵛ–3.

Persons, Robert, *The Warn-Word to Sir Francis Hastinges wast-word* (Antwerp, 1602).

— *A quiet and sober reckoning with M. Thomas Morton [. . .] also adjoyned a peece of a reckoning with Syr Edward Cooke* (London, 1609).

Plato, *Republic*, trans. G. M. A. Grube, rev. C. D. C. Reeve; in John M. Cooper (ed.), *Plato. Complete Works* (Indianapolis, 1997), 971–1223.

— *Theaetetus*, trans. M. J. Levett and Myles Burnyeat, in John M. Cooper (ed.), *Plato. Complete Works* (Indianapolis, 1997), 157–234.

Pliny the Elder, *Naturalis Historiae Libri XXXVII*, ed. Karl Friedrich Theodor Mayhoff, 6 vols (Leipzig, 1906).

Plowden, Edmund, *Les Comentaries, ou les reports de Edmonde Plowden* (London, 1571).

Plutarch, *The Lives of the noble Grecians and Romanes compared*, trans. Thomas North (London, 1579).

— *Brutus*, in Bernadotte Perrin (ed. and trans.), *Plutarch's Lives*, 11 vols (Cambridge, MA, 1961), 6: 125–247.

Porter, Henry, *The Pleasant History of the Two Angry Women of Abington* (London, 1599).

Preston, Thomas, *The Life of Cambises, King of Percia* (London, 1569), in Robert Carl Johnson (ed.), *A Critical Edition of Thomas Preston's 'Cambises'* (Salzburg, 1975).

Prynne, William, *Histriomastix, the players scovrge or actors tragedie [. . .]* (London, 1633).

Pulton, Ferdinando, *De pace Regis et regni viz. A treatise declaring vvhich be the great and generall offences of the realme* (London, 1609).

Puttenham, George, *The Arte of English Poesie* (London, 1589).

Pykering, John, *A Newe Enterlude of Vice*, in Marie Axton (ed.), *Three Tudor Classical Interludes* (Cambridge, 1982), 94–138.

Pynchon, Thomas, *The Crying of Lot 49* (London, 2000).

Quintilian, *Institutio Oratoria*, ed. and trans. Harold Edgeworth Butler, 4 vols (Cambridge, MA, 1922).

Rainalds, John, *Th'overthrow of stage-playes* (London, 1599).

Rainolde, Richard, *The Foundacion of Rhetoric* (London, 1563).

Raithby, John (ed.), *The Statutes at Large, of England and of Great Britain*, 20 vols (London, 1811).

Ralegh, Walter, *The History of the World*, in William Oldys and Thomas Birch (eds), *The Works of Sir Walter Ralegh*, 8 vols (Oxford, 1829), contained in vols 2–7.

Randolph, Thomas, *The Muse's Looking-Glasse*, in *Poems with the Muses Looking-Glasse; and Amyntas* (Oxford, 1638).

Rankins, William, *A Mirrour of Monsters* (London, 1587).

Rastell, John, *Les Termes de la ley* (London, 1527).

Reed, Isaac, Samuel Johnson, George Steevens (eds), *The Dramatic Works of William Shakespeare*, 10 vols (New York, 1818).

Rhys Roberts, R. (ed.), *Demetrius on Style. The Greek Text of Demetrius De Elocutione Edited after the Paris Manuscript* (Cambridge, 1902).

Richalm of Schöntal, *Liber revelationum de insidiis et versutiis daemonum*, in

Bernhard Pez (ed.), *Thesaurus anecdotorum novissimus*, 6 vols (Augsburg, 1721–29), I/ii.
Richardson, H. G. and G. O. Sayles (ed. and trans.), *Fleta*, 3 vols (London, 1954–84).
Robertson, Thomas, *Lillies Rules Construed* (London, 1633).
Romei, Annibale, *The Courtier's Academie*, trans. John Kepers (London, 1598).
Rowlands, Samuel, *Greenes Ghost haunting conie-catchers* (London, 1602).
Rutter, Carol Chillington (ed.), *Documents of the Rose Playhouse* (Manchester, 1999).
Saviolo, Vincent, *Vincentio Saviolo his practise, In two bookes. The first intreating of the use of the rapier and dagger. The second, of honor and honorable quarrel* (London, 1595).
Sclater, William, *A Key to the Key of Scripture* (London, 1611).
Scot, Reginald, *The Discovery of Witchcraft* (London, 1584).
Seneca, *Thyestes*, trans. Jasper Heywood, in Thomas Newton et al., *Seneca his tenne tragedies* (London, 1581), 21–39.
— *Agamemnon*, in Rudolf Peiper and Gustav Richter (eds), *Tragoediae* (Leipzig, 1921), 241–78.
— Seneca, 'Epistle 70', in Richard M. Gummere (ed.), *Seneca ad Lucilium Epistulae Morales*, 3 vols (Cambridge, MA, 1962), 2: 56–73.
Shakespeare, William, *The Tragedy of King Richard II*, ed. Peter Ure, Arden 2nd ser. (London, 1956).
— *King John*, ed. E. A. J. Honigmann, Arden 2nd ser. (London, 1967).
— *Measure for Measure*, ed. J. W. Lever, Arden 2nd ser. (London, 1967).
— *Romeo and Juliet*, ed. Brian Gibbons, Arden 2nd ser. (London, 1980).
— *King Henry IV, Part 2*, ed. A. R. Humphreys, Arden 2nd ser. (London, 1981).
— *Antony and Cleopatra*, ed. John Wilders, Arden 3rd ser. (London, 1995).
— *Titus Andronicus*, ed. Jonathan Bate, Arden 3rd ser. (London, 1995).
— *King Lear*, ed. R. A. Foakes, Arden 3rd ser. (London, 1997).
— *Macbeth*, ed. Kenneth Muir, Arden 2nd ser. (London, 1997).
— *Troilus and Cressida*, ed. David Bevington, Arden 3rd ser. (London, 1998).
— *The Tempest*, ed. Virginia Mason Vaughan and Alden T. Vaughan, Arden 4th ser. (London, 1999).
— *The Winter's Tale*, ed. J. H. P. Pafford, Arden 2nd ser. (London, 1999).
— *King Richard II*, ed. Charles R. Forker, Arden 3rd ser. (London, 2002).
— *Othello*, ed. E. A. J. Honigmann, Arden 3rd ser. (London, 2006).
— *The Tragical History of Hamlet, Prince of Denmark*, ed. Ann Thompson and Neil Taylor (London, 2006).
— *Julius Caesar*, ed. David Daniell, Arden 3rd ser. (London, 2011).
Shakespeare, William [and Thomas Middleton], *Timon of Athens*, ed. H. J. Oliver, Arden 2nd ser. (London, 1984).
Shirley, James, *The Cardinal*, ed. E. M. Yearling (Manchester, 1986).
Sidney, Philip, *The Countess of Pembroke's Arcadia (The New Arcadia)*, ed. Victor Skretkowicz (Oxford, 1987).
Silver, George, *Paradoxes of defence wherein is proved the true grounds of fight to be in the short auncient weapons* (London, 1599).
Smith, Emma (ed.), *Five Revenge Tragedies. Kyd, Shakespeare, Marston, Chettle, Middleton* (London, 2012).
Smith, Thomas, *De Republica Anglorum* (London, 1583).

Southwell, Robert, 'Life is but Losse', in James H. McDonald and Nancy Pollard Brown (eds), *The Poems of Robert Southwell, S. J.* (Oxford, 1967), 50–1.
Spenser, Edmund, *The Shepheardes Calender*, in Ernest De Sélincourt (ed.), *The Poetical Works of Edmund Spenser*, 3 vols (Oxford, 1910), 1–121.
St Augustine, *Confessions*, ed. R. S. Pine-Coffin (Baltimore, 1961).
S., Mr, Master of Art [William Stevenson?], *Gammer Gurton's Needle* [1553?], ed. Charles Whitworth (London, 1997).
Stocker, Thomas, *A Tragicall Historie of the troubles and civile warres of the lowe Countries, otherwise called Flanders* (London, 1583).
Stow, John, *The Chronicles of England from Brute unto this Present Yeare of Christ, 1580* (London, 1580).
Stubbes, Phillip, *The Anatomie of Abuses* (London, 1583).
Studley, John (trans.), *The Eyghth Tragedye of L. Annaeus Seneca, Entituled Agamemnon*, in Thomas Newton et al., *Seneca his tenne tragedies* (London, 1581).
Sutcliffe, Matthew, *The Practice, proceedings, and lawes of armes* (London, 1593).
Tasso, Torquato, *The Housholders Philosophie*, trans. Thomas Kyd (London, 1588), in Frederick Boas (ed.), *The Works of Thomas Kyd* (Oxford, 1951), 231–84.
Taylor, Gary, John Lavagnino et al. (eds), *Thomas Middleton. The Collected Works* (Oxford, 2007).
Tennenhouse, Leonard (ed.), *The Tudor Interludes 'Nice Wanton' and 'Impatient Poverty'* (London, 1984).
Terence, *Hecyra*, in Edward St John Parry (ed.), *Publii Terentii Comoediae Sex* (London, 1857), 328–94.
'The Lord Mayor and Aldermen to the Privy Council, 28 July 1597', *MSC* 1.
'The Lord Mayor to Lord Burghley, 12 June 1592', in *MSC* 1.
Thomas, John Henry and John Farquhar Fraser (eds), *The Reports of Sir Edward Coke, Knt., in Thirteen Parts*, 6 vols (London, 1826).
Thompson, Ann and Neil Taylor (eds), *Hamlet: The Texts of 1603 and 1623* (London, 2006).
Thynne, Francis, 'Of the Same', in Hearne (ed.), *A Collection of Curious Discourses*, 2: 113–16.
Topsell, Edward, *Times Lamentation* (London, 1599).
Tyndale, William, *Tyndale's New Testament*, ed. David Daniell (New Haven, 1995).
Udall, Nicholas, *Respublica*, ed. W. W. Greg (Oxford, 1952).
van Rodenburgh, Theodor, *Wraeck-Gieriges Treur-spel* (Amsterdam, 1618).
Waghenaer, Lucas Janszoon, *The Mariners Mirrour* (London, 1588).
Webster, John, *The Works of John Webster. An Old-Spelling Critical Edition*, ed. David Gunby, David Carnegie, Antony Hammond, and MacDonald P. Jackson, 3 vols (Cambridge, 2004).
— *A Monumental Column*, in Webster, *Works*, 3: 373–86.
— *Monuments of Honor* (London, 1624), in Webster, *Works*, 3: 253–94.
— *New Characters (drawne to the life) of severall Persons, in severall qualities* (1615), in Webster, *Works*, 3: 459–85.
— *The Duchess of Malfi*, in Webster, *Works*, 1: 467–575.
— *The White Devil*, in Webster, *Works*, 1: 139–254.

Webster, John and William Rowley, *A Cure for a Cuckold* (London, 1661).
West, William, *The first part of Simboleography* (London, 1615).
Westerman, William, *Two Sermons of Assise the one intituled A prohibition of revenge, the other, A sword of maintenance* (London, 1600).
Wever, Richard[?], *An Enterlude Called Lusty Iuventus, liuely describing the frailtie of youth: Of nature, prone to vyce: By grace and good councell traynable to virtue*, ed. Helen Scarborough Thomas (New York, 1982).
Whately, William, *Prototypes* (London, 1640).
Wiggins, Martin (ed.), *A Woman Killed with Kindness and Other Plays* (Oxford, 2008).
Wriothesley, Charles, *A Chronicle of England during the Reigns of the Tudors, from A.D. 1485 to 1559*, 2 vols (London, 1877).
Xenophon, *Oeconomicus*, in E. C. Marchant (ed. and trans.), *Xenophon*, 7 vols (London, 1968), 4: 361–526.

Secondary Literature

Abel, Lionel, *Metatheatre: A New View of Dramatic Form* (New York, 1963).
Abrahamse, Wouter, *Het toneel van Theodore Rodenburgh (1574–1644)* (Amsterdam, 1997).
Adorno, Theodor W., *Ästhetische Theorie*, in Rolf Tiedemann et al. (eds), *Gesammelte Schriften*, 20 vols (Frankfurt a. M., 1986), 7.
— *Minima Moralia. Reflexionen aus dem beschädigten Leben*, in Rolf Tiedemann et al. (eds), *Gesammelte Schriften*, 20 vols (Frankfurt, 1986), 4.
Agamben, Giorgio, *The Kingdom and the Glory. For a Theological Genealogy of Economy and Government* (Homo Sacer II, 2) (Stanford, 2011).
Agnew, Jean-Christophe, *Worlds Apart: The Market and the Theater in Anglo-American Thought, 1550–1770* (Cambridge, 1986).
Alexander, Gavin, 'Prosopopoeia: The Speaking Figure', in Sylvia Adamson, Gavin Alexander and Katrin Ettenhuber (eds), *Renaissance Figures of Speech* (Cambridge, 2007), 97–112.
Amussen, Susan, 'Punishment, Discipline, and Power: The Social Meanings of Violence in Early Modern England', *Journal of British Studies* 34:1 (1995), 1–34.
Anderson, Linda, *A Place in the Story: Servants and Service in Shakespeare's Plays* (Newark, 2005).
Anon., Unsigned Review, *Westminster Review* 86, new series 30 (Oct., 1866), 269–71.
Archer, William, 'John Webster', *The Nineteenth Century* 87 (Jan., 1920), 126–32.
— *The Old Drama and the New: An Essay in Re-Valuation* (London, 1923).
Aston, Margaret, 'Iconoclasm in England: Official and Clandestine', in Clifford Davidson and Ann Eljenholm Nichols (eds), *Iconoclasm vs. Art and Drama* (Kalamazoo, 1989), 47–91.
Atwell, David, 'Property, Status, and the Subject in a Middle-Class Tragedy: *Arden of Faversham*', *English Literary Renaissance* 21 (1991), 328–48.
Auerbach, Erich, 'Figura', *Archivum Romanicum* 22 (1938), 436–89.
— 'Figura', *Neue Dantestudien* (Istanbul, 1944), 11–71.

— 'Figura', *Gesammelte Aufsätze zur romanischen Philologie* (Berlin, 1967), 55–92.
— 'Figura', trans. Ralph Manheim, in *Scenes from the Drama of European Literature: Six Essays* (Minneapolis, 1984), 11–76.
— *Dante als Dichter der irdischen Welt* (Berlin, 2001).
— *Mimesis. Dargestellte Wirklichkeit in der abendländischen Literatur* (Tübingen, 2001).
Baker, John, 'Review: *The Tudor Law of Treason*', *American Journal of Legal History* 24:3 (July, 1980), 275–6.
— *The Oxford History of the Laws of England. Volume VI. 1483–1558* (Oxford, 2003).
— 'The Changing Concept of a Court', in *Collected Papers on English Legal History* (Cambridge, 2013), 413–41.
— *The Reinvention of Magna Carta 1216–1616* (Cambridge, 2017).
Balme, Christopher, '"Geschichtliches Wissen muss einfach gesichert und tradiert werden" Interview mit Christopher Balme [. . .]', in Jens Ilg and Thomas Bitterlich (eds), *Theatergeschichtsschreibung. Interviews mit Theaterhistorikern* (Marburg, 2006), 116–24.
Bate, Jonathan, *Shakespeare and Ovid* (Oxford, 1994).
Bates, Katherine Lee, *The English Religious Drama* (London, 1893).
Baumbach, Sibylle, *Shakespeare and the Art of Physiognomy* (Leicester, 2008).
Beckwith, Sarah, *Signifying God: Social Relation and Symbolic Act in York's Play of Corpus Christi* (Chicago, 2001).
Beier, A. L., *Masterless Men: The Vagrancy Problem in England, 1560–1640* (London, 1985).
Bell, Catherine, *Ritual Theory, Ritual Practice* (Oxford, 1992).
Bellamy, John, *The Tudor Law of Treason* (Abingdon, 2013).
Belsey, Catherine, 'The Case of Hamlet's Conscience', *Studies in Philology* 76:2 (Spring, 1979), 127–48.
Benjamin, Walter, *Das Passagen-Werk*, in Benjamin, *GS* V/i.
— *Ursprung des deutschen Trauerspiels*, in Benjamin, *GS* I/i.
Berger, Thomas L., William C. Bradford and Sidney L. Sondergard (eds), *An Index of Characters in Early Modern English Drama: Printed Plays, 1500–1660* (Cambridge, 1998).
Bergeron, David M., 'The Wax Figures in *The Duchess of Malfi*', *SEL 1500–1900* 18:2 (1978), 331–9.
Bergman, Gösta M., *Lighting in the Theatre* (Stockholm, 1977).
Berry, Ralph, *The Art of John Webster* (Oxford, 1972).
Bevington, David, *From 'Mankind' to Marlowe: Growth of Structure in the Popular Drama of Tudor England* (Cambridge MA, 1962).
Biddick, Kathleen, *The Typological Imaginary: Circumcision, Technology, History* (Philadelphia, 2003).
Bishop, T. G., *Shakespeare and the Theatre of Wonder* (Cambridge, 1996).
Blayney, Peter W. M., 'The Publication of Playbooks', in John D. Cox and David Scott Kastan (eds), *A New History of Early English Drama* (New York, 1997), 383–422.
Bloomfield, Morton W., *The Seven Deadly Sins: An Introduction to the History of a Religious Concept, with Special Reference to Medieval English Literature* (East Lansing, 1967).

Bossy, John, *Peace in the Post-Reformation. The Birkbeck Lectures 1995* (Cambridge, 1998).
Bowers, Fredson, *Elizabethan Revenge Tragedy* (Princeton, 1940).
Bradley, A. C., *Shakespearean Tragedy: Lectures on* Hamlet, Othello, King Lear, Macbeth, 3rd edn (New York, 1992).
Brand, Paul, 'Henry II and the Creation of the English Common Law', in Christopher Harper-Bill and Nicholas Vincent (eds), *Henry II: New Interpretations* (Woodbridge, 2007), 215–41.
Brecht, Bertolt, 'Bemerkungen zu einem Aufsatz', in *Gesammelte Werke*, 20 vols (Frankfurt a.M., 1967), 19.
— *Kleines Organon für das Theater*, Gesammelte Werke, 20 vols (Frankfurt a.M., 1967), 16.
Brie, Friederich, '*Horestes*', *Englische Studien* 46 (1912), 68–71.
Bristol, Michael, 'How Many Children Did She Have?', in John J. Joughlin (ed.), *Philosophical Shakespeares* (London, 2005), 19–34.
Brooke, Rupert, *John Webster & the Elizabethan Drama* (London, 1917).
Brooks, Harold F., '*Richard III*: Antecedents of Clarence's Dream', *Shakespeare Survey* 32 (1979), 145–50.
Broude, Ronald, '*Vindicta Filia Temporis*: Three English Forerunners of the Elizabethan Revenge Play', *Journal of English and Germanic Philology* 72:4 (Oct., 1973), 489–502.
Bruns, Gerald L., *The Material of Poetry. Sketches for a Philosophical Poetics* (Athens, 2005).
Bruster, Douglas, 'Shakespearean Spellings and Handwriting in the Additional Passages Printed in the 1602 *Spanish Tragedy*', *Notes & Queries* 60:3 (2013), 420–4.
Bryson, Anna, *From Courtesy to Civility: Changing Codes of Conduct in Early Modern England* (Oxford, 1998).
Buckley, W., *The Jurisdiction and Practice of the Marshalsea & Palace Courts* (London, 1827).
Burnett, Mark Thornton, *Masters and Servants in English Renaissance Drama and Culture* (London, 1997).
— 'Review of *Shakespeare, Love and Service*, by David Schalkwyk', *Shakespeare Quarterly* 60:2 (Summer, 2009), 230.
Butterfield, David, *The Early Textual History of Lucretius' De Rerum Natura* (Cambridge, 2013).
Butterworth, Philip, *Magic on the Early English Stage* (Cambridge, 2005).
Calderwood, James L., *Shakespearean Metadrama. The Argument of the Play in* Titus Andronicus, Love's Labour's Lost, Romeo and Juliet, A Midsummer Night's Dream, *and* Richard II (Minneapolis, 1971).
Camille, Michael, *The Gothic Idol: Ideology and Image-Making in Medieval Art* (Cambridge, 1989).
— *Image on the Edge: The Margins of Medieval Art* (London, 1992).
Campbell, Lily B., 'Theories of Revenge in Renaissance England', *Modern Philology* 28:3 (Feb., 1931), 281–96.
Carroll, Stuart, *Blood and Violence in Early Modern France* (Oxford, 2006).
Cavanagh, Dermot, *Language and Politics in the Sixteenth-Century History Play* (Basingstoke, 2003).

Cavell, Stanley, *Disowning Knowledge in Seven Plays of Shakespeare* (Cambridge, 2003).
Chalk, Brian, 'Webster's "Worthyest Monument": The Problem of Posterity in *The Duchess of Malfi*', *Studies in Philology* 108:3 (2011), 379–402.
Chambers, E. K., *The Mediaeval Stage*, 2 vols (Oxford, 1903).
— *The Elizabethan Stage*, 4 vols (Oxford, 1923).
Charalabopoulos, Nikos G., *Platonic Drama and its Ancient Reception* (Cambridge, 2012).
Charalampous, Charis, *Rethinking the Mind–Body Relationship in Early Modern Literature, Philosophy and Medicine. The Renaissance of the Body* (London, 2016).
Clemen, Wolfgang, *English Tragedy before Shakespeare. The Development of Dramatic Speech* (London, 1961).
Cloud, Random, '"The very names of the Persons": Editing and the Invention of Dramatick Character', in David Scott Kastan and Peter Stallybrass (eds), *Staging the Renaissance. Reinterpretations of Elizabethan and Jacobean Drama* (New York, 1991), 88–96.
— 'What's the Bastard's Name?', in George Walton Williams (ed.), *Shakespeare's Speech-Headings* (Newark, 1997), 133–209.
Cockayne, Emily, *Hubbub. Filth, Noise & Stench in England* (New Haven, 2007).
Cockburn, J. S., 'Patterns of Violence in English Society: Homicide in Kent 1560–1985', *Past & Present* 130:1 (Feb., 1991), 70–106.
Collins, John M., *Martial Law and English Laws, c.1500–1700* (Cambridge, 2016).
Collinson, Patrick, *From Iconoclasm to Iconophobia. The Cultural Impact of the Second English Reformation* (Reading, 1986).
— 'The Monarchical Republic of Queen Elizabeth I', *Bulletin of the John Rylands University Library of Manchester* 69:2 (1987), 394–424.
Coolidge, John S., *The Pauline Renaissance in England: Puritanism and the Bible* (Oxford, 1970).
Cooper, Helen, 'The Afterlife of Personification', in Ruth Morse, Helen Cooper and Peter Holland (eds), *Medieval Shakespeare: Pasts and Presents* (Cambridge, 2013), 98–116.
Cormack, Bradin, *A Power to Do Justice. Jurisdiction, English Literature, and the Rise of Common Law, 1509–1625* (Chicago, 2007).
Corssen, Stefan, 'Die Anfänge der deutschsprachigen Theaterwissenschaft', in Gesellschaft für Theatergeschichte (ed.), *Max Hermann und die Anfänge der deutschsprachigen Theaterwissenschaft* (Berlin, 1992), 20–8.
Cox, John D., *The Devil and the Sacred in English Drama, 1350–1642* (Cambridge, 2000).
Craig, Hugh, *Shakespeare, Computers, and the Mystery of Authorship* (Cambridge, 2009).
Crawford, Charles, 'The Authorship of *Arden of Faversham*', *Jahrbuch der Deutschen Shakespeare-Gesellschaft* 39 (1903), 74–86.
Creizenach, Wilhelm, *Geschichte des Neueren Dramas*, 5 vols (Halle a. S., 1893–1916).
Crosbie, Christopher, '*Oeconomia* and the Vegetative Soul: Rethinking Revenge in *The Spanish Tragedy*', *English Literary Renaissance* 38:1 (2008), 3–33.

Crow, Andrew, 'Mediating Boys: *Two Angry Women* and the Boy Actor's Shaping of 1590s Theatrical Culture', *Shakespeare Quarterly* 65:2 (Summer, 2014), 180–98.
Crowley, John E., *The Invention of Comfort: Sensibilities and Design in Early Modern Britain* (Baltimore, 2001).
Culbertson, Philip L., *A Word Fitly Spoken. Context, Transmission, and Adoption of the Parables of Jesus* (Albany, 1995).
Cushman, L. W., *The Devil and the Vice in English Dramatic Literature before Shakespeare* (Halle a. S., 1900).
Davis, Tracy C. and Thomas Postlewait, 'Theatricality: An Introduction', in Tracy C. Davis and Thomas Postlewait (eds), *Theatricality* (Cambridge, 2003), 1–39.
de Grazia, Margreta, 'Hamlet's Smile', in Peter Holland and Stephen Orgel (eds), *From Performance to Print in Shakespeare's England* (Basingstoke, 2006), 231–42.
Dessen, Alan C., *Shakespeare and the Late Moral Play* (Lincoln, NE, 1986).
Diehl, Huston, *Staging Reform, Reforming the Stage* (Ithaca, 1997).
Dolan, Frances E., 'The Subordinate('s) Plot: Petty Treason and the Forms of Domestic Rebellion', *Shakespeare Quarterly* 43:3 (Autumn, 1992), 317–40.
Dover Wilson, John, 'The Duel in *Hamlet*', *Times Literary Supplement*, 18 January 1934, 44.
— *What Happens in* Hamlet (Cambridge, 1937).
Dowd, Michelle M., *Women's Work in Early Modern Literature and Culture* (Basingstoke, 2009).
— 'Desiring Subjects: Staging the Female Servant in Early Modern Tragedy', in Michelle M. Dowd and Natasha Korda (eds), *Working Subjects in Early Modern English Drama* (London, 2011), 131–44.
Drake, Ryan, 'Wonder, Nature, and the Ends of Tragedy', *International Philosophical Quarterly* 50:1 (197) (March, 2010), 77–91.
Dudley, Scott, 'Conferring with the Dead: Necrophilia and Nostalgia in the Seventeenth Century', *ELH* 66:2 (Summer, 1999), 277–94.
Dunne, Derek, *Vindictive Justice. Shakespeare, Revenge Tragedy and Early Modern Law* (Basingstoke, 2016).
Edelman, Charles, *Brawl Ridiculous: Swordfighting in Shakespeare's Plays* (Manchester, 1992).
Eden, Kathy, *Hermeneutics and the Rhetorical Tradition. Chapters in the Ancient Legacy and its Humanist Reception* (New Haven, 1997).
Edwards, Kathryn A., 'The History of Ghosts in Early Modern Europe: Recent Research and Future Trajectories', *History Compass* 10:4 (2012), 353–66.
Efal, Adi, *Figural Philology: Panofsky and the Science of Things* (London, 2016).
Elias, Norbert, *Die Höfische Gesellschaft. Untersuchungen zur Soziologie des Königtums und der höfischen Aristokratie mit einer Einleitung: Soziologie und Geschichtswissenschaft* (Berlin, 1969).
— *The Civilizing Process*, trans. Edmund Jephcott (Oxford, 1994).
Erne, Lukas, *Beyond the Spanish Tragedy. A Study of the Works of Thomas Kyd* (Manchester, 2001).
— *Shakespeare as Literary Dramatist* (Cambridge, 2003).
— *Shakespeare's Modern Collaborators* (London, 2008).

Eskew, Doug, '"Soldiers, Prisoners, Patrimony": *King Lear* and the Place of the Sovereign', *Cahiers Élisabéthains* 78 (2010), 29–38.

Evett, David, *The Discourses of Service in Shakespeare's England* (Basingstoke, 2005).

Faber, Riemer A., 'The Description of the Palace in Seneca *Thyestes* 641–82 and the Literary Unity of the Play', *Mnemosyne* 60 (2007), 427–42.

Fineman, Daniel (ed.), *Maurice Morgann: Shakespearian Criticism* (Oxford, 1972).

Fleming, James Dougal, 'Making Sense of Science and the Literal: Modern Semantics and Early Modern Hermeneutics', in Kevin Killeen and Peter J. Forshaw (eds), *The Word and the World. Biblical Exegesis and Early Modern Science* (Basingstoke, 2007), 45–60.

— *The Mirror of Information in Early Modern England. John Wilkins and the Universal Character* (Basingstoke, 2017).

Fletcher, Anthony J., 'Honour, Reputation and Local Officeholding in Elizabethan and Stuart England', in Anthony J. Fletcher and John Stevenson (eds), *Order and Disorder in Early Modern England* (Cambridge, 1985), 92–115.

Flögel, Karl Friedrich, *Geschichte der Hofnarren* (Leipzig, 1789).

Forker, Charles R., *Skull beneath the Skin: The Achievement of John Webster* (Carbondale, 1986).

Fortier, Mark, *The Culture of Equity in Early Modern England* (London, 2005).

Frangoulidis, Stavros A., *Handlung und Nebenhandlung. Theater, Metatheater und Gattungsbewußtsein in der römischen Komödie* (Stuttgart, 1997).

Frevert, Ute, *Men of Honour: A Social and Cultural History of the Duel*, trans. Anthony Williams (Cambridge, 2007).

Fumerton, Patricia, *Unsettled. The Culture of Mobility and the Working Poor in Early Modern England* (Chicago, 2006).

Genette, Gérard, *Seuils* (Paris, 1987).

Geuss, Raymond, 'Poetry and Knowledge', *Arion* 11:1 (3rd ser.) (Spring/Summer, 2003), 1–31.

Giles-Watson, Maura, 'The Singing "Vice": Music and Mischief in Early English Drama', *Early Theatre* 12:2 (2009), 57–90.

Gill, William Arthur (ed.), *Morgann's Essay on the Dramatic Character of Sir John Falstaff* (London, 1912).

Girard, Dale Anthony, *Actors on Guard: A Practical Guide for the Use of Rapier and Dagger for Stage and Screen* (London, 1997).

Goffman, Erving, *The Presentation of Self in Everyday Life* (New York, 1959).

Goldie, Mark, 'The Unacknowledged Republic: Officeholding in Early Modern England', in Tim Harris (ed.), *The Politics of the Excluded, c.1500–1850* (New York, 2001), 153–94.

Gomes, Rita Costa, *The Making of a Court Society: Kings and Nobles in Late Medieval Portugal*, trans. Alison Aiken (Cambridge, 2003).

Goodacre, E. B., 'The Duel in *Hamlet*', *Times Literary Supplement*, 11 January 1934, 28.

— 'The Duel Scene in *Hamlet*', *Times Literary Supplement*, 8 February 1934, 38.

Goth, Maik, '"Killing, Hewing, Stabbing, Dagger-Drawing, Fighting, Butchery":

Skin Penetration in Renaissance Tragedy and its Bearing on Dramatic Theory', *Comparative Drama* 46:2 (2012), 139–62.
Graves, R. B., *Lighting the Shakespearean Stage, 1567–1642* (Carbondale, 1999).
Green, Thomas A., 'The Jury and the English Law of Homicide, 1200–1600', *Michigan Law Review* 74 (1976), 413–99.
Greenblatt, Stephen, *Shakespearean Negotiations. The Circulation of Social Energy in Renaissance England* (Berkeley, 1988).
— *Hamlet in Purgatory* (Princeton, 2001).
— 'Shakespeare and the Ethics of Authority', in David Armitage, Conal Condren and Andrew Fitzmaurice (eds), *Shakespeare and Early Modern Political Thought* (Cambridge, 2009), 64–79.
Greene, Douglas G., 'The Court of the Marshalsea in Late Tudor and Stuart England', *The American Journal of Legal History* 20:4 (Oct., 1976), 267–81.
Griffiths, Paul, *Youth and Authority: Formative Experiences in England, 1560–1640* (Oxford, 1996).
— *Lost Londons. Change, Crime, and Control in the Capital City, 1550–1660* (Cambridge, 2008).
Guarino, Raimondo, *Shakespeare: la scrittura nel teatro* (Rome, 2010).
Guerzoni, Guido Antonio, 'Use and Abuse of Beeswax in the Early Modern Age. Two Apologues and a Taste', in A. Daninos (ed.), *Waxing Eloquent: Italian Portraits in Wax* (Milan, 2012), 43–59.
Gunby, David, 'The Life of John Webster', in Webster, *Works*, 1: 3–17.
Gundolf, Friedrich, *Shakespeare und der deutsche Geist* (Berlin, 1920).
Gurr, Andrew, *The Shakespearian Playing Companies* (Cambridge, 1996).
Hacking, Ian, *The Emergence of Probability. A Philosophical Study of Early Ideas about Probability, Induction, and Statistical Inference* (Cambridge, 1975).
Halliday, Paul, 'Birthrights and the Due Course of Law', in Lorna Hutson (ed.), *The Oxford Handbook of Law and Literature, 1500–1700* (Oxford, 2017), 587–603.
Halpern, Richard, 'The Classical Inheritance', in Michael Neill and David Schalkwyk (eds), *The Oxford Handbook of Shakespearean Tragedy* (Oxford, 2016), 19–34.
Hamilton, Clayton M., '*The Duchess of Malfi* Considered as a Tragedy of Blood', *Sewanee Review* 9:4 (Oct., 1901), 410–34.
Hamilton, Donna B., 'The Spanish Tragedy: A Speaking Picture', *English Literary Renaissance* 4:2 (Spring, 1974), 203–17.
Hamilton, Ross, *Accident: A Philosophical and Literary History* (Chicago, 2007).
Hanssen, Beatrice, 'Philosophy at its Origin: Walter Benjamin's Prologue to the *Ursprung des deutschen Trauerspiels*', *MLN* 110:4 (Sept. 1995), 808–29.
Happé, Peter, 'The Vice and the Folk-Drama', *Folklore* 75 (1964), 161–93.
— 'The *Vice*: A Checklist and an Annotated *Bibliography*', *Research Opportunities in Renaissance Drama* 22 (1979), 17–35.
— 'Laughter in Court: Four Tudor Comedies (1518–1585), from Skelton to Lyly', *Tudor Theatre* 6 (2002), 111–27.
— 'The Vice, 1350–1605: An Examination of the Nature and Development of a Stage Convention', PhD thesis, University of London, 2006.

— 'Deceptions: "The Vice" of the Interludes and Iago', *Theta* 8 (2009), 105–24.
Harding, Alan, *Medieval Law and the Foundation of the State* (Oxford, 2002).
Hawkes, David, *Idols of the Marketplace. Idolatry and Commodity Fetishism in English Literature, 1580–1680* (Basingstoke, 2001).
Hazard, Mary E., 'An Essay to Amplify "Ornament": Some Renaissance Theory and Practice', *SEL, 1500–1900* 16:1 (Winter, 1976), 15–32.
Hazlitt, William, *A Review of the English Stage; Or, A Series of Dramatic Criticisms*, in P. Howe (ed.), *The Complete Works of William Hazlitt*, 21 vols (London, 1930–4), 5: 169–424.
Heath, James, *Torture and English Law. An Administrative and Legal History from the Plantagenets to the Stuarts* (London, 1982).
Hegel, G. W. F., *Vorlesungen über die Ästhetik III*, in Eva Moldenhauer and Karl Markus Michel (eds), *Werke*, 20 vols (Frankfurt a.M., 1990), 15.
— *Elements of the Philosophy of Right*, ed. Allen W. Wood, trans. H. B. Nisbet (Cambridge, 1991).
Heinemann, Margot, *Puritanism and Theatre* (Cambridge, 1980).
Herlihy, Anna Friedman, 'Renaissance Star Charts', in David Woodward (ed.), *The History of Cartography, Volume Three, Part 1: Cartography in the European Renaissance* (Chicago, 2007), 99–122.
Hill, Christopher, *Society and Puritanism in Pre-Revolutionary England* (London, 1966).
— *Change and Continuity in Seventeenth-Century England* (New Haven, 1991).
Hill, Eugene D., 'Senecan and Vergilian Perspectives in *The Spanish Tragedy*', *English Literary Renaissance* 15 (1985), 143–65.
Hillman, David, *Shakespeare's Entrails. Belief, Scepticism and the Interior of the Body* (Basingstoke, 2007).
Holdsworth, William, *A History of English Law*, ed. A. L. Goodhart and H. G. Hanbury, 16 vols (London, 1936–72).
Horder, Jeremy, 'The Duel and the English Law of Homicide', *Oxford Journal of Legal Studies* 12 (1992), 419–30.
— *Provocation and Responsibility* (Oxford, 1992).
Hornby, Richard, *Drama, Metadrama and Perception* (London, 1986).
Hotson, Leslie, 'The Adventure of the Single Rapier', *Atlantic Monthly* 148 (July 1931), 26–31.
House, Anthony Paul, 'The City of London and the Problem of the Liberties, c.1540–c.1640', DPhil thesis, Oxford, 2006.
Hunniset, R. F., *The Medieval Coroner* (Cambridge, 1962).
Hunzinger, Christine, 'La Notion de θῶμα chez Hérodote', *Ktèma* 20 (1995), 47–70.
Hutson, Lorna, *The Invention of Suspicion: Law and Mimesis in Shakespeare and Renaissance Drama* (Oxford, 2007).
— *Circumstantial Shakespeare* (Oxford, 2015).
Ibbetson, David, 'Sixteenth Century Contract Law: *Slade's Case* in Context', *Oxford Journal of Legal Studies* 4:3 (1 December 1984), 295–317.
Ingram, Martin, *Church Courts, Sex and Marriage in England, 1570–1640* (Cambridge, 1987).
Jackson, James L., '"They Catch One Another's Rapiers": The Exchange of Weapons in *Hamlet*', *Shakespeare Quarterly* 41:3 (Autumn, 1990), 281–98.

Jackson, MacDonald P., *Determining the Shakespeare Canon: Arden of Faversham and A Lover's Complaint* (Oxford, 2014).
Jakacki, Diane K., '"Canst paint a doleful cry?": Promotion and Performance in the *Spanish Tragedy* Title-Page Illustration', *Early Theatre* 13:1 (2010), 13–36.
James, Mervyn, 'English Politics and the Concept of Honour', in Paul Slack (ed.), *Society, Politics and Culture: Studies in Early Modern England* (Cambridge, 1986), 308–415.
Jarrett, Joseph Christopher, 'Mathematics and Late Elizabethan Drama, 1587–1603', PhD thesis, University of Cambridge, 2017.
Jarvis, Simon, 'For a Poetics of Verse', *PMLA* 125:4 (Oct., 2010), 931–5.
John, Evan, 'The Duel in *Hamlet*', *Times Literary Supplement*, 25 January 1934, 60.
Johnson, J. H., 'The King's Wardrobe and Household', in James F. Willard and William A. Morris (eds), *The English Government at Work: 1327–1336*, 3 vols (Cambridge, MA, 1940), 1: 243–5.
Jones, Ann Rosalind and Peter Stallybrass, *Renaissance Clothing and the Materials of Memory* (Cambridge, 2000).
Jones, W. R., 'The Court of the Verge: The Jurisdiction of the Steward and Marshal of the Household in Later Medieval England', *Journal of British Studies* 10:1 (Nov., 1970), 1–29.
Kannengiesser, Charles, *Handbook of Patristic Exegesis. The Bible in Ancient Christianity*, 2 vols (Leiden, 2006).
Keenan, Siobhan, *Travelling Players in Shakespeare's England* (New York, 2002).
Kerrigan, John, *Revenge Tragedy. From Aeschylus to Armageddon* (Oxford, 1996).
— *Archipelagic English. Literature, History, and Politics 1603–1707* (Oxford, 2008).
— *Shakespeare's Binding Language* (Oxford, 2016).
— *Shakespeare's Originality* (Oxford, 2018).
Kibbey, Ann, *The Interpretation of Material Shapes in Puritanism* (Cambridge, 1986).
Kiernan, V. G., *The Duel in European History: Honour and the Reign of Aristocracy* (Oxford, 1988).
Killeen, Kevin, *The Political Bible in Early Modern England* (Cambridge, 2016).
Kingwell, Mark, 'Husserl's Sense of Wonder', *Philosophical Forum* 31:1 (Spring, 2000), 85–107.
Knapp, Jeffrey, *Shakespeare's Tribe. Church, Nation, and Theater in Renaissance England* (Chicago, 2002).
Knapp, Robert, 'Horestes: The Uses of Revenge', *ELH* 40 (1973), 205–20.
Knight, A. H. J., '*Der bestrafte Brudermord* and *Hamlet*, Act V', *Modern Language Review* 31:3 (July, 1936), 385–91.
Knight, Leah, *Reading Green in Early Modern England* (London, 2014).
Kurath, Hans (ed.), *Middle English Dictionary* (Ann Arbor, 2001).
Kussmaul, Ann, *Servants in Husbandry in Early Modern England* (Cambridge, 1981).
Lamb, Charles, 'On the Tragedies of Shakespeare, Considered with Reference

to their Fitness for Stage Representation' [1818], in E. V. Lucas (ed.), *The Works of Charles and Mary Lamb*, 7 vols (London, 1903–5), 1: 97–111.

Landauer, Carl, '*Mimesis* and Erich Auerbach's Self-Mythologizing', *German Studies Review* 11:1 (Feb., 1988), 83–96.

Lane, Christopher, 'The Poverty of Context: Historicism and Nonmimetic Fiction', *PMLA* 118:3 Special Topic: Imagining History (May, 2003), 450–69.

Laslett, Peter, *Family Life and Illicit Love in Earlier Generations* (Cambridge, 1977).

— 'Family and Household as Work Group and Kin Group: Areas of Traditional Europe Compared', in Richard Wall et al. (eds), *Family Forms in Historic Europe* (Cambridge, 1983), 513–63.

— *The World We Have Lost: Further Explored* (London, 1988).

Latour, Bruno, 'On Interobjectivity', trans. Geoffrey Bowker, *Mind, Culture, and Activity* 3:4 (1996), 228–45.

Leech, G. N., 'Linguistics and the Figures of Rhetoric', in Roger Fowler (ed.), *Essays on Style and Language: Linguistic and Critical Approaches to Literary Style* (London, 1966), 135–56.

Lezra, Jacques, *Unspeakable Subjects: The Genealogy of the Event in Early Modern Europe* (Stanford, 1997).

Librett, Jeffrey S., *The Rhetoric of Cultural Dialogue. Jews and Germans from Moses Mendelssohn to Richard Wagner and Beyond* (Stanford, 2000).

Lindley, Arthur, *Hyperion and the Hobbyhorse: Studies in Carnivalesque Subversion* (Newark, 1996).

Lomax, Marion, *Stage Images and Traditions: Shakespeare to Ford* (Cambridge, 1987).

Loughnane, Rory, 'The Artificial Figures and Staging Remembrance in Webster's *Duchess of Malfi*', in Andrew Gordon and Thomas Rist (eds), *The Arts of Remembrance in Early Modern England: Memorial Cultures of the Post Reformation* (London, 2013), 211–28.

Low, Jennifer A., *Manhood and the Duel: Masculinity in Early Modern Drama* (Basingstoke, 2003).

Lupton, Julia Reinhard, *Afterlives of the Saints: Hagiography, Typology, and Renaissance Literature* (Stanford, 1996).

— 'The Pauline Renaissance: A Shakespearean Reassessment', *The European Legacy: Towards New Paradigms* 15:2, Special Issue: Shakespeare and the Ethics of Interpretation (2010), 215–20.

Lupton, Julia Reinhard and Kenneth Reinhard, *After Oedipus. Shakespeare in Psychoanalysis* (Ithaca, 1993).

Lynch, Deirdre, *The Economy of Character. Novels, Market Culture, and the Business of Inner Meaning* (Chicago, 1998).

Lyne, Raphael, 'Shakespeare, Perception and Theory of Mind', *Paragraph* 37:1 (2014), 79–95.

Machosky, Brenda, *Structures of Appearing. Allegory & the Work of Literature* (New York, 2013).

Mahood, M. M., *Bit Parts in Shakespeare's Plays* (Cambridge, 1992).

Maitland, Fredric William, *Domesday Book and Beyond. Three Essays in the Early History of England* (Cambridge, 1907).

Mann, J. C., 'The Orphic Physics of Early Modern Eloquence', in Howard

Marchitello and Evelyn Tribble (eds), *The Palgrave Handbook of Early Modern Literature and Science* (London, 2017), 231–56.
Manning, Roger B., 'The Origins of the Doctrine of Sedition', *Albion* 12:2 (Summer, 1980), 99–121.
— *Swordsmen: The Martial Ethos in the Three Kingdoms* (Oxford, 2003).
Marcus, Leah S., *Unediting the Renaissance. Shakespeare, Marlowe, Milton* (London, 1996).
Mares, Frances Hugh, 'The Origin and Development of the Figure Called the "Vice" in Tudor Drama', B.Litt. thesis, University of Oxford, 1954.
— 'The Origin of the Figure Called "The Vice" in Tudor Drama', *Huntingdon Library Quarterly* 22:1 (1958), 11–29.
Marshall, Peter, *Beliefs and the Dead in Reformation England* (Oxford, 2002).
Martin, Randall, '"Arden winketh at his wife's lewdness, & why!": A Patrilineal Crisis in *Arden of Faversham*', *Early Theatre* 4 (2001), 13–33.
Marx, Karl, *Das Kapital*, in *Marx-Engels-Werke*, 43 vols (Berlin, 1956–90), vols 23–5.
Maus, Katherine Eisaman, *Inwardness and Theater in the English Renaissance* (Chicago, 1995).
Maxwell, Lynn, 'Wax Magic and *The Duchess of Malfi*', *Journal for Early Modern Cultural Studies* 14:3 (Summer, 2014), 31–54.
McBain, Graham, 'Modernising the Law of Murder and Manslaughter: Part 1', *Journal of Politics and Law* 8:4 (2015), 9–97.
McIntosh, Marjorie M., 'Immediate Royal Justice: The Marshalsea Court in Havering, 1358', *Speculum* 54:4 (October, 1979), 727–33.
McLynn, Frank, *Crime and Punishment in Eighteenth-Century England* (London, 1989).
Merleau-Ponty, Maurice, 'The Primacy of Perception and its Philosophical Consequences', trans. James M. Edie, in James M. Edie (ed.), *The Primacy of Perception and Other Essays on Phenomenological Psychology, The Philosophy of Art, History and Politics* (Evanston, 1964), 12–42.
Merritt, Karen Maxwell, 'The Source of John Pikeryng's *Horestes*', *Review of English Studies* 23 (1972), 255–66.
Meyer, Liam J., '"Humblewise": Deference and Complaint in the Court of Requests', *Journal of Early Modern Studies* 4 (2015), 261–85.
Miksch, Walter, *Die Verfasserschaft des Arden of Feversham* (Breslau, 1907).
Miller, William Ian, *Eye for an Eye* (Cambridge, 2006).
Milne, Drew, 'Electra Traces: Beckett's Critique of Sophoclean Tragedy', *Didaskalia, Ancient Theatre Today* 5:3 (Summer 2002), available at www.didaskalia.net/issues/vol5no3/milne.html.
Mitterauer, Michael, *Sozialgeschichte der Jugend* (Frankfurt a.M., 1986).
— 'Servants and Youth', *Continuity and Change* 5 (1990), 11–38.
Montagu, Elizabeth, *An Essay on the Writings and Genius of Shakespeare* (London, 1810).
Mooney, Michael E., *Shakespeare's Dramatic Transactions* (Durham, NC, 1990).
Moretti, Franco, *Signs Taken as Wonders: On the Sociology of Literary Forms* (London, 2005).
Morris, Irene, 'A Hapsburg Letter', *MLR* 69:1 (Jan., 1974), 12–22.
Morris, Joseph, 'John Webster', *Fortnightly Review* 77 (June, 1902), 1064–78.

Mosse, George L., 'The Influence of Jean Bodin's *République* on English Political Thought', *Medievalia et Humanistica* 5 (1948), 73–83.

Nardizzi, Vin, *Wooden Os: Shakespeare's Theatres and England's Trees* (Toronto, 2013).

Nares, Robert, *A Glossary; or collection of words, phrases, names [...]* (London, 1822).

Neill, Michael, 'Monuments and Ruins in *The Duchess of Malfi*', in James Redmond (ed.), *Drama and Symbolism* (Cambridge, 1982), 71–87.

— *Issues of Death: Mortality and Identity in English Renaissance Tragedy* (Oxford, 1997).

— *Putting History to the Question. Power, Politics, and Society in English Renaissance Drama* (New York, 2000).

— '"He that knowest thine": Friendship and Service in *Hamlet*', in Richard Dutton and Jean E. Howard (eds), *A Companion to Shakespeare's Works*, 4 vols (Oxford, 2003), 1: 319–38.

— 'Ich Dien', *London Review of Books* 31:20 (22 October 2009), 11–16.

Nelson, William, *Fact or Fiction: The Dilemma of the Renaissance Storyteller* (Cambridge, MA, 1973).

Northway, Kara, "[H]urt in that service": The Norwich Affray and Early Modern Reactions to Injuries during Dramatic Performances", *Shakespeare Bulletin* 26:4 (Winter, 2008), 25–46.

Nowell-Smith, David, *On Voice in Poetry. The Work of Animation* (Basingstoke, 2015).

O'Connell, Michael, *The Idolatrous Eye. Iconoclasm and Theater in Early Modern England* (Oxford, 2000).

O'Sullivan, Neil, 'Aristotle on Dramatic Probability', *The Classical Journal*, 91:1 (Oct.–Nov. 1995), 47–63.

Oberth, Iris, 'Appropriating France in Elizabethan Drama', in Gabriela Schmidt (ed.), *Elizabethan Translation and Literary Culture* (Berlin, 2013), 275–98.

Oizumi, Akio, *A Complete Concordance to the Works of Geoffrey Chaucer*, 15 vols in 21 books (Hildesheim, 1991–2008).

Ong, Walter J., *Orality and Literacy: The Technologizing of the Word* (New York, 1982).

Oppitz-Trotman, George, 'Shakespeare's Abandoned Cave: Bertolt Brecht and the Dialectic of "Greatness"', in Giovanni Cianci and Caroline Patey (eds), *Will the Modernist: Shakespeare and the European Historical Avant-Gardes* (Oxford, 2014), 165–86.

— 'Adorno's Hamlet', *New German Critique* 43:3 (Nov., 2016), 175–201.

— '"Into that geere the rope": Notes on the Early Modern Halter', *Sixteenth-Century Journal* 47:1 (Spring, 2016), 53–73.

— *Stages of Loss. The English Comedians and their Reception* (forthcoming).

Orgel, Stephen, 'What is a Character?', *Text* 8 (1995), 101–8.

Orlin, Lena Cowen, 'Man's House as his Castle in *Arden of Faversham*', *Medieval and Renaissance Drama in England* 2 (1985), 57–89.

Owens, Margaret E., 'John Webster, Tussaud Laureate: The Waxworks in *The Duchess of Malfi*', *ELH* 79:4 (Winter, 2012), 851–77.

Palfrey, Simon and Tiffany Stern, *Shakespeare in Parts* (Oxford, 2007).

Panzanelli, Roberta, 'Compelling Presence. Wax Effigies in Renaissance

Florence', in Roberta Panzanelli (ed.), *Ephemeral Bodies. Wax Sculpture and the Human Figure* (Los Angeles, 2008), 13–40.

Passannante, Gerard, *The Lucretian Renaissance. Philology and the Afterlife of Tradition* (Chicago, 2011).

Pathmanathan, Sri, 'Death in Greek Tragedy', *Greece and Rome* 12 (1965), 2–14.

Paxson, James J., *The Poetics of Personification* (Cambridge, 1994).

Peltonen, Markku, *The Duel in Early Modern England: Civility, Politeness and Honour* (Cambridge, 2003).

Perry, Curtis, 'The Uneasy Republicanism of Thomas Kyd's *Cornelia*', *Criticism* 48:4 (Autumn, 2006), 534–55.

Pervukhin, Anna, 'Deodands: A Study in the Creation of Common Law Rules', *The American Journal of Legal History* 47:3 (July, 2005), 237–56.

Pollnitz, Aysha, *Princely Education in Early Modern Britain* (Cambridge, 2015).

Pollock, Frederick and Frederic William Maitland, *The History of English Law before the Time of Edward I*, 2 vols (Cambridge, 1898).

Pollock, Linda A., 'Honor, Gender, and Reconciliation in Elite Culture, 1570–1700', *Journal of British Studies* 46 (2007), 3–29.

Porter, James I., 'Disfigurations: Erich Auerbach's Theory of *Figura*', *Critical Inquiry* 44 (Autumn, 2017), 80–113.

Potter, Robert, *The English Morality Play: Origins, History, and Influence of a Dramatic Tradition* (London, 1975).

Prosser, Eleanor, *Hamlet and Revenge* (Stanford, 1971).

Prynne, J. H., *They that Haue Powre to Hurt: A Specimen of a Commentary on Shake-speares Sonnets, 94* (Cambridge, 2001).

Pugliatti, Paola, *Beggary and Theatre in Early Modern England* (London, 2003).

Rappaport, Steve, *Worlds within Worlds: Structures of Life in Sixteenth-Century London* (Cambridge, 1989).

Reich, Hermann, *Der Mimus. Ein litteratur-entwicklungsgeschichtlicher Versuch*, 2 vols (Berlin, 1903).

Reumann, John, 'οικονομια as "Ethical Accommodation" in the Fathers and its Pagan Backgrounds', *Studia Patristica* 3 (1961), 370–9.

Richter, Gerhard, *Oikonomia. Der Gebrauch des Wortes Oikonomia im Neuen Testament, bei den Kirchenvätern und in der theologischen Literatur bis ins 20. Jahrhundert* (Berlin, 2005).

Ricks, Christopher, 'The Moral and Poetic Structure of *The Changeling*', *Essays in Criticism* 10 (1960), 290–306.

Riffaterre, Michael, 'Prosopopeia', *Yale French Studies* 69 (1985), 107–23.

Rist, Thomas, *Revenge Tragedy and the Drama of Commemoration* (London, 2008).

Rivlin, Elizabeth, *The Aesthetics of Service in Early Modern England* (Evanston, 2012).

Roach, Joseph, *Cities of the Dead. Circum-Atlantic Performance* (New York, 1996).

Robinson, Josh, *Adorno's Poetics of Form* (New York, 2018).

Rose, Gillian, *Hegel contra Sociology* (London, 2009).

Rosenmeyer, Thomas G., '"Metatheater": An Essay on Overload', *Arion: A Journal of Humanities and the Classics* 10:2, 3rd ser. (Autumn, 2002), 87–119.

Round, J. Horace, *The King's Serjeants & Officers of State with their Coronation Services* (London, 1911).
Russell, Jeffrey Burton, *Lucifer: The Devil in the Middle Ages* (Ithaca, NY, 1984).
Sacks, Peter, 'Where words prevail not: Grief, Revenge and Language in Kyd and Shakespeare', *English Literary History* 3 (Autumn, 1982), 576–601.
Salingar, Leo G., '*The Revenger's Tragedy* and the Morality Tradition', *Scrutiny* 6 (1937–8), 402–22.
Sallis, John, '"A wonder that one could never aspire to surpass"', in Kenneth Maly (ed.), *The Path of Archaic Thinking. Unfolding the Work of John Sallis* (Albany, 1995), 243–74.
Salmon, J. H. M., 'Precept, Example, and Truth: Degory Wheare and the *Ars Historica*', in Donald R. Kelley and David Harris Sacks (eds), *The Historical Imagination in Early Modern Britain. History, Rhetoric, and Fiction, 1500–1800* (Cambridge, 1997), 11–36.
Schalkwyk, David, *Shakespeare, Love and Service* (Cambridge, 2008).
— '"Love's Transgression": Service, Romeo, Juliet, and the Finality of the You', in Graham Bradshaw, T. G. Bishop, Alexander Cheng-Yuan Huang and Jonathan Gil Harris (eds), *Placing Michael Neill: Issues of Place in Shakespeare and Early Modern Culture*, Shakespearean International Yearbook 11: Special Issue (Farnham, 2011), 111–48.
Schlegel, August Wilhelm, *Über dramatische Kunst und Litteratur: Vorlesungen*, 2 vols (Heidelberg, 1809–11).
Schoch, R., 'Inventing the Origin of Theatre History: The Modern Uses of Juba II's "teatriké historia"', *Journal of Dramatic Theory and Criticism* 27:1 (2012), 5–23.
Schrickx, Willem, *Foreign Envoys and Travelling Players in the Age of Shakespeare* (Gent, 1986).
Schumacher, Meinolf, 'Catalogues of Demons as Catalogues of Vices in Medieval German Literature: *Des Teufels Netz* and the Alexander Romance by Ulrich von Etzenbach', trans. Edward Potter, in Richard Newhauser (ed.), *In the Garden of Evil: The Vices and Culture in the Middle Ages* (Toronto, 2005), 277–90.
Scott, James C., *Weapons of the Weak: Everyday Forms of Peasant Resistance* (New Haven, 1985).
Scragg, Leah, 'Iago – Vice or Devil?', *Shakespeare Survey* 21 (2002), 53–66.
Skura, Meredith Anne, *Shakespeare the Actor and the Purposes of Playing* (Chicago, 1993).
Sear, Frank B., 'Vitruvius and Roman Theater Design', *American Journal of Archaeology* 94:2 (Apr., 1990), 249–58.
Sedley, David, 'Lucretius' Use and Avoidance of Greek', *Proceedings of the British Academy* 93 (1999), 227–46.
Serres, Michel, *Statues. The Second Book of Foundations*, trans. Randolph Burks (London, 2015).
Shapiro, James, '"Tragedies naturally performed": Kyd's Representation of Violence. *The Spanish Tragedy* (c.1587)', in David Scott Kastan and Peter Stallybrass (eds), *Staging the Renaissance. Reinterpretations of Elizabethan and Jacobean Drama* (Abingdon, 1991), 99–113.

Shepard, Alexandra, *Accounting for Oneself: Worth, Status, and the Social Order in Early Modern England* (Oxford, 2015).
Siemon, James R., 'Sporting Kyd', *English Literary Renaissance* 24:3 (Autumn, 1994), 553–82.
Simpson, A. W. B., *A History of the Common Law of Contract. The Rise of the Action of Assumpsit* (Oxford, 1975).
Skinner, Quentin, *Forensic Shakespeare* (Oxford, 2014).
Slater, Niall M., *Plautus in Performance* (Amsterdam, 2000), 10.
Smith, David Chan, *Sir Edward Coke and the Reformation of the Laws. Religion, Politics and Jurisprudence, 1578–1616* (Cambridge, 2014).
Smith, Emma, 'Author v. Character in Early Modern Dramatic Authorship: The Example of Thomas Kyd and *The Spanish Tragedy*', *Medieval & Renaissance Drama in England* 11 (1999), 129–42.
Spivack, Bernard, *Shakespeare and the Allegory of Evil: The History of a Metaphor in Relation to his Major Villains* (New York, 1958).
Staley, Gregory A., *Seneca and the Idea of Tragedy* (Oxford, 2009).
Stallybrass, Peter, 'Naming, Renaming and Unnaming in the Shakespearean Quartos and Folio', in Andrew Murphy (ed.), *The Renaissance Text. Theory, Editing, Textuality* (Manchester, 2000), 108–34.
Steenbrugge, Charlotte, *Staging Vice. A Study of Dramatic Traditions in Medieval and Sixteenth-Century England and the Low Countries* (Amsterdam, 2014).
Steiner, George, *The Death of Tragedy* (New Haven, 1996).
Stern, Tiffany, '"The Curtain is Yours!" The Lord Chamberlain's Men at the Curtain', in Helen Ostovich, Holger Schott Syme and Andrew Griffin (eds), *Locating the Queen's Men, 1583–1603: Material Practices and Conditions of Playing* (Aldershot, 2009), 77–96.
— '"A ruinous monastery": The Second Blackfriars Playhouse as a Place of Nostalgia', in Andrew Gurr and Farah Karim-Cooper (eds), *Moving Shakespeare Indoors. Performance and Repertoire in the Jacobean Playhouse* (Cambridge, 2014), 97–114.
Stewart, Alan, 'Purging Troubled Humours: Bacon, Northampton and the Anti-Duelling Campaign of 1613–1614', in Stephen Clucas and Rosalind Davies (eds), *The Crisis of 1614 and the Addled Parliament: Literary and Historical Perspectives* (Aldershot, 2003), 84–97.
Stewart, Frank Henderson, *Honor* (Chicago, 1994).
Stoichita, Victor I., *A Short History of the Shadow*, trans. Anne-Marie Glasheen (London, 1997).
— *The Self-Aware Image. An Insight into Early Modern Metapainting*, trans. Anne-Marie Glasheen (London, 2015).
Stoll, Elmer Edgar, *John Webster: The Periods of his Work as Determined by his Relations to the Drama of his Day* (New York, 1905, repr. 1967).
Stone Peters, Julia, *Theatre of the Book 1480–1880. Print, Text, and Performance in Europe* (Oxford, 2003).
Sugden, Edward H., *A Topographical Dictionary to the Works of Shakespeare and his Fellow Dramatists* (London, 1925).
Sullivan, Jr, Garret A., '"Arden lay murdered in that plot of ground": Surveying, Land, and *Arden of Faversham*', *English Literary History* 61 (1994), 231–52.
Sutton, Dana Ferrin, *Seneca on the Stage* (Leiden, 1986).

Syme, Holger, 'Unediting the Margin: Jonson, Marston, and the Theatrical Page', *English Literary Renaissance* 38:1 (Feb., 2008), 142–71.

Taylor, Barry, *Vagrant Writing: Social and Semiotic Disorders in the English Renaissance* (Hemel Hempstead, 1991).

Taylor, Gary, 'Did Shakespeare Write *The Spanish Tragedy* Additions?', in Gary Taylor and Gabriel Egan (eds), *The New Oxford Shakespeare: Authorship Companion* (Oxford, 2017), Chap. 15.

Taylor, Hillary, 'The Price of the Poor's Words: Social Relations and the Economics of Deposing for One's "Betters" in Early Modern England', *Economic History Review* (forthcoming).

Thaler, Alwin, 'In My Mind's Eye, Horatio', *Shakespeare Quarterly* 7:4 (Autumn, 1956), 351–4.

Thomson, Peter, *On Actors and Acting* (Exeter, 2000).

Thorndike, A. H., 'The Relations of *Hamlet* to Contemporary Revenge Plays', *PMLA* 17:2 (1902), 125–220.

Thrush, Andrew, 'EGERTON, Sir John (c.1551–1614)', in Andrew Thrush and John P. Ferris (eds), *The House of Commons 1604–1629*, 6 vols (Cambridge, 2010), 4: 178–81.

Tillyard, E. M. W., *Shakespeare's Last Plays* (London, 1938).

Tribble, Evelyn, *Cognition in the Globe. Attention and Memory in Shakespeare's Theatre* (New York, 2011).

— *Early Modern Actors and Shakespeare's Theatre. Thinking with the Body* (London, 2017).

Trusler, John, *The London Advisor and Guide* (London, 1790).

Turner, Henry S., *The English Renaissance Stage. Geometry, Poetics, and the Practical Spatial Arts, 1580–1630* (Oxford, 2006).

Turner, Timothy A., 'Torture and Summary Justice in *The Spanish Tragedy*', *SEL 1500–1900* 53:2 (Spring, 2013), 277–92.

Turner, Victor, *From Ritual to Theatre. The Human Seriousness of Play* (New York, 1982).

Unruh, Daniel B., 'The Predatory Palace: Seneca's *Thyestes* and the Architecture of Tyranny', in Adam M. Kemezis (ed.), *Urban Dreams and Realities in Antiquity* (Leiden, 2014), 246–72.

Usher, Abbott Payson, *A History of Mechanical Inventions: Revised Edition* (New York, 1988).

Vallelly, Neil, 'Being-in-Light at the Early Modern and Reconstructed Theatres', PhD thesis, University of Otago, 2015.

Vickers, Brian, 'The Emergence of Character Criticism, 1774–1800', *Shakespeare Survey* 34 (1981), 11–22.

— 'Thomas Kyd, Secret Sharer', *Times Literary Supplement*, 18 April 2008, 13–15.

von Schlosser, Julius, 'Geschichte der Porträtbildnerei in Wachs', *Jahrbuch der Kunsthistorischen Sammlungen des Allerhöchsten Kaiserhauses* 29 (1910/11), 171–258.

Walsh, Brian, *Shakespeare, the Queen's Men, and the Elizabethan Performance of History* (Cambridge, 2009).

Walsham, Alexandra, *Providence in Early Modern England* (Oxford, 1999).

Ward, Adolphus William, *History of English Dramatic Literature, to the Death of Queen Anne*, 3 vols (London, 1899).

Watson, R. N., *The Rest is Silence: Death as Annihilation in the English Renaissance* (Berkeley, 1994).
Wayland, Scott, 'Religious Change and the Renaissance Elegy', *English Literary Renaissance* 39:3 (2009), 429–59.
Weil, Judith, *Service and Dependency in Shakespeare's Plays* (Cambridge, 2005).
Weimann, Robert, *Shakespeare and the Popular Tradition in the Theater*, ed. Robert Schwartz (Baltimore, 1978).
— *Author's Pen and Actor's Voice. Playing and Writing in Shakespeare's Theatre* (Cambridge, 2000).
Weimann, Robert and Douglas Bruster, *Prologues to Shakespeare's Theatre. Performance and Liminality in Early Modern Drama* (London, 2004).
— *Shakespeare and the Power of Performance: Stage and Page in the Elizabethan Theatre* (Cambridge, 2008).
Wells, Stanley, 'Staging Shakespeare's Ghosts', in *Shakespeare on Page and Stage. Selected Essays* (Oxford, 2016), 255–70.
Wernham, R. B., *After the Armada* (Oxford, 1984).
West, Russell, *Spatial Representations on the Jacobean Stage: From Shakespeare to Webster* (Basingstoke, 2002).
Whigham, Frank, *Seizures of the Will in Early Modern English Drama* (Cambridge, 2009).
White, Hayden, *Figural Realism. Studies in the Mimesis Effect* (Baltimore, 2000).
White, Martin, '"When torchlight made an artificial noon": Light and Darkness in the Indoor Jacobean Theatre', in Andrew Gurr and Farah Karim-Cooper (eds), *Moving Shakespeare Indoors* (Cambridge, 2014), 115–36.
Whitney, Charles, '"Usually in the Werking Daies": Playgoing Journeymen, Apprentices, and Servants in Guild Records, 1582–92', *Shakespeare Quarterly* 50:4 (Winter, 1999), 433–58.
Wilson, Luke, *Theaters of Intention: Drama and the Law in Early Modern England* (Stanford, 2000).
— 'Renaissance Tool Abuse and the Legal History of the Sudden', in Erica Sheen and Lorna Hutson (eds), *Literature, Politics and Law in Renaissance England* (Basingstoke, 2005), 121–45.
Withington, Robert, 'The Ancestry of the "Vice"', *Speculum* 7 (1932), 525–9.
— 'Braggart, Devil, and "Vice"', *Speculum* 11 (1936), 124–9.
— 'The Development of the "Vice"', in *Essays in Memory of Barrett Wendell* (New York, 1967), 155–67.
Witmore, Michael, *Culture of Accidents: Unexpected Knowledges in Early Modern England* (Stanford, 2001).
Wizisla, Erdmut, *Benjamin und Brecht. Die Geschichte einer Freundschaft* (Frankfurt a.M., 2004).
Wood, Andy, 'Fear, Hatred and the Hidden Injuries of Class in Early Modern England', *Journal of Social History* 39:3 (Spring, 2006), 803–86.
— *The 1549 Rebellions and the Making of Early Modern England* (Cambridge, 2007).
— 'Deference, Paternalism and Popular Memory in Early Modern England', in Steve Hindle, Alexandra Shepard and John Walter (eds), *Remaking English*

Society: Social Relations and Social Change in Early Modern England (Woodbridge, 2013), 233–53.

Woodbridge, Linda, *English Revenge Drama: Money, Resistance, Equality* (Cambridge, 2010).

Worthen, W. B., 'Drama, Performativity, and Performance', *PMLA* 113:5 (Oct., 1998), 1093–107.

— *Print and the Poetics of Modern Drama* (Cambridge, 2005).

Wrightson, Keith, *Earthly Necessities: Economic Lives in Early Modern Britain* (New Haven, 2000).

— '"These which be participant of the common wealth": Class, Governance, and Social Identities in Early Modern England', unpublished working paper.

Zaller, Robert, *The Discourse of Legitimacy in Early Modern England* (Stanford, 2007).

Zika, Charles, 'The Witch of Endor: Transformations of a Biblical Necromancer in Early Modern Europe', in Charles Zika and F. W. Kent (eds), *Rituals, Images and Words: The Varieties of Cultural Expression in Late Medieval and Early Modern Europe* (Turnhout, 2005), 235–59.

Zimmerman, Susan, *The Early Modern Corpse and Shakespeare's Theatre* (Edinburgh, 2007).

Zmora, Hillay, *The Feud in Early Modern Germany* (Cambridge, 2011).

Zoran, Gabriel, *Bodies of Speech. Text and Textuality in Aristotle* (Cambridge, 2014).

Zurcher, Andrew, 'Spenser's Studied Archaism: The Case of "Mote"', *Spenser Studies* 21 (2006), 231–40.

— 'Consideration, Contract, and the End of *The Comedy of Errors*', *Law and Humanities* 1:2 (2007), 145–65.

Zysk, Jay, *Shadow and Substance. Eucharistic Controversy and English Drama across the Reformation Divide* (Notre Dame, 2017).

Index

Abel, Lionel, 165, 210–15, 220; *see also* metatheatre
Abelard, Peter, 111
absolutism, 36, 44, 54, 76
accident
  Aristotelian, 77
  epistemology of, 12, 65, 92–3, 170
  in scholastic ontological sense, 1, 74, 80, 127
  in sense of unintended action, 32, 65, 82, 170
  undoing plans, 76–8
actor *see* player
Adorno, Theodor W., 1, 17, 181, 219
Aeschylus
  Agamemnon, 176
  kidnapped, 213
  Libation Bearers, 204
  Orestes, 211
affray, 86–7, 90, 98, 99, 147; *see also* duelling
Agamemnon, 6, 176, 213
agency
  and authority, 54
  discernment of, 77, 117
  of player *see* player
  and providence, 40
  and service, 131, 147, 149–50
  and villainy, 31, 112
allegory, 15, 18, 44, 50, 107, 114, 156, 175; *see also* psychomachia
amateurism, 12, 103, 213; *see also* professionalism
Amleth, 72, 79
anachronism, 17–18, 72, 102–3, 209
Anderson, Anthony, 185
anthropology, 4–5
antitheatre
  as catalyst to art, 119, 215
  and iconoclasm, 103, 188
  and Plato, 9
  and prejudice, 149, 189
  and Puritanism, 202
  and Reformation, 119
  and secularisation, 105
Antony & Cleopatra, 2, 5, 88
Apollo, 52, 67, 111, 176
apostrophe, 183; *see also* eidolopoeia; prosopopoeia
Appletree, Thomas, 32
apprenticeship
  and abuse, 159
  and commonwealth, 133
  and complaint, 134
  and disorder, 52–3, 62, 149
  and service, 129, 130, 159
  and theatre, 10, 149
  underground, 154
Arden of Faversham, 204–8
Ardern, John, 32
Aristotle
  De Anima, 172
  Metaphysics, 182–3
  Poetics, 3
  Politics, 47, 48
  Rhetoric, 7
Armada, 27
Articuli super Cartas, 29–30; *see also* Magna Carta; Verge
assumpsit, action at common law, 55–6, 145–6; *see also* contract; debt
astronomy, 20, 176–8; *see also* constellations
atavism, 13, 47–8, 73, 78–9, 155, 216
atomism *see* Lucretius
Auerbach, Erich, 167, 186, 187–92, 193–4, 203, 212
authenticity, 16, 80, 103, 117, 189, 215, 218; *see also* essences
axes *see* blades

Bacon, Francis, 27, 34–5, 45, 90, 141
Bale, John, 102
bathos, 66, 69–70, 75, 79, 190
Belleforest, François de, 79
Benjamin, Walter, 2, 14–16, 20, 21, 45, 92, 175, 181, 216
Bentley, John, 87, 99
Bentley, Thomas, 154
Bernard of Clairvaux, 113
Bestrafte Brudermord, Der, 76
blades
  axes, 72
  bare, 53, 67–8, 81
  bodkins *see* bodkin
  daggers, 64, 72–4, 78, 83, 115, 205; *see also* rapier *(below)*
  drawn *see* bare *(above)*
  and intent, 64–93 *passim*
  knives, 64, 88
  rapier: as anachronism, 18, 72, 80, 115; and anger, 68, 72, 83, 91; with dagger, 72, 73–4, 78, 83–4, 86, 89; essentiality of, 65, 68, 70; fashion for, 67–9, 70, 74; and improvisation, 83–8, 89, 91; lethality of, 64–5, 69, 72, 82, 165; and manslaughter, 82–3; and metaphor,

blades (cont.)
  rapier (cont.)
    64, 72, 79, 88; and mimesis, 90–2, 115; negligibility of, 64, 69–70, 87–8; as prop, 76, 80, 90, 92–3; versus sword, 69, 72, 99; and technique, 67, 73–4, 77–80, 91; and wit, 64, 73
  scalpels, 64, 92, 208–10
  sheathed, 67, 79, 83
  swords: and bravery, 72, 126–7; and epic, 67–8, 75–6; and hesitation, 67–8; and honour, 66, 69, 70, 84, 148; and legitimacy, 76, 79; as props, 35, 86, 92; versus rapier, 69, 72, 99; and theatre, 65, 67, 85–6, 88, 164–5
Blague, Thomas, 64
blinding *see* eyes
bodies
  artistic inhabitation of, 9
  capable of work, 149, 162
  and causation, 114, 186
  dead, 11, 3, 95, 164, 187, 192, 206
  diseased, 2
  eaten *see* cannibalism
  first, 186
  sounds within, 171
  economic, 48
  imprint of, 207, 218
  invisible, 117
  metaphysical, 1, 6, 110, 113
  noble, 73–4
  partially real, 19, 114, 194
  player's *see* player
  pneumatic, 9, 171
  political, 182
  removal of, 164, 168, 170, 206
  rotting, 16, 155, 164
  royal, 33, 47, 50
  singular and infinite, 10, 110, 194
  as subject of rhetoric, 43, 192
  supplemented, 50, 126–7, 187, 194
  vicious *see* Vice
Bodin, Jean, 48
bodkin
  hair-pin, 69
  metaphor for judgement, 92
  and suicide, 67
  tool: in textile industries, 69; in bookbinding, 69, 195
  see also blades
borough, 47–8, 61
boundaries
  critical, 24, 29
  crossing of, 38, 166
  dramatic, 44, 111–12, 176, 206–7
  of games, 84
  intriguers at, 114, 140, 155
  legal *see* law: and jurisdiction
  and substances, 42, 47, 59
  see also Verge
brawling *see* duelling
Brecht, Bertolt, 8–9, 16, 91
Breton, Nicholas, 72
Burbage, Richard, 10, 12, 70, 104, 142–3
burial
  and clowning, 66, 87, 113
  and disinterment, 169
  and sound, 170–1
  as theme of tragedy, 11, 155

Calvinism, 188; *see also* providence
Campion, Edmund, 32

candles *see* light
cannibalism, 175, 176
Carey, Henry, 32
catharsis, 12, 54, 114
causation
  and action, 80
  and materiality, 114, 116, 186
  and semblance, 21, 112, 116, 127, 142, 159, 195
  and universal law, 15
  see also motive
Cawdrey, Robert, 181–2
Cecil, Robert, 32
Cecil, William, 88
Chambers, Edmund Kerchever, 107
chance-medley, 82; *see also* manslaughter
Chapman, George
  The Revenge of Bussy D'Ambois, 24
  The Tragedy of Bussy D'Ambois, 75, 97
character
  its afterlife, 2, 5, 11, 13–14, 28, 65, 135, 168
  charactery, 104, 140, 191
  and conscience, 114, 155, 213
  and dramatic person, 5, 12, 109, 130, 150, 168, 174
  and function, 130, 147, 150, 204
  as idol, 104, 106, 109, 116, 134, 168, 178, 190, 210–12
  and perception *see* physiognomy
  and pity, 7, 168, 184, 185
  player as hidden premise of, 13, 18, 73, 91–2, 138, 157, 192
  as real people, 3, 8, 9, 18, 116, 127, 134, 157, 190
  as textual formations, 4, 6, 7, 65, 126–7, 156
Cheke, John, 133
Chettle, Henry, *Hoffmann*, 17, 139–40, 146, 156, 205
chivalry *see* honour
Churchyard, Thomas, 72
Cicero, 37, 103, 172, 192
circumstance
  and form, 29, 44, 71
  and legal inquiry, 38, 80, 184
  and motive, 43, 187
  rhetorical term, 37, 43–4, 46, 192
civility
  after the Reformation, 71
  and anachronism, 71
  and class, 77, 90, 148
  and gesture, 73, 88–9
  theory of, 85
class, 16, 109, 129, 135, 160, 218
Cleaver, Robert, 135, 136
cloth *see* textiles
clothes
  in candlelight, 180
  as consideration, 145, 153
  and destitution, 153
  dyed black, 117, 142
  and inauthenticity, 117
  monopolised, 112
  see also livery
clowns
  and celebrity, 109, 149
  and death, 66, 76, 88
  and dexterity, 85, 86
  and improvisation, 87, 106
  and popular tradition, 107, 109–10, 151
Cocke, John, 104
cognition, 9, 185, 201, 216; *see also* misrecognition

Index   251

Coke, Edward, 30, 33, 82, 145, 148
Collins, Wilkie, 166
colonialisation, 188
comedy, 137, 146, 166–7, 209; *see also* tragedy
commonwealth
 and duelling, 75
 family as origin of, 48–9
 and household *see* household
 and neighbourliness, 53, 75
 player's part in *see* player
 as preferred word, 61
 and property, 134, 136
 and rebellion, 77
 and revenge, 151
 and service, 133, 137–8, 143
 and vagrancy, 137, 139
community *see* polis
confession, 67–8, 84–5, 88, 115
conscience, 11, 70, 74, 85, 87, 115, 127; *see also* Vice
consideration *see* contract
constellations, 14, 20, 110, 130, 157, 192, 194, 212; *see also* astronomy; Benjamin, Walter
contamination *see* infection; plague
contract
 and consideration, 145–6, 150–1
 disruption of, 129, 139
 erotic potential of, 150
 Hegel's category, 131, 145
 and identity, 131
 length of, 152
 of service, 134, 137, 145
 in the theatre, 129
 and words, 142
 working to, 137
coroner, 30, 93, 208–10
corregidor, 36, 41
Cosin, Richard, 46
Cotton, Robert, 33
court
 ancient, 30, 33, 54
 Anglo-Norman, 31
 as audience, 1, 39, 65, 89, 194
 of Chivalry, 72
 clown at, 88
 of Common Pleas, 88
 corrupt, 42, 54, 88, 140, 155, 216
 Danish, 1
 etymology of, 33, 48
 exclusion from, 27, 39, 41, 52, 55, 114, 140, 155
 image of, 140, 168–9
 inferior/superior, 31, 57
 of King's Bench, 31, 32, 34, 55–6
 and literary form, 15, 38, 44, 45, 216
 of Marshalsea *see* Verge
 mythical, 36
 Palace *see* Verge
 Portuguese, 36, 38, 49
 and revenge, 114
 and semblance, 44
 servants in, 130
 Spanish, 27, 36, 38, 42, 49
 structure of, 28
 Tudor, 27–8
 of the Verge *see* Verge
 see also law
cowardice, 72, 90–1, 211–12
Croke, George, 31
Crooke, Helkiah, 182, 186
cues, 91, 126, 147, 168
cultural materialism, 109, 132

daggers *see* blades
Dante Alighieri, 193–4
Darell, Walter, 136, 137
David, king of Israel and Judah, 34, 126, 138
Day, John, 81, 83, 137, 138
Deacon, John, 102
death
 acting of *see* player
 beyond knowledge, 66, 69, 92
 by clown, 88
 disappointing, 70
 escape from, 32
 in France, 65
 instant, 66
 investigation of *see* coroner
 lingering, 164–8, 205
 of one's literary rivals, 85
 of people: Agamemnon, 114, 213; Ananias and Sapphira, 46; Antonio, 12, 170; Arden of Faversham, 205; Bosola, 166, 170, 174; Claudius, 77; Clois Hoffman, 205; Clois Hoffman's father, 205; Duchess of Malfi, 128, 168; The Duke, 205; Ferdinand, 155; Flamineo, 164–5; Gertrude, 73; Hamlet, 1, 82, 176; Henry Porter, 69; Hippolito, 191; Ithocles, 205; Julia, 205; Julius Caesar, 69, 80, 187; Laertes, 75; Mercutio, 91; Otho, 205; Polonius, 69, 91; Priam, 67; Prince Henry, 196; Richard Burbage, 104; Richard Tarlton, 86; Serberine, 37; servants, 135, 159; spectators, 51; Tybalt, 91
 personified, 68
 prophylaxis against, 96
 threat of, 66
 in tragedy, 164–6, 195
 unforeseen, 95
 Webster's alleged obsession with, 165, 167
 see also manslaughter; murder; suicide
debt, 5, 15, 34, 41, 65, 118, 136, 140, 145, 152, 217
Dekker, Thomas, 54, 141
Demetrius of Phalerum, 6
Democritus, 190
demons, 110, 111, 115, 116–18, 181, 190; *see also* evil; Vice
deodands, 93, 100
Descartes, René, 171, 172
Devereux, Robert, Earl of Essex, 32–3, 36
Devil
 its material shape, 102, 142, 181, 182
 metaphysical encounter with, 113
 on the stage, 102, 109, 115
 see also Vice
di Grassi, Giacomo, 69, 72, 78, 94, 96
disease *see* infection; plague
disguise
 and duty, 127–8, 155
 ethics of, 149–50
 and essential evil, 102, 119
 high office made into, 40–1, 52
 of name, 101
 and personhood, 9, 104, 156, 157
 and strangers, 101, 119, 151, 185
 see also player
Drake, Francis, 27
duelling
 and brawling, 77–8, 82–3
 criticism and control of, 65, 81, 97
 in France, 65, 83–4
 legal status of, 65, 75, 81–3
 political implications of, 75–80

duelling (*cont.*)
  and warding, 83, 86, 88–9
  see also blades; fencing
dumbshow, 29, 35, 80, 128–9, 164, 171–5, 215

echoes
  and figuration, 10–11, 168–9, 174
  literary, 117, 169, 178
  and tragic ground, 35, 168–9
editorial science
  attribution, 217
  excision, 218
  glossing, 89, 118
  and historicism, 173
  interpolation, 39, 58
  naming, 7, 126
Egerton, John, 34
Egmont, Count of, 36
eidolopoeia, 6, 170, 176, 183; *see also* prosopopoeia
Elias, Norbert, 71
Eliot, T. S., 165
Elizabeth I, queen of England, 32, 54, 112
emotions *see* semblance
emulation *see* mimesis
enargeia, 50, 192; *see also* rhetoric
English Comedians, 85–6
Enterlude of the Godly Queene Hester, 112
Epicurus, 182; *see also* Lucretius
epicycle, 177; *see also* astronomy
epilogue
  alleged liminality of, 4, 176, 218
  to *Arden of Faversham*, 205, 206–8
  to *Horestes*, 119–20, 153
  and metatheatre, 214
  to *The Tempest*, 152, 176
equity *see* law
essences
  belief in unchanging, 104, 110
  and character, 191
  fundamental property, 68, 70, 183
  noble, 148
estate *see* land
ethics
  absolute or relative, 213–14
  Christian, 65
  and figuration, 11, 71, 126–7, 164
  and form, 74
  and materiality, 13, 71
  and revenge, 21, 79, 93, 156, 213–14
  and service, 128, 131–5, 156
Euripides
  Electra, 204
  Hecuba, 6
  Orestes, 67
evil, 32, 111, 118, 120, 129, 138, 211
exegesis, 46, 193, 207
eyes
  emanations from, 6, 103, 128, 165, 174, 205
  for eyes, 195
  impairment of, 177, 178–9, 181, 182, 185, 186, 213
  and judgement, 138, 139, 141, 143, 182, 185
  metaphysical, 181–2, 184
  open, 167
  removal of, 83–4, 126–9, 144
  strained, 20, 178, 183, 199

faces *see* masks; physiognomy
Falstaff, Sir John, 30, 107, 210–12

family *see* household
fathers
  and ancestors, 6, 79, 112, 136, 176
  and citizens or officers, 38
  John Webster's, 167
  as motive, 66, 72, 90, 114, 140
  spectral, 41–2, 90, 116–17, 181–2, 185
  and the State, 47–9, 133
  Thomas Kyd's, 43
Feake, James, 83
fear
  acting of, 212
  of conformity, 187
  and courage, 67, 71–2, 97, 149
  of disease, 27
  of legal action, 27, 139
  of remembrance, 2, 5
  of satire, 70
  of servants, 138, 141, 142
  of Spain, 36
  of vagrants, 153
  see also ghost
fencing
  and grace, 72, 75, 77
  masters of, 69, 86
  schools of, 78
  technique of, 69, 77–9, 83–5
  and theatre, 85
  see also duelling
feud, 71, 90
Fit, John, 135
Fitzherbert, Anthony, 30
Flögel, Karl Friedrich, 107
footprints, 180, 204, 206; *see also* imprinting
Ford, John
  The Broken Heart, 205
  on *The Duchess of Malfi*, 175
  'Tis Pity She's a Whore, 17, 146–9
formalism, 209, 212
Fossett, Thomas, 138
Foxe, John, 102
Frankfurt am Main, 85
Fraunce, Abraham, 43, 46, 59n81
freedom
  from contract, 152–3, 155–6
  and fate, 93, 205
  illusory, 213
  of interpretation, 9
  and liminality, 22
  political, 133–4
  and social death, 119, 133, 153
  and suicide, 64
Fulwell, Ulpian, 118, 119

Gammer Gurton's Needle, 119
Garter, Thomas, 111
Gdańsk, 85
genealogy
  arboreal symbolism of, 50
  of fool, 109
  of text, 20
  of Vice *see* Vice
genre
  dialectical concept of, 21, 205
  of metatheatre, 210, 220
  and *mimus*, 108
  and reflexivity, 205, 209
  and scheme, 193, 195
  and social order, 83, 157
ghost
  and causation, 64, 89–90, 116, 187
  of Don Andrea, 50, 114

Index   253

and figure, 18, 116, 169, 174, 176–86, 190, 194
of Julius Caesar, 178, 187
as object of scholarship, 15, 176–7, 201
of Old Hamlet, 8, 64, 89, 116–18, 176–86
as prologues, 176, 183–5, 186, 212
recognition of, 89–90, 115, 178, 180–2
of Richard Tarlton, 87
of Seneca, 176–7, 189
solid, 17, 117–18, 182–5, 187
of Tantalus, 184
of Thyestes, 176
and Vice, 114–18, 182
Gifford, Humphrey, 137
Gosson, Stephen, 51–2, 104; see also antitheatre
Gouge, William, 136, 138, 143
Gratwicke, Steven, 102
graves see burial
Graz, 83
Green, John, 83–6, 89
Greenblatt, Stephen, 10, 126, 176
Greene, Robert, 74, 87, 90
Griffith, Matthew, 138
Gundolf, Friedrich, 3

Hall, Joseph, 168, 191
halters, 32, 36, 153–4
Hamlet
abroad, 85
as art, 65, 90, 92, 210
and atavism, 67, 73, 79–80
and atomism, 182, 186
and bodies, 11
and commonwealth, 75
editions of, 7, 70, 177, 185, 216
and extravagance, 59
and failure, 92
first quarto of, 66, 77, 80, 87, 144
and the future, 1–3, 7, 14, 77, 90, 95, 186, 195, 217
and the Ghost see ghost
and Hamlet: actor of, 12, 73, 91, 104; alive, 8, 9, 12, 91, 212; and Brutus, 70, 80; clown, 87; conscience of, 67–8, 73, 74, 82, 115, 118; fatness of, 89; and Fortinbras, 90; grace of, 72–3, 75; his intent, 71, 77, 79–80, 91; incapacity of, 66, 70, 90, 103, 210; as melancholic, 117, 142; myth of, 3, 7, 79, 212; name of, 1, 5–6, 7, 12, 73, 74; paleness of, 116–17; and Shakespeare, 9, 190, 212; and voice, 10
and literary history, 213, 219
and maimed rites, 78
and mathematics, 198
opening scene of, 177–86
and philosophy, 92–3, 182–3, 186, 210
and purgatory, 176
and the Queen's Men, 86
readers of, 65, 79, 216
as revenge tragedy, 21, 205, 207
and rhetoric, 183
and slander, 64
sources for, 79–80, 87, 90, 116–17, 177, 181–2
and suicide, 68–70
and symbolism, 64
as tragedy, 18, 210, 213–14, 220
and Vice see Vice
hands
dead, 173, 175, 179, 180, 185, 187
full of speeches, 177

handwriting, 25–6, 191
holding rods or staffs, 36, 58
holding wax, 172, 209
holding weapons, 53, 67–8, 76, 79, 80, 87, 96, 144
and idols, 103–4, 187
and illegitimate work, 144, 154
and intent, 74, 79, 80, 126
moulded to, 143–4
ready, 152
removal of, 31
and restraint, 126, 144
and skill, 74, 77–8, 103, 134, 144
and small props, 88
solid, 185, 187
synecdochic, 179
Harman, Thomas, 154
Hazlitt, William, 113
Hegel, G. W. F., 131, 145, 213, 214, 215
Henricpetri, Adam, 36
Henry IV, Part 2, 30
Henry VII, king of England, 31
Henry VIII, king of England, 31
hent, 67–8, 70–4
Herbert, Frank, *Dune*, 95
Heywood, Jasper, 49, 76, 189
Heywood, John, 106, 107, 111, 113, 123
Heywood, Thomas, 118, 196, 198
historicism
its concept of history, 167
and *figura*, 189
immanent critique of, 14, 130
invulnerability of, 173, 176–7
and task, 172–4
Holinshed, Ralph, 68, 205–6, 218
honour
and citizenship, 49, 75, 76
corruption of, 66, 72, 74–5, 84
through death, 70, 71, 165–6
defence of, 65–6, 72–4, 90, 91, 149
feudal, 18, 71
loss of, 1–2, 66, 69, 72, 75, 82
martial, 28, 72, 83
and neo-Platonism, 1, 6
private, 65, 75, 77
as satanical illusion, 66
as semblance, 74, 85, 91, 155
theorisation of, 71, 76, 82–3
Horace, 85
household
economics see *oikonomía*
royal see Verge
its salience in early modern thought, 48–9, 132–3
and State, 47, 49, 138
and theatre-house, 51
vulnerability of, 53, 134–8, 140, 149
see also private sphere
Howard family, 34
humanism, 13, 66, 182, 187
Hutson, Lorna, 28–9, 43, 80, 192–3, 204

iconoclasm
and art, 188, 215
and genocide, 188
identity see non-identity
idolatry, 102–3; see also eidolopoeia
imitation see mimesis
imprinting, 186, 194, 195, 211
wax, 140, 143, 171, 187
improvisation, 2, 80–8, 106, 126, 127; see also clowns; duelling

infection, 27, 38, 52, 80, 118, 144, 175, 186
insanity
  of duelling, 72
  of Ferdinand, 155, 174
  of Hieronimo, 45, 194
instruments, 87–8, 144
intention
  discernment of, 43, 71, 92, 93, 184
  and improvisation see improvisation
  and language, 68, 142
  mimesis of another's, 88–90, 143
  obscure, 2, 65, 69, 80
  as question of law, 66, 82–3, 86
  and reflection, 181
  and reflexes, 65, 81, 82, 92
  as special question in revenge tragedy, 207
  and weapons, 68, 74, 77–9, 82
interludes, 52, 54, 102, 107, 111–12
intriguer
  and competence, 89
  and servant, 18, 135, 146, 149
  and Vice, 108
  and Walter Benjamin, 15
inwardness, 41, 91–2, 146; see also character

Jonson, Ben
  and books, 216
  duel with Gabriel Spencer, 83, 93
  Every Man Out of his Humour, 74
  as Hieronimo, 54
  and the Vice, 115, 125
Julius Caesar, 2, 66, 69, 70, 80, 178, 187
Justices of the Peace, 81

Kerrigan, John, 12, 20, 29, 77, 142
killing see murder
King John, 181
King Lear, 68, 126–7, 130–1, 133, 153
Knevet, Edmond, 31
Knight Marshal, 27–35; see also office-holding; Verge
knives see blades
Kyd, Thomas
  his career, 59
  Cornelia, 36
  Don Horatio (lost), 35
  reception of Seneca, 49–50
  The Householder's Philosophy, 48
  The Spanish Tragedy: additions to, 20, 45, 164, 178; choric element in, 114–15, 208, 215; figural logic of, 194–5; its influence, 21, 166; Painter in, 205; printing of, 59, 60; its relation to *Hamlet*, 20–1

labyrinths, 49–51, 150
Lactantius, 104
Lamb, Charles, 113
Lambarde, William, 81
land
  attainder, 49; see also treason
  enclosure of, 133
  and inheritance, 140, 178
  and property, 35–6, 44, 60, 133–4, 205
  and providence, 206, 218
  purification of, 34, 47
  and rights, 133–4, 136, 138, 162
  scot and lot, 53
  yardland, 35
  see also commonwealth; Verge
Langton, Stephen, Archbishop of Canterbury, 102
Laslett, Peter, 132–3

law
  and art, 83, 212–14
  availability of, 30, 42, 66, 136
  canon, 46
  change in, 33–4, 81–2, 133, 145
  corruption of, 34, 42, 97, 102, 125, 137
  and equity, 41, 54, 213–14
  of the house see oikonomía
  and judgement, 83, 86, 93
  and jurisdiction, 31, 33–5, 59, 60
  and land see land
  martial, 28, 33
  natural, 74, 138, 152
  obscurity of, 32, 93, 100
  and origins, 47, 61, 100, 212
  pedantry of, 66, 82, 154
  and providence, 205–6
  and revenge, 27, 38, 49, 75, 213–14
  and rhetoric, 43, 59
  and sovereignty, 17, 30, 75–6
  sumptuary, 148
  universal, 15, 102, 213
  see also contract; debt; murder; trespass
letters, 38, 45–6, 79, 113, 130, 150, 187
light, 173–82, 205, 215
  in art, 180
  candlelight, 20, 174, 177–80, 184, 199
  electric, 7, 178, 180, 204
  lanterns, 16, 173, 174
  and shadow, 194
  stage, 180
  sunshine, 20, 180–2, 200
liminality, 4–5, 6, 42, 139, 176; see also boundaries
limits see boundaries
literary unity, 44, 50, 54, 105–6, 111, 183, 213
livery, 140, 147–9, 153; see also servant
Lodge, Thomas, 116–17
London
  Cheapside, 125, 167, 204
  crime in, 32, 125, 205
  Liberties of, 52
  migration to, 135–6
  oligarchy of, 51, 52–3
  playhouses of see playhouses
  preaching in, 100
  public events in, 2, 21, 78, 196
  sailors returning to, 27
  St Paul's, 125, 196, 204
  Southwark, 53–4, 204; see also playhouses
Lord Chamberlain, 53
Lucretius, 177, 182, 186–7, 190
Lukács, György, 16
Lupton, Thomas, 106

Macbeth, 77, 182, 190
Machiavelli, Niccolò, 43, 45, 112
Maddalena, Maria, 83, 86
magic see witchcraft
Magna Carta, 29–30
Mankind, morality play, 105, 117, 118
Manningham, John, 88
manslaughter, 18, 31, 81–3, 93, 98, 134
Marlowe, Christopher
  Dido, Queen of Carthage, 87–8
  Doctor Faustus, 190
Marowe, Thomas, 82
Marx, Karl, 133–4, 146, 153; see also class
Masaccio, 180
masculinity, 65, 88; see also duelling

masks, 5, 15, 103, 107, 115, 116–17, 122, 149, 156–7, 172
masterless men *see* vagrancy
masters
  as arbitrators of honour, 74
  being sought, 119, 139, 151, 156
  of fencing *see* fencing
  hurt, 126, 142, 155, 156
  litigated, 134, 135
  originating household, 50
  and slaves, 61, 128, 134, 140, 142–5, 152
  supervising punishment, 32, 38, 154
  their perspective, 130, 132–3, 136, 139
  vicious, 143, 146, 159
  see also fathers; household; servant
melancholia
  and clothes, 142
  and intriguer, 39
  and service, 155
  and *theatrum mundi* conceits, 214
  as vice, 117
Meres, Francis, 189
Merleau-Ponty, Maurice, 9–10; *see also* phenomenology
metatheatre, 2, 166, 170, 173–4, 208–15, 219
Middleton, Thomas
  The Changeling (part author), 17, 141, 150–1
  on *The Duchess of Malfi*, 165
  The Revenger's Tragedy, 17, 41, 85, 143–5, 156, 167–8, 205
  Women Beware Women, 191
Milton, John, 187
mimesis, 7–8, 9, 44, 50, 75, 88–91, 104, 108–9, 128, 168, 175, 180, 192; *see also* Auerbach, Erich; player
mimus, 108–10; *see also* clowns; player
Mirror for Magistrates, 42
mirrors, 90, 184; *see also* mimesis
misrecognition, 7–9, 14, 41, 115, 118–19, 126–7, 129, 130, 138, 157, 182
modernity, 131, 137–8, 157
money
  corrupting effect of, 131, 142, 143
  and modernity, 131
  stolen, 142
  wages, 134, 137, 150, 153, 163
Montaigne, Michel de, 186
monuments, 13, 167–9, 175, 187, 193, 196; *see also* ruin
morality plays, 102, 105–7, 110, 111, 115, 121; *see also* Vice
More, Thomas, 153–4
More, William, 52
Morgan, Edward, 34
Morgann, Maurice, 211–12
motes, 176–86
motion
  celestial *see* astronomy
  and emotion, 91, 178, 183
  first, 80, 187
  mischievous, 114, 178
  muddled, 82
motive
  arbitrarily imputed, 126, 211
  figured, 114, 117, 140, 183, 216
  natural, 74
  see also causation; circumstance
Munday, Anthony, 51; *see also* antitheatre
murder, 69–70, 81, 83, 85, 98, 127, 128, 144; *see also* manslaughter
Murder of John Bowen, The, 40

Nashe, Thomas, 87, 134, 177, 184
  Pierce Penniless, 6
  Terrors of the Night, 182
nature, 49–50, 74, 139, 148, 152, 169
Neill, Michael, 130–2, 133
Neo-Aristotelianism, 200, 211
Neo-Kantianism, 15–16
Neo-Platonism, 1, 104, 184
New Historicism, 10; *see also* cultural materialism; Greenblatt, Stephen; historicism
nobility *see* honour
non-identity *see* masks
Norris, John, 27
Norwich, 86–7, 90, 99, 147; *see also* affray
Nuremberg, 85

office-holding, 39–40, 49
oikonomía, 46–50, 60, 138, 192, 205
Orlando Furioso, 186
Othello, 1, 67, 110, 131, 179–80
Overbury, Thomas, 147, 191
Ovid, 172, 188, 189

Painter, William, 149
painting, 168, 180, 188, 204–5, 207, 215
patches, 116–17, 177, 184
paternalism, 133–4, 135–6, 146
pathos, 53, 70, 128–9; *see also* eyes: emanations from
patriarchy *see* fathers
peace, 32, 34, 36, 41, 47–9, 61, 81, 135; *see also* justices of the peace; Verge
Peacham, Henry, 148, 192
performance
  and accident, 12, 87, 92
  and action, 37, 66, 114, 127, 171
  of contract, 51, 129, 137, 141, 145–7, 150–2, 163
  as erotic conceit, 141, 143, 144–5, 150–1
  and failure, 92, 150, 166
  as hidden premise, 2, 13, 19, 77, 91, 93, 112, 113, 157, 176, 216
  and identity, 110, 116, 127, 130, 148–9, 150–1, 163, 166, 170
  and literature, 13, 166, 178, 212, 216–17
  and possession, 145, 147, 150, 174
  and ritual, 5
  and space, 38, 44, 50–3, 85, 105, 111, 138
  and witchcraft, 185
  see also player
Perkins, Richard, 117–18, 165
Persons, Robert, 106, 148
phenomenology, 9–10, 14, 17, 20, 127, 138, 157, 171–2, 177, 182–8, 216; *see also* eyes; semblance
philology, 189, 210
  German, 106, 108, 122
Phoebus *see* Apollo
physiognomy, 15, 42, 102, 138, 140–2, 143, 191; *see also* faces; masks
pies, 16, 175, 176; *see also* cannibalism
pipes, 87–8
pity, 6–8, 128; *see also* pathos
plague, 27, 51–2, 118, 153, 167, 169; *see also* infection
Plato
  Menexenus, 6
  Republic, 9
  Theaetetus, 172, 182

player
  agency of, 18, 54, 101, 149–50, 170
  appearance of, 54, 90–2, 119–20
  body of, 104, 119, 170, 184, 194
  common, 12–13
  and death, 166, 174
  partial reality of, 19, 194
playhouses
  architecture of, 51
  Blackfriars, 2, 169
  critics of see antitheatre
  The Curtain, 85
  The Globe, 2, 70, 169, 180
  The Rose, 52–3
Pliny, 184, 194
Plowden, Edmund, 43
poetics, 3–4, 29, 43, 50, 157, 177, 183; see also Aristotle
poetry, 3–4, 10–11, 45, 192–3, 214; see also poetics
poison, 66, 68, 73, 76, 77, 79, 80, 82, 95, 144, 166, 191, 204–5
polis, 46, 165, 206; see also commonwealth; public sphere
political economy, 46–8, 213; see also household; Marx, Karl; oikonomía
Porter, Henry, 69, 81–2, 83
poverty see vagrancy
practice (also practise), 51, 74, 76, 89–90, 100, 104–5, 132, 137, 168, 173, 190, 191, 212, 215, 220; see also player; skill
premeditation, 77, 81–3, 85, 98, 155; see also murder
Preston, Thomas, 118–19
private sphere, 24, 45, 48–50, 53; see also household; public sphere
Privy Council, the, 32, 52
professionalism
  of playwright, 164, 190
  of theatre see player
  trades: 9, 12, 129, 147
  see also amateurism; skill
prologues
  and actors, 104
  and the dead, 6, 176, 183–6
  and didacticism, 102
  and liminality, 4, 218
  and metatheatre, 210, 214
props
  and epistemology, 86, 90, 118
  and risk, 76, 82, 92
  and tragedy, 35, 88
prosopography, 135, 156
prosopopoeia, 5–6, 11, 134, 156–7; see also eidolopoeia
providence, 40, 46, 77, 92, 204–5
Prynne, William, 104–5, 120–1; see also antitheatre
psychoanalysis, 212
psychomachia, 107–8, 113–14, 117, 185
public sphere, 9, 12, 21, 28, 48, 50, 51, 53, 70, 85, 87, 103, 166, 167; see also commonwealth; private sphere
purification, 52, 54, 93; see also catharsis; infection
Puttenham, George, 5–6, 54, 129, 192
Pykering, John, Horestes, 17, 106, 113–19, 151–3
Pynchon, Thomas, 166
Pythagoras, 189

Quintilian, 6, 191–2, 212; see also rhetoric

Rainald, John, 51
Rainolds, Richard, 6, 192
Rankins, William, 51, 104; see also antitheatre
rapier see blades
rebellion
  of 1549, 31, 133
  and commonwealth, 77
  suppression of, 31, 57
recognition see misrecognition
Reformation, 165, 176, 183, 190, 215
regicide see tyrannicide
Reich, Hermann, 108–9, 110, 122
reputation, 1, 53, 72–4, 86, 89, 91, 97, 136, 140, 142, 148–9
Return from Parnassus, The, 10
revenge tragedy, preliminary definitions of, 13–14, 19–21, 24
rhetoric
  and affect, 7–8, 105, 114–15, 212
  and corpses, 66, 183, 192
  and deception, 134, 156
  dispositio, 46
  forensic, 43, 183
  and orality, 5, 192
  reception in England, 191–2
  and remembrance, 11
Richard II, 44–5, 88
riot, 27, 53, 57, 62; see also rebellion
ritual
  and effigies, 175
  failed, 78
  and origin of theatre, 109
  theory of, 5, 22
  and violence, 67, 73–5
Romanticism, 212
Romeo & Juliet, 91
Rose, Gillian, 24, 59, 213–15
Rowlands, Samuel, 147
Rowley, William, part author of
  A Cure for a Cuckold, 75
  The Changeling, 17, 141, 150–1
Royal court/household, 33, 49
ruin, 9, 10, 34, 45, 49, 70, 80, 82, 102, 116, 155, 164, 168–71, 176, 196, 205; see also monuments

sailors, 27
Sainct Didier, Henry de, 77–8
St Augustine of Hippo, 113
St Peter, 46
Saviolo, Vincent, 68–9, 73–4, 91
Saxo Grammaticus, Gesta Danorum, 72, 79
scalpel see blades
scepticism, 155, 169, 171–2, 215
Schalkwyk, David, 132, 133
science
  of astronomy see astronomy
  broken optic of, 181
  economic, 46
  of fencing, 66
  fiction, 95
  and form, 92–3
  mathematical, 198
  molecular, 177
  prosopographical, 156
  social, 16, 189, 195, 198
Scot, Reginald, 185; see also ghost; witchcraft
Scott, James C., 130
scripture, 51, 65, 126, 132, 138, 181, 185, 193
sedition, 62, 77, 102; see also rebellion; treason; tyrannicide

semblance
  artistic, 15, 110, 175, 216
  of a duel, 71, 74
  of a love scene, 141
  and resemblance, 8, 112, 117, 189
  theatrical, 42, 102
Seneca, 76, 195, 204
  Agamemnon, 198
  ghost of, 189
  and gloom, 182, 204
  Medea, 184
  reception in England, 113, 176, 177, 204
  and suicide, 64
  Thyestes, 49–50, 61, 62, 176, 184, 189
sensationalism, 21, 166–7, 172
Serres, Michel, 10, 164
servant
  abuse of, 159
  as animal, 126, 129, 135, 137, 138, 140, 142, 157
  concept of, 129–30, 134–5, 157, 158, 193
  and contract, 128, 131, 134, 145, 150
  denotation of, 126, 130, 141
  dismissed, 151–6
  as ethical person, 131–3, 156
  feudal, 18, 127, 130, 146
  as group identity, 128, 135
  idle, 136, 148, 149
  impoverised, 154, 163
  as intriguer, 84, 119, 125, 129–30, 135, 146
  and land, 133, 136
  loyalty of, 139–40, 146–7
  obedience of, 128, 142, 147
  procured, 135–45
  treasonous, 134, 138, 151–2, 154
  wages, 131–6, 142–3, 146, 148–9, 150, 153
  see also vagrancy
shadow
  and character, 157
  and figure, 184, 190, 193, 200
  foreshadowing, 50, 69–70, 141, 193
  as ghost, 176, 183–4
  player as, 157, 190, 194
  and rhetoric, 184
  and substance, 104, 184
  see also ghost; light
Shakespeare, William *see individual works*
Shirley, James, *The Cardinal*, 41
Sidney, Philip, 59, 69
sight
  astronomical *see* astronomy
  and cowardice, 72
  deception of, 185
  and desire, 150
  divided, 182
  and *figura*, 185
  first, 39, 87, 211
  hindsight, 166, 171
  judgement, 93, 183, 215
  master's, 139, 141
  pleasing, 50
  reformation of, 103
  royal, 93, 126
  social, 188
  spiritual, 184
  see also eyes
Silver, George, 78
skill, 77–9, 84, 89, 104, 109, 128, 146, 149, 168, 190
skin, 165, 208–10
Skinner, Quentin, 183

slander, 32, 64, 90, 148
  and the Court of Chivalry, 72
Smith, Thomas, 48, 49, 137
Society of Antiquaries, 33, 47
Sonnets (Shakespeare), 184
Sophocles, 213
Southwell, Robert, 68
sovereignty
  of dramatic art, 44, 54, 65
  and legalism, 30, 76
  and private justice, 75–7
  and space *see* Verge
Spencer, Gabriel, 83
Spenser, Edmund, 67–8
stage-directions, 106, 139, 161, 164, 167, 173, 179
State
  as body, 182
  and commonwealth, 61; *see also* commonwealth
  and household *see* household
  theorisation of, 46–8
  tragic reconstruction of, 93
statues
  of Brutus, 186–7
  as instruments of prefiguration, 193–4
  wax, 172–5
Stocker, Thomas, 36
Stoichita, Victor, 180, 215
Stoicism, 42, 65; *see also* Seneca
Stow, John, 31
Stubbes, Phillip, 104, 188; *see also* antitheatre
Stukeley, Thomas, plays about, 36
suicide, 66–9
sumptuary law, 148; *see also* livery; textiles
supersession, 193
suspension of disbelief, 9, 173
swords *see* blades; duelling

Tantalus, 6, 111, 184
Tarlton, Richard, 86–7, 110, 149; *see also* clowns
Tasso, Torquato, 48
Tempest, The, 152–3, 176
Terence, *Hecyra*, 210
textiles, 69, 140, 147, 148, 151
  and costume, 112
textuality, 4–8, 17, 19, 92, 110, 157, 171, 173, 180, 185, 189, 191, 205, 207, 210, 216–17
theatre
  companies, 19, 24: Chamberlain's Men, 86, 87; Children of the Chapel, 24, 35, 70; King's Men, 148; Queen's Men, 86–7, 147
  criticism of *see* antitheatre
  houses *see* playhouses
  itinerancy of, 54
  origins of, 108
  performer *see* player
theatrum mundi, conceit of *see* metatheatre
Theophrastus, 191
Thynne, Francis, 47
Titivillus, 117; *see also* demons; evil; Vice
Titus Andronicus, 6, 24, 64, 175
topography, 33, 50
Topsell, Edward, 51
trade *see* professionalism
tragedy
  classical, 155; *see also* Seneca
  its historical alteration, 7, 14, 17, 21, 213–14
  negation of, 69–70, 79, 88, 164
  Roman theory of, 50
  see also catharsis; pathos; *Trauerspiel*

translation
  and comedy, 137
  and etymology, 47, 107, 181, 186
  of revenge narrative, 149
  of Seneca, 62, 184
  and Thomas Kyd, 36–7, 48–9
  and Thomas Middleton, 85
  and William Shakespeare, 79
Trauerspiel
  and baroque courts, 45
  and martyrdom, 216
  and theatricality, 16
  versus tragedy, 21
  see also Benjamin, Walter
treason, 32, 73, 80
  petty, 134, 138, 151, 154
  see also sedition; tyrannicide
trees, 50, 152
trespass, action at common law, 30–1, 33, 41, 56–7, 139, 146
Triall of Treasure, The, 111
Turner, Victor, 4–5, 22, 139; *see also* liminality
Tyndale, William, 181
tyrannicide, 62, 76, 77, 80, 129; *see also* sedition; treason

Udall, Nicholas, *Respublica*, 101, 102, 113
unmasking *see* masks
Ur-*Hamlet*, 20, 76, 79, 86

vagrancy
  legislation, 52, 135, 139
  and poverty, 129, 154, 163
  and service, 25, 125, 129, 134–5, 153
  and theatre, 134, 149, 153
  and Vice, 119
  see also servant
van der Doort, Abraham, 172
Verge
  and banishment, 30, 39–40
  corruption of the, 49–50, 53
  Court of the, 28–35
  exemption from the, 26, 30, 39–40, 42
  and land law, 36, 44–5
  and the Liberties of London, 52
  and the Marshalsea: Case of, 34, 55–6; Court of, 28, 28–35, 37, 56–7; prison, 27, 32, 34; as space, 29
  mechanical, 45
  as origin of political thought, 48–9
  and private law within, 26, 30, 40–2, 49
  of sight, 139
  and *The Spanish Tragedy*, 27–54 *passim*
  as staff of authority, 35–6
  as subject, 43, 51–2
  as substance, 42
Vice
  and conscience, 112–18
  denotation of, 101, 111–12, 115, 193

  and the devil, 106, 115
  and doubling, 115
  and folk plays, 107, 122
  and genealogy, 106, 110, 115, 116, 117
  and morality plays, 106
  and origins, 106, 113
  as player, 101–5, 119
  and the popular tradition, 108–10
  props of, 115
  and Reformation, 102, 119
  and revenge motive, 106, 113
  of sight, 139, 177
  and sin, 106, 111–13, 123
  solidity of, 118
  as vagrant servant, 119, 124–5, 143, 151
  and Virtue, 105, 118
  and work, 103, 112, 136
Virgil, 67
virtue *see* Vice
visage *see* faces; masks
Vitruvius, 51
voice
  and affect, 10, 23, 128
  devocalisation, 10, 75, 166, 169
  and figures, 9–12, 127–8, 151, 164, 180
  player's, 4–5, 9, 10, 169
  poetic, 5, 9, 10, 18
  revocalisation, 1, 6, 10, 74, 168–9, 171

wages *see* money; servant
Watch, the, 37–8, 139
wax, 128, 140, 171–5, 178, 187, 201
weapons *see* blades
Webbe, William, 52–3
Webster, John
  and acting, 91, 165–6
  A Cure for a Cuckold (part author), 75
  and dead things, 167
  The Duchess of Malfi, 10–12, 17, 128, 140–3, 149–50, 155, 164–6, 168, 172, 174, 180, 187
  New Characters, 191
  The White Devil, 164–5
Weimann, Robert, 4–5, 107, 108, 109, 110
Wentworth, William, 136
Westermann, William, 154
Wever, Richard, 111
Whateley, William, 136
Wily Beguiled, 184–5
Winter's Tale, The, 92, 173
witchcraft, 104, 142, 152, 173–4, 182, 185, 187; *see also* demons; devil
Wolsey, Thomas, 112
wonder, 86, 182–3, 200
Woodbridge, Linda, 20–1, 167
Wycliffe, John, 181

Xenophon, 47–8

Zeno, 172

EU representative:
Easy Access System Europe
Mustamäe tee 50, 10621 Tallinn, Estonia
Gpsr.requests@easproject.com

www.ingramcontent.com/pod-product-compliance
Lightning Source LLC
Chambersburg PA
CBHW052058300426
44117CB00013B/2182